3/06

No
Ordinary
Joe

Missouri Biography Series

William E. Foley, Editor

No
Ordinary
Joe

A Life of
Joseph Pulitzer III

Daniel W. Pfaff

University of Missouri Press
Columbia and London

Library of Congress Cataloging-in-Publication Data

Pfaff, Daniel W.
    No ordinary Joe : a life of Joseph Pulitzer III / Daniel W. Pfaff.
        p.   cm. — (Missouri biography series)
    Summary: "Examines that life and career of Joseph Pulitzer III, editor and
publisher of the St. Louis Post-Dispatch. Pulitzer was the head of the Pulitzer
Publishing Company, and he served as chairman of the Pulitzer Prize Board at
Columbia University for thirty-one years"—Provided by publisher.
    Includes bibliographical references and index.
    ISBN-13: 978-0-8262-1607-6 (alk. paper)
    ISBN-10: 0-8262-1607-2 (alk. paper)
    1. Pulitzer, Joseph, 1913–   2. Newspaper editors—United States—
Biography.   3. Publishers and publishing—United States—Biography.
I. Title.   II. Series.
    PN4874.P82P43 2002
    070.4'1'092—dc22   2005018185

㊰™ This paper meets the requirements of the
American National Standard for Permanence of Paper
for Printed Library Materials, Z39.48, 1984.

Designer: Kristin Caplinger
Typesetter: Phoenix Type, Inc.
Printer and binder: Thomson-Shore, Inc.
Typefaces: Palatino and Galliard

Publication of this book has been assisted by generous
contributions from the Pulitzer Foundation and the
Sprint Foundation.

Photographs and illustrations were provided courtesy
of the *St. Louis Post-Dispatch,* Emily Rauh Pulitzer,
Joseph Pulitzer IV, William F. Woo, and Sarah Dunn.

For my family,
Eileen, Mark,
Andy and *Tova,*
and *Jesse Noah*

Contents

Sources and Acknowledgments

This biography was made possible by Emily Rauh Pulitzer, widow of Joseph Pulitzer III, who generously opened the papers of her late husband to me. I am deeply grateful to Mrs. Pulitzer, executor of her husband's estate, for granting me access to these essential primary materials. Joe, whom I first met in 1984, consented to the biography in 1993, shortly before his death. I first proposed it to him in 1989, after completing a biography of his father, Joseph Pulitzer II. He demurred, but left an opening. "I would prefer to be sitting on a cloud, playing a zither when that is done," he replied.

I am particularly indebted to two grandsons of the first Joseph Pulitzer: Michael E. Pulitzer, half-brother of Joseph Pulitzer III, who succeeded him as chairman and chief executive officer of Pulitzer Publishing Company, and David E. Moore, a cousin of J. P. III and Michael, who served as a voting trustee of the company and a member of its board of directors. Both provided essential information. Joseph Pulitzer IV, son of J. P. III, who worked for nearly twenty years at the *Post-Dispatch* in both journalistic and business positions, was an invaluable source of information about his family and aspects of company operations with which he was closely familiar.

I began reading in the papers of Joseph Pulitzer III at the *Post-Dispatch* in the summer of 1994. They cover more than fifty years, and form the core of the biography. The papers of Joseph Pulitzer II, held by the Library of Congress and available on microfilm, provided essential information on the early years of the third Joseph Pulitzer's life.

In 1984, Joseph Pulitzer III agreed to assist me in gathering material for the biography of his father, published in 1991. He was extraordinarily helpful, and made clear from the beginning that he did not approve of authorized biographies because "they smack of too much PR and are suspect." We quickly agreed that I would have final control over the manuscript. I asked, however, that he read early drafts of chapters for accuracy, and he generously agreed. I have enjoyed the same understanding and working relationship with Pulitzer family members, company employees and advisers, and friends interviewed for this biography, a total of more than seventy individuals. Michael Pulitzer, Emily Rauh Pulitzer, and Joseph Pulitzer IV all granted multiple interviews and read several chapters in draft dealing with topics about which they had direct knowledge. Similar assistance was provided by William F. Woo, who worked closely with J. P. III for many years, first as editor of the *Post-Dispatch* editorial page and then as the paper's editor; Glenn A. Christopher, one of the closest associates of J. P. III, who held several major executive positions during his fifty-year career in the company; James M. Snowden, Jr., a company financial adviser; Richard A. Palmer and William Bush, company counsel; and Richard Gaddes, a close friend of Joe and Emily. The suggestions of all these people significantly improved the accuracy and depth of detail herein. The late Kate Davis Pulitzer Quesada, a sister of Joseph Pulitzer III, provided essential information in interviews about the family, her brother's early life, and various events in later years. Among those interviewed, many agreed to follow-up sessions. William F. Woo, who consented to ten, holds the record for those.

Throughout the years-long process of producing this biography, I enjoyed the unfailing cooperation of James V. Maloney, former assistant to Joseph Pulitzer III and subsequently secretary and director of shareholder relations for the Pulitzer Publishing Company and its successor, Pulitzer Inc. He both accommodated and anticipated my needs and made many helpful suggestions during the production of this and the J. P. II biography.

I offer special thanks to Mary Jane Roach Masters for giving me access to letters she wrote to her mother in the summer of 1929 when she was a twenty-year-old college student. The letters deal with the activities that summer of Joseph Pulitzer II and family at Chatwold, the family's summer home at Bar Harbor, Maine, when the then Miss Roach was employed as a companion for Kate Davis. She gave me copies of the letters to J. P. III and Emily in 1992, with permission for their quotation.

I sincerely appreciate the patience and encouragement of all who granted interviews, wrote me letters, or both. In addition to those identified above, they were: Adam Aronson, Walter W. Barker, G. Duncan Bauman, Jerry Berger, Arthur R. Bertelson, Benjamin C. Bradlee, Bob Broeg, Charles E. Buckley, Robert Burnes, James D. Cherry, Foster Davis, Patricia Degener, Sally Bixby Defty, Irving Dilliard, Richard Dudman, Robert W. Duffy, Thomas F. Eagleton, Ken J. Elkins, Margaret W. Freivogel, James Fox, Evarts A. Graham, Jr., Katharine Graham, George H. Hall, John M. Harney, Howard H. Hayes, Robert B. Hentschell, Edward A. Higgins, John Hohenberg, Diane Johner, Helen F. Jones, Marvin Kanne, Robert Lasch, James K. Lawrence, Harry Levins, David Lipman, Ruth McClenahan, George R.

McCue, Joan M. McSalley, Robert and Lois Orchard, Nicholas G. Penniman IV, Selwyn Pepper, Frank L. Peters, William J. Polk, Jr., Elkhanah Pulitzer, Peter W. Quesada, Euretta Rathbone, Nelson A. Reed, Peter J. Repetti, Ronald H. Ridgway, Martha Schomburg, Florence Shinkle, Martha Shirk, Robert Brookings Smith, Margaret Stearns, Emily Stone, Richard K. Weil, Jr., Joe M. Whittington, Harry Wilensky, and Ronald H. Willnow.

Donald L. Smith, professor emeritus of journalism at Penn State University, a superb editor and a longtime friend and colleague, read the entire manuscript in draft and provided many excellent suggestions for its improvement. George Juergens, professor emeritus of history at Indiana University, Bloomington, reviewed the manuscript prior to its acceptance for publication and offered expert advice.

I am grateful to the editors and staff of the thirty-five-year-old *St. Louis Journalism Review* for their coverage of and editorial commentary about the *Post-Dispatch* during and beyond the tenure of Joseph Pulitzer III. Staff members of the Missouri Historical Society in St. Louis and the Western Historical Manuscript Collection of the University of Missouri–St. Louis kindly helped me locate various details about life in the city and some of the prominent local individuals with whom J. P. III was associated. Professor Michael D. Murray, then chair of the Department of Communication at the University of Missouri–St. Louis, made every effort to make my stay in St. Louis as pleasant and productive as possible.

The Institute for Arts and Humanistic Studies at Penn State under former director George Mauner awarded a faculty research fellowship that provided substantial assistance during the sabbatical I spent doing research and interviews in St. Louis. The College of Communications at Penn State University provided travel assistance over several years. I wish particularly to thank former Dean Terri Brooks for her support and encouragement as the project took shape.

My wife, Eileen, helped in many ways, including research assistance, the transcription of many tape-recorded interviews, critical reading of draft chapters, and countless odds and ends that made the going much smoother. Our son Mark kept our balky computer functioning as long as possible beyond its natural span before offering the inevitable and wise advice to replace it and get some new software. Our son Andrew and daughter-in-law Tova, parents of our first grandchild, Jesse Noah, provided encouragement throughout the years it took to finish the book.

The most cordial and professional staff of the University of Missouri Press was as helpful as humanly possible from the beginning to the end of the publication process. I offer most sincere thanks to Beverly Jarrett, director and editor-in-chief; Jane H. Lago, managing editor; John Brenner, copyeditor; Cathy Birk, advertising and design manager; Kristin Caplinger, designer; Karen D. Renner, marketing manager; and marketing staff members Beth Chandler and Eve Kidd.

This biography would never have come into print without the generosity of those named here and of uncounted others not identified, who helped in important ways to keep the wheels turning. All deserve only praise. I take full responsibility for any and all shortcomings.

Abbreviations

The following abbreviations are used in the footnotes:

ARB	Arthur R. Bertelson
ARK	Arch R. King
ATP	Alexander T. Primm III
BHR	Benjamin H. Reese
CEB	Charles E. Buckley
CJH	Charles J. Hentschell
DBS	Dell B. Stafford
DEM	David E. Moore
DG	Donald Grant
DL	David Lipman
EAG	Evarts A. Graham, Jr.
EP	Elkhanah Pulitzer
ERP	Emily Rauh Pulitzer
FFR	Fred F. Rowden
GAC	Glenn A. Christopher
GDB	G. Duncan Bauman
GH	George H. Hall (always used GH)
GMB	George M. Burbach
GRM	George R. McCue
HOG	Harold O. Grams
HPJr	Herbert (Peter) Pulitzer, Jr.
ID	Irving Dilliard
JFH	Joseph F. Holland
JH	John Hohenberg
JHK	Julius H. Klyman
JKL	James K. Lawrence
JMS	James M. Snowden, Jr. ·
JVM	James V. Maloney
JPII	Joseph Pulitzer, Jr. (II)
JPIII	Joseph Pulitzer III ("Jr.")
JPIV	Joseph Pulitzer IV
JVM	James V. Maloney

KDPQ	Kate Davis Pulitzer Quesada
KJE	Ken J. Elkins
MEP	Michael Edgar Pulitzer
MWC	Marquis W. Childs
NGP	Nicholas G. Penniman IV
OKB	Oliver Kirby Bovard
PJR	Peter J. Repetti
RAP	Richard A. Palmer
RBS	Robert Brookings Smith
RC	Ralph Coghlan
RD	Richard Dudman
RFT	*Riverfront Times*
RGB	Richard G. Baumhoff
RHR	Ronald H. Ridgway
RL	Robert Lasch
RLC	Raymond L. Crowley
RPB	Raymond P. Brandt
RPJr.	Ralph Pulitzer, Jr.
SBD	Sally Bixby Defty
SJR	*St. Louis Journalism Review*
SLBJ	*St. Louis Business Journal*
SMC	Stuart M. Chambers
SP	Selwyn Pepper
SS	Samuel J. Shelton (always used SS)
WB	William Bush
WJP	William Julius Polk, Jr.
WW	William F. Woo (always used WW)

No
Ordinary
Joe

Introduction

The identity of Joseph Pulitzer III and the principles of the *St. Louis Post-Dispatch* were inseparable. "He was very aware of being Joseph Pulitzer," said Robert W. Duffy, who knew him both as an employer and a friend. "There was a bearing that was quite noble. He just had a sense of himself that recognized that he was the heir to a very great tradition in the newspaper business in this country that his grandfather started and his father had continued and that he was responsible for carrying on." People who observed him from a distance often described him as aloof, reserved, probably shy. Such judgments were mistaken but understandable in Duffy's opinion: "It was just that there was a very aristocratic bearing about him that was immediately noticeable. You knew that this was somebody who just wasn't an ordinary Joe."[1]

Nor were his predecessors. His grandfather, the remarkable Hungarian immigrant Joseph Pulitzer (1847–1911), founded the *St. Louis Post-Dispatch*, the *New York World* newspapers, the Columbia University Graduate School of Journalism, and the Pulitzer Prizes in journalism, letters, and music. He never doubted his abilities or sidestepped controversy and was, he admitted, "crazy about politics." His namesake son, Joseph Pulitzer II (1885–1955), was twenty-six when he succeeded to leadership of the St. Louis property in 1911, and remained at the helm for forty-three years. He both followed and reinforced the founder's principles during the first half of the twentieth century, guiding the *Post-Dispatch* to wide distinction—including five "meritorious public service" Pulitzer Prizes. (The *World* newspapers were sold in 1931.)[2]

The third Joseph Pulitzer (usually referred to hereafter as Joe) worked in journalism from 1936 to 1993. He was born two years after his grandfather's death. Before succeeding his father in 1955 at the age of forty-one, he had fifteen years of hands-on instruction in the liberal editorial outlook of Pulitzer journalism, colorfully articulated by his grandfather in the self-invented word "indegoddampendent." Joe worked in every department

---

1. Interview with Robert W. Duffy, October 5, 1994, St. Louis.
2. Daniel W. Pfaff, *Joseph Pulitzer II and the Post-Dispatch: A Newspaperman's Life*, passim.

of the *Post-Dispatch*, attended his father's executive meetings, and was a pupil of the company's top journalists and business executives. By the time he took charge, he recalled, "I had attended countless conferences where policy matters were discussed or debated. I had access to all my father's papers, journalistic or business. . . . The thread of continuity established by my predecessors gave me no problem. The [liberal] tradition, practices, point of view, aspirations, idealism, and also the pragmatism and accountability were engraved on my consciousness from long experience."[3] He served as chief executive of the Pulitzer Publishing Company for thirty-eight years, and concurrently for thirty-one of those years as editor and publisher of the *Post-Dispatch*.

The newspaper's platform, written by his grandfather in 1907, was his touchstone across that span, as it had been his father's for the previous forty-three years. He agreed with his father that as the guide for formulating editorial opinion, the platform should be interpreted as a mandate for reasoned rather than shrill liberalism. Unlike the first J. P., who encouraged "fighting" editorials, the second and third usually chose a more deliberative approach, considering it more likely to win readers' careful consideration. Even so, there was plenty of resistance. "I think that there is no question but there existed in the minds of many St. Louisans a sense that this paper was highbrow," said William F. Woo, the paper's editorial page editor under Joe for eleven years. Woo found that Joe "appreciated and greatly revered competent analysis of the issues," and believed that the paper should give significant space to the thought of intellectual leaders in government, business, and universities on topics of the day. Consequently, the paper conveyed "an element of self-conscious intellectualism that [Joe] encouraged, appreciated and demanded."

The competing *St. Louis Globe-Democrat*'s motto was "Fighting for St. Louis," based largely on the claim that it published more local news than the *Post-Dispatch*, an assertion Woo and his colleagues disputed, but neither paper attempted to test statistically. Whatever the numbers might have shown, Woo conceded that "paradoxically," the *Globe-Democrat* "presented itself very successfully as the paper of the little person" even though analysis of its editorials, news analysis, and political endorsements "would show that [it] was a paper very much of the political elite, the corporate elite, a very Republican paper." To Woo, the *Post-Dispatch* was the more egalitarian and therefore actually "the paper of the little person," even if most St. Louisans did not recognize it as such.

---

3. Address by J. P. III to the Newcomen Society, St. Louis, December 1, 1988, Papers of Joseph Pulitzer III, *St. Louis Post-Dispatch* (hereafter JPIII Papers.)

As could be expected, the paper got much of its applause from readers outside of St. Louis. A 1927 *American Mercury* article characterized the *Post-Dispatch* as "easily the strongest force in St. Louis fighting for enlightenment and personal liberty, while opposing official lawlessness. It is the city's one live contact with the outside world, without which St. Louis would be like a submarine without a periscope." The *Wall Street Journal* observed in 1982, near the end of Joe's tenure as editor-publisher, that while many newspapers "now are limiting editorials to parochial issues or avoiding opinions entirely," *Post-Dispatch* editorials "take the liberal side of issues ranging from the death penalty (against), to abortion ('pro-choice') and whether welfare recipients should be required to work for their benefits (against.)" As a result, the *Journal* noted, the paper's "liberalism infuriates a spectrum of interests, from anti-abortion groups to pro-Israeli organizations."[4] Joe took the criticisms in stride, endorsing the oft-heard expression: "It is a newspaper's duty to print the news and raise hell." As he saw it, the paper was obligated "to comment on events with vigor, sound reasoning, and moral purpose irrespective of the popularity of the views expressed or by denunciations that might thunder from high places of authority."[5] "Never trust the establishment," he cautioned subordinates.

To a point, certainly, he was part of the St. Louis establishment, but he drew a line where the paper's independence might be compromised by favoring any special interest group. He avoided civic affiliations except for those with cultural concerns. He was a lover of art, music, and theater, his greatest interests being the St. Louis Art Museum, St. Louis Symphony, and the Harvard University Art Museums. He served on their advisory boards and was a major benefactor of all three. He expanded coverage of the arts in the *Post-Dispatch*, but kept his personal involvement as much as possible out of public view. He was largely invisible as well as chairman of the Pulitzer Prize Board at Columbia University during the thirty-one years he was editor and publisher. He found the work interesting and at times stressful, but for the most part enjoyed it.

In directing the *Post-Dispatch* and the company, he had his finger on every pulse. Subordinates who worked directly with Joe quickly learned to do their homework before writing him a memorandum or going into a meeting. They found that his keen memory would quickly spot inconsistencies in things they told him across time. The going was difficult during much of his tenure as the *Post-Dispatch* and the Pulitzer Publishing

4. Arthur Strawn, "A Short View of St. Louis," *American Mercury,* April 1927, 474; *Wall Street Journal,* August 23, 1982.
5. Joseph Pulitzer [III], "The Press Lives by Disclosures," *Nieman Reports,* July 1961 (reprint), JPIII Papers.

Company entered the greatest period of change and challenge in American journalism since his grandfather's day. It is fair to say that he faced more trials during his leadership than either of his predecessors—though not to suggest that either of them had it easy.

On the journalistic side, social and economic turbulence countrywide clamored for reconsideration of longstanding practices. On the business side, new technologies created competitive pressures and required new financial strategies. The outlook for newspapers was not promising, as growing numbers of readers shifted to other sources for news, opinion, and, especially, entertainment. As readership declined, so did the number of newspapers nationwide. Some closed, while others consolidated with rival papers or were sold to chain owners, their individual personalities disappearing in the process. The *Post-Dispatch* could not, of course, rise wholly above these realities. Instead, Joe chose a course that valued survival to fight another day over capitulation to forces not easily controlled, and requiring some compromises.

The first of these compromises emerged in tandem with his succession as editor-publisher. The *Post-Dispatch* and *Globe-Democrat,* both privately owned, were the only two dailies in St. Louis by 1955, down from six in 1911. The morning *Globe-Democrat* was faltering. That, plus diminishing advertising support in the St. Louis market, led to a cost-cutting joint operating arrangement between the two newspapers. A combination of belt-tightening by the newspaper and expansion and diversification of the company beyond St. Louis—particularly into television—sustained the *Post-Dispatch* through this period, significantly enlarging the company and strengthening it financially. The *Globe-Democrat* was sold in 1983 and closed in 1986. St. Louis became another city without competing daily newspapers. By that time, there were competing dailies in only about thirty-five cities and towns in the United States.[6]

Undoubtedly the most substantial measure of Joe's determination to keep the company intact was the rejection in 1986 of a $625 million offer from an outside buyer for all of the company's stock. The offer was arranged by a minority group of family shareholders who, believing their shares were undervalued and their dividends too low, wanted to sell their holdings at a "fair market" price. A dispute about this had been simmering for fifteen years, and in the end became both acrimonious and public. Ultimately, a coalition of Joe, the largest shareholder, his brother, Michael E. Pulitzer, and cousin, David E. Moore—all grandsons of the founder—

6. *Wall Street Journal,* May 1, 1986.

arranged to buy out the minority's shares for $189 million, taking the company public in the process.

The move from private to public ownership in order to save the 108-year-old company deeply disappointed Joe. As one who closely associated family ownership with editorial independence, it was hard for him to see the company move into the open marketplace. He was seventy-three and chose to step down as editor and publisher when the change took place, appointing editorial page editor Woo and general manager Nicholas G. Penniman IV as the first people outside the family to hold those positions. He remained chief executive and chairman of the board. Joe's brother Michael, fifty-six, vice president and chief operating officer since 1979, became chief executive officer in 1988.[7]

Joe's business responsibilities did not keep him from enjoying a range of other activities. He loved parties, and he and his first and second wives gave and attended many. He was a favorite dinner guest. He took up skiing in his forties and enjoyed the sport for more than thirty years. To all who knew him—and many who only knew of him—Joseph Pulitzer III was associated with both journalism and art. He was internationally recognized for what he called his "avocation" or "hobby"—as a major collector of and expert on modern and contemporary art. He began collecting while a class of 1936 fine arts major at Harvard University. Had he not been in line to assume leadership of the family business, many doubted he would have chosen newspaper journalism. When he became editor of the *Post-Dispatch* in 1955, "there was among the staff a great deal of speculation about 'How's this guy going to be when he succeeds the old man?'" said Evarts Graham, Jr., who spent forty-three years on the *Post-Dispatch*, eleven of them as managing editor under J. P. III. "In St. Louis at the time," Graham explained, "he was widely denigrated and vilified as a no-good art freak who would never get on to the facts of life and didn't know anything about what the world was . . . because all he cares about is art. Well, I knew better." Graham had been around him long enough to know that "he cared about newspapers."

Some of the dismissive remarks got back to Joe, but he made no issue of them. "One of the ways in which Joe defended himself from all this," said friend and businessman Robert Orchard, "was this sort of retreat from public display. He really tried in his social world and his aesthetic world [to portray] a delicacy that belied the strength that was there. The public

7. *St. Louis Post-Dispatch,* April 12, 1979; *St. Louis Business Journal,* November 7, 1988; description of MEP career, November 1988, JPIII Papers.

perception of Joe was never this tremendously powerful financial intellect. Occasionally amongst friends, he would let that mask drop." In a conversation with Orchard, Joe revealed that when he was in his twenties he told his father that he wanted to work for the *Post-Dispatch* and eventually succeed him as editor-publisher. His father replied, Orchard recounted, "that he felt that was a marvelous idea but for one thing—that he thought Joe's aesthetic sensitivities were perhaps greater than would be possible for a newspaper publisher. And Joe's words were: 'My father said, Joe if you want to do this, you have to have rhinoceros hide. I'm not sure you have rhinoceros hide.' And Joe said, 'Well, I'll develop rhinoceros hide.'"[8] Later in life he would say on occasion, "My hide is elephantine, reinforced with scar tissue."

8. Interview with Robert H. Orchard, April 18, 1995, St. Louis.

One

Growing Up

For the man third in succession to bear the name of Joseph Pulitzer, it was difficult not to feel the weight of history. "I have grown up in the shadow of two giants,"[1] Joseph Pulitzer III wrote on succeeding to the positions of editor-publisher and president of the Pulitzer Publishing Company as they passed to him in 1955. He had long accepted by the time he took charge at age forty-one, this plain truth: In the ordinary course of things, he really hadn't any choice in the matter. He and his father never "in any exact formal way discussed my future," he recalled, "but we certainly, I think, had an unwritten instinctive expectation that I would carry on a family tradition. I understood it, but without it being written in stone, without it being elaborated as a dictum of that kind. It just sort of grew up."[2] His first duty in that line had been at age three and a half, when he had patted into place the mortar for the cornerstone of the new *St. Louis Post-Dispatch* building at Twelfth Boulevard and Olive Street. His father had used the same silver trowel twenty-seven years earlier, in 1889, in laying the cornerstone of his grandfather's grandiose new *World* building in New York, at that time the tallest in the city.

His grandfather and father were indeed tough acts to follow.[3] Though their careers were not identical, there was a strong ideological bond between the first two J. P.s. Long before 1955, the family name had become a household word through its identification with the prestigious prizes in journalism, letters, and music established by the first Joseph Pulitzer. Yet third-in-line J. P. Jr., as he was known throughout his life even though his

1. *P-D Notebook*, April 1955, 1.
2. William F. Woo interview with JPIII, March 9, 1993. Transcription given to author by Woo.
3. Unless otherwise indicated, the historical survey and descriptive material about family members in this chapter is from George Juergens, *Joseph Pulitzer and the New York World*; Pfaff, *Joseph Pulitzer II and the Post-Dispatch*; Julian S. Rammelkamp, *Pulitzer's Post-Dispatch 1878–1883*; Don C. Seitz, *Joseph Pulitzer: His Life and Letters*; W. A. Swanberg, *Pulitzer*; and interviews with these relatives of Joseph Pulitzer III: Kate Davis Quesada and Elinor Hempelmann (sisters), Michael E. Pulitzer (brother), Joseph Pulitzer IV (son), and Emily Rauh Pulitzer (widow).

father was the actual "junior,"[4] knew, as had his father, that despite ties of blood and assumptions about destiny, no one can or should follow the same path as his predecessor. It proved as true in his case as it had in the previous generation. J. P. II had experienced the world differently than had his father and had responded accordingly and not always as his parent might have done. Yet in their individuality there was a certain continuity. If the three Joseph Pulitzers had one thing in common, it was a strong sense of self-possession—some might call it independence. Each knew himself well enough by early adulthood to trust his own judgments and desires. At the same time, each hoped to be able to gratify his goals in ways worthy of thoughtful respect. And so, when the solemn opportunity came, the third J. P. stepped forward with a bow of humility toward the past followed by a firm assertion of confidence that he and his subordinates also could make a creditable record during their watch. He had no illusion that it would be easy.

Joseph Pulitzer III was born May 13, 1913, in St. Louis at 3836 Lindell Boulevard, his parents' rented first home. He died not far from there, at 4903 Pershing Place, his longtime city residence, almost exactly eighty years later, on May 26, 1993. At his birth, his father, Joseph Pulitzer II, was twenty-eight years old and had been editor and publisher of the *Post-Dispatch* for just over eighteen months. The third J. P. never knew his grandfather, who founded the *Post-Dispatch* in 1878 and died in October 1911 having achieved wealth, renown, and notoriety as the proprietor of the hugely successful *New York World*, which he bought in 1883 and in three years remade into the most profitable and influential newspaper ever published to that time.[5]

Young Joe's father, the second J. P., had not impressed his own father as having the intellect, interest, or drive to succeed him at the helm of the *World*. So he was banished to St. Louis and the *Post-Dispatch*, where, his father believed, he could do the least harm. But in 1931, the *World*, a business failure under the founding Pulitzer's eldest and youngest sons, Ralph and Herbert, disappeared into a merger while the *Post-Dispatch* was well on its way to eminence among American newspapers.[6] For reasons both personal and professional, Joseph Pulitzer II considered himself lucky to

4. J. P. II dropped "Jr." from his name in 1922 and thereafter signed his name as Joseph Pulitzer or J. P.

5. Obituary, Joseph Pulitzer III, *St. Louis Post-Dispatch*, May 27, 1993; Frank Luther Mott, *American Journalism* (New York: Macmillan, 1962), 436.

6. On being sold by the founder's three sons for five million dollars to the Scripps-Howard chain. This required court action to break their father's will, which had stipulated that the *Post-Dispatch* could be sold, but never the *World*. The buyer killed the once distinguished morning and Sunday editions and combined the *Evening World* with its own evening paper to form the *New York World-Telegram*.

have landed in St. Louis. He had gotten most of his newspaper training at the *Post-Dispatch* after doing so poorly during two years at Harvard that his father pulled him out of college in 1906 and put him to work at his midwestern property. In 1910, he married Elinor Wickham of St. Louis. Their first child was Joseph III, followed by two daughters, Kate Davis, born in 1916 and given her paternal grandmother's full maiden name, and Elinor, born in 1922 and named after her mother.

Although nothing suggests that the marriage was calculated on this basis, the alliance with the prominent Wickhams of St. Louis, several generations deep in the tobacco business,[7] was important in establishing the second-generation Pulitzers in the city's upper tier. The Pulitzer name was prominent, too, but it was not uniformly respected. Theirs was not old money. Moreover, their money had been accumulated by the practice of the founding Pulitzer's lusty, loud, and irreverent publicity—more glaringly so in New York than in St. Louis—that became known as "modern American journalism." There were two aspects to this. The first was brassy, bright reporting and illustration tailored to achieve wide popular appeal, huge circulation, and a dependable stream of advertising revenue. The second was crusades for democratic reform of social and political institutions. The editorial positions linked to the crusades generally ran contrary to the interests of the moneyed classes, even though Joseph Pulitzer himself was in that category. He accepted the fact that the *World* would be "detested by those who profited from [the] injustices" and would be portrayed "as cheap, lying, proletarian and revolutionary."[8]

This seeming irony is explainable, however, because although Joseph Pulitzer, born of Hungarian Jewish parents in 1847, had grown up in comfortable circumstances, he also went through some hard times.[9] His father was a successful grain and produce merchant in Mako. The family moved to Budapest, where private tutors educated him. But his father died when he was eleven years old and his mother remarried. Joseph did not like his stepfather and in effect exiled himself from the family when he was sixteen by leaving home with the hope of having a military career. After being rejected as an unlikely physical specimen by several European armies,

7. Elinor Wickham's mother was a Catlin, a family that made its money in tobacco manufacturing in St. Louis. Her father was a descendant of the eminent Carter family of Virginia. Telephone interview with C. Wickham Moore, nephew of Elinor Wickham Pulitzer, October 5, 1985.

8. Swanberg, *Pulitzer*, 99.

9. Csillag, "Joseph Pulitzer's Roots in Europe: A Genealogical History," 54–64. Csillag's research in Hungary verified that both of Pulitzer's parents were Jewish. Two biographies published prior to 1987 identified his father as Jewish and his mother as Austrian-German Catholic. See also Pfaff, *Joseph Pulitzer II*, 400n7.

the seventeen-year-old skin-and-bones six-footer with weak eyesight was accepted in 1864 as a bounty soldier for service with the Union Army in the United States Civil War. He served for one year.

He went through a series of menial jobs both in New York and St. Louis, where he migrated in 1866. But thereafter he rose swiftly. He became a naturalized U.S. citizen, read law and was admitted to the bar, added mastery of English to his fluency in German, French, and Hungarian, and rose from newspaper reporter to proprietor in St. Louis between 1868 and 1878 while intermittently holding elective and appointive governmental offices. He was a millionaire in his early forties. He saw his success as a realization of the American dream, and considered himself a prime example for others on how to achieve it. He designed the *World* to appeal to the thousands of poor immigrants then crowding New York and who, he immodestly believed, he could help achieve better lives through his newspaper and his personal example. As he saw it, "True Americans, having no aristocracy, are ready to worship the aristocracy of virtue and the royalty of genius."[10] While critics questioned the virtue of the *World*'s circulation-building sensationalism and Pulitzer's megalomaniac tendencies, few if any doubted his genius. Those who considered themselves "respectable" journalists—and others—were particularly put off by his battle-in-kind for circulation supremacy with flamboyant William Randolph Hearst's *New York Journal* before and during the Spanish-American War of the 1890s. Although anti-Semitism influenced some detractors, Pulitzer never responded to such published taunts as "*Jew*seph Pulitzer" and "Joey the Jew," choosing instead to side-step the issue. He never practiced Judaism, and was at best a casual Christian. He became a nominal Episcopalian, his wife's affiliation, and his children were reared within the rites of that denomination.[11]

In time, he substantially diminished his papers' sensationalism by infusing the news and editorial columns of his beloved morning *World* with intellectual grist, while the *Evening World* continued to cater to popular tastes in trivial entertainment and sinful behavior. The *Post-Dispatch*, supervised largely by lieutenants rather than by Pulitzer himself, fell somewhere in between the extremes of its New York sisters. For the most part, the St. Louis paper mainly carried news and comment on issues of government and social affairs that would interest the city's substantial middle class. But it also provided liberal helpings of scandal, gossip, comics,

10. Swanberg, *Pulitzer*, 125.
11. See Juergens, *Joseph Pulitzer and the New York World*, 245; Seitz, *Joseph Pulitzer*, 19; and Swanberg, *Pulitzer*, 38–39, 412.

sports, and light entertainment. This changed gradually under the second J. P., who balanced the popular features with more broadly based civic discussion and editorial advocacy in line with his interpretation of his father's liberal ideals. These were expressed when the senior Pulitzer nominally "retired" in 1907, writing of the *Post-Dispatch:* "I know my retirement will make no difference in its cardinal principles, that it will always fight for progress and reform, never tolerate injustice or corruption, always fight demagogues of all parties, never belong to any party, always oppose privileged classes and public plunderers, never lack sympathy with the poor, never be satisfied with merely printing news, always be drastically independent, never be afraid to attack wrong, whether by predatory plutocracy or predatory poverty." Since Pulitzer's death in 1911, that statement has been the newspaper's editorial platform.

In their personal lives, second- and third-generation Pulitzers experienced nothing of the hardships against which the platform inveighed. The homes in which they grew up were staffed with nursemaids, companions, governesses, and a variety of household servants. They were privately educated and socialized with others who were being reared as they were. They summered at Chatwold, a palatial "cottage" on Frenchman Bay at Bar Harbor, Maine, purchased in 1894 by the first J. P. and passed on by his widow in the 1920s to the namesake son after eldest son Ralph declined it. Worried that the children might contract polio in the muggy St. Louis summers, most years J. P. II kept the family in Maine until after the first frost, usually in mid-October. Because school started in September, the children were tutored while they stayed in Maine.

The earliest available record of the elementary education of young Joe Pulitzer III is for 1921, when he entered second grade at Rossman School in St. Louis. Two spinster schoolteachers had founded the coeducational private school four years earlier, the dominant one being Mary B. Rossman. It was housed in a converted three-story brick home at 5438 Delmar Boulevard in the fashionable Central West End, from which the school drew many of its pupils and where the third J. P. eventually bought a home. Miss Rossman emphasized the basics of reading, writing, and mathematics and insisted on the memorization of such facts as the value of *pi* and the number of feet in a mile. Perhaps of greatest value for the future editor who became a fluent writer, she required the students to diagram sentences, a subject on which she coauthored a text. She and the teachers also gave strong reinforcement to moral values and proper conduct. Misbehavior was not tolerated and therefore seldom seen. Alumni readily recalled being taught to respect elders and to be considerate of others, pay attention, be prompt and obedient, work hard, admit mistakes, and never cheat, because "cheating was considered much worse than failing." There was a prayer and the singing of a hymn at the start of each school day. The few existing grade reports of young Joe indicate that he was a bright pupil, his lowest grade being a "passable" in spelling, though he received "excellent" in writing. School records show that he was skipped from fourth to sixth grade.[12]

He took his final year of elementary education in 1925–1926 at Miss Evans's School of Individual Instruction in the St. Louis suburb of University City, locale of Washington University. The purpose was to prepare him to meet the entrance requirements for St. Mark's Preparatory School in Southborough, Massachusetts, where his father and uncles had gone. Most of his grades at Miss Evans's were "good," with the exception of arithmetic, and, as at Rossman, spelling, which were "average." A teacher at Miss Evans's wrote a largely complimentary report on his reading that year, but thought he needed to be challenged more. "I perhaps have expected more of the boy because of his future responsibilities and his present fine mind," the teacher wrote. "Joe is no average child. He is artistic, takes delight in finishing a composition to his satisfaction. He has a great capacity for work and I feel needs to be thrown upon himself more. He needs to think. . . . Joe is too soft in his reading! He needs something to think over. . . . He says he does not care for poetry, but he does." Joe left Miss Evans's School with its confidence that his "stability and well-rounded development" should carry him successfully through prep school and college.[13]

By the time Joe entered elementary school, his family was living in the country home his parents had built in St. Louis County on a hundred-acre site they named Lone Tree Farm. The property was adjacent to the prestigious St. Louis Country Club, to which his father belonged mainly for the benefit of the children. The area is now the bustling upscale St. Louis suburb of Ladue, but in those days the roads were unpaved and neighboring homes were some distance apart. Asked in his seventies to describe his childhood years there, Joe replied, "fun and empty."[14] To be with children

12. Shirley Swanson, *A Portrait of Rossman School 1917–1992* (St. Louis: Gene-Del Printing; privately printed booklet), 22 and passim; Rossman School "Report for Joseph Pulitzer," Joseph Pulitzer II Papers, Library of Congress, microfilm copy, reel 5, frame 47. Hereafter, items from this source will be identified as coming from JPII Papers, and by correspondents, date, and microfilm reel and frame numbers. Telephone interview with Diane Johner, director of development and public relations, Rossman School, May 17, 1995.
13. Reports from Miss Evans's School, 1925–26, JPII Papers, reel 5, frames 266–69, 284.
14. Charlotte Bry questions for History of Ladue, "mailed 8–26–86," JPIII Papers.

their ages, Joe and Kate Davis, three years apart in age, and eventually
Elinor, nine years Joe's junior, were taken into the city for such things as
dance lessons and to see friends. Friends also were brought to the farm.
On Saturdays, Joe and Kate Davis would have dance lessons for an hour
in the morning—boys and girls separately at first, then together for ballroom instruction. Both became excellent ballroom dancers. Years later, an
admiring sometimes partner wrote in a note to him, "You can dance like
an elegant serpent."[15] Joe and Kate Davis also had riding lessons from a
retired cavalry officer at the country club stables who "made you sit up
and pay attention," Kate Davis remembered. "The big social event of the
week" was on Saturday afternoon "when all the little children that we
were supposed to be nice to" came to the Pulitzer home to watch movies,
often cowboy-and-Indian features. There might be as many as twenty children, seated on pillows on the living room floor. Part of the fun was toss-
ing the pillows around while reels were changed.

The most disagreeable thing Joe had to do in those years was try to
learn golf, also at the country club. The first hole was just beyond the
Pulitzers' driveway, where the family's Chesapeake Bay retriever evoked
the ire of club members by fetching balls. But Joe did not enjoy the game
and never played in later life. Ditto for tennis, even after his father had
expensive courts installed at Chatwold and hired private instructors. He
was not a competitive or team athlete, but did enjoy riding, swimming,
sailing in Maine, and bird shooting with his father and others. As an adult
he became an avid skier.

Wanting the boy to develop some competitive attributes, his father,
who had boxed and played football as a youth, made a concerted but
unsuccessful effort to convert his son to similar interests. When Joe was
eleven, his father wrote a St. Louis summer camp counselor that Joe "needs
to be stimulated into a greater understanding of what constitutes manliness. . . . He needs to learn to stand up under grueling physical exercise
and [to overcome] physical fatigue, discomfort, exposure, anything and
everything to make him realize that a soft life is really not worth living."
The summer before Joe went off to St. Mark's, his father had him examined by a St. Louis psychologist, who reported, "Your son, Joe, appears to
have a very keen ability for criticism and a marked interest in everything
dramatic. If he is given encouragement, I shall look for him to do creditable work in this field." Apparently in answer to a specific question, she
also wrote, "I saw no evidence, during my short examination of him, that
his pleasure in dressing up in various costumes was other than that of

15. Virginia [no last name given] to JPIII, September 13, 1987, JPIII Papers.

impersonating different characters. I hope he has had an opportunity to express himself in this way during the year." The same summer, J. P. II wrote a camp counselor in Maine that "Joe is a thoroughly good kid at heart but has many effeminate mannerisms, knows very little about sports and needs roughening up. That was my principal reason for sending him to you." The counselor replied that "Joe seems to be coming out of his mannerisms quite noticeably and is getting quite chummy with some of the other boys. . . . I think he will come right along in the way you want him to." Seeking to reinforce this, his father wrote a coach when Joe was fourteen and at St. Mark's the following year that he wanted his son to take boxing lessons "as often as his schedule will permit." He asked the coach to do all he could "to make him pitch in and take his boxing seriously." Years later he advised younger son Michael to "concentrate on boxing as your principal indoor sport." But boxing appealed to neither boy. When Joe was seventeen and in his fourth year at St. Mark's, his father wrote him, "I hope you will make the second football team this year. There is nothing that would give Mommie and myself greater pleasure."[16]

Mommie was Joe's stepmother, the former Elizabeth Edgar, a St. Louisan his father married in 1926, the year after his first wife died at age thirty-five of injuries suffered in an automobile accident in New York City. Joe was eleven at the time, and felt the loss of his mother the most deeply of the three children. He recalled his reaction after his father hired Miss Sedric Williams, a woman Joe described as "a ghastly governess-type. Awful. She was there after my mother died as a kind of woman in the house. She was sort of stiff . . . very pompous, but not much fun. I thought she was horrible. I used to set paper afire and put it under her door."[17] Kate Davis, on the other hand, took an instant liking to Miss Williams.

Fortunately, their stepmother's temperament was such that all three children came quickly to love her. She was particularly attentive to Joe after he went to St. Mark's, writing him nearly every day. During the six years he spent there—from 1926 to 1932—he made some friends, but on the whole frankly hated the place. One of his friends was John Cromwell, who became an important actor and playwright. "Our closest bond was our distaste for St. Mark's and we conspired in every way to break every

16. JPII to William Goodall, January 12, 1925; JPII to Henry Richards, July 7, 1926; Henry Richards to JPII, July 10, 1926; Ethel M. Riddle to JPII, March 12, 1927; JPII to Thomas Pinckney, January 24, 1927; JPII to MEP, February 11, 1944, JPII Papers, reel 5, frames 174, 275–76, 283, 286; reel 7, frame 245. JPII to JPIII, September 17, 1930, JPII Papers, reel 5, frame 399.
17. Interview with JPIII, July 17, 1984, St. Louis.

rule of the school without being expelled," Joe recalled.[18] Counter-conspiracies of a sort were set in motion from home. One year Joe's step-mother promised him he could choose whatever site he wished for Easter vacation if he could get onto any team at the school. He did—which team no one remembers—and he got his wish to go to Palm Beach, Florida.[19]

Even so, his father persisted in attempting to graft his conception of manliness onto his son. In 1930, Joe's fifth form year at St. Mark's, he tried a covert maneuver by asking the headmaster to thwart his son's plan to room with a boy Joe's father thought was not a sufficiently rough-and-ready type. Although leaving the decision to the headmaster's judgment, he wrote:

> I have nothing whatsoever against -----, and I have the impression that he is a rather unusually intelligent boy. Probably that is what makes him and Joe congenial. I do believe, however, from the little that I have seen of him, that -----, like Joe, lacks vigor, manliness and stamina, and that they both have a somewhat overdeveloped, and I fear false, sense of appreciation of the artistic and of the aesthetic. We believe Joe is pe-culiarly easily influenced by his associates, and we see signs this sum-mer of his having grown away from his namby pamby tendencies through association with a group of virile boys. I cannot help feeling that Joe would be better off without ------ as a roommate, and that ------ would be better off without Joe.

The headmaster, who was new that year and did not know either boy well, discussed with them their wish to room together and concluded that this was perfectly understandable. He wrote Joe's father that because "their tastes are similar... it would be a rather irritating hardship to separate them and might easily do more harm than good. They apparently have a taste for literature and collect first editions together in a small way, and I am sure that you would not want those tendencies discouraged."[20] That ended the matter.

In other ways his father was encouraging, particularly when Joe did some writing for the school publication, the *Vindex*. "I thought your last story... was really fine and easily the best thing that you have ever done," he wrote in 1931. "You made an interesting character of that old woman, and I was glad that there were not as many jade clocks and incense burners

18. JPIII to Mrs. David E. Moore, Sept. 13, 1979, JPIII Papers.
19. Interview with William Julius Polk, Jr., June 11, 1994, St. Louis.
20. JPII to Dr. Francis Parkman, September 14, 1930, Parkman to JPII, September 25, 1930, JPII Papers, reel 5, frames 408 and 403 respectively.

in it as usual. In all seriousness, it was a mighty good story. I do hope the hard work you say you have been doing has been recognized." It was. He received two prizes given by the prep school: the William Otis Smith Prize for English Verse and the Cammann Music Prize. While at St. Mark's, Joe continued piano lessons, which he had begun in St. Louis. "I am very anxious indeed to give whatever aptitude for music he possesses the fullest opportunity for development," his father had written his teacher.[21]

Despite those positives, Joe's aversion to St. Mark's was real and had some foundation. Benjamin Bradlee, who became famous as the *Washington Post*'s managing editor during the Watergate episode of the 1970s and later became the paper's executive editor and a company vice president, attended the school a few years after Joe. It "was one of a dozen citadels of WASP culture that dotted the New England countryside, each giving absolutely first-class educations to young boys preparing to join a world that was slowly ceasing to exist," Bradlee observed in his autobiography. The Episcopalian institution catered to the richest families, and "specialized," he explained, "in fitting round pegs into round holes, fine-tuning good students and good athletes into better students and better athletes, turning them on to new opportunities like social work, debating and extracurricular activities in general." At the time, most of this appealed to Bradlee—a self-described round peg—but he recognized that others, including his own brother, were "square pegs" who "just wouldn't fit into those round holes." So it was for Joe Pulitzer, who generally appreciated the academics and to a certain extent the religious discipline, but little else. His grades across all subjects usually averaged somewhat above 7 (for satisfactory). He did best in English and French, often near or above 8 (good). Still, "he had a miserable time at St. Mark's," Bradlee recalled Joe telling him when they knew each other in later life. "He wasn't a jock, which is how to make friends and influence fellow students at those schools." Looking back at age seventy-one, Joe remembered it as "a very restricted and limited place. It was all very structured, and you did everything that everybody else did. There weren't options and electives and that sort of thing that you get into at college. . . . It was okay, but I was not enthused about it at all."[22] It is virtually certain that St. Mark's was the

---

21. JPII to JPIII, May 7, 1931, JPII Papers, reel 5, frame 458; Robert W. Duffy and George R. McCue, "The Pulitzer Art Collection Earned Worldwide Respect," *St. Louis Post-Dispatch*, May 27, 1993; JPII to William H. Marr, November 19, 1926, JPII Papers, reel 5, frame 278.

22. Bradlee, *A Good Life*, 30, 35; St. Mark's grade reports for JPIII, 1926–1931, JPII Papers, reel 5, frames 277, 279, 313, 361, 445; Telephone interview with Benjamin C. Bradlee, March 31, 1999; JPIII interview, July 17, 1984.

model for a short novel he wrote at Harvard titled *Moth and Rust*. Paragraphs from the novel's prologue introducing "St. Stephan's" reflect his assessment of the prep school:

> On September 15, 1889 the doors of St. Stephan's School open to a selected group of boys. Sons of respectable, land owning, trust funded, pedigreed families form an orderly community of an orderly state.
>
> Football and Latin, hazings and God, a sound mind in a healthy body, self-respect, self-reliance are given equally to all members of the school. A stout-hearted young man is turned out to face the dazzling reality of living. A new and colorful world opens before him, a world of choosing, where Latin is left behind, where cigarettes and spirits exist, where wicked New York beckons, where gaily dressed whores drink champagne at the Waldorf, where things live and breathe....
>
> Into this institution pass father and son in traditional succession, there to be fitted for Harvard and adult life, there to fight for the school flag, cheat at lessons, pray to God, get confirmed amid the smell of lilies and expensive perfumes, the sound of solemn singing and a few tears.[23]

The story almost certainly gives a snapshot of J. P. III as he coped with St. Mark's. He likely named his main character Brook Taurus because Joe was born under the astrological sign of Taurus, a fact he mentioned occasionally all his life. At the outset, his protagonist is a lonely, observant first-former who methodically considers his situation—including how much he looks forward to letters from his mother—and ruminates on the motivations and behavior of the other students, the teachers, and the headmaster. Taurus feels alienated from most of what he observes, particularly the pranks of his peers and the resigned boredom of the masters. Taurus and another boy attempt to run away from the school, but are stopped. Still, they are strengthened by their boldness in the attempt and by the fact that they gain some stature in the eyes of other boys, making life at St. Stephan's more tolerable. Among the instructor's comments on the novel is that there is too much interior monologue. "If you were to take the course over I'd insist on your leaving introspective boys alone," he wrote. However, this interview between Taurus and one of the masters captures some of the young Pulitzer's main impressions of the prep school's narrowness:

> "The trouble, I think, is that you have come to school with the wrong idea. You seem to feel that we are trying to force you against your will

23. Manuscript, *Moth and Rust*, undated, JPIII Papers.

to do all sorts of things, to participate in a life here that you—that is uncongenial to you. Isn't that so?"...

Mr. Culner cleared his throat.

"I think, my boy, that after you've been here a while, you will see that there is quite a tradition about the school, quite a thing to live up to. We must all do our part to cooperate and form part of the life of the school, if you see what I mean....I think in time you and your class mates [will see that you] are a growing body, a team, if I may say so, where every man must do his share if the play is to work right, like in football, you know."

"Yes, sir."

"You see, we come here to learn how to live, and if every one does his share we turn out a fine type of boy who can handle himself in the outside world, a man in fact."...

Brook fumbled to the door, saying "thank you" and Mr. Culner's eyes...seemed to have a look in them that meant you have to make the best of it. A kind look, but he must get out, away from him, he hadn't come here to live; no, it wasn't true. They weren't a team; he didn't want that. He didn't want a team, nor to live here—learn to live.

Part of Joe's difficulty in adjusting undoubtedly lay in the contrast between the relatively Spartan atmosphere of St. Mark's and his environment at home. If life at St. Mark's did not equate with the "real world" as the adolescent imagined it, his life while he was away from prep school during holidays and summers was even further from that norm. The family's life at Bar Harbor had a fairy tale quality, with genteel luxury at every turn. An insider's view of this was preserved in letters to her mother written by Mary Jane Roach, a twenty-year-old St. Louis college student who was hired by the Pulitzers in the summer of 1929 to accompany them to Chatwold as a companion and tutor to Kate Davis. Joe was sixteen that summer, Kate Davis twelve, and Elinor seven. Joe's personality was transformed in these surroundings. Miss Roach described him as "extrovert to the Nth degree. He is a dear and highly diverting; at once naive and subtle, unconscious and calculating. Also, he has a first class sense of humor.... He's really a card—and can even laugh at himself."[24] He frankly enjoyed luxury, telling Miss Roach, "It's nice to have money. I haven't any, but Father has some, and one can have yachts and so forth." "So forth" included his own car, a black Ford with red wheels and white tires. She also observed that he was very close to his stepmother, taking "all his little

24. Mary Jane Roach to her mother. Among typewritten copies of letters written in July and August, 1929, by Mary Jane Roach Masters and given to Joseph Pulitzer III in 1992, JPIII Papers.

thoughts and plans to 'Mommy' because he talks well and at great length about himself, anyway, under the slightest pressure. He is crazy about his own reactions."

Miss Roach was dazzled by the posh life at Chatwold, with its twenty-six rooms and seven bathrooms plus a separate dwelling for servants, a caretaker's cottage, a greenhouse, and a large stable on fifteen acres. A Swiss chef ran the kitchen. She was treated like a member of the family, with a sitting room of her own filled with flowers. She had meals with the family. The breakfast table settings included a fresh gardenia for each person to wear in a buttonhole. "The grownups, including Joe, all dress formally for dinner." She was given a copy of the *Post-Dispatch* daily. Among her favorites of the family's guests were Joe's aunt and uncle, Mr. and Mrs. William S. Moore, who had five sons and also had their own cottage nearby. "I listened to an awfully interesting conversation today between Mr. Moore and 'Daddy' [J. P. II]", she wrote. "All about everything. They say Owen D. Young is going to be the next president, even if he is a Democrat. Everyone here, even the servants, are Democrats." Recalling a dance she attended with Randall Creel, a Harvard senior employed as a companion for the Moore boys, she wrote, "I have never seen such gorgeous clothes in my life. Really, Mother, like the movies—glorious clothes." The dance was held at "the swimming pool, the fashionable hangout for young Bar Harbor." An orchestra played there as well in the afternoons.

She was impressed perhaps most of all by the frequent outings with the family on board their almost-new yacht, *Discoverer*, a seventy-five-foot schooner built in 1924 for fifty-three thousand dollars. It had a crew of six—captain, three sailors, cook, and cabin boy—and was equipped with a galley, bathroom, bunks, and even "tiny chintz parasols to keep the sun off your back." One afternoon they cruised around Mount Desert Island, on which Bar Harbor is located, then had a fish dinner on board and left the boat to see a play in Blue Hill. "Mr. and Mrs. Pulitzer spent the night on the yacht, but Joe, K. D. and I motored home with [butler Albert] Gould, who came for us in the 'Packard for Country Use.' Gray and unspeakably lovely. So we didn't get to bed until about 12:30—but such a beautiful day. You can't imagine how perfect it is to lie around on cushions on deck, covered with a rug, and listen to pretty records on the gramophone, or sleepily read 'The Autobiography of Benvenuto Cellini.'"

While most of what she saw was idyllic, on at least one occasion Miss Roach observed that the Pulitzers could mete out discipline. She had difficulties at first with temperamental Kate Davis, and after several provocations called her bluff by reporting to the girl's stepmother a discourteous rejoinder the girl had made to her. As a result, "a court martial was held, presided over by ma and pa, whereat K. D. and I each spoke her little piece, and as K. D. never lies, she admitted she'd been rude." She was punished by being excluded from a cruise down the coast on the yacht. Relations between young lady and companion improved, and Mrs. Pulitzer assured Miss Roach that she expected and appreciated discipline. Not long thereafter, however, Miss Roach had reason to be grateful for her charge's sharp tongue. She wrote to her mother—and also told Kate Davis and Joe—that Basil Rudd, at that time the private secretary Mr. Pulitzer always took with him to Maine to help with *Post-Dispatch* matters, "attempted to throw a necking party" after taking her out to dinner one evening. He apologized, but she vowed never to go out with him again. "K. D. and Joe were furious, too. K. D. especially gave him a long lecture. It was killing, but so to the point!"

After her daughter made several references in letters to how much she enjoyed Joe's company, Miss Roach's mother cautioned her to keep up her guard. The young lady replied, "Don't bother your dear head about him."

> If anything, I am thought to be too prim and proper, and he is a cute little boy who sees the funny side of everything, and through all pretenses. Nothing in the nature of a crush is in danger of developing. He would think it too screamingly droll for anything. Our friendship is based on this admirable entente of sensing the ridiculous in everything, and never transcends the realm of pure fun.
>
> Romantically, too, he has at least 5 irons in the fire already, and he composes many love letters a day to them, all of which he reads to me. You may be sure we enjoy them thoroughly. He is a dear and a boon for entertainment. As for informality, no one could possibly be formal with him. He is not, however, in the least familiar, so don't worry about the informality. It just breaks the ice for the entire family, and they love it. They are not a bit serious, at heart, I find.

The regular use of alcohol may have contributed to the family's relaxed mood. However, she never saw "the slightest evidence of tightness or even an edge on" except in the case of secretary Rudd, concluding that "drinking matters are so sanely handled here." Even though Prohibition, on the books from 1919 to 1933, was still in force, it was widely ignored. Joe was regularly served a cocktail before dinner, Miss Roach reported, and a dinner-dance given by Kate Davis for twenty-eight children featured "12-year-olds in full dress suits, a twelve-piece 500 dollar orchestra, and brandy in the punch." She once discussed drinking with Joe, who told her "no gentleman ever drinks enough to be able to feel it at all. It's to be treated with no more excess than coffee."

Joe and his parents left Chatwold in August to spend a few weeks in Europe before his return to St. Mark's. When they were a few years older, he and Kate Davis spent more time in Europe than in Maine during summers. Both were glad to expand their horizons beyond the Bar Harbor routine, especially the tennis and golf lessons, which neither enjoyed. Joe's father had offered him seventy-five dollars if he could beat cousin Clement Moore at tennis that summer. This motivated him to practice, but Miss Roach did not record whether he got the reward.

Two

Harvard

During the months spent with the Pulitzers in Bar Harbor, Mary Jane Roach formed some opinions about family dynamics and the destinies of the two oldest children: "Joe and K. D. are both entirely too worldly-wise, and almost ruined by spoiling and servants. Joe is cut out for a life-long dilettante, and K. D. will be a Society Lion, I'm afraid." Her prediction about Kate Davis turned out to be mostly correct. She eventually married an Air Force lieutenant general and became a notable in Washington society. She was mistaken, however, in concluding that Joe would be little more than a dabbler in various pursuits. In addition to his life's work in journalism, he achieved a place among the relative few in the 1930s then dedicated to establishing the significance and appreciation of modern art, an interest that continued throughout his life. Miss Roach also concluded that "Papa gets along with K. D. best, but is more interested in Joe, the son."

Joe's presumed future role in the family business of course explained this. He was the only son until age seventeen, when his half brother, Michael Edgar Pulitzer, was born in 1930, two years before Joe entered Harvard in the Great Depression year of 1932. Although the economic crisis reduced *Post-Dispatch* revenues for most of the decade, the newspaper remained profitable and the family's lifestyle was unaffected. The blueprint for Joe's succession to leadership of the family business was virtually identical to his father's: first, boarding school at St. Marks, then a Harvard degree, then a newspaper apprenticeship consisting of rotation among the various departments.

As it happened, Joe stayed more closely on course than had his father, who stumbled badly on the first two steps. J. P. II had been expelled from St. Mark's when he was sixteen for slipping away from the school with some friends and buying beer. This so angered his father that he vowed to end the young man's formal education then and there, but relented and paid for private tutors so he could pass Harvard's entrance exams. But once at Harvard, the gregarious young man majored mainly in having fun, cut many classes, overspent his allowance, got low grades, and was put on academic probation in 1906 during his sophomore year. Harvard was willing to give him a chance to rectify his situation, but his father had had enough. He pulled his son out of college, assigned him to the *World* for a time—mostly to observe while others worked, which bored him—and then sent him to the *Post-Dispatch*. There J. P. II stayed, except for a short stint back in New York, which he disliked because he missed St. Louis and his bride-to-be. Especially after being allowed to work as a reporter, he took to journalism as a duck to water. His father received glowing reports about his performance, which he discounted as exaggerated and possibly false. The elder Pulitzer focused on disturbing examples of headstrong individualism—never mind how closely these reflected his own makeup—that made him doubt his son's abilities as a journalist or businessman. One of these incidents was taking a five-day vacation from his St. Louis duties without his father's permission to attend a Harvard-Yale football game. Another was bluntly writing his father that fraudulent and misleading medical advertising should be banished from his newspapers. The advice was rejected in a scalding reply. (After inheriting control, J. P. II established at the *Post-Dispatch* the strictest advertising acceptability standards in the country.)[1]

In 1909 Joseph Pulitzer changed his will, leaving only 10 percent of the income from his newspapers to Joseph II, down from 60 percent in the earlier will. Herbert, the youngest son and a schoolboy of fourteen at the time, was to get 60 percent, Ralph, 20 percent, and principal editors and managers 10 percent. After their father's death, the three sons amicably rectified the differences in their incomes. Most importantly, they agreed in 1931 that the *Post-Dispatch* under Joseph II was the only viable Pulitzer newspaper, got court permission to break their father's will, and sold the *World*.[2]

The academic career of Joe III and some aspects of his personality are more closely comparable to those of his Uncle Ralph than to his own father. Ralph, quiet and poetic in temperament and no athlete, also did his time at St. Mark's and earned a Harvard degree, class of 1900.[3] Although they saw relatively little of each other and Ralph died when Joe was in his twenties, the two were alike in being reserved, unprepossessing, and timid among people they did not know well. Both, as eldest sons, were presumed successors, and each surely stood in some awe of the assured self-confidence of his respective father. It is likely as well that Ralph would have agreed with Joe's complaint that at St. Mark's "you did everything

1. Daniel W. Pfaff, "Joseph Pulitzer II and Advertising Censorship, 1929–1939."
2. Pfaff, *Joseph Pulitzer II*, 28–147. They had to get court permission to do this, for their father's will forbade sale of the *World*, but not the *Post-Dispatch*.
3. Obituary, Ralph Pulitzer, *New York Times*, June 15, 1939.

that everybody else did" and had welcomed the greater freedom of choice available at college.

The relative freedom of college was so inviting to Joe that once at Harvard he shed the role of reluctant conformist he had felt forced into at prep school by choosing to major in fine arts. He also slacked off so much in his first semester that he ended up on academic probation, receiving a D in, of all things, one of two English courses. In the other he earned a B. "There is no excuse in the world for his D," his father wrote assistant dean Wilbur J. Bender, noting that Joe had entered Harvard with "an honor" in English. He pledged both to write and telephone his son with a stiff reminder of his responsibilities and suggested that Joe be shown the letter, which also contained these lines:

> Government 1, which I insisted upon his taking in preparation for what I hope will be a life work in journalism, will be a difficult course for him, as he seemingly has little interest in the subject. That, of course, only means that he will have to work all the harder on that course.
>
> He is a boy of good character and in many respects has an original and creative mind, but unless interested he is irresponsible and inclined to let things slide.[4]

Bender's reply was that he did not think Joe's difficulties were serious. He attributed them to his not having worked hard enough and giving too much time to social activities. Bender might not have realized how pointedly this particular parent took his meaning when he added: "You realize, of course, that this happens to a great many Freshmen." And so the matter evaporated. Despite Joe's somewhat wobbly start, his father's own gregarious social temperament no doubt figured in his decision to permit Joe to have an automobile in his second semester and for the rest of his time at Harvard. The first vehicle was a 1931 Auburn Phaeton, replaced two years later by a new 1934 Ford Cabriolet.[5]

Joe's father almost certainly was inclined to object that a fine arts major was an effete and impractical choice for someone on his career path, but J. P. II kept it to himself. Joe's stepmother was instrumental in this, considering his interest in art legitimate and encouraging it. There were times, Kate Davis remembered, when Mommie intervened in Joe's behalf when Daddy protested about his preoccupation with art. "Let him alone. Let

---

4. JPII to Assistant Dean W. J. Bender, December 2, 1932, JPII Papers, reel 5, frame 483.

5. Wilbur J. Bender to JPII, December 8, 1932, JPII Papers, reel 5, frame 482; JPII to JPIII, September 23, 1933; Laclede Insurance Agency to Lincoln Hockaday, April 2, 1934, JPII Papers, reel 5, frames 572 and 621.

him do what he wants. It's fine," she would say.[6] And—at least to him-self—his father would have had to admit that Joe had after all chosen a genuine academic pursuit over his own preferences while at Harvard to lounge around with fraternity pals during the week and go to parties and ball games on the weekends. His tolerance also may have been bolstered by his own aversion toward becoming the dictator his father had been in attempting to direct his children's every move. Still, J. P. II did not leave to chance Joe's getting the message that his future in journalism was set-tled. "I always felt that was the profession I should stay in and that it was a family thing and that it had three generations," Joe said in 1984. "I felt the third generation thing. I felt it was important to try."[7]

The strong bond of admiration and respect Joe developed for his father—plus a good measure of fear of displeasing—no doubt cemented that deci-sion, although both Kate Davis and lifelong St. Louis friend William Julius Polk, Jr.—known to his friends as Polky—agreed that he did not reach it without some vacillation.[8] In the end, art took the prominent second place in his life. As if to ensure this, his father saw to it during his son's college years that there were periodic reminders about the future. In early 1933 he asked *Post-Dispatch* chief Washington correspondent Charles G. Ross to spend two days showing "my very immature and, alas, unpolitically minded nineteen-year-old son Joe around Washington . . . giving him a chance to see the wheels go round and teaching him as much as you can about the low-down of American political life."[9] He wrote Joe that he would enjoy meeting Ross and the two other men in the bureau, Paul Y. Anderson and eventual bureau chief Raymond P. Brandt. "You will soon discover that Anderson thinks along different lines from those followed by the fathers of your St. Mark's friends," he noted. Anderson, at that time probably the country's best investigative reporter and a man who had only contempt for the pretentious and hypocritical, had won a Pulitzer Prize for uncovering facts behind what became known as the Teapot Dome scandal of the 1920s.

In July 1935, between his junior and senior years, Joe's father arranged for him to get his first hands-on daily newspaper experience by working for a month at the *San Francisco News* under editor W. H. Burkhardt, do-ing mostly reporting and writing. Before proposing the assignment to

6. Interview with Kate Davis Pulitzer Quesada, April 27 and 28, 1995, Hobe Sound, Florida.
7. Interview with JPIII, July 17, 1984, St. Louis.
8. Interviews with KDPQ, April 27, 1995, and WJP, June 11, 1994, St. Louis; William J. Polk, Jr., and John W. Curley, *Uncle Polky*, 35.
9. JPII to Charles G. Ross, January 23, 1933, JPII Papers, reel 95, frame 615.

Burkhardt, Joe's father asked Henry Niemeyer, who wrote from the West Coast for the *Post-Dispatch*, to check out the *News*. Although it had the smallest circulation of any San Francisco paper, Niemeyer reported, "newspaper men consider it the most reliable paper on the coast where the [sensationalistic] curse of the Hearst press hangs heavily over the heads of all newspapers out here. The *News* is a typical Scripps-Howard paper, which means that it is understaffed. That, for Joe, Jr., is fortunate, for he will get a world of experience in every line." In asking Burkhardt to take Joe on, J. P. II wrote the editor: "Whether he has any aptitude for journalism, I do not know. . . . It goes without saying that I should much prefer that he be given no special consideration as to hours, discipline, etc., and indeed I should rather see him given if anything the worst of it, for the sooner he realizes how very little he knows and how much he has to learn the better."[10]

Burkhardt obliged. One assignment was to report on the effort of an unemployed father to find work. Joe found it "very depressing. It's rather tough for a young reporter to go into a family that's going through tough times and to keep asking, 'How's it going?'" Day after day, the response was the same: still struggling, no change. But the tough city editor to whom Joe reported this kept insisting otherwise: "Oh goddammit, there has to have been a change!"[11]

This exposure to a family so unlike his own underscored his father's point that Joe had much to learn. Yet as doubtful as J. P. II may have been about his son's career readiness at age twenty-two, Joe and his father clearly had a much closer relationship, both professionally and personally, than had existed between his father and grandfather. Grandfather was a brilliant bundle of nervous energy who had always been a voracious reader and appreciated good music, art, and the theater. But by midlife his newspapers and politics dominated his attention and his health was failing. He was virtually blind by the age of forty-two and grew so sensitive to noise that he spent almost no time in New York, and none in St. Louis. For the rest of his life he traveled restlessly among his homes in Bar Harbor, Maine, Jekyll Island, Georgia, and Cap Martin, France. From 1907 on, he spent much time cruising between America and Europe on his 269-foot steam yacht, *Liberty*, specially built for $1.5 million to shield him from noise. He was accompanied everywhere by a corps of male secretaries who read to him many hours daily and handled the constant stream of

10. Henry Niemeyer to JPII, May 19, 1935, JPII Papers, reel 5, frame 641; JPII to W. H. Burkhardt, April 30, 1935, JPII Papers, reel 5, frame 644.
11. Steve Friedman, "Pulitzer," *St. Louis Magazine*, August 1987, 28; WW interview with JPIII, March 9, 1993, St. Louis.

memorandums and letters he dictated to his editors, managers, and family members. He genuinely loved his wife and children, but because of his condition spent limited time with them.

The second J. P. gradually lost all but about 20 percent of his vision and also had to be read to, but at the same time had what Joe III remembered as a *"joie de vivre"* instead of his grandfather's "brooding and melancholy character." Despite his visual handicap, Joe's father was an outdoorsman who particularly enjoyed fishing and bird shooting. Even in his later years, he could shoot ducks if they were silhouetted against an overcast sky. Joe recalled that when he was in prep school and college, "my father was rather inclined not to talk business at home. He would talk public affairs or journalism, but he didn't like talking office at home. I think he had enough [and] wanted something else that would be diverting. He was quite determined on this point: To have fun in life as well as having a responsible and important career." To Joe, this seemed a form of permission to him to give both his vocation and other interests full play. That made room for art—a riveting, passionate interest that came from deep inside him rather than from any outside person or influence. "Joe saw art as an integral and essential part of his daily life," art historian Angelica Zander Rudenstine commented.[12] This set him apart as an individual and earned him international standing as an authority on and collector of modern and contemporary art.

Although his father's temperament and poor vision prevented him from understanding his son's love of art, Joe pressed on. Within a year of his graduation from college he had acquired about a dozen paintings and was allowed to have display space at home, thanks largely to his stepmother's influence over his father. Joe redecorated a rather large room over the garage at Lone Tree Farm as both his bedroom and a backdrop for his pictures. Nationally prominent St. Louis designer Victor Proetz supervised this and created some chairs, tables, lamps, and other furniture especially for it. The tables, which Joe kept in his home ever afterward, have intaglio decorations of a mandolin and guitar, forms copied from Picasso paintings. The walls, carpeting and furniture, and drapes and blinds were all in neutral colors, mostly gray. "It looked a little like a mortuary," Kate Davis said. "Daddy, whose eyesight was very bad, wandered upstairs one day while Joe was away and he came back and said to my stepmother, 'My God, he must be sick! Have you seen his room? His room

12. M. Hayward Post, Jr., M. D., to Carlos F. Hurd, *Post-Dispatch* reporter, May 22, 1947, JPIII Papers; Telephone interview with JPIII, May 23, 1986; Rudenstine's remarks at the funeral of JPIII, May 29, 1993, JPIII Papers.

is the most depressing thing I've ever seen in my life. It's just a great big gray box with all the shades pulled down.'" Others reacted differently. Asked if he was impressed by Joe's early collection, Robert Brookings Smith, a longtime St. Louis friend with an interest in the arts, replied: "Of course, you couldn't help it." Initially, Joe bought pictures he could afford on the allowance he received—this was $3,000 in 1933—just because he liked art, not because he planned to become a collector. When he was twenty-one and just finishing his sophomore year, he got an inheritance from his grandfather's estate, as did all the grandchildren on coming of age. Joe received the income on some $700,000. Kate Davis described it as "a nice little sum" that Joe used to buy art. The family attorney suggested to J. P. II that Joe's payments be $5,000 a year while he was at Harvard, then raised to $10,000 on his graduation and to $15,000 at age thirty. He suggested that the full income be paid him from age thirty-five on "for by then he will undoubtedly have acquired a knowledge of the value of money, unless too large an income is paid to him at the outset."[13]

A friend recalled that in later life, Joe enjoyed telling how "his father would take General [Leif] Sverdrup [head of a St. Louis engineering company] and his other friends who were square, macho guys, upstairs and show them the art in Joe's room and say: 'This will teach you not to leave your money to your young grandchildren.'" When a 1949 *Post-Dispatch* file draft of his father's obituary identified his father rather than Joe as a collector of "the young masters, starting with Picasso," Joe wrote the managing editor: "This is not correct. J. P. [II] instinctively dislikes modernism in any form and I am sure does not consider himself as a 'collector.' It is true that he has a fondness for color and he has satisfied that inclination through bright sporting prints, very often Currier and Ives, bright chintzes and fresh cut flowers. He has always been fond of English and American furniture but never—I repeat—'modern.'"[14]

His father was "convinced," Joe believed, "that I had been fleeced by shrewd and unscrupulous New York art dealers."[15] This was to be expected. "Nobody in St. Louis when Joe started [collecting] understood him or had any appreciation of contemporary art," recalled Euretta (Rettles) Rathbone,

    13. Interview with WJP, June 11, 1994; Interview with Robert Brookings Smith, September 22, 1994, St. Louis; Memorandum to J. P. II from [no first name] Anderson dated 1933, JPII Papers, reel 105, frame 504; JPII to John G. Jackson, September 13, 1933, Jackson to JPII, September 20, 1933, JPII Papers, reel 5, frames 590–91.
    14. Interview with Adam Aronson, May 30, 1995, St. Louis; JPIII to BHR, January 24, 1949, Papers of JPIII.
    15. Robert W. Duffy and George McCue, "The Pulitzer Art Collection Earned Worldwide Respect," *St. Louis Post-Dispatch*, May 27, 1993.

whose husband, Perry T. Rathbone, directed the St. Louis Art Museum from 1940 to 1955. "Joe was very brave in that because . . . nobody understood what he was collecting until Perry came." Rathbone helped educate the community by bringing modern and contemporary art to St. Louis while Joe saw that the new artists got attention in the *Post-Dispatch*.[16] When it became apparent that Joe's selections were both important and valuable, his father asked him how he had known what to buy. "Because you sent me to Harvard," he replied, adding that he had been able to visit the finest museums in Europe in the summers during his prep school and college years and at Harvard had studied under some of the best art professors anywhere. Modesty no doubt kept him from adding what those knowledgeable about art would say: that he was gifted with "a great eye."

Pablo Picasso was one of the artists Joe most admired and one his father could not understand. Joe received honors for his senior thesis on Picasso. These are the concluding paragraphs:

> We have laid a foundation for an understanding of the art of Pablo Picasso. The development leading up to contemporary painting has been surveyed. The spiritual attitude of modern European painters and of Picasso has been suggested. We have looked at Picasso's life and at representative pictures from his many periods.
>
> What can we say of this genius of painting that his pictures do not say more eloquently? Nothing. We avoid the words "intense," "sensitive," "beautiful" and the like because, already exhausted, they are still undefined.
>
> We do say this: that Picasso has been truthful to what he has felt; that he has reflected courageously a breathless era; that he has painted, like the great masters of all periods, with control and intelligence.
>
> Time, I suspect, will substantiate his greatness. Of this I am certain: that students one hundred years from today when they are asked, "Who ushered in twentieth-century French painting?" will necessarily answer: "Picasso."[17]

Those passages contain themes relevant to more than art, including approaches that might be taken in newspaper journalism. For one thing, they show that the author was interested in making connections, just as a fact-gatherer does in pulling bits of information together into an article. For another, they suggest intellectual forcefulness and curiosity to get

---

16. Interview with Mrs. Perry T. Rathbone, July 17, 1999, Cambridge, Massachusetts.
17. Portion of Harvard thesis, JPIII Papers.

beyond the obvious and superficial and to ponder deeper, more elusive issues of human existence. This is done in a certain detached, inquiring, and respectful way, without shades of arrogant expertise. The language shows a facility for direct, clear, engaging expression. Seen in this light, the education of Joseph Pulitzer III, no matter what his major, was less a departure into the impractical than it might have seemed to his father and some others.

Evidence of his critical and expressive abilities shows up in his work in Harvard English classes, despite the D as a freshman. Most of this is in the form of short stories, in which the writer's personal experience is clearly evident. The writing itself is crisp and clean. "This is very clear," a Professor Kempton commented on one story. "You have a priceless gift of observing details and transmitting them without change." In a section of the story "Tide Cycle," David, a prep school boy, has just finished a solo cross-country run:

> Gasping for breath, he at last dropped onto a wooden bench outside the gymnasium. His heart was beating fast, and sweat glistened on his forehead. The healthy weariness of running overcame him, made him feel at peace with the school he tried so often to forget. He would have a different sense of freedom in four days. New York. Exciting. The unbelievable end of the long school term was at hand. Once more he would be an individual. He thought of the towering buildings, of the people with unnatural, pallid faces under the lights of Broadway, of the long, hushed galleries of art; the tomb-like corridors of paintings where couples passed, whispering as if in the presence of the dead. A dance at Pierre's with girls and music and laughter. And it would be wonderful to see girls again. He'd be timid in their presence and awed by their delicacy, by their softness.[18]

As that passage, other things he wrote at Harvard, and Miss Roach's account of the summer of 1929 suggest, Joe developed a lively interest in the opposite sex in adolescence and early adulthood. He saved a letter suggestive of a gentle turndown with his Harvard English stories. It was signed "Peg" and includes these lines:

> Why do you always ask me, Joe, whether I think you're an idiot? You must know I like you—or do you think I'd have taken any beau home with me?(!) (that night). . . . I couldn't fall in love with you, it would be too painful. . . . You're a playboy and can't be taken seriously now tho

---

18. From "Tide Cycle," JPIII Papers.

you may be different later on. I wouldn't want you to fall for me either. I'm afraid I'm not a lucky number to take a chance on.[19]

However, most of his Harvard experience Joe chose to preserve has to do with his education. One of his favorite English classes was in contemporary literature, also with Kempton. Near the end of the course he wrote some lines of poetry titled "Epistle to Dr. Kempton." These are some of its passages:

> Surveying facile lines of Pope inspired
> Our writing comments we have long desired
> We first present a laurel to James Joyce:
> The modern writer's peremptory choice. . . .
> We linger with the turgid Gertrude Stein
> To call her writing merely asinine.
> We skip the foreign Wasserman and Proust
> To settle with Virginia Woolf to roost.
> She is the lady who experiments,
> Producing novels none of us resents. . . .
> Returning to America we find
> Maturing writers of a different kind.
> There's William Faulkner's sordid Tennessee
> With every woman steeped in pregnancy. . . .
> John Dos Passos and Ernest Hemingway
> Keep frantic imitators well at bay.

"Neat but not fiery," Kempton commented. "An achievement, unquestionably. You leave Faulkner too abruptly. You are a very mild Pope, a very impersonal Pope. But if this amused you to write, it pleases me to read." He graded the work "A." On another story a professor—possibly Kempton—wrote: "Butterfield has just phoned me that you wrote the best book in Eng. 95. Good stuff."

That Joe's interests in art and music also set him apart from the general run of Harvard undergraduates is evident in several of his stories. One is about an art counterfeiter whom a friend fails to persuade to produce and market original work of his own; in others there are scenes in galleries or museums. He drew the scenes from firsthand experiences both at home and abroad. Kate Davis, who visited him often at Harvard, said classmates considered him "somewhat quaint" because of his fine arts major and because "on weekends everybody would go to football games. That was the big deal. Have a girl up and go to the football game. Well, he would

---

19. "Peg" to JPIII, undated [approx. 1935], JPIII Papers.

get on the train and go down to New York and go to art galleries. . . . No one else wanted to go to an art gallery." Joe was just as disdainful of football, as comes through in this passage from another of his Harvard stories: "A nice fellow, Ollie; but what a mind. How could one play football all fall and then live with a roommate who managed football? And then discuss football all winter at the club, or maybe hockey? God."[20]

His sister recalled that the attractive furnishings in his Harvard room further confirmed his reputation as an atypical collegian. "His college mates thought he was quite eccentric, really. . . . He had a carpet on the floor. That was like living at the Ritz." Sidney Freedberg, who had more in common than most with Joe as a fellow fine arts major, and who became a distinguished curator and a fine arts professor at Harvard, remembered the room as striking:

> Joe's rooms in Eliot House (in those days students might still have suites) were a fitting frame for him. . . . [They] contained one piece of furniture that was, even in those days, unusual in a student's room: a baby grand piano. The room conveyed the effect, also unusual in a student's room, of recessive elegance. Joe's own instinctive elegance could not, without a conscious effort, be suppressed; it was apparent in his manner, in his dress and in his speech, which carried the flavor of the great New England Episcopal boarding schools, . . . but uttered through a slightly drawling baritone voice. . . .
>
> The Eliot suite was the locale of a discreet number of cocktail parties, attended by Joe's undergraduate Harvard and Radcliffe friends and a few older friends as well. After these parties, it was Joe's habit to adjourn with a small core group to the Ritz bar, in those days entirely a pretty glitter of fake Louis Quinze, where we would entrench ourselves in a corner and consume, occasionally to mild but not extreme excess, the delicious concoctions of the Ritz bartender.[21]

Joe made regular use of the piano, having become proficient in some works of the classical composers and at jazz improvisation. He played at home for his own pleasure more than for others, and on occasion for friends. His sister remembered one rather public display of her brother's skill. They and friends were at a dance where the music was provided by society pianist Eddie Duchin and his orchestra. Also there was Eve Symington, wife of Stuart Symington, then head of Emerson Electric in St. Louis and later a Democratic U.S. senator from Missouri. Mrs. Symington was a

20. From "The Empty Spaces," JPIII Papers.
21. Talk by Sidney Freedberg at Harvard tribute to J. P. III, October 1993, JPIII Papers.

popular singer at New York night spots, and during the evening Joe and Duchin sat at two pianos and played while she sang. There is a glimpse of Joe's musical literacy and his critical flair in this passage from one of his Harvard stories:

Sitting down at the piano, [Anna Whetherby] ran her fingers wildly over the keyboard: minor scales, the whole tone scale, all cried out with mad frivolity. Paul glanced at the music on the rack: Chopin, a Bach fugue, Rachmaninoff, Lizst, a suite of Debussy, Grieg, Beethoven, a sonata of Syril Scott, The White Peacock by Griffes, even a transcription of Stravinsky, and tossed over these a tone-poem by Leo Ornstein. Paul was surprised; the music of Leo Ornstein and Anna Whetherby clashed like shell-pink and brick-red, but infinitely more seriously, like two orbits yanked out of place, battling for supremacy, or like a madman rising in a church, and with deadly serenity and perfect calm, pronouncing the great untruth, God is Satan, Satan is God. Leo Ornstein and Anna Whetherby; this was chaste and pure dissimilarity. These names were as discordant together as the music of Leo Ornstein is dissonant![22]

During his Harvard years he also helped to establish the Little Symphony in his hometown. This group, begun in 1934, augmented the summer incomes of some St. Louis Symphony musicians, thus keeping them from seeking employment elsewhere. Little Symphony concerts were first given in the amphitheater of a private school and then on the quadrangle at Washington University. Robert Brookings Smith, son of a St. Louis broker and investment adviser who eventually followed his father into that business and became a longtime financial adviser to the Pulitzer Publishing Company, was the first Little Symphony president. Joseph Pulitzer III was the second.[23] His old friend Polk also was heavily involved. In a lighthearted letter after Joe missed a Little Symphony directors meeting, Polk wrote about some of the vexations with which the board was grappling. He reported that the symphony came within ten dollars of meeting its $3,340 costs for the season, and continued that in putting together programs it is

impossible to please everybody... if you play the moderns, inevitably old ladies would write in canceling their subscriptions, and if you played the classics, the young would pout and say they wanted to know what was going *on* in the world.... But isn't music lousy with politics? God

22. "Number 17 Ashley Street," JPIII Papers.
23. Wells and McIntosh, *Symphony and Song: The St. Louis Symphony Orchestra,* 66; Interview with Robert Brookings Smith, September 22, 1994, Clayton, Missouri.

knows what cankering jealousies may be smoldering away in the hairy breasts of Arnold Maremont or Milton Mendle, only to flare into some fearful flame by Labor Day. What horrid baby viper may not be coddling in Mrs. Goldstein's jet-trimmed bonnet or coiling around the sleek curves of Chloe Sherman? Oh well![24]

Obviously able to weather all that, Joseph Pulitzer III was for the remainder of his life an important patron and benefactor of the St. Louis Symphony, serving on its governing board for many years. (Both his father and grandfather had been major contributors as well.) While keeping his own connection as quiet as possible, he was a constant source of memorandums suggesting symphony coverage to *Post-Dispatch* staff members.

He also began paying attention while at Harvard to the annual awarding of the Pulitzer Prizes, particularly those in the arts. His father was on the Advisory Board on the Pulitzer Prizes, chaired by his Uncle Ralph, which made the final decisions based on recommendations of juries in each category. "Everyone is asking why, why, why," Joe wrote his father after the 1935 drama prize went to *The Old Maid*, by Zoe Akins, "in this year of social crisis is the Pulitzer drama award given to a play about mother love in the eighteen thirties? Obviously, a more cooked-up saccharine and unimportant play rarely has been seen. If 'The Old Maid' represents 'the power and educational value' of the stage, I misunderstand the meaning of these terms. I should be very interested to know what mad humor prompted the Advisory Council's decision." His father, who was not to speak out of school on these matters but occasionally did, replied confidentially that he too found the play "a very dull thing to sit through," and had told the board he did not think giving it the prize would sit well with the public. Nevertheless, a board majority went along with the jury's recommendation. His father added: "It is a curious fact that the awarding of prizes is really an extraordinarily difficult undertaking."[25] Joe learned that firsthand later during his long tenure as Advisory Board chairman.

Joe received his degree at Harvard in the spring of 1936. During his final year at college, he made his first major art purchase, the painting *Elvira Resting at a Table*, by Amedeo Modigliani. It was not a spur-of-the-moment decision, but carefully considered and acted on only after he consulted art professor Paul J. Sachs, who encouraged him to buy it, even if he had to borrow the money. Kate Davis recalled that he did, probably

24. WJP to JPIII and Louise Pulitzer, July 22, 1939, JPIII Papers.
25. JPIII to JPII, undated [1935], JPII to JPIII, May 11, 1935, JPII Papers, reel 5, frames 661–63.

from a bank, certainly not their father: "Oh no! Daddy thought modern art was degenerate!"

Perry Rathbone, who met Joe when both were fine arts students at Harvard and went on to direct the St. Louis Art Museum and then the Boston Museum of Fine Arts, had a sharply different perspective. He saw Joe's first dozen acquisitions, including the Modigliani, as evidence of "courageous independence."[26] Other paintings in this group included four Picassos, the *Corsage Jaune* of 1907 being the most famous, and works by Braque, Rouault, and Bonnard. They "would have pleased the collector's grandfather, the great journalist," Rathbone suggested, "however firmly he might have disagreed with his namesake's taste." The small group of paintings in Joe's room, he noted, became the foundation of his collection. And that room was the place where "his contemporaries, as well as the older generation, had their first opportunity to see modern art in St. Louis." By the time he went into the Navy at age twenty-eight, he had purchased twenty works of art, most of them pieces of lasting importance.[27]

26. Perry T. Rathbone, "Journalist-Collector: A Nose for the New," *Art News*, April 1957, 32, 62.

27. Sidney Freedberg, "Remembering Young Joe," unpublished tribute delivered at Harvard University, October 1993.

Three
Executive Apprentice

Joe sailed for Europe shortly after graduation, staying there until late September. He stopped on the return trip at Villanova, Pennsylvania, to be a groomsman in cousin Frances McKittrick's wedding. Back home, his father was eager to move his son's education in its primary direction. J. P. II had alerted *Post-Dispatch* Washington bureau chief Raymond P. Brandt to make arrangements for Joe to tour on the presidential campaign trains in the fall so he could "inhale the pure air of American politics and find out how little he knows about it." Brandt assigned him to accompany correspondent Marquis Childs. His father gave his standard admonition that his son was to be shown no favoritism or special treatment and instructed Brandt that when Joe was not on a campaign trip "please do whatever you can to keep him busy and interested and stimulated by taking him with you whenever possible on your rounds in Washington." His salary was twenty dollars a week. J. P. II wrote Joe that besides accompanying incumbent Franklin D. Roosevelt and his Republican opponent, Alfred M. Landon, "it would be instructive and well worth your while" to cover speeches by Socialist Norman Thomas and Communist Earl Browder as well as Father Charles Coughlin, the Roosevelt-hater and anti-Semite, and Francis Townsend, who advocated providing two hundred dollars a month to everyone sixty or older. He and Childs got the opportunity to cover only Thomas, whom, Joe recalled in 1993, he found "a very delightful man, very charming and civilized," who "didn't look like a wild guy socialist." His father's point, he added, had been to broaden his political understanding, especially that the country "wasn't strictly a society made up of capitalists."[1]

1. Miss McKittrick was the daughter of Joe's Aunt Emily, his late mother's sister. Kate Davis also was in the wedding party. *New York Times*, September 27, 1936, section II, page 5. JPII to RPB, May 13, 1936, JPII Papers, reel 101, frame 642; JPII to RPB, September 23, 1936, JPII Papers, reel 5, frame 687; JPIII to author (by telephone), September 29, 1987; JPII to JPIII, September 25, 1936, JPII Papers, reel 5, frame 681; WW interview with JPIII, March 9, 1993, St. Louis.

J. P. II telephoned Childs for reports on how Joe was doing. In early October he asked about what probably was the first of Joe's stories to be published. Because Joe was in the room at the time, Childs demurred and sent a letter. It reported that Joe wrote the story at about 1 a.m., drawing on notes he had made during the day, then showed it to Childs, who suggested a few changes in the lead paragraph. "I thought the lead would stand up through the day," Childs explained, "but the Jersey City demonstration was so remarkable that I suggested . . . that he write a new lead. This he did in the press stand just back of the speaker's stand, and I did not even see it before he sent it. He wrote it, as one always writes such stories, just as fast as possible, handing two or three paragraphs at a time to the telegraph operator. I wish you might have seen your son. He was sweating like a trooper and completely oblivious to his surroundings."[2]

The lead read:

> Arriving at Jersey City Medical Center for dedication ceremonies, President Roosevelt was met today by a tremendous crowd which lined the streets four to 10 deep for three miles. Mayor Frank Hague had got out a crowd estimated at 200,000, made up mostly of school children.

The second paragraph included this visual detail:

> It became more apparent each moment that a great theatrical performance was being staged. Church steps and tenement steps were packed; windows, pasted with photographs of the President, bulged with admirers; fire escapes swarmed with people.

His report of a Landon appearance in Cleveland on October 13 opened:

> Ticket holders began to pour into the barrel-vaulted Public Hall at 7 o'clock last night to hear Gov. Alf M. Landon. Flags were distributed to the crowds as they entered. A large percentage of women and Negroes could be seen among the spectators. A jazz band played popular tunes. One or two flags waving would start 10,000 flags waving.[3]

The stories' bylines identified the writer only as "a staff correspondent of the Post-Dispatch."

2. Marquis W. Childs to JPII, October 6, 1936, JPII Papers, reel 5, frame 683.
3. "Jersey City Greets Roosevelt Rousingly," "Cleveland Crowd Two Hours Early," *St. Louis Post-Dispatch*, October 2 and 13, 1936; JPII Papers, reel 5, frames 684–85.

When the campaign ended, Childs wrote J. P. II that he had enjoyed having the young man with him and that because Joe's interests in "the arts and contemporary literature coincided with my own interests to a certain degree" they sometimes turned to those topics "in the brief interludes when we were not writing or observing." He was guardedly complimentary for the most part:

> I think that Joe wants to be genuinely interested in newspaper work and I feel he will eventually overcome a certain diffidence toward public affairs that he now has. He has a preeminent interest in ideas, and therefore, as he well realizes, most people, particularly those who do not speak his own language, bore him. He is aware of this, however, as a handicap. He is timid about making requests and seeking people out, but no more than many beginning reporters. My impression is that he learns very rapidly when he has a mind to learn. He has an excellent eye for detail, for the curious and phenomenal, which, I believe, will be sharpened as he continues in newspaper work and will constitute one of his chief assets.
>
> The campaign trips were to him in a certain degree a hardship—the long, irregular hours, the uncertain living conditions, etc.—but I heard him do no grumbling about it. He took it like a good sport.

Yet in some important respects Childs found deficiencies, mainly the need to gain "an understanding of the importance of exact names, exact addresses, correct spelling and those details which are acquired through routine reporting." Childs recommended "the discipline of routine work for a considerable period of time" even though "the prospect is distasteful to him." He also pointed out that the young man "is not a newspaper reader" and is familiar only in "a broad way with national affairs." Childs was cautious about predicting the future, but said he found two key qualities in the young man: "I have great respect for his intellect and for his capacity to form his own opinions." Others had said the same things about Joe's grandfather. But where Joe's abilities might lead him, Childs was not sure: "[H]e wants very earnestly and seriously to become a newspaperman and assume his responsibility. But I think he would be perfectly candid with himself if he thought he had failed after a sufficient time. If, plus his intellect, there is the goad of ambition, I should say he will go far in whatever field he settles down in."[4]

In his father's mind, his son was being groomed to succeed, period. Failure was not an option. Knowing this, the prospect of his future respon-

4. MWC to JPII, November 4, 1936, JPII Papers, reel 5, frame 679.

sibilities made Joe uneasy. "I always approached it with a good deal of modesty and trepidation," he recalled. "Because I think third generation—there was a lot of weight hanging over you."[5] His father made him a director of the Pulitzer Publishing Company six months after he graduated from Harvard. In 1939 he became first vice president and, on the death of his Uncle Ralph that year, joined his father and Uncle Herbert as one of the company's three trustees. Joe recognized that his father wanted this done "to make me aware of the business responsibilities that I would someday be confronted with and also make me aware of what was going on at the Pulitzer Publishing Company. . . . He did that for a very good reason: He exposed me to all these discussions and business." Even so, "it was in a way hard, because if you're on the board, and you're a trustee, with no specific job, you're just an observer. There's a sort of awkwardness about that." For his first few years as a trustee, Joe received no commission, as did his father and uncle, getting instead an equivalent ten-thousand-dollar annual salary from the *Post-Dispatch*.[6]

Much as his father's newspaper training had been arranged by J. P. I, Joe's St. Louis assignment during the late fall of 1936 was as an observer in the paper's various departments. His parents were away part of that time, shooting pheasants in Hungary and visiting elsewhere in Europe. Shortly before they were to return, Joe sent his father a summary of "my apprentice work on the eighth floor," the location of the business offices. "I think I've been learning quite a bit about how the wheels turn around," he reported. He had spent two weeks with company treasurer James T. Keller "going through his files pretty thoroughly and listening to long sad lectures" on the paper's mounting expenses. On his own, he decided to make graphs of the expenses of all the paper's departments "which gave me a good but alarming picture of how expenses have been running for the last ten years." He noted in another report: "I believe it was at my suggestion that a summary of the revenues, expenses and Nelson [his grandfather's code word for 'net profit'] of the company less interest on investment and radio was made." This turned up "evidence of extravagance." For example, 1936 expenses of $566,000 were $4,000 ahead of revenues and net profits were that much behind 1935. Keller was delighted with these insights, Joe reported: "He said any number of times, 'I'm tickled to death to see you getting into these things. . . . You're the only person around here who pays any attention to me. I have to keep hollering

5. Interview with JPIII, July 17, 1984, St. Louis.
6. JPII to JPIII, August 31, 1942, JPII to Herbert Pulitzer, September 9, 1942, JPII Papers, reel 6, frames 66 and 68.

all the time.'"[7] Keller showed him how he determined the size of the paper each day according to how much advertising had been sold. He also showed Joe comparisons of advertising lineage in the *Post-Dispatch* and the competing *Globe-Democrat* and *Star-Times,* and had an assistant "clear up for me the intricate workings of the daily cash book."

Joe spent time as well in the circulation and mechanical departments, most of whose procedures he was able to comprehend, except for the photoengraving process: "I still don't know how a copper plate is made and doubt if I ever will." In sum, he appreciated the overview assignment "despite its undefined and vague nature"—unknowingly echoing a lament of J. P. II to his father about the lack of hands-on experience in his early newspaper education. Joe emphasized that he was keeping pace in his training even amidst "a very hectic debutante season here with parties three or four times a week. Somehow I manage to rip myself from my bed at quarter to seven. If it weren't for the routine I wouldn't be able to do it."[8]

He soon got a lesson in the harsh realities of *Post-Dispatch* proprietorship that stayed with him the rest of his life. Bradford Shinkle, Jr., the same age as Joe and one of his closest friends, caused two major accidents in 1936 while driving drunk. A man was killed and another injured in the first. Four people were injured in the second, one woman severely. Young Shinkle, like Joe, was an heir to a family fortune and preparing to take a place in his family's business. What became the Johnson, Stephens and Shinkle Shoe Company had been established in St. Louis in 1914 by his maternal grandfather, Jackson Johnson. The Pulitzers and Shinkles moved in the topmost circle in the city and saw each other often. This ended when unrelenting *Post-Dispatch* publicity in the aftermath of the accidents shattered their relationship. The paper reported the story in detail, publishing many articles during 1937, while Shinkle's lawyers maneuvered his case through the courts.[9] The St. Louis County grand jury twice refused to indict Shinkle in the death of Emmett J. O'Brien, a city worker, and the serious injury of his passenger. Shinkle ultimately was acquitted on a manslaughter charge after the trial was moved out of St. Louis and "a jury of Osage County farmers . . . found he had not shown 'utter disregard of human life'" in O'Brien's death, the *Post-Dispatch* reported. His only penalties in the O'Brien case were an $850 fine and a six-month suspen-

---

7. JPIII to JPII, December 3, 1936, JPII Papers, reel 88, frame 71. In 1922, J. P. II had established radio station KSD in St. Louis as an adjunct of the *Post-Dispatch.* JPIII to JPII, undated (probably early 1937), JP II Papers, reel 88, frames 18–19.

8. JPIII to JPII, December 3, 1936, JPII Papers, reel 88, frame 71.

9. The *Post-Dispatch* published the full progress of events on February 12, 1938.

sion of his driver's license.[10] His lawyers reached settlements of four damage suits. The paper's description of the second accident said Shinkle "was returning in his Packard in top hat, white tie and tails from a Halloween party at the St. Louis Country Club" when his "6,000-pound, 12-cylinder" vehicle struck and overturned a Ford, injuring all four of its passengers. Melba Peterson, a twenty-seven-year-old former saleswoman, suffered two skull fractures and a broken pelvis. One of her eyes had to be removed. A jury awarded her $100,000, breaking the record for a personal injury damage suit in St. Louis courts. The paper made an example of Shinkle in editorials against drunken driving.[11]

Shinkle's parents saw this as a betrayal of friendship, recalled Florence Shinkle, a niece of Bradford Jr. "My family felt that they had never prosecuted any of these breaches that were almost condoned in their group before" when the *Post-Dispatch* "landed on [the families'] closest alliance"—the friendship of their up-and coming sons—"and they were royally ticked."[12] The Shinkles "wanted to keep it down, and the Pulitzers decided that it was time to prosecute drunken driving." This "was considered by those people in the upper crust as the voice of Mr. Pulitzer [J. P. II]. It was he who could dictate the paper's policies, so it was taken very personally when it came out against Brad Shinkle on the editorial page, and my family cut off all relations. It must have been very hard to do. At that time the social and economic power in St. Louis was all in the hands of the same families.... There were about fourteen families that ran everything. They must have thought they were in heaven or Argentina. It was a great life." At one point young Shinkle's sister Jane, whom Joe also knew well, was prompted by her family to ask Joe if he could do anything to stop the flow of what they saw as malicious publicity. "As far as I can tell, he didn't do anything," Ms. Shinkle said. The Shinkles moved to Phoenix, Arizona, after the first accident, but kept their St. Louis home in prestigious Portland Place.

Joe recalled the case in a 1993 interview as "a very painful thing for both families because they had friendships and social relations for many, many years." For him personally, "it was a matter of real embarrassment and concern to be involved with a young man that I had a casual

10. *St. Louis Post-Dispatch*, March 17, 1937.
11. Commenting on the man's long record on February 26, 1937: "How many offenses must a motorist be guilty of . . . before he is adjudged a public menace, incompetent to drive and his license is revoked?" On March 18, 1937, an editorial headed "Betrayal of Public" criticized the grand jury's failure to indict "in the flagrant Shinkle case."
12. Interview with Florence Shinkle, June 19, 1995, St. Louis.

relationship with until this break. . . . I was made quite aware that irresponsible behavior by any sector of the public was just not going to be tolerated—for the benefit of the public." This went for Pulitzers too. When Kate Davis and Joe were fined for speeding violations, stories appeared in the *Post-Dispatch*. When J. P. II, an avid bird hunter, was fined five hundred dollars in 1943 for shooting more ducks than his limit, the story was on page one. Managing editor Evarts Graham handled the matter routinely in 1976 when a personal friend of J. P. III complained that the paper should not have reported that police had killed the son of "an old, respected St. Louis family" during an apparent robbery attempt. "We published the story because it was news, and it was news exactly for the reason you cited. The young man was a member of an old, respected St. Louis family," Graham explained.[13]

In 1970, Florence Shinkle was hired by Joe as a *Post-Dispatch* reporter even though she had no journalism experience. She succeeded as a reporter, but believed she never would have gotten the job without the long-ago family connection: "I thought I was a medium by which [Joe] made something bad into something good. And I thought that was rather endearing that he had to keep his loyalty and his allegiances to the group [and] at the same time . . . be a journalist. It was a real squeeze on his life, I think." She believed Joe's "great struggle—that he succeeded at, I think, to a good degree—was to maintain this enormous emphasis on etiquette and right behavior and a certain snob appeal, and at the same time to behave in a professional manner." In the case of Brad Shinkle it meant "he voted his conscience on something and lost his friend."

Starting in 1937, J. P. II assigned Joe to read copies of all his father's internal memorandums and other correspondence to familiarize him with the full range of the chief executive's duties. He frequently included his son as an observer in meetings with various executives. The most important executive was haughty, imperious Oliver Kirby Bovard, who media observers even in his own time ranked as an exemplary managing editor. Bovard had been at the *Post-Dispatch* since 1898, rising from reporter to city editor in just two years and to managing editor eight years later, in 1908.[14] He had started in journalism at the *St. Louis Star*, but aspired, as did many newspapermen, to a career on a Pulitzer newspaper in St. Louis or New York. "To work in the Pulitzer organization was to be tempered in fire," wrote James Markham, Bovard's biographer. "If a man had real abil-

13. WW interview with JPIII, March 9, 1993, St. Louis; *St. Louis Post-Dispatch*, November 11, 1937, November 26, 1941, October 8, 1943, January 24, 1964; S. E. Freund to JPIII, EAG to S. E. Freund, June 10, 1976, JPIII Papers.
14. For the first two years he was "Acting Managing Editor."

ity (or 'capacity,' as Bovard termed it) this was the kind of experience that brought it out. Pulitzer's ideals demanded competence. Under his system, men and their performance were carefully measured and continually subjected to tests. If one fell short of what was expected, he was fired or shifted."[15]

Bovard had negotiated his hiring by the *Post-Dispatch* by offering it a story of his the *Star* had rejected as unproved. The story told how bribes of city officials had secured exclusive control of the street railway franchise in St. Louis. Checking by *Post-Dispatch* editors proved him right in every detail; he had uncovered a web of corruption. This became his forte, and under his editorial leadership it became the kind of journalism at which the *Post-Dispatch* excelled for more than thirty years, winning the newspaper wide recognition as one of the top four or five newspapers in the country. His contribution to the quality of the *Post-Dispatch* was widely recognized. Bovard had a defining role in the training of young Joseph Pulitzer II, starting in 1906. Once the young man became editor and publisher, he gave Bovard virtually free rein over the news operation and rewarded him generously. Bovard's compensation was second only to Pulitzer's, peaking at seventy-five thousand dollars a year in 1932, triple that of the next highest paid executive, treasurer Keller. "My judgment is emphatically in favor of holding on to Bovard," Pulitzer said in 1922, "not because he is invaluable to us, but because he would be infernally valuable to a competitor."[16]

Yet while J. P. II respected and wanted to keep Bovard, he was innately self-confident and enjoyed being in charge. Thus he was not, as were virtually all others, intimidated by what Markham termed Bovard's "cold temperament, which equally held at a distance his staff and his visitors. His manner was aloof, domineering, and at times even arrogant. He gave no confidences and invited none." The managing editor had only a grammar school education and was virtually self-taught in his craft, but was so impressive in imparting that knowledge that he became to those under him "a one man school of journalism."[17]

It was therefore natural for Joe's father to want his successor to absorb all he could from this extraordinary newsman. It was just as natural that Bovard would take a dim view of the journalistic prospects of a cultured young man with a Harvard fine arts degree. Once, after J. P. II asked Bovard to speak with Joe and then give him his estimate of the young man,

15. Markham, *Bovard of the Post-Dispatch*, 20.
16. JPII to Florence D. White, April 5, 1922, JPII Papers, reel 50, frame 384.
17. Markham, *Bovard*, 58–59.

Bovard reported that he thought Joe should "stick to his violin." This did not deter the publisher from putting the master and neophyte together. When the time came for Joe to do his apprenticeship turn in the newsroom, his father saw to it that he was given a desk at the very nerve center of the operation, between Bovard and city editor Benjamin Reese. His father required daily reports from Joe of his observations of the news apparatus. He also assigned him various specific projects, one of which was to compare "how well or how badly" the *Post-Dispatch* and *Star* were doing in the selection of local pictures. He let Bovard know that Joe was capable of making some useful suggestions, such as that some of the picture cutlines did not adequately explain why a picture had been printed. He sent his brother Ralph a copy of one of Joe's reports, with a note that "he learns quickly and his observances for the most part are sound." Ralph agreed, calling the report "very promising indeed."[18] Ralph remarked particularly on a suggestion of Joe's that the appearance and readability of the front page could be improved if there were more spacing between the lines of type. The idea was not adopted, but it anticipated changes many newspapers made several decades later, when more open, horizontal layouts with larger body type were recognized as more visually appealing than the traditionally cramped, vertical display of most papers.

It was not surprising, of course, that the visual appearance of the paper would attract Joe's attention, or that his father would recognize and promote this as a way of giving his son a sense of fitting in and having something to contribute. He complimented Joe in mid-1937 for his work on a picture page and for the advice he had given a staff artist, saying that if she would continue to produce work of the quality he had recently seen, "I should feel that the credit is all yours for making a real artist out of her and for getting her away from her old stereotyped style." On the business side, he added, "you did a good job in increasing automobile allowances and cutting hours in the business department. Congratulations." When Joe told his father that he had some ideas on how the paper's typographic design could be improved, his father was doubtful but encouraged him to try them out in an edition for two or three days "and see how you and the men around the office like them. My guess is that if you then take a vote you will go down under a landslide. However, maybe I am old-fashioned." Joe agreed with that but kept it to himself. He responded that he "could not do this in two or three days' makeup" because he needed to experi-

18. BHR to James W. Markham, January 23, 1952, JPII Papers, reel 18, frames 33–34; JPII to JPIII, January 28, 1937, JPII Papers, reel 88, frame 58; JPII to Oliver Kirby Bovard, March 24, 1937, JPII Papers, reel 88, frame 83; JPII to Ralph Pulitzer, March 29, 1937, Ralph Pulitzer to JPII, April 2, 1937, JPII Papers, reel 6, frames 599 and 601.

ment with type faces, sizes, and combinations and then refine the results "to convince you that we can improve the general appearance without being freakish." He had to bide his time. The paper's makeup remained largely unchanged until after Joe succeeded his father, in part perhaps because Joe didn't press the issue even though, he later said, "I thought the typography was awful."[19]

Although he put nothing in writing about them, Joe's father probably was pleased by his son's responses to his assignment to assess the backgrounds, personalities, and growth potential of several top business executives. Joe called this "a big order," but obliged with insights reminiscent of the character sketches he wrote in college. Of Keller:

> [A] person of keen judgment and executive ability. This has often come out in the way he can make a baffling subject clear by a few words or figures and by his ability to make illuminating comparisons. Of course his poker face is the thing that makes him difficult to deal with. He uses it to wither salesmen who approach him with a new typewriter or a new ink.... He hates to pay Anderson $15,000 a year when he isn't producing. He would much rather leave Anderson off the payroll than leave a negro porter off who gets say $15 a week and cannot show up because he happened to slip on the ice. This did happen and Mr. Keller made some such comparison in his conversation with me.... I didn't realize that a man of such meagre intellectual development could be such a whiz at his own business.

Of business manager Albert G. Lincoln:

> [T]he most intelligent, clear-thinking man, outside of Mr. Keller, on this floor. He has a tenacious thoroughness and inquisitiveness which leads him to the core of whatever problems he deals with. He is a conservative spender and is always looking for ways to cut down waste. An example of this is his examination of the waste caused by indulging the advertisers in resetting their ads several times. This comes to as much as $75,000 to $100,000 a year.

Of advertising manager George M. Burbach:

> Mr. Burbach is the back-slapper, the Rotarian, the self-centered, busy, aggressive, club-loving businessman. He is not as intelligent as Mr. Lincoln and not as devoted to the paper as the other men. He jumps to conclusions

19. JPII to JPIII, July 15, 1937, JPII Papers, reel 88, frame 35; JPII to JPIII, July 28, 1940, JPIII to JPII, August 1, 1940, JPII Papers, reel 88, frame 230; JPIII interview, July 17, 1984.

and then gets up figures to convince himself that he is right....He is extravagant....Despite his obvious weaknesses, he makes a good advertising man because of his energy, his aggressiveness and ambition....He is tough and vivid and I believe will continue at top speed indefinitely. [Burbach proved of inestimable value to the company well beyond his tenure by seeing to it that J. P. II got into and stayed in television. He did this by means of some creative accounting to convince the publisher that Pulitzer station KSD-TV was showing a profit sooner in 1949 than was the case.][20]

Joe's competence and confidence in evaluating key employees grew after that. He advised his father a few years later that recently hired production manager Charles J. Hentschell showed potential for higher executive responsibility. Hentschell had suggested in mid-1941 that three thousand already printed copies of the *Post-Dispatch* which did not carry the news that Germany had attacked Russia be destroyed because there was still time to make changes and include this news in all editions. Business manager Lincoln agreed, and this was done. Hentschell eventually became business manager, a company vice president, and the first non-Pulitzer member of the company's board of trustees. He shared Joe's belief that the paper's typography should be modernized.[21]

His father did not ask Joe to assess Bovard, but the young man got a close-up view of him during what turned out to be Bovard's final year at the *Post-Dispatch*. Starting in mid-1937, Joe handled a number of editing assignments of feature material under those in charge of the Sunday and women's magazines. This included editing and condensing copy, writing headlines, doing layouts, writing picture cutlines, and making last-minute changes in the composing room. His father read the published results in Bar Harbor. "[Y]our work has been excellent," he wired Joe, instructing him to ask Bovard "to go over your work critically." Joe's memory years later of his interaction with the managing editor was that he was there "as a powerful presence, and I would sometimes have my work raked over by Bovard disapproving me."[22] In March 1938 Joe was put in full editorial charge of the Sunday magazine for several weeks. J. P. II asked Bovard for his opinion of those issues and got this lukewarm reply:

20. JPIII to JPII, undated (probably early 1937), JPII Papers, reel 88, frames 29–32; Pfaff, *Joseph Pulitzer II*, 335.
21. JPIII to JPII, June 25, 1941, JPIII Papers.
22. JPII to JPIII, August 18, 1937, JPII Papers, reel 88, frame 15; WW interview with JPIII, March 9, 1993.

It is more like a college newspaper than a professional newspaper. But what more could be expected? The editor is only a student of journalism. In my opinion, editing cannot be learned by cramming. However, I think the experience must have been distinctly valuable to the young man. I think it must have given him some self-confidence and some sense of responsibility. The generally lower tone of the magazine would hurt the paper if permanently adopted. But these few issues probably have done no harm. He might have done much worse. I doubt that any of the other young men of his age on the staff would have done much better.[23]

If this seemed tinged with malice, J. P. II knew it stemmed mainly from the deteriorating relationship between himself and Bovard rather than with the managing editor's doubts about the heir apparent. By 1938 the managing editor was on a collision course with the editor-publisher because of what Bovard saw as J. P. II's misguided pro–New Deal editorial policy toward the issues of the Great Depression. Bovard considered President Roosevelt's approaches incapable of keeping the country out of such calamities in the future. He had visited both Sweden and Russia and came back impressed by what seemed to him to be great economic and social advances under socialism. He thought the *Post-Dispatch* should lead the way in advocating sharp changes in that direction, starting with nationalization of utilities and other public services. He dubbed his program "practical economics" and presented its details in a "thesis" of sixty-two double-spaced pages titled "Forward with Socialism and Democracy." The managing editor was convinced that the United States was too much in the grip of the holders of inherited wealth. The thesis made clear that, among others, he held both Roosevelt and newspaper publishers—including his own—responsible for the economic crisis.

Bovard had handed his thesis to J. P. II just a few weeks before being asked to evaluate Joe's work on the Sunday magazine. He wanted his tract to be the paper's editorial touchstone on the Depression, and he wanted the editor-publisher to hand full authority in this matter to him. Not wanting to lose Bovard and hoping he might moderate his views, J. P. II stalled in replying, then refused. Bovard resigned on July 29, 1938.[24] City editor Reese succeeded him. Reese's assessment of Bovard—not expressed until several years after Bovard's death in 1945—was that he

23. OKB to JPII, March 25, 1938, JPII Papers, reel 88, frame 12.
24. Details on these events are from Pfaff, *Joseph Pulitzer II*, 195–215 and Markham, *Bovard*, 166–78.

had indeed been a great editor until the last three or four years of his career, when "he became too possessed, too egotistic, too know-it-all, too settled into a pattern. Being human, he made mistakes of judgment—news and otherwise."[25]

While the Bovard drama was playing out, plans were made, then dropped, for Childs to take Joe on an extensive European tour in mid-1938 to acquaint him with international issues. Instead, Joe, Julius Polk, and Kate Davis toured parts of Europe, starting in Paris, where Joe and Polk met up with Kate Davis, who had been attending school there. They drove through Germany to Austria, stopping at the music festival in Salzburg, where they spent time with some American friends. They then went to Vienna, which Kate Davis found "a very depressing place. The Jewish people had to wear the Star of David . . . and Nazis were all around." While they could not fathom the ominous meaning of what they were seeing, Joe told Polk that because of his Jewish heritage and connection with a newspaper he was certain they were being watched. They decided to leave for Budapest, where they had letters of introduction to Hungarian relatives, none of whom turned out to be in the city at that time. After several days there, they moved on to Italy to join longtime friends Brooke and Charles (Buddie) Marshall at their villa in Portofino. (After Marshall's death, Brooke married Vincent Astor. As Astor's widow, she dispensed nearly two hundred million dollars across thirty-seven years as head of the Vincent Astor Foundation, closing it when she reached age ninety-five in 1997.)[26]

Probably the most important stop for Joe that summer was in Ireland, where the three St. Louisans joined a group of young people at Glenveagh Castle, the summer home of Henry J. McIlhenny, president of the Philadelphia Art Museum. Louise Vauclain, whose family from the Philadelphia suburb of Haverford was friendly with McIlhenny, had arranged for the young Pulitzers and several other friends to stay at the castle. She had known Kate Davis and Joe for several years. In 1939, Joe and Lulu, as Louise was known by her friends, were married.[27] Kate Davis had brought

25. BHR to Markham, January 23, 1952, JPII Papers, reel 18, frames 33–34.

26. MWC to JPIII, May 17, 1965, JPIII Papers; Interviews with Kate Davis Pulitzer Quesada, August 12, 1985, Bar Harbor, Maine, and April 27 and 28, 1995, Hobe Sound, Florida; Interview with William J. Polk, Jr., June 11, 1994, St. Louis; Brendan Gill, "A Party for Brooke," *New Yorker*, April 21, 1997, 72.

27. McIlhenny was an art history student at Harvard when Joe was there and ushered at Joe and Lulu's wedding. He became a curator of the Philadelphia Art Museum, and eventually was chairman of the museum's board of directors. Obituary, Henry P. McIlhenny, *New York Times*, May 13, 1986; "Main Line Belle June Bride," *Philadelphia Inquirer*, June 3, 1999.

them together. She had met Lulu through mutual friend Margaret Dorrance (later Mrs. George Strawbridge II) at Bar Harbor and then introduced Joe and Lulu when he was in college. Lulu was a granddaughter of Samuel Matthews Vauclain, chairman of the Baldwin Locomotive Works of Philadelphia, and a daughter of Mr. and Mrs. Jacques Leonard Vauclain. She entered society in 1932, "a debutante who could have come out of Phillip Barry's 'The Philadelphia Story,'" Childs wrote of her. "The Main Line, location of those beautifully manicured small estates that summed up the proper life of the proper Philadelphian, this was her background."

The couple was married in the late afternoon of June 2, 1939, at the Church of the Redeemer in Bryn Mawr by the Episcopal Bishop of Pennsylvania, the Right Reverend Francis M. Taitt. A poolside reception followed at Broadlawn, the Rosemont estate of Lulu's grandfather. The newlyweds, their parents, and members of the wedding party—including Kate Davis as maid of honor and Polk as best man—received the guests under green awnings while a string orchestra played from an upper terrace. The next day the couple embarked from New York aboard the Italian liner *Rex* for Europe, gradually making their way to Portofino, where they had rented the Marshalls' villa for the month of August.

One of their stops was an art auction house in Lucerne, Switzerland. There, twenty-six-year-old Joseph Pulitzer III saw—and decided he must have—Henri Matisse's painting *Bathers with a Turtle*, done in 1908. It was one of many paintings banished from Germany by the Nazis as "degenerate" and put up for sale. Curt Valentin, a New York art dealer who had persuaded Joe to attend the sale, and Pierre Matisse, the artist's son, accompanied him. Pierre Matisse, who considered the work one of his father's masterpieces, placed the bid on Joe's behalf. The work subsequently came to be regarded as one of the most important contributions to modern art. Joe paid twenty-four hundred dollars for it. It was estimated that the painting was "easily worth 10,000 times that amount," or twenty-four million dollars, at the time of his death in 1993. He donated the picture nearly thirty years earlier to the St. Louis Art Museum.[28]

Details about the marriage and wedding trip are from interviews with Mrs. Kate Davis Pulitzer Quesada, April 12, 1985, at Bar Harbor, Maine, and April 27 and 28, 1995, at Hobe Sound, Florida; Marquis W. Childs, obituary of Louise Vauclain Pulitzer, *St. Louis Post-Dispatch*, December 22, 1968; articles in the *Post-Dispatch* of April 16, May 14, and June 4, 1939; accounts in the Philadelphia *Record*, June 4, 1939; Philadelphia *Inquirer*, June 3, 1939; and *New York Sun*, June 9, 1939; and Pfaff, *Joseph Pulitzer II*, 243–44.

28. Lynn H. Nichols, *The Rape of Europa* (New York: Alfred A. Knopf, 1994), 1; Angelica Zander Rudenstine, "Words of Commemoration," funeral service for JPIII, May 29, 1993, privately printed; Obituary, JPIII, *New York Times*, May 27, 1993; *The St. Louis Art Museum Magazine*, July–August 1993, 7.

Kate Davis joined Joe and Lulu at Portofino. J. P. II wrote Joe there that he had "arranged, provided you want the jobs," to have him elected a trustee and first vice president of the company. Joe replied that he was "naturally... pleased and glad" to take on those responsibilities.[29] He reported that life at Portofino was "casual—lots of swimming and excursions by boat to nearby fishing villages." At the end of August the three of them departed for Paris so Lulu could select winter clothes and she and Joe could look for furniture, but their plans were cut short. Germany and Italy were now Axis Pact partners, and war seemed likely. This news threw Joe's father into a panic about the children. He cabled them to come home immediately, and wanted frequent reports as they made their way to France. He sought the help of Secretary of State Cordell Hull in booking them passage on the British liner *Andora Star* out of Cherbourg. To their surprise, Brooke Marshall, who had been traveling in Europe, ended up on the same ship, and the group crossed together. The liner was blacked out at night and followed a zigzag course during the eleven-day crossing as a precaution against German submarines.

The young travelers had discounted the talk of war they heard in Italy. At first, Joe and Kate Davis were certain their father was overreacting in demanding that they come home. The Italians with whom they talked expressed dislike of Germans and Germany. This made them doubt that an Italian-German alliance would hold and that Germany would back off. Their opinion changed once they reached France. Military preparations were in full swing. French soldiers were everywhere, and from the highway they saw anti-aircraft guns and their crews in the fields. On August 31, they learned that the Germans had crossed the Polish border in four places, and they felt lucky to have gotten the last available spaces on the boat, which left the next day.[30] The wedding trip was to have continued three more weeks, including time for furniture shopping in London and a week at Henry McIlhenny's castle in Ireland.

29. JPII to JPIII, August 9, 1939, JPIII to JPII, August 19, 1939, JPII Papers, reel 7, frames 53, 57. The other trustees were his father and Uncle Herbert.

30. "Joseph Pulitzer Jr. Tells of Getting Out of War Zone," *St. Louis Post-Dispatch*, September 13, 1939.

Four
Wartime

Back at the *Post-Dispatch*, Joe found his father at loggerheads with new managing editor Reese and editorial page editor Ralph Coghlan. J. P. II thought the editors were giving inadequate space and prominence to the hostilities in Europe. The two chief sub-editors supported a widely popular opinion that the United States should stay out of foreign entanglements. This was dramatically demonstrated when Coghlan—without consulting J. P. II—published an editorial in June 1940 harshly criticizing Roosevelt's shift of U.S. war policy from "neutrality" to "nonbelligerency." *Post-Dispatch* readers flooded the newspaper with letters and telephone calls of approval. The editor-publisher interpreted the response as more emotional than realistic, but did not assert his more hawkish viewpoint until late September, when he told Reese and Coghlan he could not support "blind isolationism." The *Post-Dispatch* is "not for peace at any price," he declared. Instead, the paper had a duty to let readers know "that we see all too clearly the menace of Hitler and Hitlerism and that our one and only objective is [that] WE MUST GET READY FOR WAR." During 1941, J. P. II moved closer to advocating intervention. But Coghlan, especially, resisted until Germany's attack against the Soviet Union persuaded him that the editorial page should make a gradual pro-war shift.[1] The Japanese attack on Pearl Harbor on December 7 eliminated all doubts.

Until that calamity, probably the year's most unpleasant experience for Joe came in a stinging criticism from his father for suppressing pertinent information about a prominent woman's suicide. J. P. II was then summering at Bar Harbor and, as always, keeping up with the *Post-Dispatch*. His secretary read him a two-paragraph item at the bottom of page three on June 24 reporting that Mrs. Catherine Dameron Weakley, wife of State Representative William B. Weakley of Pike County, had "ended her life today at her home." J. P. II dictated a memorandum to Reese asking why the item had not appeared on page one and had not included the method of death, hanging, which he had learned about from a friend. Joe wrote

1. Pfaff, *Joseph Pulitzer II*, 248, 240–55.

the answer, explaining that he had requested the treatment after Theron Catlin, a friend of the Weakley family, asked "if the paper could handle the story with restraint. In view of Mrs. Weakley's long illness, it seemed to me that we could give consideration to the request."[2] On that basis he asked Reese to omit "hanging." His father responded that "under the Pulitzer philosophy" of journalism

> [Y]ou were guilty of an unforgivable journalistic sin when you asked [Reese] to suppress a salient fact—the fact that she hanged herself in the story of Mrs. Weakley's suicide.... It is at the very heart and core of what I regard as journalistic honesty—honesty with the readers and honesty with the staff. Showing reasonable consideration for families in distress is one thing...but the reader was definitely entitled to know how she ended her life. I would not suppress such a fact in the case of a member of my own family and I hope and feel sure that you will never again do so, no matter how much anguish it may cause them and you.
>
> Another point is that suppression in the long run never does any good and often, through permitting untrue gossip to be circulated, does more harm than good.[3]

He said he would have given the story a half column of space on page one under a two-column headline and with a picture. He instructed Joe to have Reese explain to him how other requests, "reasonable and unreasonable," had been handled in the past.

The incident made a lasting impression on Joe, but the war became the major preoccupation of everyone at the *Post-Dispatch* for the next four years. Within a month of Pearl Harbor, fourteen regular newsroom employees were in military service, another was to leave soon, and five more expected to be called.[4] Without waiting for a call, Joe entered naval officer training, similar to the course his father had followed in World War I. However, his father only completed training and did brief ground duty in the naval aviation corps before the armistice was signed in 1918. Navy Ensign and then Lieutenant Junior Grade Joseph Pulitzer, Jr.—he did not use III—ended up with nearly four years of active service. He was first assigned to Washington, D.C., for naval intelligence training.

He and Lulu rented a house in Washington, and he was able to keep his hand in art collecting while there by running up to New York occasionally to check out some of the galleries. Kate Davis remembered visit-

2. *St. Louis Post-Dispatch*, June 24, 1941; JPII to BHR, June 30, 1941, JPII Papers, reel 93, frame 120; JPIII to JPII, July 3, 1941, JPII Papers, reel 88, frame 214.

3. JPII to JPIII, July 9, 1941, JPIII Papers.

4. BHR to Albert G. Lincoln, January 8, 1942, JPII Papers, reel 93, frame 419.

ing them one time when he returned from New York with a painting by Paul Klee that he proudly showed his wife and sister, who reacted by teasing him. To them, she said, it appeared to depict "a lot of little people running along a street under umbrellas—sort of stick people. 'What in the world do you want with that thing?'" they asked. "We thought it was simply horrible. He was so disappointed." But he had again, Kate Davis realized later, followed his own instincts about art, from which family criticism never deterred him. "He just went straight out and did what he wanted."[5]

His first duty after his intelligence training was as a press relations officer in Hawaii for seven months. Other than missing Lulu, he wrote his parents, he found life there "very pleasant." He made several friends, including distant cousin Eleanor Carter of St. Louis, related to him through the Wickhams. She was working for the Army. Despite blackouts, gasoline rationing, and a 10 p.m. curfew, "I have been very hospitably received," he wrote his parents. He also was able to do some reading, and recommended to his father, as a member of the Advisory Board for the Pulitzer Prizes, that the novel prize be awarded to *The Song of Bernadette* by Franz Werfel. "In case you haven't read it," he explained, "the story is based on the life of Bernadette Soubirous, the French mystic whose visions at Lourdes resulted in the founding of that famous shrine. The book is a profession of faith in the dignity of the human personality—one of the things we're fighting for." He thought John Steinbeck's *The Moon Is Down* the likely runner-up, "but to my mind is nowhere near as powerful or lasting a work of art." He thought no novel prize should be given except to Werfel, but it went to Upton Sinclair for *Dragon's Teeth*, about Germany under national socialism. His recommendation for the drama prize, Thornton Wilder's *Skin of Our Teeth*, did win, though his father voted against it as being "too mystic for my feeble imagination."[6]

The Hawaiian assignment was temporary, as Joe had expected. He was next assigned to the destroyer U.S.S. *Hailey* at Seattle. The ship was being outfitted and he was being trained for supervising men in all means of secure communications. Lulu joined him in Seattle, and then migrated to

5. Obituary, Louise V. Pulitzer, *St. Louis Post-Dispatch*, December 22, 1968; Interviews with KDPQ, April 27 and 28, 1995, and WJP, June 11, 1994. During his training for sea duty on the West Coast, J. P. III stayed in touch with New York dealers such as Pierre Matisse, son of painter Henri Matisse. Matisse to JPIII, December 21, 1942, JPII Papers, reel 6, frame 61. Emily Pulitzer identified the work as *Protected Children* by Klee, purchased in 1942. ERP to author, March 24, 2005.

6. JPIII to Daddy and Mommie, April 17, 1943, JPII Papers reel 6, frame 90; JPII to JPIII, May 24, 1943, JPII Papers, reel 6, frame 89.

San Diego, where the ship moved for its shakedown cruise prior to sea duty. She stayed in a hotel, and they were able to be together when he did not have to be on board. While they were there, Joe's father sent him five hundred cigars, including five boxes of Punches, Winston Churchill's favorite, with the admonition, "don't get nicotine poison." Lulu returned to Washington when Joe shipped out and served as codirector of the Stage Door Canteen, established by the American Theatre Wing. She often put in fourteen-hour days recruiting actors, musicians, and others for the shows attended by thousands of servicemen each month at the Belasco Theatre on Lafayette Square.

Joe enjoyed destroyer training, especially after Lulu came to Seattle. But his life at sea proved disagreeable. After six months aboard the *Hailey*, he requested and was granted land duty. "You must have guessed that Bell Bottom Trousers is not my theme song according to the tone of my letter requesting a transfer from the Hailey," he wrote his parents. "I was awfully low at the time, brought on by being 20 pounds underweight and also tired and fed up with the high strung temperaments in command of that ship." The destroyer took part in the Marshall Islands campaign, where it engaged in assaults on Kwajalein, Eniwetok, Guam, and Saipan. It then moved to the Solomon Islands and finally into New Ireland waters, whose climate Joe described as "warm, moist and guaranteed to rot or mildew everything including the human body." The natives, he found, "are small black people who like to dye their hair with laundry bleach which they barter for native trinkets." He made trades for "a couple of native spears that are not quite good enough to put on my fine arts policy." He stayed in the Pacific after leaving the ship, assigned to writing, selecting graphic material, and editing reports on Japanese installations for a geographic section of Naval Intelligence. He liked the work and wished he had been in it from the start. "I will never be regular Navy— God forbid—but as jobs go in the service, it is a welcome one," he wrote.

He was assigned for two months in early 1945 to lead a study team of enemy defensive installations within the Third Marine Division zone of action on Iwo Jima while it was still under enemy fire. In a Japanese foxhole, he found a book of the art of Vincent Van Gogh. "I thought of some desperate Japanese soldier trying to escape the horrors of war, and all that was left was this book," he recalled. "It sobered me up."[7] He wrote his father about some other experiences there, including encountering a Japanese soldier in a shell hole:

7. Quoted in Steve Friedman, "Pulitzer," *St. Louis Magazine*, August 1987, 28.

Emaciated and in need of water, he put up no resistance but did, after we had divested him of two hand grenades and unloaded his rifle, try to induce us to kill him. Pointed to our guns, to his throat and then held his hands together in an attitude of prayer. But what amused me was his sidelong look to see if we would take him up on the proposal. We turned him over to the stockade and felt pleased to have turned in one of the few combatant prisoners taken by the division . . .

Today I was invited to lunch with the Japanese language officers at the stockade. The meal was prepared and served by one of the Japanese prisoners and the food was Japanese which has been captured during the campaign. The cook was typical of a Jap cartoon—all smiles and sibilant mutterings and he backed out of our tent in a half-bowed position which would have done justice to an Oriental servant in a story by Somerset Maugham. The officers chatter away with the prisoners in fluent Japanese, which is a credit to the language schools the Navy started some months ago. If it isn't confidential, the story might make interesting reading in the paper and I imagine could be got from Public Relations in Washington.

My reaction to the lunch was mixed. The canned sardines were delicious. The rice with vegetables and soy sauce quite edible, but I couldn't go for the sweet pickled turnip which [had] a dead taste which reminded me of corpses—of which we have seen enough. Unfortunately the Japs must have drunk all their Saki during the campaign as nothing but empty bottles have been recovered.[8]

When the assignment ended, the Marine colonel in charge said the work of Joe's team was "outstanding at all times and it is with distinct regret that we see them leave." Lieutenant Pulitzer received several commendations during his Navy tour, and at war's end he wore five battle stars on his Pacific campaign ribbon.[9] Two of his cousins—Aunt Edith's sons Army Private First Class William S. Moore and Marine Private First Class Richard W. Moore—were killed in the war. William died in France, Richard on Okinawa. Kate Davis's first husband, Air Force Captain Henry W. Putnam, to whom she had been married at Bar Harbor in 1941, died in a night air raid over Tokyo in May 1945. Kate Davis was pregnant with their second daughter at the time. The initial information to the family was that Putnam was missing in action. Joe requested a transfer to

8. Correspondence about Navy service of JPIII between August 29, 1942, and March 21, 1945, JPII Papers, reel 6, frames 69–132; Naval correspondence of JPIII, March 20 and May 9, 1945, and undated, JPIII Papers.
9. JPIII obituary, *St. Louis Post-Dispatch,* May 17, 1993.

Washington preceded by thirty days' leave on hearing of this, and his father—without Joe's knowledge—asked Navy Secretary James Forrestal to support the request. It was not granted because of a shortage of replacement personnel in the Pacific.[10]

Joe's military career might have been cut short or otherwise altered had he been given a chest X ray on entering the Navy. While he was being processed for separation from the service in August 1945, an X ray revealed "possible healed tuberculosis in both upper lobes" of his lungs.[11] He had shown no symptoms of the disease, although he lost twenty pounds and had night sweats during his time on the *Hailey* in the first half of 1944. These stopped, however, and he regained the weight. Even so, the Navy held him in active duty status until its doctors were satisfied that there was no active disease. He and Lulu lived for four months at the Ritz-Carlton Hotel in Boston, where, he wrote a fellow Naval officer, they spent their "subsistence allowance on Martinis at the bar,"[12] while he made required monthly visits for X rays at nearby Chelsea Naval Hospital. These confirmed that he'd had the disease, and that it had healed. Using the considerable backlog of leave time he had accrued, Joe and Lulu went to Mexico for two months and then visited Kate Davis in Florida for a month, returning to St. Louis and civilian status in the spring of 1946.

During his last months in the Navy, Joe confided to Kate Davis, he and Lulu went through a period of indecision about their future. Did he want to return to the *Post-Dispatch* or make art his career? It was perhaps inevitable that the appeal of days immersed in art had hit him with particular force at war's end, as he and Lulu pondered the future against events of the past four years. So while they were in Mexico, as Kate Davis remembered it, "he very seriously thought that what he would like to do would be an art historian or director of a museum—in other words devote his life to the field of art, which was, I guess, his primary interest." At the same time, he "felt an obligation to the paper and family and Daddy and his grandfather, and so he decided to stay on." Kate Davis said he may have realized—though he did not discuss it with her—that by staying at the *Post-Dispatch* he would have "the wherewithal to be able to collect art, which otherwise, as a curator or director, he certainly wouldn't have." But there was no doubt in her mind that her brother's postwar introspection settled once and for all that "his main interest, other than the paper, was art. He

10. Pfaff, *Joseph Pulitzer II*, 260–61; JPIII to JPII, June 16, 1945, JPII to Forrestal, June 24, 1945, JPII Papers, reel 6, frames 125–26.
11. "Report of Medical Survey," U.S. Naval Hospital, Chelsea, Massachusetts, January 16, 1946, JPIII Papers.
12. JPIII to John W. Esau, January 17, 1947, JPIII Papers.

was seriously interested in art from then on. And whenever he had a nickel, he put it into art." This was never as investment speculation, he emphasized some years later. "I don't use investment counselors for art," he explained. "I buy only what I like and what I consider significant. Otherwise, my collection would have neither character nor individuality."[13]

Polk agreed that Joe went through the art-versus-journalism struggle Kate Davis described, but in his view largely resolved it before rather than after the war. This seems likely. He was not divorced from *Post-Dispatch* concerns while in the Navy, getting periodic reports from the office prior to going to sea. In late 1944 he requested and received from his father's secretary a report on the company's earnings and dividends for 1942 and 1943 and the prospects for 1944. The earnings averaged $611,000 for each of the three years, virtually all of which was paid out in dividends. The secretary also sent him brief reports from all department heads and said he would gladly send anything else Joe wanted. At the same time, Joe did not set art collecting aside during the war years. The catalog of a 1957 show at Harvard's Fogg Art Museum of about half the approximately 140 works he and Lulu had collected by that time contains twenty-four acquired between 1936 and 1943, six of them Picassos. (Picasso's monumental *Les Demoiselles d' Avignon* was *not* among them, although the *New York Times* erroneously reported in his obituary in 1993 that it had been and that he had donated the work to the Museum of Modern Art in New York. He was shown the picture when it was for sale in 1937 for thirty thousand dollars, but remembered being told the Museum of Modern Art had reserved it. "In any event, I did not feel I could afford the price at the time. Either then or at some later date the instinct prevailed to recognize that a painting of this majestic importance belonged to the public.") Whatever the exact timing of his decision to stay in journalism, an observation Joe made about his father provides a strong "like father, like son" rationale for choosing to give art its due: "He was a lively man and liked to have a good time. You can see that right through his whole life. I mean, he damn well had his boat and his fishing and he loved and harbored his privacy."[14] With the substitutions of art, music, and skiing, that statement also describes Joseph Pulitzer III.

One of Joe's first acts in pursuit of his art avocation on returning from the war was to instruct Reese that "when consistent with good journalism,

13. "Collector's Choice," *Time*, April 15, 1957, 98.
14. JPIII to Arch R. King, December 4, 1944, King to JPII, January 3, 1945, JPII Papers, reel 6, frames 103 and 136; Charles Scott Chetham, *Modern Painting, Drawing and Sculpture Collected by Louise and Joseph Pulitzer, Jr.*, vol. 1 (New York: Knoedler and Company, 1957); William Rubin, Helene Seckel, and Judith Cousins, *Les Demoiselles d' Avignon*

I should like to see us cooperate in giving publicity to the Little Symphony Concerts Association of which I am a member...I have asked their publicity man to communicate with the city desk when they have news or feature material." That he was giving such directions to the managing editor amounted to a signal that he would be taking an even more active role in the paper's operation. A few weeks later, *Time* magazine asked its St. Louis correspondent, who also was a *Post-Dispatch* reporter, if J. P. II, then sixty-one, was stepping down and giving his job to his son. The rumor, whose source was not revealed, was quickly quashed, but the magazine, which had nothing about him in its files, asked for a biographical sketch of J. P. III.[15]

Joe knew his father enjoyed his position and would keep it as long as his health permitted. But he had been assuming greater responsibility, especially during the summers, when J. P. II left St. Louis for recreation and to escape the heat. His father was away each year for about four months starting in June, first for a month of salmon fishing in Canada, then three months at Bar Harbor. During his absences, he always had a reader/secretary with him and stayed in touch with the office by telephone, telegram, and letter, entrusting Joe with day-to-day decision making in St. Louis.

At the end of his father's 1947 salmon outing, Joe sent him a nine-page report on the month's activities. There had been several major news developments: the worst flood of the Missouri and Mississippi valleys in 103 years, a transportation strike in the city, and battles in Washington over the Taft-Hartley bill to regulate labor unions and the Marshall Plan for European reconstruction. Joe had worked on both foreign and domestic issues with the editorial page staff. There had been no policy disagreements, he reported, "in contrast to the spot I was in a year ago when [editorial page editor Ralph] Coghlan still had hopes that Russia could be sold on international cooperation and I felt that Russia's actions indicated otherwise."[16] Perhaps his most interesting decision was to suggest an editorial on the colonial resources of Western European powers in light of "an interesting straw in the wind"—that France and Siam "would promote a union of Southeast Asia. The move still is in the talking stage, but could develop into important news. We are watching it." (In 1954, less than a year before J. P. III became its editor-publisher, the *Post-Dispatch* became

---

(New York: Museum of Modern Art, 1994), 199; Telephone interview with JPIII, August 16, 1984.

15. JPIII to BHR, June 17, 1946, JPIII to JPII, July 2, 1946, JPIII Papers.

16. JPIII to JPII, July 11, 1947, JPII Papers, reel 68, frame 195 ff.

one of the first American newspapers to oppose U.S. involvement in what became the Vietnam War. It did so throughout the conflict.)

On the business side, Joe reported signing multiyear salary contracts with Washington Bureau Chief Brandt, business manager Hentschell, and editorial writer Irving Dilliard. He advanced Brandt and Hentschell in steps to $20,000 a year; Dilliard to $12,500. There were successful wage settlements with all the mechanical unions. He dispatched the paper's chief labor negotiator to attend a meeting in New York with his counterparts from other major papers. He did this, he explained, believing that the potential benefit of gaining labor relations information outweighed concern that *Post-Dispatch* participation might dampen the morale of some of the paper's union employees. The most vexing problem was a shortage of newsprint because of a loss of supply from Canada, forcing the newspaper to reduce advertising space for a week. Should further such reductions be necessary to rebuild the newsprint inventory, he predicted a decline in profit of between $50,000 and $100,000 for the year. Sunday retail advertising rates were increased to compensate in part for an increase in expenses and a decline in profits. Joe pledged to find ways to effect economies of any "presumably controllable expense."

A cost well worth incurring, in his judgment, was the deficit the company was running in introducing the infant medium of television to St. Louis. As soon as he returned from the Navy he had urged his father not to give up on television, into which J. P. II had taken the plunge just five months before, even though doubtful about its future. No one else in the city was willing to give it a try, and there were only four television sets in St. Louis at the time. The elder Pulitzer's pessimism so far was justified— the station, KSD-TV, was more than $40,000 in the red. But the younger J. P. saw it differently. "The television broadcast of the U.S. Open Golf Championship at the St. Louis Country Club made a very favorable impression on me," he wrote. "I am convinced that this medium has inherent dramatic possibilities which will result in ultimate financial success. The present operating loss on television is at the annual rate of $100,000. In my opinion, it is only a question of time until network programs can be established and sold profitably to advertisers. The baseball games and particularly the golf tournament have caused much favorable comment." His confidence was impressively affirmed as broadcasting grew to contribute the majority of the company's earnings in subsequent years.[17]

17. Across more than four decades—during most of which J. P. III was in charge— the company expanded its investment in television as well as radio, first in St. Louis and then in other markets. The company's broadcasting profitability surpassed that of the *Post-Dispatch* and other newspaper properties the company had acquired. See Epilogue.

Five

Associate Editor

In April 1948, two years after Joe's return from the Navy, his father asked him for a report on his progress. The report was to summarize how he had contributed to "the policy and content of the Post-Dispatch" and how he had performed as acting editor when his father was away. Joe wrote a long reply, though it is unlikely that he told his father much that was not already known. He noted that as a vice-president, director, and trustee of the company, "I have additional responsibilities for the business conduct of the company, sharing responsibility when you are in town and taking full responsibility for decisions made in your absence. Since returning from the Navy I have taken a 'refresher course' ... and have got the 'feel' of what this newspaper is trying to do. I have a grasp of the problems confronting the business. I can confidently—and I have—exercised authority and made decisions for the newspaper and for the business."

Knowing his father was interested mainly in his journalistic activities, he began with those, noting that he had "naturally gravitated toward foreign affairs; naturally because of education, travel, war service and taste. Foreign affairs have inevitably led my interest to national affairs. I have consciously tried not to neglect the local scene." He said he considered a foreign staff for the newspaper highly desirable as a "long-term objective" once economic constraints were overcome. He knew his father was lukewarm about setting up foreign bureaus, believing the paper was adequately supplied by the wire services and through contracts with newspapers that already had bureaus. (That view prevailed. Even after J. P. III became editor and publisher, the paper established no foreign bureaus, although *Post-Dispatch* reporters occasionally were given special assignments abroad.)

Joe took credit for establishing a book page and for suggesting a number of successful feature stories, with arts and letters subjects predominating. Among them were interviews with St. Louis–born playwright Tennessee Williams and blues singer Ethel Waters, a profile of St. Louis Symphony conductor Vladimir Golschmann and wife—who became close friends of Joe and Lulu—and a picture feature on paintings by Picasso in St. Louis.

"Without riding my hobby, I make it a point to advise the city desk on art activities in the community which might not otherwise get in the paper," he explained.

As for the editorial page: "In general, I have followed the course previously charted. Shortly after returning from the service, I was glad to see the paper recognize the threat of Russia's expanding communism and support the Administration in containing communism." He endorsed positions taken in favor of universal military training, a sound national economy, and "for world collaboration of free peoples either within the United Nations or otherwise. During your absences, I have underscored editorial policies designed to preserve personal liberty and discourage war." When the Santa Fe Railroad sought permission to provide service to St. Louis, he and editorial page editor Coghlan visited the president of Santa Fe to get further details. The paper subsequently opposed the application, which was not approved.

He took credit for being the "principal spokesman for the office" on two trips to Montreal with circulation manager George Carvell to discuss newsprint needs with International Paper Company executives. They got guarantees of additional supplies and "may well have prevented International's requesting to reduce our order, as they have some of their other customers." He reported authorizing increases in advertising and subscription rates. While these were accepted with "few protests" and the paper's advertising percentage was ahead of the previous year's, he was cautious about the fiscal future. "The financial operation of the company falls short of security," he wrote. "The enterprise should earn 10 percent and in a banner year more than 10 percent to offset inevitable lower earnings in poor years. Correction of the present condition will require new revenue including a fifteen cent Sunday city price, reduced expenses, elimination of excess personnel, a hold-the-line policy on payroll."

There was more: "The business organization has been loose. A business manager with authority is badly needed. While teamwork is essential, there is the old saying, 'too many cooks spoil the broth.'" Here he was actually underscoring criticisms his father had heard a few weeks earlier—and had discussed with his son. They had come from Sam Shelton, formerly a crack *Post-Dispatch* investigative reporter and now the editor-publisher's most trusted management adviser. J. P. II had asked Shelton for an "entirely frank" dissection of the business organization. This was to include mistakes attributable to the publisher "for delays or for any form of loose play or failure in the operation of our business machine." Shelton responded in terms that would in the terminology of later years identify his boss as a "micromanager"—one who was so accessible to major department heads that they gravitated to him both for approval and attention and failed to work cooperatively with one another to solve problems. To remedy this, he recommended a kind of super-publisher, describing this individual as

> a general business executive of stature and influence who can command the respect and good will of all employees; who understands all phases of the business; who will be constantly on the job; who can reconcile conflicts within the organization; who will play no favorites; who will expect and require that all subordinate executives will put the welfare of the institution ahead of their personal welfare, being himself a shining example in this respect, who has the stamina, courage and patience to execute broad, forward-looking, long-range policies.
>
> You are partly responsible for the looseness of the organization. Very properly you wish to retain final authority both editorially and for business management in your own hands. In doing so you have failed to set up clear and positive lines of authority for those who are directly responsible for the execution of day by day operations.
>
> You expect a coordinated, efficient management, and yet you have some department heads reporting at times directly to you, at other times to the business manager, sometimes to J. P. [III] . . .
>
> You are the editor and publisher, with a wealth of background and experience and peculiar talent, and it is in that capacity, not leaded down with details, that you are worth all that you can get out of the business.[1]

The mercenary tone of "all that you can get out of the business" should not be misinterpreted. The Pulitzer philosophy—despite the sensationalistic lapse of the founder—never had been to make as much money as possible, but to strike a balance between profit and public service. Shelton, like the two J. P.s with whom he worked, thought a consistent 10 percent profit—not then the norm for the company—was reasonable but not excessive.[2] Like Shelton, Joe deeply respected his father, but at the same time, experience had fortified his self-confidence. He now saw the relationship with his father as being more collaborative than as strictly teacher-and-pupil. This is evident in the relaxed candor of the final paragraph of Joe's report to his father: "This newspaper and publishing company have not lost vitality. I hope as much can be said for the reader of this report."

This evidently set well. In October, managing editor Reese notified two subordinates that a story was to be run at the top of a column on the soci-

1. Samuel J. Shelton to JPII, March 19, 1948, JPII Papers, reel 98, frames 293–95.
2. During the forty-three-year tenure of J. P. II, the company averaged an annual net profit of 11.3 percent of revenues. The highest point was 18.9 percent in 1929; the lowest 4.8 percent in 1948. Pfaff, *Joseph Pulitzer II*, 324–25.

ety page announcing "that J. P. [III] has been appointed Associate Editor of the Post-Dispatch. I have written the headline and edited the copy. No changes are to be made in it."[3] The apparent reason for running the item on the society page was to assure its being seen by the community's more prominent citizens, to whom such pages catered in those days. The new title did not include "publisher," in line with the creed of the first J. P. that the news and editorial functions were primary, however vital sound financial management was to staying in business. Joe was well aware of this, and there were periodic reminders, as when his father pointed out that when an advertiser "gets into trouble . . . we would print the news regardless of whether or not he is an advertiser."[4]

All the same, business got its due, and J. P. III functioned as associate publisher as well as editor. "Yesterday I approved sale of the lower right hand corner of the daily magazine page to Stag Beer," he informed his father in December. "The ad, which will have clean copy and be the same size as Wrigley's, will produce $31,000 additional annual revenue, which is equivalent to selling 300,000 lines of additional advertising printed on spot market newsprint."[5] When the industry magazine *Editor & Publisher* asked Joe for an interview a few months after his appointment, his father advised him to "suit yourself," though "I have always denied interviews and sought to avoid publicity" and "I have always thought of Editor and Publisher as a cash register, business office medium." Like his father, Joe—with few exceptions—shunned personal publicity throughout his career. He was most emphatic that his art interests be soft-pedaled. "I prefer when possible to avoid publicity," he told one of the paper's art critics. "The reason for this reticence is the desire to avoid creating a mistaken impression that I encourage personal publicity in the *Post-Dispatch*. In addition, and possibly more important, the *Post-Dispatch* is a balanced newspaper and it would be unfortunate if my hobby, art, through publicity were to convey the mistaken impression that the *Post-Dispatch* is or may become an 'arty' newspaper. Please try to ignore my art activities."[6]

His publicity shyness manifested itself in other ways and contributed to the perception of Joseph Pulitzer III as an essentially private individual.

3. BHR to Meek and Clarke, October 20, 1948, JPIII Papers.

4. JPII to JPIII, December 6, 1946, JPIII Papers.

5. JPIII to JPII, December 17, 1948, JPIII Papers. A postwar shortage of newsprint had created competition for newsprint on the "spot market" in addition to that contracted from paper companies at set prices. Interview with Charles J. Hentschell, July 16, 1984, St. Louis.

6. JPII to JPIII, May 18, 1949, JPII Papers, reel 88, frame 187; JPIII to Howard Derrickson, April 7, 1952, JPIII Papers.

He was if anything more dedicated than his father to the belief that the financial affairs of their privately held business should be as confidential as possible. For example, in a 1951 memo to his father, he advised against a company policy of 50 percent pensions for executives recommended by treasurer Stuart M. Chambers because it smacked of "special treatment" and because a pension that high to all employees "would clearly represent an impossible burden which no company to my knowledge has attempted.... This leads me to believe we should try in the future to avoid special arrangements and, if unavoidable, then they should be strictly confidential understandings between the publisher and the individual, with a minimum of paper work and that not in the general file." The same memo shows that as of 1951 J. P. III was the third-highest-paid executive in the organization, at $40,000. He was just $2,000 behind treasurer Chambers. His father's compensation, which varied with the company's fortunes, generally exceeded $200,000 and was more than double that in the early 1950s, near the end of his career.[7]

A step virtually certain to enhance the company's fortunes was taken in June 1951 with the purchase by the *Post-Dispatch* of its ailing afternoon competitor, the *Star-Times*. With his father in Canada fishing for salmon, Joe was in charge of the final negotiations and signed the $5,058,000 sales agreement with *Star-Times* publisher Elzey Roberts. *Post-Dispatch* business manager Charles Hentschell scouted the deal once it became known that Roberts would consider selling. Foremost in his mind was that the *Globe-Democrat* should not get the other afternoon daily. "We just damn well can't afford that," Hentschell told J. P. II.[8] The purchase would give a big boost to Pulitzer Publishing, which estimated that *Post-Dispatch* circulation would increase by some 90,000 daily, about half the *Star-Times* total of 180,000. The additional circulation would justify an increase in advertising rates and the loss of the *Star-Times* to its advertisers would create a substantial gain in advertising for the *Post-Dispatch*. The Pulitzers did not want these tangibles to fall into the hands of the morning *Globe-Democrat*— on the purchase of which Joe's father had put out unsuccessful feelers in the late 1940s. The matter was so hush-hush that it was discussed only outside the office, initially in the library at Lone Tree Farm with just the two Pulitzers, Hentschell, and controller Dell B. Stafford present. The actual negotiations took place at various St. Louis hotels. Joe made the surprise announcement on June 15. The *Star-Times* printed its last issue the next

7. JPIII to JPII, February 2, 1951, JPIII Papers; Pfaff, *Joseph Pulitzer II*, 245.
8. Interview with CJH, May 5, 1984, St. Louis.

day. By mid-September, the *Post-Dispatch* led the *Globe-Democrat* in circulation by about 90,000 daily and 100,000 Sunday.[9]

The nationwide decline of newspaper voices through consolidation of properties and group ownership was well established and accelerating by 1951. All three St. Louis dailies carried hybrid nameplates, as did those in many cities. In an editorial, the *Post-Dispatch* cited the usual reason for the demise of its afternoon competitor—"the steadily mounting costs of newspaper production."[10] The editorial noted that there were 703 fewer dailies in the United States in 1950 than there had been in 1910, adding: "Those newspapers which have survived . . . are, however, vastly improved in facilities for gathering and presenting the news over those of a generation ago. This every adult newspaper reader knows. Even so, the fact remains that fewer newspapers mean fewer voices in the formulation, assembly and expression of public opinion." Group ownership contributed significantly to the decline of independent newspaper voices in subsequent years. By 1990, groups owned 75.5 percent of the 1,611 daily newspapers, accounting for 81 percent of total daily circulation.[11]

Star-Times managing editor Norman Isaacs viewed the sale from a special perspective. Although a competitor, Isaacs had developed a good relationship with some *Post-Dispatch* people, including J. P. II and especially managing editor Ben Reese, who retired shortly before the sale. The two lunched together occasionally, Isaacs recalled, to discuss "our mutual headaches." His centered on his boss, Elzey Roberts, whom he described as "a terrible bastard publisher," on whom he frequently threatened to quit. "Every time I said 'I've had enough, I'm getting the hell out of here,' Elzey would promptly rush to amend my contract and say he'd never do that again. Of course he did."[12] Reese had no complaints against his publisher. The bond between the two managing editors lay in each being "a professional son of a bitch," Isaacs said, "and I concede without any reservation that I deserved the reputation. . . . I could be rough as a cob." Reese, he pointed out, trained under and emulated the fearsome Bovard.

9. Pfaff, *Joseph Pulitzer II*, 338–39; CJH interview, July 16, 1984; "P-D Notebook," July 1951, 1–2.

10. *St. Louis Post-Dispatch*, June 15, 1951.

11. There were 8 groups in 1900 controlling 27 papers. The numbers rose to 63 with 328 papers by 1935; 109 with 560 papers by 1960, and 135 with 1,228 papers by 1990. Along the way, some larger groups bought out smaller ones. There were 135 groups in 1990, 32 fewer than in 1978, when there were 167. Michael Emery and Edwin Emery, *The Press and America*, 8th ed. (Needham Heights, Massachusetts: 1996), 538.

12. Telephone interview with Norman E. Isaacs, October 23, 1984.

Immediately after the sale, J. P. II invited Isaacs to his office to discuss three things. Pulitzer first informed Isaacs that the possibility of his being invited to join the *Post-Dispatch* had been considered and rejected. Raymond Crowley, Reese's recent successor as managing editor, opposed hiring him. "I don't blame him," Isaacs replied. "Don't worry about me . . . I'm not over here looking for a job." He thought—but did not say—that he expected Crowley lacked the self-confidence of predecessors Bovard and Reese and was in no mood to deal with Isaacs: "I was considerably younger and tougher, and if I had been in Crowley's position, I would have said 'I don't want him around.'" Pulitzer next asked Isaacs if there were any *Star-Times* staff members the *Post-Dispatch* might hire. Isaacs gave him some names. The *Post-Dispatch*, already well staffed, hired one or two of these. The third item was the *Post-Dispatch* itself. Pulitzer wanted Isaacs's opinion of the newspaper's weaknesses, not its strengths, because he already knew those. "Well, the number one thing is arrogance," Isaacs replied, by which he meant snobbishness and discourtesy by reporters and others, including operators who answered *Post-Dispatch* telephones. They seemed to think the paper's high reputation entitled them to be rude, he charged. As to arrogance, Pulitzer answered, "I happen to agree with that." But he was not receptive to Isaacs's criticism of the editorial page. Isaacs called it "one of the stuffiest looking pages you ever saw in your life." Pulitzer brushed this aside, saying in effect, "the editorial page is mine and I don't want to discuss it. . . . I'm satisfied with it."

Even so, editorial-page makeup, among other subjects, came up again in a "competitor's analysis" J. P. II asked Isaacs to write following their meeting. Knowing the publisher's paternalistic view of the page, Isaacs was more conciliatory in writing, saying the makeup was "certainly distinctive . . . but hardly modern," and predicting that changes would come gradually over time. Isaacs's main recommendation was that with its afternoon rival gone the *Post-Dispatch* must work to "avoid the same fate that has overtaken so many 'monopoly' newspapers—slowness of movement, apathy, a slackening of editorial vigor." He advised putting "a prize on speed and alertness," because the paper "is going to have to struggle harder than ever to sharpen those qualities." He did not note that the *Globe-Democrat* competition remained, with the growing advantage of readers' preference for a morning paper. Overall, he described the *Post-Dispatch* "as a newspaper institution. I was always conscious of the fact that I was fighting a giant. . . . Sure, I could see what I considered to be faults . . . but to me it was a tough, rugged and two-fisted competitor." He also pointed out "that the Post-Dispatch's great, overpowering strength [is] in its massive, solid and thoughtful approach—in its complete lack of sensationalism." This matched compliments from many quarters during the tenure of J. P. II.

As for other faults, "I had to go about probing for weaknesses," Isaacs confessed, but he found several. While no one then could know, with J. P. III taking over in three-plus years, Isaacs's views were to be more pertinent to him than to his father, should he choose to act on the criticisms. There is little indication that he did, although he definitely agreed with Isaacs that the paper's makeup—on the editorial page and elsewhere—was "stodgy" and uninviting to the eye. But he did not share Isaacs's opinion that the typography, on which Joe and his father differed, gave the paper a dignified "look" amounting to "one of its greatest strengths." Yet when Joe succeeded his father and could update the paper's appearance, Isaacs said, "very little changed." Joe in effect admitted this to Isaacs several years later when they met at the Kentucky Derby in Louisville. "Do you remember that report you wrote?" Joe asked. "You know, it's just as valid today as it was then."[13] Isaacs attributed the slowness of change to the bureaucratic resistance to modernization found in most newsrooms. In time, the paper got several layout and design makeovers under Joe.

It is evident that by the time of the *Star-Times* purchase, Joe, almost forty, had formed a concept about his family heritage and his position in the chain of succession. In it was a degree of insecurity. This had developed over years, likely dating from his time at St. Mark's. He objected in July 1951 when his father proposed making advertising manager Fred Rowden second vice-president of the company. He believed only family members should be vice presidents and that if Rowden became one "my title automatically is diluted and something intangible is done to the idea of [president and vice president] being members of one family. I further think that the title, second vice-president, is meaningless as far as advertisers are concerned. The title suggests the proliferation of vice-presidents in small positions in large banks."[14] His opinion eventually changed. When he was president, board chairman, and CEO, non-family members were named vice presidents.

---

13. Isaacs interview. Isaacs left St. Louis to work on the *Times* and the *Courier-Journal* in Louisville, both owned by the Bingham family. He became executive editor of both papers. Their meeting at the Kentucky Derby probably was between 1956 and 1960, when Joe's brother Michael was working as a reporter at the *Courier-Journal* before moving to the *Post-Dispatch*. See also Susan E. Tifft and Alex S. Jones, *The Patriarch: The Rise and Fall of the Bingham Dynasty*. Isaacs's perspective on the sale and his recollections about J. P. III come from the Isaacs interview and from his letter to the assistant to J. P. II: Isaacs to Sam Shelton, July 19, 1951, JPIII Papers. See also Norman E. Isaacs, *Untended Gates: The Mismanaged Press*.

14. JPIII to JPII, July 18, 1951, JPIII Papers.

His sense of self and family showed up the next year, when he rejected the notion that families such as his were part of a small ruling elite. This happened in an exchange with Julius Klyman, a longtime *Post-Dispatch* reporter who for many years edited the paper's distinguished "Pictures" section. Klyman lived in the same upscale St. Louis suburb of Ladue where both J. P. II and J. P. III had homes, but fancied himself a working-class radical. If he wasn't a Communist—as some suspected and he denied— he unquestionably was a Socialist. In a meeting he and J. P. III attended, Klyman tried to discredit as "myth" that a "managerial class" actually runs the country's business enterprise. To further explain his theory, Klyman sent the associate editor a letter after the meeting. "[A] sizable group of boss boys getting big salaries now exists. But they are not the real powers," he explained. "They work for somebody and I don't mean that multitude of little stockholders the public relations mountebanks like to drool about. They work for Morgan or Kuhn, Loeb or Mellon or Rockefeller or du Pont or one of a few other great houses." He called the managerial class a creation "hand tailored for public consumption. Its psychological basis is the same as 'any boy can be president,' or in this case any boy can become a manager. And these 'self made' managers are proof of the American way.... [T]hey work for the millions of stockholders, little stockholders, that prove that just about everybody is one hell of a capitalist.... It all makes beautiful propaganda and does its part to soothe the savage breast of the proletariat."[15]

To this, Joe replied: "I hold no brief for the 'managerial class,' but I believe its members exert considerably more power than you suggest in relegating them to the position of glorified office boys for the Morgans, the Rockefellers, etc." He cited the cases of the heads of two companies, Edgar Queeny of Monsanto—headquartered in St. Louis—and Fowler McCormick of International Harvester in Chicago: "Queeny, who owns less than five percent of the stock of Monsanto is certainly not suppressing the management of Monsanto when he is on a photographic expedition in Africa. The wheels continue to turn to the benefit of labor, consumers and stockholders, including Queeny." And "McCormick steps out of International Harvester, which his family founded, because he disagrees with management—not a defeat for the hired hands." He recalled a "silly book" titled *America's Sixty Families*,[16] published in 1937, that "undertook

15. Julius H. Klyman to JPIII, undated (probably Fall 1952), JPIII Papers.
16. Ferdinand Lundberg, *America's Sixty Families*, 283. Lundberg had several harsh things to say about specific Pulitzers, singling out particularly the decline of the *World* under Ralph and Herbert. He was kinder to the *Post-Dispatch* under Joseph II: "Although never a performer in the stalwart old Pulitzer tradition, the *Post-Dispatch* has done

to prove the sinister control of American business by sixty families. The author was so hard up for names he included the Pulitzers who previously had sold the broken down *New York World* for salvage. This theory of monopolistic control reminds me of *Pravda*, something which it might report but which it doesn't believe—like the Russian invention of baseball." He observed that no managers of some eighteen hundred independent oil companies in the United States work "for the Rockefellers. Perhaps I should have said the House of Rockefeller. I have often wondered why these conspirators of enormous wealth (these operatives of capitalism)—the Rockefellers, the Morgans, etc.—seem to operate from their houses. It suggests they cannot afford offices." He found it surprising that "the sinister capitalists and power-mad money men with American industry in their hip pockets have been unable to elect a President for twenty years. Perhaps they will slip one over with Ike, but that might be the exception to prove the rule." He nudged Klyman to consider his own lifestyle, noting that "no longer does one have to be a Rockefeller or a Mellon to play golf or drive a station wagon. Out your way around Ladue the golf courses and station wagons suggest the strong ascendancy of the 'managerial class.'" He concluded that "the owners of great wealth today exert a fraction of the influence associated with the robber barons of the old free enterprise days" and that the managerial class "probably contributes more to the community... in civic enterprise... charitable and cultural fields than other segments of society."[17]

He could have reminded Klyman of *Post-Dispatch* obedience to his grandfather's command—a mixture of business pragmatism and kind-heartedness—that the newspaper be generous in improving St. Louis. And he could have given a current example. During his six years in St. Louis, Isaacs recalled, J. P. II "used to drive the other publishers crazy by his expenditures for news and... his generosity towards the community. He just made them look silly. They couldn't afford to match him.... [He] was bold when it came to... revitalizing downtown St. Louis and St. Louis generally. He threw a lot of money into it." The year before buying the *Star-Times*, the *Post-Dispatch* promoted sweeping downtown redevelopment in a thirteen-week series, "Progress or Decay? St. Louis Must Choose."

---

some excellent things in an era when the press as a whole has functioned as the first line of defense for political and financial rapists." It gave as examples that the *Post-Dispatch* "alone insisted that the Teapot Dome investigation continue in 1924" and opposed the executions of Sacco and Vanzetti in 1927—who ultimately were vindicated fifty years later.

17. JPIII to JH, October 16, 1952, JPIII Papers.

A major goal was to replace slum areas with affordable low-income hous-ing. The newspaper pledged $250,000 toward the project and called for other businesses to join, which they did, providing some $2 million. Two years later, J. P. II asked his son's opinion on giving $50,000 a year for ten years to the St. Louis Symphony in memory of the founding J. P., who loved symphony music. Joe advised against it, explaining that an "angel" con-tributor almost always "discourages community support by relieving citi-zens of their individual responsibility" because they think the angel will "bail them out."[18] He recommended instead that the company make gen-erous contributions over the years if "X number of large firms [do] like-wise," a proven approach in sustaining other orchestras.

18. Harry Wilensky, *The Story of the St. Louis Post-Dispatch,* 25; JPII to JPIII, February 27, 1953, JPIII to JPII, March 4, 1953, JPIII Papers.

Joe, about two years old, with grandmother Kate Davis Pulitzer.

Joe, age three and a half, laid the cornerstone of the *Post-Dispatch* building at Twelfth and Olive Streets, St. Louis, in 1916, with Mayor Henry Kiel presiding. Joe's father, J. P. II, used the same trowel at age four in laying the cornerstone for the *New York World* building in 1889.

Joseph Pulitzer III, about twelve years old.

Elinor Wickham Pulitzer, Joe's mother, died in an automobile accident when he was eleven.

Joseph Pulitzer II and second wife Elizabeth Edgar Pulitzer at Kate Davis's debut, 1934.

William Polk, Jr. ("Polky"), Joe's friend from childhood; his sister Kate Davis; and Joe's wife, Louise ("Lulu"), about 1939.

Joe in the late 1930s with two of his early art acquisitions. *Still Life*, by Georges Braque, is in front of *Woman in Yellow*, by Pablo Picasso.

St. Louis friends William Polk, Jr., and Robert Brookings Smith, a
Post-Dispatch company financial adviser, during Navy service in
World War II, about 1942. Courtesy of Sarah Dunn.

Joe and his father in the lobby of the old *Post-Dispatch* building
with a plaque containing words from 1904 by the first J. P., beginning: "Our Republic and its press will rise and fall together. An
able, disinterested, public-spirited press . . . can preserve that
public virtue without which a popular government is a sham
and a mockery."

Cantankerous managing editor Oliver K. Bovard was frosty toward Joe during his apprenticeship years.

Marquis W. Childs mentored Joe during the 1936 presidential campaign and became *Post-Dispatch* Washington Bureau chief and a syndicated columnist.

Irving Dilliard, editorial page editor from 1949 to 1957, clashed with both Joe and J. P. II over interpretation of the *Post-Dispatch* platform. Joe relieved him of the editorship.

J. P. II and J. P. III with Rodin bust of J. P. I, late 1940s. Joe was associate editor.

Raymond C. Crowley, managing editor from 1951 to 1962, did not like taking orders from Joe.

Joe and Lulu with son Joseph Pulitzer IV, 1950.

Joe hands a retirement gift to Sam J. Shelton, special assistant and confidant to both J. P. II and J. P. III, in 1956, as Charles J. Hentschell looks on. Hentschell, a longtime Pulitzer executive, was Joe's primary business adviser from 1955 to 1970.

Post-Dispatch newsroom about 1960, before computers.

From left: Louise Pulitzer; Arch King, Joe's secretary; Joseph Holland, his special assistant; and Robert Lasch, editorial page editor, after the 1962 cornerstone ceremony for the renovated former *Globe-Democrat* building. Pulitzer Publishing Company bought the building in 1959, when the *Post* and *Globe* reached a joint printing agreement.

Bill Mauldin, Pulitzer Prize–winning World War II editorial cartoonist, worked for the *Post-Dispatch* from 1958 to 1962. He admired the newspaper's editorial philosophy, but left the paper for more money, a decision he later regretted.

Arthur R. Bertelson, managing editor from 1962 to 1968.

Joe and J. P. IV aprés-ski in Switzerland, March 1966.

Six

Succession

Joe naturally had concerns outside the *Post-Dispatch*. One of the biggest after the war was that he and Lulu had been unable to conceive a child until nearly ten years after their marriage. She was approaching thirty-five, and they had sought medical advice. She "went though an awful lot of medical things to be able to have the baby," her friend Euretta ("Rettles") Rathbone recalled.[1] Following the birth of Joseph Pulitzer IV on December 21, 1949, Joe and Lulu were told that there could be no more children. The newest "young Joe"—a robust eight-pounder—became a presumptive heir in the chain of family succession, but as events transpired, this did not come to pass. The four generations of "Joseph Pulitzer" were memorialized in a 1955 photograph showing J. P. second, third, and fourth flanking John Singer Sargent's portrait of the founder.

Despite the long wait for a child, the birth of their son did not create major changes in the lives of the new parents, especially Joe. While he loved his son, he did not enjoy the company of small children and was not interested in doing fatherly things. Part of this was settled in family custom as well as general practice among the wealthy. Hired help had always tended Pulitzer offspring while their parents continued their lives much as they had before children arrived. As Michael Pulitzer saw it growing up, business and adult company came ahead of children in his father's life. "I felt he never did anything that other fathers did, his lifestyle was such. And I felt that the family tradition was such that being a child was unacceptable; the quicker you grew up, the better off you were. The house definitely was not organized for a child, although as far as nursemaids and toys and stuff like that, there never was any deprivation."[2]

Joe IV's experience was essentially the same. He was around his parents regularly during his early years, but a nanny, Stella Rowan, with whom he bonded, cared for him most of the time. "She was really a surrogate parent," he said. "I was under the care of my nanny pretty much the whole

1. Interview with Euretta Rathbone, July 17, 1999, Cambridge, Massachusetts.
2. MEP interview, July 19, 1985.

time." His parents traveled frequently, most often to Europe and Mexico. When Joe and Lulu decided the boy no longer needed Ms. Rowan and let her go, he was so unhappy that they hired her back until he went away to prep school at thirteen. As he grew older, he saw more of his mother and father, usually during school vacations and holidays.

Monday was Ms. Rowan's day off when Joe IV was a small child. He then had time with his mother, who in the evening sometimes prepared lamb chops, one of his favorite meals. On other days, he would be with her when she dressed for dinner or to go out for the evening. "I would pick out a pair of gloves for her or something like that." Until he started preschool at age three, he and his mother sometimes had outings in her Plymouth station wagon. A favorite destination was Forest Park, the largest green space in St. Louis, where the city zoo, art museum, and other attractions are located. He remembered those days as carefree times when he and his mother sometimes joined in song as they drove along.

He had few childhood memories of his father, and those that he had were mainly from when he was older and in school. They usually were together in the mornings. "He'd be shaving and he'd want to know about my homework. It was pretty awful, actually. I'd be interrogated while he was shaving." He was enrolled in kindergarten at Rossman School, his father's elementary school, at age four, where he attended through fourth grade. From fifth through eighth grade he attended private Country Day School, where many prominent St. Louisans sent their children. He then followed his father and grandfather to St. Mark's. Like them, he spent part of every summer at Bar Harbor. Until he was about nine, he traveled there with his nanny. He and Ms. Rowan stayed at a motel, and occasionally visited his parents during the day at Beechcroft, the smaller cottage J. P. II purchased after high-maintenance Chatwold was torn down in 1947. He started attending summer camps at age seven, first in the daytime at Country Day, and then at residential camps in Maine from the age of eight. He experienced some homesickness as an eight-year-old, but soon adjusted. At camp he learned to sail, was active in sports and other activities, and grew more self-sufficient.

His father was coming ever closer to his succession as editor and publisher during Joe IV's childhood years. There were indications that this could happen at any time. J. P. II began to have health problems in 1953, when he was sixty-seven, undergoing surgery twice that year. A benign stomach tumor was removed in the first procedure and a benign colon polyp and his appendix in the second.[3] An aneurysm was discovered in

3. Unless otherwise noted, material on the illness and death of JPII is from Pfaff, *Joseph Pulitzer II*, 375–79.

his main abdominal aorta in the first operation, but it was not considered life threatening. He was well enough by June 1954 to go salmon fishing in Norway. The following October an obstruction of the right carotid artery to the head was found after he had a small stroke that caused a transient loss of vision. At the time, no surgical techniques existed to remove such obstructions. There are two accounts of the gravity of this finding. In the first, Dr. Sam Grant, his physician, saw no cause for alarm. Grant told J. P. II confidant Sam Shelton—after his boss asked the doctor to do so—about the publisher's condition. Shelton's notes say that the doctor believed anticoagulant medication could give him another ten or fifteen years if he slowed down by delegating some details to others. In the second account, recalled thirty years later by Charles Hentschell, Grant had delivered a stark message directly to J. P. II in approximately these words: "Joe, I am not going to kid you. You've had a stroke and that generally precedes another stroke with generally fatal consequences. You might live one month; you might live six months. I wouldn't bet on more than six months." Hentschell's source for this was Arch R. King, J. P. II's main secretary.

Less than four months after the stroke J. P. II died, but not of a stroke. The abdominal aneurysm ruptured sometime while he was working in his office on March 30, 1955. He went home not feeling well, collapsed shortly after dinner, and was rushed to Barnes Hospital. He died in the emergency room. With him were his wife, Joe and Lulu, and his two physicians. His seventieth birthday nine days earlier had been marked by a party attended by immediate family and twenty-five employees, each of whom had served the longest in his or her department. A photo from the party shows a visibly concerned Elizabeth Pulitzer watching her husband rather than the camera. In another, he is embracing five-year-old J. P. IV.

Arguably, Joe should have been informed immediately about his father's stroke, but was not. J. P. II told only his wife and Shelton about the obstructed carotid artery and admonished them to keep it "graveyard secret." Fearing cancer would be discovered during the 1953 stomach operation, he had consulted Shelton, Hentschell, and Raymond Crowley about contingency planning, but not his son and heir.[4] Shelton's record of that session noted that J. P. II "was concerned as to whether Joe [III] was competent to carry on." There is no evidence that he actually doubted this himself. He may have wanted the executives to affirm their confidence in his son. This they did, pledging to give their all in helping him. J. P. II then requested and got from his brother Herbert, a trustee, assurance that he would support

4. To ensure that he would not be deceived about the outcome of this operation, he ordered that a story be printed in the *Post-Dispatch* revealing whatever was found. It said "a small benign tumor" was removed. *St. Louis Post-Dispatch*, February 6, 1953.

"ample and generous compensation for [the] heavy responsibilities" Joe would assume on becoming head of the company. In July 1954 Hentschell was named a company trustee, joining J. P. II, Herbert Pulitzer, and J. P. III.[5] Adding a fourth member provided insurance that there would be three trustees, as usual, should one die.

Even without all the medical facts, Joe could tell that his father "was not in top form the last two or three years" of his life. In early 1954, after the second operation, a reunion of immediate family was arranged at Herbert's home in Palm Beach, Florida. Children and grandchildren attended, but Joe could tell that his father was not having a good time. "He was very depressed, but he didn't tell me about it. He was not acting normal." He knew his father was taking anticoagulant medication, but not why, because "health was something he considered very private" and had never discussed with his children.[6]

Approximately five hundred people attended his funeral at Christ Church Cathedral on April 2, 1955. The service followed Episcopal practice in line with requests J. P. II had made, with Joe supervising every detail. He described the funeral in a letter to cousin Ralph Pulitzer, Jr., who could not attend, as "the most impressive service I can remember, organ music by Bach, white flowers on the altar, carefully chosen white flowers on either side of the choir stalls with some color leading to the altar tastefully arranged, the casket with a profusion of spring flowers, and the Episcopal service was not interrupted by hymns or extra unnecessary prayers. It was a dignified tribute, yet simple and in keeping with my father's inherent good taste."[7] Although a burial plot beside his first wife was available at Bellefontaine Cemetery in St. Louis, J. P. II chose cremation out of respect to his second wife. His ashes were scattered from the company airplane over Frenchman Bay at Bar Harbor.

Only a broad outline of the J. P. II estate was made public, undoubtedly reflecting his desire for privacy when it came to company and family financial matters. The *Post-Dispatch* reported a total value of $1,208,838, but only limited specifics. The value of his 652 company shares was "undetermined," only par values were given for unnamed securities he held, and only nominal values for art objects. (A more extensive public accounting of the founder's estate had been provided after J. P. I died in 1911, valuing it at $18,525,118—equivalent to $53,382,188 in 1955 dollars. It disclosed the expenses and earnings of the *World* and *Post-Dispatch* properties.) In

5. *St. Louis Post-Dispatch,* July 9, 1954.
6. Interview with JPIII, July 19, 1984.
7. JPIII to Ralph Pulitzer, Jr., April 11, 1955, JPIII Papers.

line with the founder's will, J. P. II established trusts providing one-fourth shares of his estate to each of his four children. Only the portions to sons Joseph III and Michael included company stock while Kate Davis and Elinor received equivalent assets. Most of the remaining stock belonged to the other male descendants of J. P. I—none of whom worked for the company. J. P. III and Michael had first refusal on any additional shares that might become available, as happened when other male heirs decided to sell shares. Herbert Jr., for example, sold all of his company stock and involved himself in several businesses, including oil and gas wells, restaurants, hotels, and Florida citrus farms.[8]

The trustees elected Joseph Pulitzer III editor and publisher of the *Post-Dispatch* and company president on April 4. He stepped boldly into his new role. He published a signed editorial "reaffirming the *Post-Dispatch* tradition and my determination to see that it is carried on" to which he received "a most gratifying response . . . from all over the nation."[9] Richard Baumhoff, a reporter and writer who became an assistant to J. P II, was assigned to produce a "memorial" issue of the paper's internal publication, *P-D Notebook*, to mark the passage of J. P. II. When Baumhoff presented a draft of the publication to J. P. III, he got an unexpected response. As Arthur Bertelson, who later became managing editor, recalled it, Baumhoff proudly

8. *New York Times*, November 22, 1912; *St. Louis Post-Dispatch*, July 26, 1955; *Editor & Publisher*, April 9, 1955, 11, 73. The Sargent portrait of J. P. I was valued at $500 and his bust by August Rodin at $100. Whatever the actual total of the J. P. II estate, figures he had compiled in 1951 estimated the inheritances of his four children at $6.6 million. The net worth of the company in 1955 was $15,366,224, and its net earnings were $2,840,860. "Children's Inheritances," May 17, 1951, JPII Papers, reel 7, frame 356; "Net Worth/Net Profit 1912–1955," prepared for the author by Pulitzer Publishing Company, 1986. The other descendants included Herbert and his son, Herbert "Peter" Jr.; Ralph's son, Ralph Jr.; the former Edith Pulitzer's sons, David and Adrian Moore; and the former Constance Pulitzer's sons, William, Gordon, and James Weir. Under the founder's will, any sons born to female descendants also would receive stock on reaching majority. Kate Davis had two daughters and two sons; Elinor had no children. Other descendants also produced children. The gradual dispersal of stock among male descendants whose only link to Pulitzer Publishing was the dividends they received created the basis for a 1986 legal battle within the family, ending with the company going public; see chapter 10. The will also provided that 10 percent of the shares belonged to principal editors and managers of the *Post-Dispatch* while they held those positions. "Last Will and Testament of Joseph Pulitzer," April 15, 1904, with codicils of March 23, 1909, January 17, 1910, May 11, 1910, and July 12, 1911; *New York Times*, April 7, 1955; *St. Louis Post-Dispatch*, July 26, 1955; JPIII to Harry Wilensky, October 28, 1970, and undated clipping from *Holland Herald*, JPIII Papers. Herbert, nicknamed Peter, gained national notoriety in the wake of a messy divorce from his second wife, Roxanne, in the 1980s. *Philadelphia Inquirer*, November 14, 1982; Roxanne Pulitzer, *The Prize Pulitzer* (New York: Ballantine Books, 1987).

9. JPIII to RP Jr., April 11, 1955, JPIII Papers.

announced, "'Here's the story of your father's death,' and Joe looked at him coolly and said, 'Mr. Baumhoff, I am the story now, not my father.' And they had to junk that issue of the *Notebook* and portray the new publisher instead of the one who had just died. My impression was that Joe [III] put on his pants both legs at once, like a real big leaguer, and from then on there was never any question who was the power of the throne, not behind it—he had ascended to the throne."[10] A story about Joe's appointment and his background, with his photograph, filled the magazine's cover page. Several stories and more photos of him started on page three.

Joe shortly got "the complimentary news" that the Advisory Board on the Pulitzer Prizes of Columbia University intended to appoint him immediately to succeed his father as chairman so that he could participate in the 1955 selections. The board's secretary, John Hohenberg, recorded in his diary that Joe was "tense" as he approached this new task. Joe had long telephone conversations from St. Louis with Hohenberg prior to his first board meeting. In the early going, Hohenberg confessed to his diary: "I can't quite figure out Joseph Pulitzer [III]." One of Joe's questions was how board members had voted for president in 1944, 1948, and 1952. "How would I know?" Hohenberg recorded. "Anyway, most of them are Republicans, I'd suppose, but if there are any Democrats outside the Pulitzers they're undoubtedly on the conservative side except for [anti-segregationist *Atlanta Constitution* editor] Ralph McGill." Hohenberg eventually found that J. P. III never based his votes for or against prizes on political considerations. In discussions, the board secretary found him to be "an articulate and liberal democrat of the old school" who took his cues from his forebears. Hohenberg observed a "distinct form of ancestor worship" in Joe's opposition to any deviation in Advisory Board decisions that might go against "conditions in his grandfather's will."[11]

Even so, he also looked ahead. Six weeks after his father's death he instructed Sam Shelton to amend a summary of the company's history from 1947 to 1954, to be sure that it made plain why J. P. III among the third-generation heirs was now in charge: "As this will be submitted to the grandsons [of J. P. I], I think it would be well to include a paragraph briefly stating that [J. P. II] devoted considerable attention to training me as his successor. In other words, I think a little reassurance as to the continuity of policy would not be out of order." Besides the reassurance, this also might be seen as a way of telling the other grandsons not to consider challenging his authority. None ever did. "Joe ran that company with an iron

10. Interview with ARB, August 19, 1993, St. Louis.
11. John Hohenberg, *The Pulitzer Diaries*, 22–24.

fist," grandson David E. Moore observed. "We didn't know what the hell he was going to do."[12]

In February 1956 Joe delivered the first Joseph Pulitzer Memorial Lecture—titled "A Tradition of Conscience"—at Columbia University. The annual lecture series had been endowed by *Post-Dispatch* staff members in memory of J. P. II. "The *Post-Dispatch* was a going concern with an established tradition before I was born," Joe began. He gave his grandfather his due, especially for the paper's platform. But he credited J. P. II with its rise to distinction during the past forty-three years largely because of "the many investigations, exposes or public services which stemmed from his suggestions." He said his father always operated in a firm but fair way, by emphasizing competence and building career-long loyalty to the newspaper. He pledged that this would continue, although unforeseen changes would require adaptations: "Fifty years ago the comparative importance of local and foreign events would be summed up by an editor who said: 'A dog fight on Main Street means more to my readers than a war in Asia.' Three wars, the airplane and a bomb have taken the bloom off that homely bit of wisdom."[13]

In fact, the *Post-Dispatch* had looked beyond Main Street for decades. The paper's reputation as one of the top five metropolitan newspapers in the country rested on its intellectual tone and its attention to national and international affairs. At the same time, its coverage of its primary circulation area in Missouri and Illinois had been vigorous as well, garnering five Pulitzer Prizes for meritorious public service during the tenure of J. P. II.[14] In his speech, Joe gave credit to the paper's thirteen-week series in 1950 titled "Progress or Decay? St. Louis Must Choose" for stimulating $2 million in gifts from businesses for urban redevelopment. Civic Progress, a group of the city's most prominent business executives, established in 1952, credited the series as "a major catalyst" in the approval of a large bond issue. The paper also favored an earnings tax enacted that year on

12. JPIII to Samuel Shelton, July 20, 1955, SS to JPIII, August 12, 1955, JPIII Papers; Interview with David E. Moore, May 22, 2000, Rye, New York. Moore was one of four sons of Edith Pulitzer Moore, a sister of J. P. II.

13. Text of "A Tradition of Conscience," delivered February 10, 1956, JPIII Papers.

14. In 1937 for exposing gross election frauds in St. Louis; in 1941 for its campaign against smoke pollution in St. Louis; in 1948 for exposing conditions leading to a coal mine explosion in Centralia, Illinois, that killed 111 miners; in 1950 (shared with the *Chicago Tribune*) for revealing that 51 Illinois editors and publishers were on state payrolls; in 1952 for exposure of widespread corruption in the Internal Revenue Bureau and other government departments. Seven other Pulitzers were awarded during the tenure of J.P. II to individual staff members. Wilensky, *The Story of the St. Louis Post-Dispatch*, 52; Harris, "The Gold-Medal Crusade Years," passim.

the salaries of people who worked in St. Louis but lived outside its boundaries. In 1955 voters approved twenty-three projects at a cost of $110.6 mil-
lion to combat blight, improve schools and highways, and build affordable housing downtown.[15] In subsequent years the "Progress or Decay"
campaign supported rehabilitating the Mississippi riverfront through
development of an industrial park and construction of the city's signature
arch and nearby Busch Stadium.

Nevertheless, St. Louis was a two-newspaper town. Whatever the *Post-
Dispatch*'s achievements, St. Louisans—most of whom called the papers
the *Post* and the *Globe*—considered the morning *Globe* the more user-
friendly, locally oriented hometown newspaper of the two. "We never
overcame the image," former *Post* managing editor Evarts Graham, Jr.,
recalled.[16] It did not matter that the *Post* devoted more staff, space, and money
to civic improvements and led in circulation. Comparisons of the amount
of local coverage in the two papers consistently showed more in the *Post*.
But the papers' front pages suggested otherwise. The *Globe*'s was almost
totally local—as were its inside pages—while the *Post*'s was largely
national and international. The *Post* put most local stories inside.

Chain ownership did not alter the public's perception of which was
the "local" paper. Samuel I. Newhouse owned ten other newspapers around
the country when he bought the *Globe* on March 24, 1955, just days before
J. P. III took charge. Well aware of the *Globe*'s declining circulation and
advertising, Pulitzer Publishing had floated an exploratory offer before
the *Globe*'s banker, David R. Calhoun, president of St. Louis Union Trust
Company. Joe, his father, and Hentschell told Calhoun just two weeks
before the death of J. P. II that "we could come close to meeting Calhoun's
figure of seven million dollars" for the *Globe*'s land, building, equipment,
and Sunday circulation lists. They were stunned when the deal went to
Newhouse for $6.25 million and included the *Globe*'s radio and television
holdings as well as the newspaper. The deal was not as favorable as it may
have seemed, however, because Newhouse also assumed $1.5 million
in debt on the television property.[17] Anticipating Federal Communications
Commission monopoly ownership objections, the Pulitzers had expressed
no interest in the station in order to avoid FCC monopoly ownership objections because they already owned KSD radio and KSDK-TV in St. Louis.[18]
Of course they knew that conservative *Globe* owner-publisher E. Lansing

15. Primm, *Lion of the Valley*, 493–96.
16. EAG interview, June 21, 1995, St. Louis.
17. The *Globe*'s television property was a minority interest in KWK-TV.
18. Pfaff, *Joseph Pulitzer II*, 340–41; JPIII, "Memorandum on Globe-Democrat,"
March 14, 1955, JPIII Papers.

Ray, who had battled the *Post* for almost forty-five years, hated the idea of selling to his liberal rival. In Newhouse, Ray thought that he had found the ideal buyer, one who cared only that his properties made money and left news and editorial policy undisturbed in the hands of local editors.

Newhouse immediately sent tested business personnel from some of his other papers to energize the *Globe*'s advertising, circulation, and production operations. When Ray died six months after the sale, Newhouse shifted Richard H. Amberg, publisher of the *Syracuse Post-Standard*, to the same position at the *Globe*. Amberg's mandate was to improve the bottom line, chiefly by eroding the *Post*'s circulation and advertising leadership. With a daily circulation of four hundred thousand, the *Post* was almost one hundred thousand ahead of the *Globe* when Newhouse took over. It had led daily circulation since 1950, and in 1955 had 67 percent of all newspaper advertising in St. Louis. Under Amberg, *Post-Dispatch* business manager Fred F. Rowden explained to an advertiser in 1958, the *Globe* "pulled out all the stops" to take advertising away from the *Post*, with little overall success. He said the *Globe* gave advertisers free color, news stories in exchange for advertising (forbidden at the *Post*), and offered some fifty special rate inducements without which "they would have less business today than under the old management." Yet this had barely reduced the *Post*'s advertising lead, dropping it only to 65 percent. Amberg's biggest success was in women's pages, where fashion and other promotions "attracted thousands of new female readers [and] millions of lines of new advertising."[19]

In late 1960, *Newsweek* and *Time* magazines published articles three months apart crediting Amberg's aggressive local boosterism for his paper's resurgence.[20] Amberg belonged to twenty-four St. Louis organizations and had made himself highly visible around town and in *Globe* photographs that showed him at public appearances and awarding *Globe* prizes to various local leaders and organizations. Joe never did such things, even requesting to be "underplayed" in *P. D. Notebook* because he did "not want to ape the ridiculous position Amberg has taken in his newspaper."[21] Neither would he curry favor with Civic Progress as did Amberg via *Globe* cheerleading, especially for its fund-raising activities. To do so would violate the Pulitzer injunction to be "drastically independent" and thus avoid charges of favoritism in coverage. Some in the newsroom, however, saw

19. FFR to Morris R. Schlensky, October 28, 1958, JPIII Papers; Richard H. Meeker, *Newspaperman*, 191.

20. "G-D vs. P-D," *Newsweek*, August 22, 1960, 55–56; "A Tough Customer," *Time*, November 14, 1960, 77.

21. JPIII to RLC, March 13, 1959, JPIII Papers.

partiality in Joe's encouragement of *Post-Dispatch* coverage of the city's art museum and symphony even though his name rarely appeared in any of the stories.

Most readers likely accepted the *Time* and *Newsweek* articles as factual even if blunt in their profiles of the competing publishers. In *Time* Amberg, forty-eight, was a "hip-shooting combination of businessman, newsman and club-joining civic promoter" and a Boy Scoutmaster who "can always find room for a moving editorial about, for example, small boys killed by lightning while selling Boy Scout circus tickets. ('Certainly there must be an especial place in Heaven for faithful little boys.')" Pulitzer, forty-seven, was "a gentle, high-minded fellow who feels infinitely more at home in an art gallery than in a city room. He has sometimes been heard to remark at dinner parties that he doesn't really like his job—except for his part in supervising the P-D's cultural articles, which he ponders in an office graced by a Rodin bust of his legendary grandfather, the founder of the P-D and the old *New York World*." *Newsweek* said J. P. III "impresses visitors with a sense of noblesse oblige" and that "according to intimates, . . . was leaning toward a career as a museum director when he inherited leadership of the paper in 1955." *Time* quoted "an old St. Louis newsman" as saying "Amberg is a bore, but he's a driving bore." Both magazines noted the *Post*'s history of distinction and commanding lead in advertising, *Time* observing that "the *Globe* has a long row to hoe before it catches up with the *Post-Dispatch* as a newspaper" because "the P-D remains more thoughtfully written and edited [and] has much superior Washington and foreign coverage."

Despite the compliments, Joe's reaction—privately—was to denounce *Newsweek* and *Time* as "news fiction" magazines and to consider suing them for libel. But first he asked managing editor Crowley "whether we should dignify the [first published] *Newsweek* story by any sort of notice to employees." A few days later employees got a dissection of the piece from *Post-Dispatch* business manager Fred Rowden. That, along with a letter from Joe, was mailed to Pulitzer family shareholders and to other individuals he thought would be interested. Joe's letter to cousin Herbert "Peter" Pulitzer, Jr., in Florida said *Newsweek*'s article was "a lot of baloney" which Rowden's report "demolished." The paper's national advertising salesmen also got the report with instructions to distribute it as they saw fit, but not to all the paper's advertisers and agencies "on the theory that to do so would dignify the *Newsweek* article."[22]

22. JPIII to Crowley, September 17, 1960, Fred F. Rowden, "To Employees," August 23, 1960, JPIII to Herbert Pulitzer, Jr., September 9, 1960, JPIII to Selwyn Pepper, September 16, 1960, JPIII Papers.

Rowden explained that the *Newsweek* reporter, Ward Just, had gotten most of his information from Amberg except for "a few brief interviews with *Post-Dispatch* executives" and "a few perfunctory calls on St. Louis businessmen, some of whom refused to discuss the newspaper situation." Relying on Amberg, Rowden wrote, "is equivalent to getting your material from Gimbel's to do a story on Macy's." Moreover, he considered the article biased because Just ignored vital available facts and could well have harbored a personal bias against the *Post*. Some of the absent facts, he wrote, were that the *Post-Dispatch* held substantial daily circulation leads in both St. Louis city and county and had been ahead on Sunday by 63 percent until the *Globe* stopped Sunday publication in 1959. "The *Globe-Democrat* investment in St. Louis today is so small that its physical facilities could likely be loaded on a couple of trucks and moved out of town within a few hours," Rowden wrote.

The bias he alleged stemmed from the fact that Ward Just was the son of F. Ward Just, publisher of the Waukegan, Illinois, *News-Sun*. A decade earlier, the *Post-Dispatch* and *Chicago Daily News* had shared a Pulitzer Prize for public service for disclosing that fifty-one Illinois newspaper editors and publishers were on the Illinois state payroll in bogus jobs paying a total of $480,000 in exchange for which they printed stories favorable to the state's Republican party. "High on the list of these questionable newspaper people were F. Ward Just, father of the *Newsweek* reporter, and his brother, William, of the *Waukegan News-Sun*. They received a total of $51,420 from the State of Illinois," Rowden reported. *Post* executives were aware of the younger Just's parentage when he interviewed them, Rowden noted, but had ignored it, deciding "that we should rely upon his honesty as a reporter and the integrity of the editors by whom he is employed." Recently, he added, Just's father had bought space in the newspaper trade publication *Editor & Publisher* to reprint a *News-Sun* editorial criticizing the *Post-Dispatch* as unethical in reviving the fact that Frank J. Prince, a prominent industrialist, had been convicted more than thirty years earlier for forgery, grand larceny, and passing bad checks.[23] The *Time* article referred to the *Post's* having reported the long ago convictions, while *Newsweek* made no mention of it. Nor did *Newsweek* report, as *Time* did, a recent example of egregious irresponsibility at the *Globe*. Before police had investigated, the *Globe* reported allegations by a white woman that three black men had raped her. Editorially, the *Globe* described the incident as

23. Managing editor Crowley had forced publication of the story over objections of city [later managing] editor Evarts Graham, Jr., who believed the long-ago convictions were not relevant. Prince had come into the news this time for making a large contribution to Washington University. EAG interview, June 21, 1995.

being "as bad as the Congo." Then the woman confessed that her story was fabricated.

As soon as the *Newsweek* article appeared, Joe assigned Joseph F. Holland, his personal assistant and community emissary, to do a damage appraisal. Holland, formerly a newsman with the *Globe, Post,* and the late *St. Louis Star,* also had a law degree. He was the city's most popular after-dinner speaker and had numerous business and political connections.[24] He sought assessments from seven highly placed St. Louisans. Only four had seen the article. Lawrence Malinkrodt, president of Scruggs, Vandervoort & Barney department stores; James Conzelman, vice president of D'Arcy Advertising Company; Joseph P. Clark, president of the St. Louis Labor Council; and Circuit Judge Robert L. Aronson all told Holland the article was unlikely to have much influence. They did, however, share the general impression that the *Globe* did a better job of local coverage. Conzelman speculated that "the man from *Newsweek* probably got a brush off at the *Post,* and the *Globe* rolled out the red carpet."[25]

The *Globe*'s next move was to send its advertisers reprints of the *Newsweek* story. That was enough for J. P. III to ask company attorney Charles B. McInnis in Washington, D.C., to "determine if the Newsweek article is libelous";[26] the same question was asked of the *Time* story after it came out. Two *Newsweek* assertions in particular offended him. The first, he told McInnis, was that although "recent national polls of editors ranked [the *Post-Dispatch*] second only to the *New York Times* . . . the paper hasn't been the same in recent years." In fact, he noted, the *Post* holds "the same position it occupied in a survey conducted by the same publicist, Edward L. Bernays, in 1952." On September 24, 1960, the *Post* ran a four-page center spread in *Editor & Publisher* displaying Bernays's identical results and the *Post*'s superior circulation and advertising figures. The *Post* mailed copies of the ad to all its advertisers and agencies.[27]

The second offending statement was that Joe "was leaning toward a career as a museum director when he inherited leadership in 1955." That, he said, "is baloney. Following my release from naval service in 1946, I rejoined the staff of the Post-Dispatch, and there was never the remotest intention of pursuing another career after that date. My art interest is, and always has been since graduation from college, an avocation, not a vocation."

24. *St. Louis Post-Dispatch,* May 19, 1967.
25. Joseph F. Holland to JPIII, September 1, 1960, JPIII Papers.
26. JPIII to McInnis, September 9, 1960, JPIII Papers.
27. *Editor & Publisher,* September 24, 1960, 63–66.

McInnis responded that it would be an "extremely close call" to establish libel, particularly against the *Post-Dispatch* as a whole rather than a claim of damage to Joe's reputation. He thought *Newsweek*—and the *Globe-Democrat*, for circulating the reprints—might be successfully sued, but that most readers would not find the *Time* article defamatory. In any case, "such a suit or suits would be expensive, and the amount of damages which the Pulitzer Publishing Company could recover is somewhat problematical." Even before McInnis was heard from, editorial page editor Robert Lasch and eight other top *Post* executives had advised against suing *Time*. Lasch thought a suit "would be most unlikely to succeed and . . . poor tactics anyway."[28] However, Marquis Childs, the veteran reporter and syndicated columnist—and Joe's mentor as a young reporter—gently expressed his displeasure to *Time* publisher Henry R. Luce, with whom he was friendly. It was "an injustice," he wrote, to assert that J. P. III was more interested in art collecting and art museums than in publishing a newspaper:

> What he has done is to expand the horizons of the *Post-Dispatch* to take in important cultural interests in the community and in the world. This is, in a sense, a new role for a newspaper in a midwestern city. I believe it is an important role . . . much like *Time* printing so much interesting and important art in color in recent years along with so much important art news.
>
> To my knowledge, Joe has sustained a very high interest in every aspect of the *Post-Dispatch*. He is a very different type of publisher from his father and grandfather. But this is not to say he does not have a very strong continuing and vital interest in the *Post-Dispatch*, not only as an institution but as a force in the community, the state and the nation.

Luce replied that he would show Childs's letter to "two or three of my senior colleagues and I hope they will be sympathetic to the points you make about the *Post-Dispatch* and Joseph Pulitzer Jr." *Time* had been mostly unsympathetic toward the *Post-Dispatch* for years, Evarts Graham, Jr., observed, "because *Time* was controlled by the China lobby and [red-baiting U.S. Senator Joseph] McCarthy, and the *Post-Dispatch* hated both."[29]

Well aware of this, Joe remarked in a letter to former managing editor Benjamin Reese that Childs's letter might foster "some improvement in the

28. McInnis to JPIII, January 5, 1961, with opinion dated December 27, 1960, RL to JPIII, November 10, 1960, CJH, "Memorandum," November 11, 1960, JPIII Papers.
29. MWC to Luce, November 14, 1960, Luce to MWC, November 16, 1960, JPIII Papers; EAG interview, June 21, 1995.

future, although I wouldn't bet on it." For a time, he considered "inspiring a friendly story about the P. D. in one of the respected national magazines" whenever the paper might "have something new to brag about," but shortly changed his mind. "I would prefer to let the initiative come from outside the office," he concluded. "As time passes I feel less concerned about smart aleck attacks against the paper and myself and am more inclined to allow favorable appraisals to originate spontaneously." Perhaps the best question he asked through all this turmoil was rhetorical, in a note to Hentschell: "Is my relatively brief editorship—five years plus—sufficient time to support this theme of a third generation, family-owned, liberal, independent, fearless, successful and idealistic newspaper adhering to its platform?"[30]

30. JPIII to BJR, November 29, 1960, JPIII to JFH, December 20, 1961, JPIII to CJH, November 11, 1960, JPIII Papers.

Seven

Michael Edgar Pulitzer

His half brother's decision to be a journalist instead of a lawyer was another unanticipated development for J. P. III during his first three years as editor and publisher. Michael—often called "Mike" by family, friends, and business associates—was working in the Boston law firm of Warren, Stackpole, Stetson and Bradlee in 1955,[1] but told Joe shortly after their father died that he wished to leave law and move into the family business. J. P. II had urged him to do this, and was greatly disappointed when Mike chose law instead. He had shown aptitude for reporting in 1947 when he was sixteen and in prep school. After a coal mine explosion at Centralia, Illinois, killed 111 miners, he accompanied a *Post-Dispatch* reporter to the scene and produced a first-person account of what he saw. It was published in the *Vindex*, St. Mark's student magazine. Mike's article provided evidence of gross neglect of mine safety regulations. Among many disturbing scenes was "a sight I'll never forget" in the washhouse building. "In the entrance...was tacked a thick sheaf of yellow inspection certificates. A lot had been torn off, but the pile was still thick. The outside one was Dec. 1946, and listed fault after fault." The *Post-Dispatch* coverage won a Pulitzer Prize for "disinterested and meritorious service." Managing editor Raymond Crowley and city editor Benjamin Reese sent J. P. II a note about Mike's account: "We think Mike did a good job, for his age and experience, in telling what he saw. When will the new reporter start?"[2]

There had been virtually no previous discussion of this subject between Mike and his father. Unlike Joe, Mike did not grow up assuming that journalism was likely to be his life's work. His relationship with his father had not been close. "My memory of him is very hazy," Mike said. "I can't really put a rounded human concept to him. I don't know if that is unusual

---

1. Which he selected on his own with no advice from his father. After his son took the job, J. P. II solicited assurances from several lawyers who worked both for him and the company that Michael had joined a good firm. JPII to Jacob M. Lashly, October 11, 1954, JPII Papers, reel 7, frame 346.
2. MEP, "Centralia Mine Disaster," *The Vindex*, undated, 1947, BHR to JPII, May 20, 1947, JPII Papers, reel 7, frame 285; Hohenberg, *The Pulitzer Prizes*, 20.

or not. I think part of it was that my relationship was kind of on an episodic basis."[3] His main male influence had been Edward Dwyer, head caretaker of Lone Tree Farm and chauffeur to J. P. II. Mrs. Dwyer was the family's cook. "It's the family story that Ed Dwyer really raised me, and I think that's a fair enough statement," Mike recalled. Dwyer took the boy to Saturday movie matinees and other activities that Mike thoroughly enjoyed: "He had a cigar in his mouth, and he was an emotional guy," he said. "He had a facade of being very rough, gruff, tough, but he was a real softie beneath that." In contrast, his father impressed him "as an autocrat and a very powerful man [who] was always behind doors."

Of course, none of this had any bearing on the fact that J. P. II expected the time would come for Mike as it had for Joe to join the Pulitzer Publishing Company. As he had done for Joe in 1935, he arranged a four-week newspaper apprenticeship for Mike in the summer of 1950, between his son's junior and senior years at Harvard. It was at the *Louisville Courier-Journal*, owned and operated by the Bingham family. The paper's news and editorial philosophies were much like those of the *Post-Dispatch*. Before Mike reported for duty, his father described Mike to *Courier-Journal* general manager (later publisher) Mark Ethridge as "a boy who gets good and rather above average marks, but with no newspaper experience. . . . I chose the *Courier-Journal* above all other American newspapers because I know that he will have an opportunity with you to get the benefit of the finest spiritual journalistic atmosphere."[4]

To his father's delight, Mike's work impressed *Courier-Journal* managing editor James S. Pope, who said the youth's only weakness was that he was somewhat lacking in aggressiveness.[5] However, this positive experience was not enough for Mike to commit to a newspaper career. Most likely to keep the subject alive and to test his son's powers of observation and description, J. P. II asked Mike after his month in Louisville for a confidential assessment of the managing editor. "Pope I think is a very shy man, but quite competent," and uniformly respected and obeyed, Mike replied. He described Pope as even-tempered, of "the strong silent type," whose "seeming aloofness impresses people," and "very interested in sports, particularly tennis."[6]

3. Unless otherwise noted, quotations from MEP in this chapter come from interviews on April 23, 1984, July 19, 1985, January 19, 1995, and June 14, 1995, all in St. Louis, and a telephone interview on July 28, 2003.

4. JPII to Ethridge, April 5, 1950, JPII Papers, reel 7, frame 320.

5. JPII to MEP, August 1, 1950, JPII Papers, reel 7, frame 312.

6. JPII to MEP, March 15, 1951, MEP to JPII, March 19, 1951, JPII Papers, reel 7, frames 320 and 365.

In Mike's last year as an undergraduate, J. P. II tried hard to move him into journalism, but met resistance. The young man had his reasons for staying at Harvard to earn a law degree. He had solid academic credentials. He had skipped the second form and graduated with honors from St. Mark's. He had enjoyed his time at prep school as much as Joe had disliked his. History was his favorite subject. "He learns and retains facts easily and can organize them well on paper," his St. Mark's adviser reported to his father. "Several masters had remarked on his dependability, geniality and humor," he added. "He seems happy and is mixing in with the other boys." After three years at St. Mark's, he entered Harvard at seventeen. "Harvard isn't nearly as grim and foreboding as they say it is. I enjoy it a lot,"[7] he wrote his father's secretary, Arch King. He majored in Government, in which he performed well, though short of the mark for honors.

A career in law seemed to Mike a logical next step, and became more appealing than journalism work after his father described the path he would need to take: "What I perceived him saying to me was, 'Son, if you're going into newspaper work, you're going to have to start out sweeping the floor. You've got to go through the grind.' And this was a time when college grads could get jobs, so the idea of grubbing around on the police beat for a couple of years really didn't appeal to me. I think I told him that, and he got very angry. But looking back on it, those three years in law school were well worth it."

Mike was not accustomed to talking back to his father, but by his senior year in 1951 he felt he could and should make up his own mind about his future. He had several reasons for wanting to stay in school. He was just twenty-one when he graduated, with the Korean conflict in progress and the draft threatening. By entering law school and joining the Navy Reserve, he could defer and perhaps avoid two years of active duty. He had married Helen Dempwolf of York, Pennsylvania, in his senior year and just over a year later was the father of Michael E. Pulitzer, Jr.[8] Also, he reminded his father, he had not "turned down newspaper work. You have not, however, ever offered me any concrete proposals or offers in that line. The future now is not the future of forty years ago and I think I will be bettering my position for any eventuality by doing graduate work rather than starting in as a cub reporter."[9]

7. MEP to Arch R. King, October 2, 1947, JPII Papers, reel 7, frame 275.
8. The couple had three sons and a daughter, and were divorced in 1970. That year Michael married J. Cecille Eisenbeis, who had two sons and two daughters from a previous marriage.
9. MEP to JPII, May 10, 1951, JPII Papers, reel 7, frame 357.

His father's response was polite but pointed. He sent his son facts and figures about his inheritance. He explained that in the best foreseeable scenario, Mike eventually would inherit $534,000 from investments and $1,175,000 from the *Post-Dispatch*. "In a nutshell, you should receive approximately $2 from the *Post-Dispatch* to every $1 you receive from investments." He agreed that if being in law school would defer military service, "no one would be more glad than I. I have often said that I would never drive a son of mine into the newspaper business who did not have a strong taste and even passion for it. That is still my conviction." But he cautioned Mike not to go into law "until you have given your future dependence on the *Post-Dispatch* the very most serious consideration."[10]

When Mike was a first-year law student, his father came up with another apprenticeship idea, hoping to lure him away from law school. He dictated a telegram to Erwin Canham, editor of the *Christian Science Monitor* in Boston, asking if he would take Mike on "to do cub reporting, research work or any other work that would give him training in the *Monitor*'s fine type of journalism? I would expect that he would receive only nominal pay."[11] But the telegram was not sent.

His father became further accepting of Mike's decision just before having stomach surgery the next year. "Mommie and I have talked it over," J. P. II explained. "I can't help agreeing with her that you should do your utmost to complete your law course." He advised Mike not to miss exams in order to be in St. Louis during the operation and recommended that he find a summer job in the legal field in the Boston area:

> I definitely do not favor your working for the *Post-Dispatch* law firm, and strongly advise that you go out on your own and make your own arrangements.
>
> As to the future, you made your decision to become a lawyer and, although in a sense that decision was disappointing to me, I admired you for making it. I now think that you should stick to that decision and do your utmost to become a lawyer and a good lawyer. Should future circumstances be such as to indicate that you could fill a useful and responsible place at the *Post-Dispatch*, I hope and believe that after I am gone the door will be open to you. That would necessarily involve a belated apprenticeship in news reporting, news editing and the entire process of evaluating the contents of a newspaper. That, I believe, is indispensable to a newspaperman, whether he is to work in the strictly

10. JPII to MEP, May 17, 1951, JPII Papers, reel 7, frame 355.
11. JPII to Erwin Canham, January 10, 1952. Marked "Not sent." JPII Papers, reel 7, frame 357.

journalistic end of the shop . . . the strictly business end of the shop or in television. Do take this advice.[12]

"A belated apprenticeship" suggests that had the *Post-Dispatch* beckoned Mike more strongly than legal training, he might—under his father—have gotten on a faster track upward in the company than turned out to be the case. However, the death of J. P. II put Joe in charge of Mike's future.

Within a few months after his father died, Mike changed his mind about a journalism career. His law firm assignments had failed to meet his expectations: "I did mostly drudge work, going to the recorder of deeds, researching titles, getting out probate files. That's the kind of work junior lawyers do." That experience and some reflection gave newspaper work a fresh appeal. "I think that as long as my father was alive, I got certain kicks out of not doing what he wanted me to do. Then after he was dead there wasn't anybody to kick against, and I really had to make a decision." He began a slow ascent over the next thirty-six years. During the final six of those years he succeeded J. P. III in steps as president, chief executive officer, and, after Joe's death in 1993, company chairman.

Their seventeen-year age difference and Joe's desire to protect his proprietorship figured in the rate of Mike's progress. Because of the gap in their ages, there had been little opportunity for them to bond as they might have if they had been children together. Joe was away at school most of the time Mike was growing up and was married when Mike was nine. Joe never shared any impressions of St. Mark's or Harvard with Mike, even though his younger brother followed him to both schools. An incident when he was fifteen indicated to Mike that his brother was not much interested in him. Joe had just returned from the Navy and was staying at a house in Bar Harbor that Kate Davis had rented. "I remember going over there with great excitement to welcome him back," Mike recalled. "He and Lulu were dressing for a party. And my impression of the reception was, 'Why are you bothering us, little boy. Go away.' So I really felt rather rejected."

Years later, after Joe succeeded their father, Mike recalled what J. P. II had said about the size of Mike's inheritance and quipped in a letter to Joe from Boston that he hoped his brother would "look after my investment." When they next saw each other in St. Louis, Joe let Mike know that he "was very offended by that and took it as a criticism of the management of the company." Joe also "took . . . as a hostile statement" Mike's use of the term "trustee management" in their conversation about the

---

12. JPII to MEP, January 30, 1953, JPIII Papers.

remark. Again he was surprised by his brother's reaction, and puzzled as well because Joe never explained it to him: "The only thing I can think of is that he thought I wanted to come into the company and question what he and [business manager and trustee Charles J.] Hentschell were doing." When he decided to join the company, Mike recalled, he and Joe had "a fairly open discussion" while climbing a mountain near Bar Harbor. "I remember that he said, 'There can only be one editor of a newspaper.' And I didn't quite understand what he was talking about because I didn't perceive myself as a threat to him." But Joe did not elaborate and Mike did not press him to do so.

From Mike's perspective, these episodes set the tone of their adult relationship as cordially businesslike rather than relaxed and informal. At times Mike saw "a certain amount of sibling rivalry" in Joe's behavior toward him, with Joe alternating between treating him as a brother and as an employee. Until about the last decade of their association, "I wasn't all that secure in my relationship with Joe," he said, admitting that he was not always as conscientious as he should have been. Excessive drinking had a part in this, he acknowledged. Alcohol use was commonplace in the family's lifestyle. Mike's parents enjoyed martinis before dinner, and wine was served at meals. The children were permitted to drink as adolescents under the assumption that they would be responsible. When Mike entered Harvard at age seventeen, J. P. II informed his son's freshman adviser that "although I have allowed him to drink, he has handled his drinking very well."[13] However, it subsequently became a problem serious enough for Joe to slow his brother's advancement until Mike stopped drinking in his early fifties. "I would say, looking back on all this," he reflected in 1995, "that I think Joe gave me an awful lot of rope, so to speak, and was very patient."

Also, their personalities differed, and they had mostly different friends. "Joe looked for kindred spirits," said a woman who knew both men. "He looked for people who were witty like him and loved what he loved. Mike is more unjudgmental friendly." Others agreed that Mike was the more casual, outgoing, and approachable of the two. He had a playful side, as when he closed a letter about his freshman expenses to his father's financial secretary Arch King with "Love and kisses." Joe was slower to warm to people, not as ready a mixer. "He was direct in dealing with people," Mike said, "but not when it was something that involved him personally or his feelings." The most frequent explanation was that he was shy. Some described him as "aloof," "a loner," "living in an ivory tower." Arthur

13. JPII to Delmar Leighton, July 26, 1947, JPII Papers, reel 7, frame 280.

Bertelson, one of Joe's managing editors, often heard such charges—especially that Joe almost never set foot in the newsroom—and disagreed: "He didn't come into the newsroom and it wasn't for shyness or anything like that. I think it was a deliberate process [as if to say:] 'I'm not going out there and have everybody come up and say hello Mr. Pulitzer.' I don't think he was being exclusive or shy. . . . I think it was planned."[14]

Michael E. Pulitzer began his newspaper education in earnest in 1956. Joe asked *Courier-Journal* president Barry Bingham to take him for several years. "I agree with your theory that it is better for a young man to get experience on a newspaper other than the one belonging to his own family," Bingham responded,[15] adding that he planned to make similar arrangements for his two sons. Joe thought Mike might spend as many as seven years in Louisville. It turned out to be four, at the end of which Mike had "mixed feelings" about leaving "because I was doing well in the job and made friends there."

Joe kept track of his progress. One of the strongest commentaries on Mike's ability came from *Courier-Journal* managing editor James Pope, writing to city editor John Herchenroeder:

> Louis Lusky, as you know, is one of our harshest and most valuable critics. When you cover a case in which Louis is one of the attorneys you'd damn sure better be rhetorically, legally, and journalistically right 100 percent. He's been a nuisance at times, but a good influence.
>
> He just called to say he'd never seen a complicated legal dustup covered as well as Mike has covered the Fehr brewery mess. It's been long and involved, with a thousand pitfalls. His tribute is a very real one. He'd cut Mike's guts out if he thought Mike had missed a step.[16]

Joe and *Post-Dispatch* managing editor Raymond Crowley visited the *Courier-Journal* twice, in 1958 and 1959, finding both times that Mike was doing exemplary work. During the second visit, they got glowing reports on his "work, progress and capabilities" from Bingham, Pope, and publisher Mark Ethridge, Crowley recorded. Pope, who mainly oversaw Mike's work, "was enthusiastic on all three counts. He was, to say the least, vigorous in his appraisal of Michael's writing ability." He also was pleased that Mike had been recognized "by news contacts outside the office"

14. Interview with Florence Shinkle, June 19, 1995; MEP to ARK, October 2, 1947, JPII Papers, reel 7, frame 275; Steve Friedman, "Pulitzer," *St. Louis Magazine,* August 1987, 28; ARB interview, August 19, 1993.

15. Barry Bingham to JPIII, January 31, 1956, JPIII Papers.

16. Pope to Herchenroeder, May 6, 1959, JPIII Papers. MEP was copied on the memo.

including sources in the federal building "who sought him out and gave him stories which otherwise might have been missed." After lunching with the executives, Joe met privately with Mike, and sent his brother a memorandum of their discussion. He said he was "gratified ... to learn that you have come along fast in your three years of journalism" and that the *Courier-Journal* "would be only too happy to consider you for a permanent staff member" if he were not destined for the *Post-Dispatch*.[17]

Mike wanted to stay in Louisville for the first half of 1960 so he could cover the Kentucky legislative session, and Joe readily agreed: "Four years of experience on a paper outside family control will give you the confidence, self-assurance and experience that will be invaluable to you when you come to the *Post-Dispatch* in taking hold with professional competence and without apology to anyone." This "was a happy decision for everybody," including the *Post-Dispatch*, Mike reflected, "because I think that they didn't really know what to do with me"—a theme he occasionally repeated in later years. When he came back to St. Louis about midyear, he proposed his next assignment—to cover the national and state election campaigns in Missouri. "I thought a national campaign with candidates criss-crossing the state was probably a pretty good way to see the state and learn about the state in a very compressed period." Following that, Joe arranged for Mike to go through tours of duty in the various *Post-Dispatch* departments, just as their father and then Joe had done. But his was to be more extensive than theirs. Mike's first year would be in the news and editorial departments, including work on the daily magazine and the "Pictures" rotogravure section. Next he would spend six months to a year becoming familiar with production, advertising, circulation, promotion, the treasurer's office, labor relations, radio and television operations, and the business manager's responsibilities involving all of these departments. Then he would go to the Washington bureau for exposure "to the widest range of national affairs—the Supreme Court, the Congress, the White House and the federal agencies."[18]

Besides these specifics, Joe added: "obviously, your name and your stock ownership in the P. D. will have a bearing on the tasks ultimately assigned to you. After your first year of indoctrination with *Post-Dispatch* news and editorial methods you would not be expected to continue as a 'working stiff,' but ... would take, provided you were qualified, a position of executive responsibility or ... would develop as a by-line writer ... as a specialist in your chosen field." Joe also said both he and Crowley hoped Mike

17. RLC, "Memorandum," April 9, 1959, JPIII to MEP, April 9, 1960, JPIII Papers.
18. JPIII to MEP, April 9, 1959, JPIII Papers.

would "want to pursue the journalistic side rather than the business side, where we believe you can make a contribution which will be more rewarding intellectually than in the business office."

Largely because of intervening events and his legal training, Mike ultimately decided the business side better matched his talents. However, about 75 percent of his time during his first four years at the *Post-Dispatch* was concentrated on news reporting, writing, and editing as well as related supervisory tasks. He spent one year rotating through the business departments and writing lengthy reports on his observations. Journalistically, he was first a reporter, handling both local and state assignments, then an assistant to city editor Evarts Graham, who wanted to keep him: "I would say that he could hold a top re-write job on any newspaper in the country."[19] He worked in the Washington bureau, on the editorial page, and for relatively short periods on the daily magazine and weekly rotogravure section. All his supervisors praised his work. The report of rotogravure "Pictures" editor Julius Klyman to Crowley typified the assessments of the department heads. Klyman had not been shy over the years in criticizing holders of inherited wealth—including his own employer—but kept it to a minimum this time. "As this is going to be a laudatory report," he began, "I want to say that it is thoroughly objective and not subconsciously colored by the desire to see a Pulitzer make good on the *Post-Dispatch*." He made these points:

> He keeps up minutely with the news. I was surprised to find how much he knows about the area and both Illinois and Missouri.
> He is a hard worker. . . . He was eager to learn about everything.
> He is a thoughtful reporter. He sees things that only a thoroughly inquisitive newspaperman would see.
> He knows how to turn a phrase and has a nice, restrained wit.
> He seems to have an overall concept of newspaper work.
> As some of the men have said to me, "You'd never guess he's one of the sons of the owner."[20]

In 1963, Mike became news editor and Joe established a new function for him—liaison between the sometimes feuding news and editorial departments. Editorial page editor Robert Lasch frequently complained about what he considered unfounded speculations and editorializing in news stories. He blamed managing editor Bertelson, who succeeded Crowley in 1962. As outlined by Joe, Mike's job was to facilitate better communications

19. EAG to RLC, June 8, 1961, JPIII Papers.
20. JHK to RLC, May 25, 1961, JPIII Papers.

between the units without infringing the authority of either editor in his domain. "I am sure you appreciate that your position will require the exercise of discretion to avoid conveying the impression to either function that you are giving an assignment," Joe told his brother.[21] The going was rocky at times, as when a complaint about the handling of a conflict reached Joe, and Mike got a memorandum. "To protect yourself against misunderstandings and to avoid any possible resentment," he advised his brother to first raise an issue "with the editor immediately concerned." For example, "a discussion of the intensity of our coverage of race relations, largely a news matter," would start with Bertelson and then be taken to Lasch. Apparently most important to Joe was that in Mike's contacts with either side he would take pains to avoid making it appear that one department was warring with the other. When *Time* reported a division at the *New York Times* in 1965 between news staff hawks and editorial page doves in the debate about U.S. involvement in Vietnam, Joe wrote to Mike: "Avoidance of this divergence within a newspaper's news and editorial departments would have denied *Time* magazine a nice little gossipy dig at the N. Y. Times but would also have prevented *Times* readers from discerning an internal disagreement which could only diminish influence on its editorial page. Liaison between news and editorial is an important function."[22]

In reporting to Joe about specific news/editorial conflicts, Mike was inclined to favor the news side, where he had worked the longest. For example, Mike disagreed with Lasch in 1964 when the city's police department and the police board clashed over the department's suspension of several senior officers for "inefficiency." Lasch argued that news had overplayed the story and published articles that were more like editorials than news accounts, and that "the city desk was waging a news-editorial campaign." The city desk "did not overplay this local controversy, which aroused a great deal of public interest," Mike wrote Joe, "and we would have been derelict if we had not covered the police fight thoroughly." Joe agreed, finding the news coverage "factual, objective and devoid of editorial coloration or bias."[23] He believed the editorial page "might have approached the subject with more caution at the outset." After observing Mike's work for more than two years, Joe decided to "institutionalize" the position of news/editorial liaison.

21. JPIII to MEP, May 20, 1963, JPIII Papers.
22. JPIII to MEP, November 6, 1963, JPIII Papers; *Time*, July 23, 1965.
23. MEP to JPIII, March 18, 1964, JPIII to ARB and RL, April 28, 1964, JPIII Papers.

At the same time, Joe had more than intramural concerns. Expansion of the company beyond Missouri was a priority now that chain-owner New- house had disturbed the status quo. Because Mike's future role as Joe's probable successor figured importantly in this, Joe began assigning Mike tasks in the wider world. In February 1964 Joe sent his brother to San Diego for a meeting of the California Newspaper Publishers' Association. "The publishers I talked to were full of gossip about properties for sale," Mike reported. "How much buying and selling there is, I don't know, but there certainly is a lot of talk."[24] He said California Governor Edmund "Pat" Brown told him "it would be wonderful if a Pulitzer paper were established" in the state. But Mike came away "with a great many reser- vations," especially about moving into southern California, "home of the extreme right wing and hardly the place for a liberal paper." He found "an even greater drawback" in "the character of the population. People there are transplanted and relatively rootless with little community identifi- cation. A newspaper is just another necessary service to these people, and I question whether a decent newspaper would be appreciated or would be worth the expense." He found the San Bernardino–Pomona–Pasadena area more appealing because it was "relatively isolated and far enough away from the *Los Angeles Times*." However, he also doubted that "a qual- ity newspaper" would impress its populace: "As an investment it would be good, as a journalistic endeavor a question mark."

This was enough, however, to spark interest at Pulitzer Publishing in the Sun Company of San Bernardino. The company published morning and evening papers daily with a combined circulation of about seventy- eight thousand and a Saturday and Sunday morning paper each with about eighty thousand. A delegation of Joe, Mike, general manager Hent- schell, treasurer Dell Stafford, and managing editor Bertelson visited the property and met its owners. Pulitzer Publishing made an offer, only to be outbid a day later by the Times-Mirror Company. "Joe was very upset about that," Bertelson recalled.[25] In part, this was because he had planned to put Mike in charge in San Bernardino. But Mike was relieved. Although

24. MEP to CJH and JPIII, February 19, 1964, JPIII Papers.

25. Interview with ARB, August 19, 1993. Joe told Times-Mirror chief executive Otis Chandler that Pulitzer would be interested in the San Bernardino papers should they come on the market in the future. In 1968, Times-Mirror was ordered to sell them to comply with anti-trust laws against geographic concentrations in media owner- ship. Pulitzer Publishing offered $13.5 million, but the Gannett chain got the papers for $17.7 million. JPIII to Times Mirror Company, September 5, 1968, JPIII to CJH, May 16, 1968, JPIII Papers.

he would have taken the assignment, Mike had told Joe he was not yet ready for the responsibility and did not want to go out there. "I looked upon it as being exiled to Siberia," he said. Joe's response, as Mike recalled it, gave him a jolt: "If you don't go out there, we are just going to have to talk about your continuing position in the company." That "scared the daylights out of me," Mike said. "It was really a bombshell." He came to see that Joe was right. First, "here I was and he didn't really know what to do with me." Second, "the experience of running a newspaper would have given me the stature to come in in a senior role sometime."

Instead, even though he knew the job well, he continued as news editor and handled some relatively undemanding tasks outside the office. After attending an American Press Institute seminar for managing and news editors in 1965, Mike reported: "The deepest impression made on me was the difference of the *Post-Dispatch* philosophy from that of the [thirty-two] other newspapers represented. . . . To oversimplify, the trend today seems to convert newspapers to magazines and leave the hard news to television and radio. The *Chicago Daily News* man, for example, said his criterion for a page one story was 'Is it readable?' It made no difference if the story were a feature or frivolous. There was little judgment or criticism of papers for underplaying or overplaying stories."[26] Seminar participants praised the *Post-Dispatch* for its news content and news analysis, sports section and coverage of culture, but found some dull and heavy news stories, poor photo reproduction, and hard-to-read headline type, he reported. He agreed with this to a point: "[T]ight, bright writing and judicious editing should be our standard. However, it is our obligation to present the news and we should not be satisfied with superficial treatment."

Although operating on a somewhat wider professional stage during the mid-1960s, Mike was adrift personally. It appeared that Joe was more concerned about his brother's future than was Mike himself. He had not yet conquered his drinking problem. Joe sometimes reprimanded him, emphasizing the responsibilities attached to their name. Mike could only agree. "I think I had a lot of growing up to do or maturing, developing, or whatever," he said. "I had problems taking responsibility at that time, and I think that obviously Joe knew that or understood that." After Mike failed in 1965 to make timely arrangements in the office to cover his need to attend the wedding of Kate Putnam, the daughter of Kate Davis by her first marriage,[27] Joe asked Bertelson to handle the matter: "Will you please,

26. MEP to ARB and JPIII, April 1, 1965, JPIII Papers.

27. To Henry Ware Putnam, an Army Air Corps officer who died in an air raid over Tokyo in May 1945. Pfaff, *Joseph Pulitzer II*, 260–61.

as his superior, take a firm stand with M. E. P. so that once and for all he will appreciate that his duties as news editor take precedence over his convenience and personal engagements, in this case a family obligation." He wanted him to attend his niece's wedding, he wrote, but "his failure to clear this in advance is indicative of a casualness which is unbecoming a young man being trained to take greater responsibility. Please convey these thoughts to him without disclosing their origin." He added that hearing the admonition from his immediate superior, just like any other subordinate, "would make a deeper impression on him than if I, as his older brother, go over your head to give him this counsel and guidance."[28]

Less than a year later, Joe struck an optimistic tone in Mike's behalf in a letter to Charles Hentschell. He said he had had "two extended conferences with my editorial successor, and I want to give you credit for opening my eyes to his very greatly increased stature which I believe was so long smothered under tradition and perhaps the dominating and unyielding personality of R. L. C. [retired managing editor Crowley]." Joe credited his brother for taking advice he had offered him and for initiating "a number of excellent stories or procedures which will contribute to the program of strengthening local coverage and making the paper more interesting and readable." Hentschell responded: "I am certainly happy to hear that our young man is fulfilling your ideas in the unhoped for eventuality. It's rather amazing to see the definite change that has taken place in his personality. His mentality was never in question."[29]

When Bertelson was elevated in 1968 from managing editor to the new position of executive editor—which he described as "work a crossword puzzle"—city editor Evarts A. Graham, Jr., became managing editor. Mike, already Graham's lieutenant, was promoted to assistant managing editor, enlarging his role in the news operation, but keeping his attention on matters he knew best. A bigger change came in April 1971, when the company bought the *Arizona Daily Star* in Tucson and Michael Pulitzer became its editor and publisher, although he had virtually no responsibilities as publisher. Joe believed his brother's training on larger newspapers would "greatly benefit the Star's journalistic performance." Mike considered the job ideal for him at the time. He had been divorced and remarried in 1970, and his second wife, Cecille Stell Eisenbeis, supported his decision to make the move. The two Tucson newspapers, the *Star* and the *Citizen*, had been in a joint operating agreement since 1940, with the morning *Star* being the dominant partner. An agency, Tucson Newspapers Incorporated, handled

28. JPIII to ARB, September 2, 1965, JPIII Papers.
29. JPIII to CJH, August 5, 1966, CJH to JPIII, August 8, 1966, JPIII Papers.

all the sales and production for both newspapers, so Mike did not have those concerns. "I think I sort of had the best of all possible worlds," he recalled. "I had the general exposure without the responsibility." There remained the issue of alcohol abuse. Mike remembered Joe saying to him just before he went to Tucson, " 'You know, you've got to watch your drinking out there,' and so, I did and I didn't." Over the next several years he gradually accepted the fact that he had a problem and got help. He first got psychiatric counseling, then rehabilitation treatment at the Hazelden Clinic in Minnesota in 1983, and stopped drinking entirely.[30]

In the meantime, the nearly seven years he spent in Tucson turned out well for both him and his family. In 1975 Joe told Mike he would like him to return to the *Post-Dispatch* in 1978, the year Joe would be sixty-five. "I feel that I am prepared professionally, physically and emotionally to accept this challenge," Mike responded.[31] He made the move in late 1977 and was named associate editor of the *Post-Dispatch* the next year, keeping the titles of editor and publisher of the *Star* in Tucson. The *Star*'s executive editor took over day-to day operations while Mike retained budgetary control. While these arrangements were being worked out confidentially, there was speculation that Joe was about to step down in favor of his brother. "It is generally believed that the transition in leadership will formally take place late next year, about the time the newspaper marks its centennial year of publication," the *St. Louis Journalism Review* reported. *St. Louis* magazine offered the same prediction, citing "family pressure" as the reason: "Joe Pulitzer is a discerning art collector and a man welcome in the most cultivated European circles. But he's not the only heir of the family's publishing empire. And there are reports that several family members believe he's too much in Europe and too much a gentleman to lead what has become an increasingly faltering circulation war against the *St. Louis Globe-Democrat*, a newspaper increasingly aggressive and rarely gentlemanly."[32] More battle-hardened and self-assured than during the sniping by *Newsweek* and *Time* seventeen years earlier, Joe had no response. As for his stepping down, that speculation was many years premature.

30. ARB interview, 1993; JPIII to CJH, January 15, 1971, JPIII Papers. Mike and Mrs. Eisenbeis were married at Joe's home in Ladue. Each had four children from their previous marriages (see note 8). *St. Louis Post-Dispatch,* April 30, 1970; MEP interview. The *Star* was a growing concern. When Pulitzer bought the paper in April 1971 its circulation was 54,245 daily and 95,235 Sunday. By 1979 the figures were 66,739 daily and 124,879 Sunday. GAC to MEP, September 11, 1980, DEM Papers. Had it not been for the drinking issue, Emily Pulitzer said she felt certain that Joe would have advanced his brother faster. MEP interviews; ERP interview, July 1, 2004.
31. MEP to JPIII, May 8, 1975, JPIII Papers.
32. *SJR*, October/November 1977; *St. Louis,* August 1978, JPIII Papers.

Eight

The Pulitzers and the Newhouses

The purchase of the *Globe-Democrat* by Samuel I. Newhouse exactly one week before J. P. II died in 1955 was a defining event in the tenure of Joseph Pulitzer III. The entry into St. Louis of a competitor with Newhouse's financial resources was the biggest challenge the *Post-Dispatch* had faced in the seventy-seven years since its founding in 1878. The first Joseph Pulitzer boldly took on four competing newspapers in St. Louis when he established the *Post-Dispatch*.[1] However, newspapers were *the* mass medium at the time, and he was correct in believing that his energies and the city's economic growth would ensure success. His paper made money from the start with the exception of 1897, after he briefly took on a minority partner. Under J. P. II, the *Post-Dispatch* never had an unprofitable year, helped, undoubtedly, by a decline in its competitors. When the *Post-Dispatch* bought and closed the *Star-Times* in 1951, only the faltering *Globe-Democrat* remained. Yet changing conditions during the next three decades forced the *Post-Dispatch* under J. P. III to struggle as never before to stay profitable—and to survive.[2]

None of that, of course, was knowable in 1955, but the new editor-publisher faced a major challenge. Newhouse, a fierce competitor, already owned ten other newspapers and had a knack for turning financially distressed properties into moneymakers. The sale surprised Joe, his father, and Charles Hentschell. Ten days before the deal was announced, they had met with a *Globe* banker to discuss making a bid. More than anything, the

1. The *Missouri Republican,* the *Star-Chronicle,* the *Times,* and the *Globe-Democrat.* See also Rammelkamp, *Pulitzer's Post-Dispatch 1878–1883;* Pfaff, *Joseph Pulitzer II.*
2. Pfaff, *Joseph Pulitzer II,* 324–25, 435n2. Information on the Pulitzer-Newhouse relationship comes from U.S. Securities and Exchange documents produced during the Pulitzer Publishing Company shareholder dispute in 1986; *St. Louis Journalism Review,* October/November 1970, January 1984, and February 1984; *Add One,* October 1–15, 1979; *St. Louis Post-Dispatch,* January 1 and 29, 1984; "St. Louis News," *Editor & Publisher,* November 12, 1983, and July 30, 2001; interviews with Michael E. Pulitzer, Peter J. Repetti, Richard A. Palmer, Glenn A. Christopher, and Ronald H. Ridgway, and specifically cited items from the JPIII Papers. See Epilogue.

Pulitzers hoped the *Globe* would not go to an outsider, especially a chain owner. Samuel Newhouse, fifty-nine when he came to St. Louis, was both. He grew up in New Jersey and as a youth worked as an office boy at the *Bayonne Times*. He then got training in bookkeeping and became the accountant for a Bayonne lawyer who subsequently got a judgeship. The judge got control of the declining *Times* and assigned Newhouse—then still in high school—to make it profitable, which he did. Newhouse negotiated, giving up his seventy-five-dollar-a-week salary in exchange for a 20 percent share of the paper's earnings, and entered the newspaper business for good. At the age of twenty-five he told an associate: "I intend to have my own chain of newspapers like Mr. Hearst."[3]

As earlier noted, Newhouse bought the *Globe-Democrat* just before the transition from J. P. II to J. P. III took place. Pulitzer executives scrambled for information about Newhouse as soon as they heard he was coming. They produced four reports on him within days of the sale. The first three were alarmist, the fourth cautiously optimistic.[4] Stuart M. Chambers, the company treasurer, Samuel Shelton, assistant to J. P. II, and Richard G. Baumhoff, a former *Post-Dispatch* reporter who advised the publisher on labor relations, did the legwork. They presented a mixture of fact, opinion, and conjecture from interviews in and around the Newhouse stronghold in New York City and northern New Jersey. The initial reports, gathered from executives of Newhouse rivals at the *Newark Evening News* and at *Newsday* on Long Island, were uniformly negative.[5] "There was an amazing unanimity of opinion as to the principles, traits, and character of Sam Newhouse," wrote Chambers. "First of all, he is undoubtedly a very smart man and a shrewd operator. He is clever, cunning and conniving, and plays his cards well. He plots his course far in advance—and thrives on war and intrigue. In a fight he is quite unscrupulous. He knows where he wants to go and will use any means, good or bad, fair or foul, to reach that end. However, he has great patience and is perfectly willing to bide his time." These sources viewed him "as a man who likes Power, Prestige, and Money—but most of all Money—which gives him Power and Prestige."

3. Lent, *Newhouse, Newspapers, Nuisances*, 18. Unless otherwise specified, information on the Newhouse organization and family comes from this and Thomas Maier, *Newhouse* and Meeker, *Newspaperman*.

4. Chambers combined his and Baumhoff's findings into one memorandum; the third was by Shelton. SMC to CJH, SS to J. P. II, both March 28, 1955. The fourth memorandum was SMC to CJH, April 2, 1955, discussed below. JPIII Papers.

5. Newhouse owned the morning *Star-Ledger* in Newark and the afternoon *Long Island Press* in Queens, New York.

In several ways, the report described Newhouse as the opposite of William Randolph Hearst and the first Joseph Pulitzer, each of whom identified himself with his holdings and even ran for elective office. Newhouse shunned publicity and had no close friends, Chambers wrote, but maintained close family ties and "makes full use of his relatives whenever he can." In the business world, he "has the ability to inspire strong loyalty" and "to have command of almost unlimited funds." Otherwise, "he carries the torch for no cause," either nationally or in the communities in which he owns newspapers.

Shelton got similarly negative appraisals from current or former Newhouse news, editorial, and promotion employees. Said one of these "who had tried" working for Newhouse: "It is too bad he didn't go in for buying up tomato canneries instead." Others said "he runs a cheap, penny-pinching operation" but "is willing to spend money more freely when he sees long-range potential." They speculated that "Newhouse might be difficult to deal with in reaching any proper understandings."

On the day of the funeral for J. P. II, Chambers produced "A New Appraisal of Sam Newhouse"[6] based on a second round of interviews and his attendance as a silent observer in a group meeting that included Newhouse himself. Although cautious, it was much kinder to the new competitor. "I can't help but believe that this...appraisal is nearer right... and that we can definitely count on anything that Sam Newhouse personally tells us," Chambers wrote. *New York Times* general manager Julius Ochs Adler and thirteen other executives had convinced him of this. "Every one of them had a good word to say for him as a businessman and for his business integrity," Chambers reported, "and they were equally agreed that he was no journalist." This was "quite a different picture than we received in Newark" and most likely "less colored than the earlier picture." Nevertheless, "there is little doubt that he is a very smart and shrewd operator and holds his local management responsible for the financial success of the newspaper without questioning too carefully the methods used locally. We must therefore differentiate between promises made by Sam Newhouse personally and those made by his individual henchmen." Nearly everyone with whom Chambers talked impressed on him the need for Pulitzer's top management to deal with Newhouse himself in order to avoid "costly fights." He predicted that Newhouse "is going to get more circulation and more advertising than the *Globe-Democrat* has had heretofore and is going to make more money than heretofore."

6. SMC to CJH, April 2, 1955, JPIII Papers.

A memorandum from Baumhoff six weeks later offered further reason for concern. He had talked with Jack Ryan, formerly a reporter on Newhouse's *Long Island Press* and then vice president of the New York Newspaper Guild, in which role he had dealt with Newhouse papers in the area. Ryan had an affinity for the *Post-Dispatch* as "one of the few liberal journals left and he doesn't want to see us harmed," Baumhoff reported. He related three predictions Ryan had made: first, that Newhouse "was likely to try to make some sort of joint deal with the *Post-Dispatch* on advertising rates, to avoid cutting each other's throats, after which . . . he would violate the agreement and try to take advantage of us." Second, that he would "try to take over the St. Louis field," including trying to buy the *Post-Dispatch*, in order to get monopoly or near monopoly control as he had done elsewhere. Third, that "there is a real danger . . . that Newhouse will pay people in the employ of the *Post-Dispatch* to supply him with information." He doubted that Newhouse would attempt to hire people away from the *Post-Dispatch*, but "that it would be instead a matter of putting some of our people in Newhouse's pay."[7]

What Newhouse actually did after taking charge was more ordinary. He immediately sent tested business personnel from some of his other papers to direct *Globe* advertising, circulation, and production. As earlier noted, he shifted Richard H. Amberg, publisher of his *Syracuse Post-Standard*, to the *Globe-Democrat* when Lansing Ray died six months after the sale. Amberg's mandate was to improve the bottom line, chiefly by eroding the *Post*'s circulation and advertising leadership. With 400,000 daily circulation, the *Post* was almost 100,000 ahead of the *Globe* when Newhouse took over and virtually impossible to beat on Sunday with a lead of 106,000.[8] The *Post* had led daily circulation since 1950, and in 1955 had 67 percent of all newspaper advertising in St. Louis, thanks in part to its Sunday dominance. It fairly rapidly lost some 30,000 daily circulation to the new regime at the *Globe*, but almost none of its advertising superiority. Under Amberg, *Post-Dispatch* business manager Fred F. Rowden explained to an advertiser in 1958, the *Globe* "pulled out all the stops" to take advertising away from the *Post*, with little overall success. He said the *Globe* gave advertisers free color, news stories in exchange for advertising (forbidden at the *Post*), and offered some fifty special rate inducements without which "they would have less business today than under the old management." Yet this had cut the *Post*'s advertising lead by only

7. RGB to CJH, May 16,1955, JPIII Papers.
8. The *Post*'s Sunday circulation was 460,501 to the *Globe*'s 354,354. Its daily circulation was 387,398 to the *Globe*'s 291,962. *Editor & Publisher International Yearbook*, vol. 88 (1955), 96.

two points, to 65 percent. Amberg's biggest success was in the women's pages, where fashion and other promotions "attracted thousands of new female readers [and] millions of lines of new advertising."[9]

Joe had plans of his own. Six weeks after the *Globe* changed hands he told Hentschell that he wanted to hire "an aggressive circulation manager" and a full-time "first class promotion manager with ideas . . . and taste." He ordered cost-control measures to pay for

(a) product improvement and (b) a full time, mean s.o.b. controller whose . . . job would be to depress extravagance, waste, duplication and unseen luxuries which do not affect the quality of the newspaper or broadcasting stations . . . and [give] careful consideration of the proposition why, by deferring increased revenues, we will bring about sooner an understanding with S. I. N. [Newhouse]. If we go out for a 20-cent Sunday, then he knows we are anxious. [But:] If we let him sit and ponder his low earnings on the *Globe-Democrat*, he may be more amenable in a few months to a working arrangement on competitive practices as well as possible one-plant arrangements for round-the-clock publication with or without his Sunday.[10]

Four years later, the latter happened—without the *Globe* on Sunday. The two newspapers reached a joint printing agreement—something Joe and his father had proposed to *Globe* lawyer Calhoun before the sale to Newhouse, and Joe had continued to pursue on his own. On February 27, 1959, the *Globe-Democrat* agreed to sell its building and equipment to the *Post-Dispatch* for $8 million or more—exact terms were not disclosed— and move into rented space a block away.[11] The *Post* would vacate its home of forty-two years at Twelfth (later Tucker) Boulevard and Olive Street, move into the former *Globe* building, and print the *Globe-Democrat* under contract. For the first time in anyone's memory, Pulitzer Publishing borrowed money in St. Louis—from Mercantile Trust Company "in strictest confidence"—to do the transaction. The company had long avoided local business arrangements, fearing that details could get around town and thus complicate its dealings with labor unions, competitors, and advertisers.

9. FFR to Morris R. Schlensky, October 28, 1958, JPIII Papers; Meeker, *Newspaperman*, 191.

10. JPIII to CJH, May 16, 1955, JPIII Papers.

11. The author did not have access to all financial records. The $8 million figure was an estimate used by published sources without authoritative attribution. A partial memorandum in the JPIII Papers says $10 million was borrowed, $1.5 million was returned to the lender. It also says $4 million was taken from company reserves "to make up the total funds needed for the purchase." Memorandum by unidentified company executive to JPIII, October 17, 1966, JPIII Papers.

In the same vein, J. P. III was uncomfortable about dealing with the New-house organization as concerns persisted about the new competitor's business methods. Samuel Newhouse was sometimes identified by his New York office address as "our Park Avenue boy" in internal Pulitzer memorandums. References in others indicate that at least some criticisms of his business methods had foundation. Phony circulation inflation by the *Globe* became a major concern, based on "numerous exhibits indicating the *Globe-Democrat*'s dishonest sales practices," and on complaints by Newhouse competitors in other cities. A specific allegation was counting unsold papers as paid circulation.[12]

Nevertheless, the joint printing arrangement was financially advantageous to both owners. The *Post* had outgrown its present space and had acquired land where it could build a new facility on Oakland Avenue facing Forest Park at an estimated cost of between $13 and $14 million. Avoiding that expense, Joe noted, "should materially strengthen the company's long-term financial position." He had a special issue of *P-D Notebook* issued in which he emphasized that the deal was "strictly a cash transaction," dismissing a rumor that Newhouse had gotten some Pulitzer stock. With no legal obligations as private companies to reveal their financial arrangements—such as the $109 per page plus paper, ink, and other overhead costs the *Globe* would pay the *Post* to do its printing—this information remained secret until congressional hearings in 1967 and 1968 on the proposed Failing Newspaper Act, eventually enacted as the Newspaper Preservation Act in 1970. The estimated $8 million it cost the *Post* to buy the building and equipment meant that in just four years Newhouse had recouped his $6.25 million purchase price for the *Globe* and the $1.5 million television debt that was part of the deal.[13] At the same time,

12. JPIII to CJH and five other company executives, September 11, 1959, JPIII to FFR, April 25, 1961, RLC to JPIII, October 4, 1955, FFR to JPIII, September 26, 1956, RLC to file, October 4, 1956, JPIII to FFR, April 25, 1961, Memo for file, JPIII, December 10, 1965, JPIII Papers.

13. *P-D Notebook,* March 1959, 1. The Newspaper Preservation Act permitted a limited exemption from anti-trust laws for the twenty-two joint operating agreements then in place. Future such agreements could be established only if the U.S. attorney general gave approval after concluding that one of the two papers was "in probable danger of financial failure." Letters submitted by JPIII, dated July 27, 1967, and March 25, 1968, and document dated February 25, 1965, submitted by *Globe-Democrat* attorney Charles Sabin to the U.S. Senate Judiciary Committee's sub-committee on anti-trust and monopoly. Reprinted in *SJR,* October/November 1970, 5. Neither newspaper published this information in its own pages. See also Paul M. Keep, "Though Upheld by Courts, Many Criticize Newspaper Preservation Act of 1971," *SJR,* January 1984, 14.

For more on the sale see chapter 6; *Post-Dispatch,* March 25, 1979, and February 26, 1984; *SJR,* January 1984, 6; JPIII to RGB, January 4, 1960, JPIII Papers. The deed filed

Pulitzer gained a monopoly on Sunday and saved several millions by not having to build a new plant. Because it was not possible to publish two Sunday papers with one set of presses, the *Globe* agreed to drop its much smaller Sunday paper and instead publish a weekend edition on Saturday.

Just a week before the mechanical consolidation was disclosed, a strike by *Globe* news and editorial employees belonging to the Newspaper Guild shut down the morning paper for ninety-nine days. The death of publisher Lansing Ray and his replacement by Amberg triggered the strike. Guild members doubted that the pension and benefits packages informally arranged by Ray would be workable under the new regime. They demanded and ultimately got a uniform employee pension plan similar to that at the *Post-Dispatch*. Incredibly, both Newhouse and Amberg blamed the strike for forcing the sale of its building and equipment, even though the sale and the Guild walkout happened almost in tandem and mechanical consolidation had been discussed privately for several years. "We had no choice," Newhouse said. "They had a gun at our heads." The Guild saw through this: "It would be fantastic to believe that the negotiations, checking of title and the various legal and financial steps necessary to such a large deal, could have been consummated in a week."[14]

After the strike, the *Globe* got back considerably more than the fifty thousand circulation it lost to the *Post* during the shutdown, cutting the *Post*'s daily circulation lead to just over seventy thousand and causing mistaken speculation that the *Globe* was the rising star in St. Louis (see chapter 6). The bigger story for nearly three decades afterward was the ever-closer secretive alliance between the Pulitzers and the Newhouses. Financial specifics of their association were closely guarded and only selectively released, many of them not until after Newhouse got Justice Department permission to sell the *Globe* in 1983. A memorandum Joe wrote in 1974 indicates that cost concerns could override the two papers' agreement to keep independent news operations in certain cases. He informed managing editor David Lipman during the Watergate hearings in Congress that the *Post-Dispatch* would run condensed versions of the testimony rather than full texts, presumably to reduce the expense—and "we will take steps to insure that the *Globe* stays in line."[15]

---

on the *Globe* sale said Newhouse sold the building to Pulitzer for "the sum of one dollar and other good and valuable considerations." The real estate valuation of the property was fixed at $7.5 million. Certified Deed, February 27, 1959; RGB to Charles McInnis, April 4, 1959, JPIII Papers.

14. *Time*, March 9, 1959, 70; "Strike Bulletin," February 28, 1959, JPIII Papers.

15. When company treasurer Dell B. Stafford suggested discontinuing the services of the Ernst and Ernst accounting firm because its 1965 bill seemed too high, Joe

Concern about what the St. Louis newspapers were doing behind closed doors dated from 1961, when the two companies, citing increased costs, established a "newspaper agency" or joint operating agreement through which they would share their profits. Technically, these agreements violated federal anti-trust laws. Yet none of them was challenged until the late 1960s, leading to adoption of the Newspaper Preservation Act in 1970. Its rationale was that communities were better served by "editorial diversity" of two newspaper voices than by one. It granted anti-trust law exemptions to allow pooling of business resources when it could be shown that without this one of the newspapers would fail. It also ratified existing agreements, as in St. Louis.[16]

In 1965, shortly after a periodic review and updating of the file obituary that had been prepared for him, Joe expressed his confidence in the agreement's soundness in a confidential memorandum to Charles Hentschell. Reading the obituary, he said, "reinforced my conviction that the moral basis for a defense of the agency arrangement is unimpeachable. Throughout, the theme of public service recurs, and I would be very pleased if I had to defend that philosophical aspect against the narrow legal contention that the agency arrangement divides the market and is, therefore, illegal under the Sherman [Antitrust] Act."[17] He continued: "If journalism of the kind enunciated by us and clarified in this obit is to be

---

vetoed the idea. "I do not believe it would be wise to discontinue their services in favor of a competing CPA, as the loss to them of this company as an account could jeopardize the confidentiality which has prevailed in connection with the agency operation." He feared there might be a "temptation, once the account were lost, to be somewhat less discreet." JPIII to DBS, October 14, 1966, JPIII Papers. Company senior vice president for finance Ronald H. Ridgway recalled in 1995, "Everything was super secret. There were a handful of people who knew whether the company made money or lost money. You just felt that everything you did around here . . . that you kept it to yourself." Interview with RHR, February 2, 1995, St. Louis. Interviewed in 1995, *Globe-Democrat* publisher G. Duncan Bauman said, "The fact is that in late 1983, the cost of newsprint being what it was, the cost of labor being what it was, the impending increases in newsprint, the impending increases in labor, and the other cost factors associated with the paper, the fact that we had priced ourselves to the maximum acceptable to the advertisers and the fact that advertising costs led to no more dollars and less lines. All of the factors that go into the economics of the function indicated that for us, not too far in the future, it would be uneconomic for two papers here. And that was the basic genesis of the decision." Interview with Bauman, May 15, 1995, St. Louis; JPIII to DL, June 27, 1974, JPIII Papers.

16. The Newspaper Preservation Act (NPA) in effect circumvented a 1968 U.S. Supreme Court ruling that had invalidated joint operating agreements. See *Citizen Publishing Company v. U.S.*, 390 U.S. 712 (1968). Under the NPA, existing agreements could continue, subject to certain provisions. Gillmor and Barron, *Mass Communications Law*, 4th ed., 648–49.

17. JPIII to CJH, January 29, 1965, JPIII Papers.

jeopardized by a breakup of a sensible business arrangement which in no way injures the public, then that disservice to the public interest would be worth a full fight and ventilation, with appeal to the highest court." The quotation in the obituary "dealing with journalism," he argued, "would be the ammunition as to morality and propriety with which we would confront an attempt to restore cutthroat competition in St. Louis, with the contestants having roughly a one-to-five financial muscle in favor of the Newhouse chain. This has clarified my thinking, and I would be completely opposed to a compromise short of a protracted, expensive and exhaustive legal contest on this question."

Be that as it may, the 1961 agreement "had many flaws" in the view of former company vice president and general manager Glenn A. Christopher, who became the point man for the Pulitzer company in relations with Newhouse after Hentschell retired in 1970.[18] The first of these, he said, was that the papers combined only their production departments, remaining independent in advertising, accounting, circulation, and delivery operations. Only news and editorial functions were separate in other cities with joint operating agreements. The profit-sharing arrangement appeared initially to favor Pulitzer, allotting it 70 percent and the *Globe* 30 percent. "But the basic, fundamental flaw in that," Christopher said, was "that the *Globe-Democrat* had no incentive to economize or to really do anything, they got such a small piece of the pie. The fact that costs were shared the same way [as profits] meant that if they had a large budget, it cost them thirty cents on the dollar." That led to "a great deal of consternation on Joe's part all through the early sixties," Christopher recalled, because "the *Globe-Democrat* actually did not contribute one cent to the profits of the joint agency." Pulitzer Publishing complained about this, and the profit-sharing split was changed to 50–50. Even though this "meant that the *Globe-Democrat* had to take a more active part," Christopher explained, what Pulitzer really wanted—and had to wait more than a decade to get— was "to combine advertising, circulation, and accounting into one system with the *Post* being responsible for all that." Reviewing the record as of 1973, Joe noted that the *Post*'s contributions to the *Globe* fluctuated between 1961 and 1973 from a low of .008 percent of *Post* operating profits in 1968 to 54.7 percent in 1973, representing overall a considerable drain on the *Post*.[19] At the same time, Christopher added, Joe was concerned about

18. Christopher held several titles during more than forty years with the company, including president and chief executive between 1984 and 1986. *St. Louis Post-Dispatch*, May 12, 1993.
19. Interview with Glenn A. Christopher, May 19, 1995. The companies agreed to the 50–50 split in 1975. It provided that each company would receive 50 percent of the

"the tremendous resources of the Newhouse company. He knew that the *Post-Dispatch* was being seriously threatened." There was an immediate impact on Joe's compensation under the agency agreement. Rather than being based on a base salary plus a percentage of *Post-Dispatch* profits, as formerly, his compensation was reduced in accordance with fluctuations in the *Globe*'s subsidy from *Post* profits. "It was unfair for his compensation to be affected by the extravagances of the *Globe-Democrat*," Christopher said. "He told me one time he was having cash flow problems." The company's directors returned Joe's compensation to the pre-agreement basis.

The agency continued to lose ground during the 1970s. Documents filed with the Justice Department reported that the agency lost $3.6 million between 1974 and 1978. The companies finally agreed in 1979 that the *Post-Dispatch* would handle advertising, circulation, and all other business functions for both papers. Only their news and editorial staffs remained independent. Pulitzer counsel Richard A. Palmer explained that the 1979 agreement also included restrictions on expenses incurred by the partners. The prior understanding was "that all monies in effect went into a pot, and allowed expenses went into a pot, and what you had left was divided or allocated. That way, if Newhouse was spending certain monies without a limitation . . . Pulitzer ended up at least paying fifty cents of those dollars." The 1979 revisions established "a standard for certain on what would be deemed reasonable expenses," and included "a procedure for challenging certain expenses "if they did not meet that standard." Yet despite this and other economy measures including wage moratoriums by unions, productivity increases, automation, and staff reductions, the *Post-Dispatch* reported, "the combined business operations of both newspapers lost money most years. . . . Taken together, the *Post* and *Globe* lost more than 30 percent of their readers between 1960 and 1980." During the two decades, the economy and population of the area declined while the

---

first $4 million in profits, and that Pulitzer Publishing Company would receive 100 percent of the profits in excess of $4 million but not in excess of $7 million. Any profit above $7 million would be divided 70 percent to Pulitzer and 30 percent to Newhouse. Each company continued to operate its own advertising, circulation, and business departments. When the 1975 agreement proved unfavorable to Pulitzer, it was amended in 1979. The 1979 amendment dropped the profit-sharing ratios and combined all business operations of the two newspapers under the supervision and control of the Pulitzer Publishing Company. Exhibit 10.1 of Pulitzer Publishing Company Exhibits to Form S-1, for the Securities and Exchange Commission 1986; JPIII to ATP, July 30, 1974, with chart "Excess of Agency Income Over Agency Operating Charges," JPIII Papers. After *Globe* losses were subtracted for those years, the *Post* got $4,746,470 and the *Globe* $2,034,202 in 1968. In 1973 the *Post* got $1,470,994 and the *Globe* $630,426. The *Post* had a profit every year from 1961 to 1973; the *Globe* in nine of the thirteen years.

number of print and broadcast competitors grew rapidly. These included a group of thirty-one free-distribution suburban weekly papers claiming a combined circulation of eight hundred thousand. Nicholas Penniman said the weeklies' advertising competition hurt the *Post* and *Globe* substantially. It was clear that even though the *Post* was doing well enough to subsidize the *Globe* and still make some profit, both newspapers were going downhill. The *Riverfront Times*, a St. Louis weekly, observed that "serious followers of the nation's dailies expect that soon no markets—except New York and Chicago—will have more than one daily not owned by the same company." It added: "Few cities, indeed, can claim the polar diversity of views St. Louis gets from its dailies, with the *Post* having a respected left-of-center editorial page and the *Globe* still mourning the fall of Joe McCarthy."[20]

People both in and outside of St. Louis shared the concern about the steady decline of competing newspapers nationwide. Most of the attention in St. Louis focused on the closed alliance between Joseph Pulitzer III and Samuel Newhouse in running their newspapers. Critics there feared that the companies' business partnership would dilute the news and editorial vigor of both papers. Both print and broadcast reporters wondered why the owners of newspapers that regularly discussed the inner workings of other companies in their pages refused to discuss those of their own. On hearing a complaint from a magazine reporter about the refusal of Pulitzer executives to talk to them, a *Post* reporter replied: "Don't feel badly. They won't let us interview them either."[21]

Philip Hochstein, who retired in 1967 after forty years in several key positions with Newhouse,[22] had opposed the newspaper preservation law.

20. RAP interview, April 13, 1995; *St. Louis Post-Dispatch*, January 29, 1984. The problem facing the company, in its agency agreement with Newhouse, Penniman explained, was how to make the *Post* and *Globe* profitable. "We would be bouncing around these little losses of a few million here, a little profit of a few million there, but were still net in the red." The reason, he said, was that contrary to what most outsiders thought, the *Post* and *Globe* were the first and third papers in St. Louis, not the first and second. The *Suburban Journals* free shopper papers were in second place, and the *Globe* was third. In rough figures, he explained, the *Post*'s advertising revenue was $125 million, the *Journals'* $80 million, and the *Globe*'s $30 million. "And here we were in a market trying to keep the first and third paper going. Had it been the first and second paper, I think we might have financially been able to swing it." NGP interview, February 2, 1995; *Riverfront Times*, February 24–March 2, 1982.

21. In 1970 J. P. III wrote a letter to U.S. Representative Emanuel Celler, chairman of the House of Representatives Judiciary Committee, supporting adoption of the newspaper preservation legislation. He "earnestly" asked that financial data he provided the committee be kept confidential. This would have included details of the 1961 agreement and amendments. *Add One*, October 10–15, 1979, 22, JPIII Papers.

22. Among them chief editorial executive and publisher of the *Newark Star-Ledger*.

"This bill would gravely prejudice any future renascence of newspaper competition flowing out of new production methods, new editorial concepts and new developments in merchandising markets," he told a U.S. Senate subcommittee. He argued that joint operating agreements damaged public confidence because the papers involved "are prone to become self-conscious, affected, and sometimes shrill, exaggerated, seldom credible." After the law was enacted in 1970, the *St. Louis Journalism Review* reproduced the stories the two newspapers published about it. Neither story revealed that the *Post* and *Globe* had a joint operating agreement going back to 1961. The *Review* commented: "Whatever the arrangement now is between the *Post-Dispatch* and the *Globe-Democrat*, the public has, to put it in terms publishers like to use, a right to know there is an arrangement and that that arrangement involves profit sharing. . . . The public has a right to wonder if two newspapers which have an agreement for the purpose of maximizing profits would indeed permit their 'independent' editorial departments to engage in a vigorous and expensive news competition."

In fact, *Post-Dispatch* editorial page editor Robert Lasch had asked Joe in 1967 if the page should editorially oppose the proposed legislation: "In the light of the *Post-Dispatch* record over many years of supporting anti-trust law enforcement in behalf of a competitive society, we would be wise to weigh carefully the pros and cons of asking for anti-trust exemption of such scope." Such an editorial, Joe replied, "appears to be out," because it "would put me in the awkward position of criticizing myself." He explained that "I am firmly committed to this legislation, believe that it is needed, [and] will protect the public interest in keeping competing editorial and news functions alive." He said he would "keep an open mind," and if evidence "does not support my thesis, we will . . . find another solution."[23]

While the agency agreement clearly played its part in sustaining the two newspapers for a period of twenty years, by 1982 the two companies were on the brink of finding "another solution." Joe reported to *Post-Dispatch* staff members that he had told the papers' labor unions "that the agency had accumulated losses of 11.5 million dollars," and that he had requested and gotten wage concessions. He also said it was not known at that point whether the *Post-Dispatch* or the *Globe-Democrat* "would go under."[24] A St. Louis weekly commented: "If St. Louis were to become a one-newspaper town in the near future, and if the *Post-Dispatch* were to be the paper to not survive the coming bad times, the loss would be the nation's almost as much as St. Louis'. Considered one of the country's

---

23. RL to JPIII, June 27, 1967, JPIII to RL, June 29, 1967, JPIII Papers.
24. Transcript of staff meeting, January 17, 1984, JPIII Papers.

very best newspapers—top five, at least—for several decades tailing off sometime in the '60s, the *Post* won 16 Pulitzer Prizes between 1925 and 1971." As for the *Globe:* "It's no secret that, among those who keep track of such things, the *Globe* is considered one of the nation's worst newspapers.... *More* magazine, a few years back, put the *Globe* in its 10 worst newspapers list."[25]

In November 1983 the Justice Department gave the Newhouse organization permission to sell the name, goodwill, and liabilities of the *Globe.* The action was initiated by S. I. ("Si") Newhouse, Jr., who had assumed control of the company following his father's death in 1979. "We determined a course of action consistent with the requirements of the Anti-Trust Division," Joe explained. "Not one step was taken without consulting with the Justice Department." The two companies were allowed "to continue jointly to publish the *Post-Dispatch*" and to maintain their profit-sharing agency agreement. At the same time, the *Post* was freed of providing production and business services to any *Globe* buyer. On February 27, 1984, it moved to morning publication, in line with reader preferences nationwide for morning newspapers. J. P. III said the company had "the complete commitment of our associate, the Newhouse organization," toward making the morning paper a circulation and advertising success. The agency agreement was to continue for fifty years, until 2034, and was renewable, indicating faith by both parties in future profitability. When asked during a press conference why Newhouse would share *Post* profits for fifty years, J. P. III replied: "They are not being rewarded for closing down."[26]

He could have added that the advertising of the free suburban "shopper" newspapers in St. Louis was soaking up so much of the available advertising that the *Globe* could not survive. As *Forbes* magazine saw it, the "small, family-owned operations almost single-handedly drove Newhouse out of St. Louis.... A full-page national ad in each of the 33 St. Louis suburbans costs $20 per 1,000 circulation. That ad in the *Globe-Democrat* is $33." The combined circulation of the "shoppers" when Newhouse sold was 820,000 against a combined circulation of 485,000 for the *Post* and *Globe.*[27]

Joe explained to staff members that Newhouse would share profits, losses, and capital expenditures as had been the case since 1979, but would have no voice in how the *Post-Dispatch* would be run: "S. I. Newhouse is a

25. *Riverfront Times*, February 24–March 2, 1982.
26. *SJR*, February 1984, 7.
27. John Heins, "Mr. Pulitzer, Meet Mr. Bick," *Forbes*, January 16, 1984, 50.

very competent businessman and he understands, as well as we do, that a newspaper must have circulation to appeal to advertisers, and this going morning is a change in roles." He said Newhouse "has given us his absolute confidence in running this paper. He has no reason to intrude. He has no role at all, except a supportive one. Now if it loses money, he pays half. If it makes money, he gets half." Asked to elaborate on that, he replied: "We are willing to take fifty percent of the earnings. Everybody is so puzzled about that. . . . It seems to be an arcane thing. I don't think it's arcane. But if you move into a situation together and you've been in it since 1961, why should one of the partners disappear?"[28] Glenn Christopher added that Newhouse had no investment in the *Post-Dispatch* until the 1979 agreement. "We agreed that if there was a capital investment that exceeded $500,000, that Newhouse had a right either to participate on a fifty-fifty basis or say 'no.' . . . But since 1979 all capital investments have been shared on a fifty-fifty basis."

Was this, as some concluded, the first time a joint operating agreement had come apart? Both yes and no. Yes because one of the papers was sold; no because the owners' profit-sharing pact continued. Overall, the venture into St. Louis was worthwhile for Newhouse—especially after the *Globe* was sold. During the fifteen years between 1984 and 1999, Newhouse's 50 percent share came to some $177 million.[29]

The *Globe* was sold the day before publication of the *Post's* first morning edition for approximately five hundred thousand dollars to thirty-two-year-old Jeffrey Gluck and his wife, Debra, of Columbia, Missouri, publishers of the *Saturday Review* and several small magazines. Under Gluck the *Globe* ran up eight million dollars in debt and went bankrupt in nineteen months. Gluck sold the newspaper to St. Louis businessmen William E. Franke and John B. Prentis for five hundred thousand dollars. Within ten months, the *Globe* failed for the last time because the owners could not secure financing to continue.[30]

Peter J. Repetti and Richard A. Palmer, corporate lawyers whose firm represented Pulitzer Publishing Company for many years, explained how the decades-long association with Newhouse worked out as it did. Faced

28. Transcript of Staff Meeting, January 17, 1984, JPIII Papers.
29. "St. Louis News," *Editor & Publisher*, July 30, 2001, 18. Profit sharing all but ceased in 2000—seven years after the death of J. P. III—when Pulitzer bought out 95 percent of the Newhouse interest for $306 million and an agreement that Newhouse would sell the remaining 5 percent in 2015 for an undetermined sum. See Epilogue.
30. *St. Louis Post-Dispatch*, January 11, 1984, and October 30, 1986; *SJR*, December 1986. Prentis, the owner of Veritas Publishing Corporation, became *Globe* publisher, and Franke, a real estate developer, became the company's chairman.

with Newhouse's entry into St. Louis, Joe and his executives developed an aggressive strategy to preserve the *Post-Dispatch* and its parent company. By far the most important decision was to expand beyond St. Louis, particularly in television. Without this, Repetti explained, Joe feared the unthinkable, that the *Post-Dispatch* could go under on his watch: "There's a good reason for that. Newhouse has infinite resources. You realize we're a peanut." Joe knew he could not resist Newhouse "to the extent he did without sufficient resources. They could wait you out forever. They really have tremendous wealth."[31] Most of all, Joe "wanted [the *Post-Dispatch*] to be independent forever and he knew he could never buy them out. He knew he couldn't do it except the way he did. He joined them, but he became the senior partner forever.... But he couldn't have done that without the revenue from other sources." As for the joint operating agreement, Joe knew "he never would have gotten the [Justice Department] to agree unless it was pretty clear that they could not exist separately. But Newhouse knew that too. He'd bleed you to death."

Yet even though J. P. III and the senior Newhouse were opposites in background and journalistic philosophy, and had limited personal contact, Repetti explained, their partnership worked because the lawyers who handled their business association worked compatibly from the beginning. The first two were Charles Sabin for Newhouse and Robert Thrun for Pulitzer. "My impression is that Bob and Charlie Sabin did a hell of a good job of keeping things very, very quiet and with no friction," Repetti said. When Thrun died in 1983, Repetti succeeded him. From a legal standpoint, he said, "the Newhouses were the best possible partners I've ever dealt with." Si Newhouse Jr. and his brother Donald were in charge by this time. "They supported everything Joe wanted to do," Repetti said. "They might have some comments, but never a veto." Emily Pulitzer recalled that "it had been a very hostile relationship up to the point when Si took over. Then he became extremely cooperative. I think from the Pulitzer point of view, the relationship has been absolutely ideal." Michael Pulitzer agreed. On a personal level, Joe and Si had in common a serious interest in contemporary art, although Si bought and sold frequently, while Joe was

31. With the firm of Fulbright and Jaworski—formerly Reavis and McGrath—in New York City. Repetti and Palmer also served successively on the Pulitzer Publishing Company board of directors. Joint telephone interview with Repetti and Richard A. Palmer, counsel to Pulitzer Publishing Company, February 14, 1995. In 1955, Newhouse's assets were estimated at $200 million; by 1993, assets of the Newhouse family were estimated at between $10 and $13 billion. Meeker, *Newspaperman*, 189; Maier, *Newhouse*, 156; Edwin Diamond, "The Boss of Bosses," *Columbia Journalism Review*, October/November 1994, 75.

a dedicated collector. For a number of years, they and their wives got together annually for dinner, alternating between St. Louis and New York. Emily Pulitzer recalled that when the dinner was held one steamy August at their summer home in Ladue, the foursome had dinner in the Pulitzers' bedroom, the only air-conditioned room.[32]

Palmer commended the Pulitzer company's strategy during the financially challenging years of the Pulitzer-Newhouse association. "The [*Post-Dispatch* had gone through very difficult times in the seventies and into the eighties," he explained. "It was Joe's backing of going into . . . the broadcasting properties which turned out to be so successful that the company was in a position to show very positive cash flow and very positive earnings." Palmer credited the Pulitzer practice of hiring and keeping quality people for this success, especially the two men who found and negotiated the broadcasting purchases. To describe what was done, Joe used the term "flying buttresses," the weight-bearing roof supports introduced by Gothic architects to allow for more windows and doors: "What could we do to ensure the central structure, which was the *Post-Dispatch*? We went deliberately into television and radio and bought the *Arizona Daily Star* to enlarge and diversify this company so that it would have the sinews and the ability in the event of a crisis to maintain the central structure. That's what I mean by 'flying buttresses': to hold up the central structure." At the end of his life the company owned nine television stations around the country and one radio station in addition to the *Post-Dispatch* and *Arizona Daily Star*.[33]

32. ERP interview, January 30, 1995.
33. Harold O. Grams, who began the company's expansion into television, and Ken J. Elkins, who succeeded Grams as director of broadcasting operations. Other key leaders were Glenn A. Christopher, company vice chairman, and Ronald H. Ridgway, senior vice president, finance. All but Elkins had their entire careers at Pulitzer. Transcript of Staff Meeting, January 17, 1984. Joe had expressed this point a decade earlier to Grams, vice president of the company's broadcasting operations: "At this time when the *Post-Dispatch* is under severe pressure we must demand the best possible performance from the subsidiaries." JPIII to HOG, September 26, 1974, JPIII Papers. The television stations were in Omaha, Nebraska; Albuquerque, New Mexico; Des Moines, Iowa; Louisville, Kentucky; Lancaster, Pennsylvania; New Orleans, Louisiana; Greenville, South Carolina; Winston-Salem, North Carolina, and Daytona Beach/Orlando, Florida. Radio: Phoenix, Arizona. Two more television stations were acquired shortly after he died. With those, broadcasting "would have provided 36 percent of the company's consolidated operating revenues and 63 percent of its operating cash flow" for 1993. To comply with federal rules against media cross-ownership in a single market, the company in 1983 exchanged KSD-TV in St. Louis for the television stations in North Carolina and South Carolina. "Pulitzer Publishing Company, 1993 Annual Report," 7; "Pulitzer, 150 Years," Pulitzer Publishing Company, August 1997, 17.

No sooner was the *Globe-Democrat* gone than forty-three-year-old newspaper mogul Ralph McAllister Ingersoll II appeared. After failing in negotiations with Gluck and then Prentis to buy the *Globe*, he decided to create a "cutting edge" newspaper in St. Louis whose distinctiveness would gain wide acceptance. His *St. Louis Sun* would be a first-of-its-kind tabloid unlike any newspaper currently published. It would be "post-modern" and "street smart," he said, sure to connect with contemporary readers, and heavy on color photographs and graphics. He dismissed the *Post-Dispatch* as an "endangered species" likely to survive—if at all—as a "boutique operation" concentrating on traditional political and crime stories from law enforcement and government sources. His newspaper would minimize this, offering readers more choices, especially about life-style issues, and would be "the best sports newspaper in the area." On September 25, 1989, the day the *Sun*'s first issue appeared, Ingersoll said, "The last thing we need in this society is more information. The market-place is sending signals that it is too much."[34]

Ingersoll came naturally by his self-assurance. He was the namesake son of brilliant, innovative, and eccentric Ralph Ingersoll, usually remembered as the mastermind of the 1940s experiment in adless newspapering, *PM*, in New York. The senior Ingersoll had titled his *PM* prospectus "A Discursive Outline of a Proposition to Invent a Daily Newspaper." *PM* failed financially after eight years, but its founder had other successes. He had been managing editor of the *New Yorker* magazine, general manager of Time Inc., publisher of *Time*, editor of *Fortune*, the guiding force in the development of *Life*, and a best-selling author. He put together a group of highly successful small- and medium-sized newspapers of which his son took charge in 1975. He lived another ten years, until 1985. By 1988 Ingersoll Publications, with revenues of $706 million, was about twice the size of Pulitzer Publishing Company, and Ralph Ingersoll II was ready to make his own attempt to "invent a daily newspaper."[35]

At that point, some $70 to $85 million of Ingersoll's revenue already was coming from St. Louis. In 1984 he had purchased the *Suburban Journals*—by then 41 weekly and twice-weekly papers in the metropolitan area—for $80 million. By 1989, privately held Ingersoll Publications owned 40 daily newspapers and more than 150 nondailies with a total circulation of 6.25 million. The company also owned 4 dailies and 39 weeklies in England and Ireland, and planned to expand in Europe. "We're going to be the Gannett of Europe," Ingersoll said, referring to the largest chain in

---

34. Quoted from the *Philadelphia Inquirer* in *SJR*, September 1989.
35. Roy Hoopes, *Ralph Ingersoll*, 157, 375–76 and passim.

the United States. He also said, "I could run any daily newspaper in my spare time."

Not so the *Sun*. He moved his family to St. Louis and spent five days a week directing the effort there. He also spent large sums of money, much of it borrowed. Reminiscent of the Pulitzer-Hearst raids on each other's staffs, Ingersoll lured Kevin Horrigan, the *Post*'s most popular columnist, and Thomas M. Tallarico, the *Post*'s general manager and a Pulitzer senior vice president, to the *Sun*, where Tallarico became publisher. The *Post* had hired Tallarico in 1986. Yet despite it all, the *St. Louis Sun* lasted just seven months, closing on April 25, 1990. It produced 213 issues and lost an estimated $25 million. Deeply in debt, Ingersoll swapped all of his American newspapers with his investment partner in exchange for sole ownership of the European holdings.[36]

The *Sun*'s reality never matched its hype. "I don't predict a happy future for the *St. Louis Sun*," said media scholar and critic Ben Bagdikian after reading early issues. He could not find anything new about the newspaper. "Not only did the tabloid fail to attract its desired readers, but its editorial identity never jelled," the *St. Louis Journalism Review* observed. Furthermore, contrary to claims Ingersoll had made, his financial condition was tenuous. "Days before Ingersoll announced the paper's closing, he was forced to extend an offer to buy back some $240 million in high-risk, high-yield junk bonds," the *Review* noted. In hindsight, Ingersoll thought his market surveys before the paper's launch had been misleading. "We did a lot of focus group testing," he said. "But so did Coca Cola when it introduced New Coke. Winning blind tastings and winning the market are two different things." He regretted not pricing the *Sun* at ten cents, a circulation builder for one of his other papers.[37]

While the Ingersoll effort was being mounted, there was reason for concern at Pulitzer Publishing. Some financial analysts lowered their earn-

36. Robert Lowes, "The Fire in the Sun," *St. Louis*, September 1989, 36 ff. Other sources about Ingersoll are the *St. Louis Post-Dispatch*, April 2, 1989; *SJR*, March 1987, April 1989, November 1989, and May 1990; *New York Times*, March 29, 1989; Associated Press dispatch, *Centre Daily Times* (State College, Pennsylvania), July 15, 1990. Tallarico wrote Joe that he joined the *Sun* because he could not pass up the "rare opportunity" of "being involved in a new organization from the very beginning." Tallarico to JPIII, March 28, 1989, JPIII Papers. Tallarico died in 1999 at the age of fifty-four. *St. Louis Post-Dispatch*, April 13, 1999. E. M. Warburg Pincus and Company had been receiving 50 percent of the profits of any newspaper deal Ingersoll made. Associated Press dispatch, *Centre Daily Times*, State College, Pa., July 15, 2001.

37. *St. Louis* magazine, January 1990, JPIII Papers; *SJR*, May 1990, 1. The other newspaper Ingersoll referred to was the *Delaware County Times*, in Pennsylvania. After converting it to a tabloid and reducing the price to a dime, its circulation grew from thirty-nine thousand to sixty-three thousand in under two years.

ings estimates for Pulitzer after Ingersoll announced his plans and that he had $100 million in reserves for the effort. Tallarico's defection was especially troubling. He "knows the *Post-Dispatch* inside out" said *Post* publisher Nicholas G. Penniman. "In his head he knows every strategy of the *Post-Dispatch*, every strength and every weakness. He knows the cost base, the revenue base, and the distribution system." Yet many at the *Post-Dispatch* were glad he left. "He was a great numbers cruncher, great budget man, not a people person," Christopher said. "He was cold and unresponsive, and it was a mistake to hire him. Fortunately, it was a mistake that cured itself."[38]

Ingersoll's father unknowingly had prophesied nearly forty years earlier the probable outcome of his son's attempt to compete against the sole daily in St. Louis: "The history of these raids on monopoly positions are monotonously similar.... How long [the] cycle takes to complete itself depends entirely on how well-heeled are the backers of the new paper. If they are both rich and stubborn, the contest will go on for a long time.... But the contest always comes out in favor of the established paper because the ultimate decision is with the readers of both papers, and the tradition of the established paper is too strong."[39]

38. Interview with GAC, May 19, 1995.
39. Hoopes, *Ralph Ingersoll*, 352.

Nine

J. P. IV: Starting Out

In a 1953 article about the *Post-Dispatch, Newsweek* observed that "J. P. [III's] son, J. P. IV, will be four years old on Dec. 21. He is likely to inherit a very live newspaper, because the P-D's crusades are backed by workmanship equaled on few papers." As a youth of thirteen in 1962, the fourth Joseph Pulitzer placed a symbolic cornerstone on a wall of the renovated *Globe-Democrat* building the *Post-Dispatch* bought after the 1959 agreement to print both papers there. The trowel he used was the same one used by his father and grandfather on similar occasions. Thirty years later, in 1992, the *St. Louis Business Journal* reported that J. P. IV "is expected eventually to become editor and publisher of the *Post,* following in the footsteps of his father, grandfather and great grandfather."[1] By then he was forty-three, two years older than his father had been on assuming leadership. His father was seventy-nine.

In fact, the fourth Joseph Pulitzer's succession to the company's leadership remained unsettled when J. P. III died in 1993. As of 1992, J. P. IV had served an active apprenticeship in journalism of eighteen years, all but two at the *Post-Dispatch,* ranging across all of the paper's news-editorial and business departments. But although often spoken of as heir apparent, he never had functioned, as had his father, as second in command or as his father's right-hand man. He took early retirement from the company in 1995, when he was one of several company vice presidents. He had concluded that he never would lead the company. A combination of circumstances contributed to this, but former *Post-Dispatch* reporter and columnist Kevin Horrigan, who had worked with him, provided a partial explanation: "Little Joe is a good guy. He's low key and lives simply. I think he drove his family nuts, though, because he was half hippie." Horrigan explained that Joe IV drove a blue 1956 Ford ranch wagon (that had belonged to his grandmother Elizabeth Pulitzer), and "wore bad clothes,

---

1. "Crusades at a Profit," *Newsweek,* December 14, 1953, 58; *St. Louis Post-Dispatch,* January 6, 1992. The *Globe-Democrat* moved to a smaller building nearby. See chapter 8. "Jay Pulitzer Climbs Ladder in Management," *SLBJ,* March 30–April 5, 1992, 1, 49.

like corduroy Levi's and shirts, ties and jackets that didn't match, and smoked roll-your-own cigarettes."[2] Elkhanah Pulitzer, the eldest daughter of Joe IV, expressed a like opinion. Her father and grandfather "had a rough time in general," she said, likely because the two never formed a close bond and because it was hard for Joe to be patient with children. "It's probably because he was so tempered and had an ability to enjoy solitude and just spend a lot of tranquil time," she said. One of her strongest memories was seeing him quietly reading newspapers and papers he brought home from the office.[3] Aside from the commonality of a powerful independent streak that may itself account for many of their differences, the third and fourth Joseph Pulitzers were, in some important respects, strangers to one another.

As noted, Joe IV was often apart from his father in his early years, and by the time he got to boarding school at St. Mark's, he was used to being on his own. He had some friends there, made more, and liked dorm life, but, typically adolescent, he also inclined toward rebellion. There were similarities and differences between his own and his father's reactions to some of St. Mark's basic assumptions. "There were things about it I did like, but it was kind of like being in jail for four or five years," he recalled. "You just sort of made the best of it." He adopted much the same coping technique his father and no doubt many others had used—resisting the system. However, nonconformity in the midst of the 1960s civil rights and Vietnam War unrest was not the largely cerebral exercise it had been for J. P. III in the late 1920s. J. P. IV saw the situation in these terms: "It was a very turbulent period . . . Everything was going on, Vietnam and drugs and social changes and free love. We were there, locked up, [but] of course we were exposed to all this when we were on vacation in the summers." There were ramifications for the prep school: "It was all boys. No girls. So you did what you could to beat the system. . . . Some of the things we'd do . . . were to get the day boys [who did not live on campus] to come and pick us up at night outside the school and sneak into town. Go to Boston, stuff like that. There were a lot of people suspended and expelled while I was there for smoking and drinking and drugs." This did not happen to him, but he did get into trouble for misbehavior, and was on probation twice. He and a troublesome classmate were not allowed to room together, and were assigned single rooms. His, behind a fire door, seemed like a cell.

Still, he graduated and was admitted to Harvard, starting there in the fall of 1968. Before the semester opened, J. P. III—likely reflecting on his

2. "Jay Pulitzer Climbs Ladder," 49.
3. Interview with Elkhanah Pulitzer, May 11, 1995, St. Louis.

own transition from prep school to more congenial Harvard—wrote the dean of freshmen about his son: "It is quite evident that as a St. Mark's graduate, moving from the restricted environment of boarding school to the freedom of a university, he would benefit from guidance administered by a professional who understands youth."[4] The letter gave an optimistic assessment of his son, but also conveyed a certain remoteness in their relationship. "Basically Joe is a boy of good character but not as yet of high academic attainment," it explained. "However, this is by no means a final judgment as we think of him as a late bloomer, an only child who was inevitably protected somewhat and reared without the competitive element of a larger family." It noted that his academic record at St. Mark's was stronger toward the end and that he had been conscientious in a summer job as an assistant stage hand at the St. Louis Municipal Theatre and as a volunteer at a camp for underprivileged children under St. Mark's direction. "Joe would benefit," he suggested, "by an adviser who would brook no nonsense, challenge him intellectually, encourage him to recognize his primary interests and give him a sense of direction and pride of achievement." These sentences suggest a lack of closeness between them: "As you know, kids today never communicate with their parents, who are considered hopelessly old fashioned and out of touch, but we hear from friends and associates that our son is capable of sustained interest and conversation. We hear favorable comment also about his lively personality." While J. P. II had written Joe's Harvard adviser of his expectation that his son would have "a life work in journalism," J. P. III was much less specific: "As to his interests, I should say drama, stagecraft, literature, journalism, history and an awakening interest in art and music are fields into which he may move. He is a casual athlete but at least cheerful about it."

The letter was written during probably the hardest year in the life of Joseph Pulitzer III. Lulu was ill with cancer of the esophagus. Relatively new radiation therapy was recommended, and she and Joe spent much of the spring at a hospital in Edinburgh, Scotland, where she took treatments. This was her second bout with the disease. She had successful surgery for cancer of the larynx in 1960, after which she always wore stylish scarves to cover the scar. Against medical advice, she continued to smoke cigarettes, but switched from an unfiltered to a filtered brand. Joe quit, and, convinced of the harmful effects of smoking by 1970, banned cigarette advertising from the *Post-Dispatch* for several years.[5]

4. JPIII to F. Skiddy von Stade, Jr., July 19, 1968, JPIII Papers.
5. The ban lasted two years and ten months, resuming in 1974. The newspaper cited "purely business reasons," noting that cigarette smoking in the St. Louis area

Lulu's radiation treatment was not encouraging. Sensing that time was growing short, she suggested that just she, Joe, and their son spend Christmas of 1967 in Zermatt, Switzerland, rather than in St. Louis. She and Joe had been going there most years during the decade so he could ski, a sport he—but not Lulu—had taken up with enthusiasm. While he was on the slopes, she would make trips to various places to see friends, and always to Paris, her favorite city, where she loved to shop. Their son returned to St. Mark's after the holiday, but his parents kept their accommodations in Switzerland until April, when they went back to Edinburgh for a final series of treatments.

Then they returned to St. Louis. She was hospitalized for a time in October, during which her son flew home during his first semester at Harvard for a weekend visit. Then she went home. Both she and Joe wanted their son to come to St. Louis for Thanksgiving. To his later regret, he made other plans, deciding instead to wait until the Christmas break. Both his parents, Joe IV recalled, "put on a good front," never telling him directly about the gravity of the situation. As part of that, his father bought his mother a Rolls Royce. When this happened, Lulu telephoned one of her many friends, Ruth "Tookie" Barker, "and said as soon as she was better she would take me to the laundromat in the Rolls. . . . She said she would get a little bundle of laundry together."[6] Although it seems unlikely in any event that Louise Pulitzer would do laundry, this never happened. She became virtually bedridden. Her son saw her alive for the last time when he came home for the Christmas holiday at the end of his first semester at Harvard. She died on his nineteenth birthday, December 21, 1968, at their Pershing Place home with her husband and son at her side. She was fifty-four. The funeral was at St. Michael and St. George's Episcopal Church in suburban Clayton with Assistant Rector John C. Danforth, later a U.S. senator from Missouri, leading the Mass. When they returned home following the service, Joe IV recalled, his father asked him to come into the master bedroom, in which Lulu had died. He took out her jewelry box, "and started going through and fingering all these wonderful jewels that she had, most of which he had bought for her. They were triggering memories for both of us." They then departed for Sun Valley, Idaho, to ski with close friends Perry and Rettles Rathbone. Afterward, Joe IV returned to Harvard.

---

had increased during the ban. JPIII, "File Memo," October 30, 1969, JPIII Papers; *Editor & Publisher*, October 26, 1974, 19.

Lulu's scarves attracted wide attention, including in *Women's Wear Daily. St. Louis Post-Dispatch*, December 22, 1968.

6. Interview with Ruth McClenahan (formerly Barker), February 24, 1995.

His father wrote his adviser there, noting that after the loss of his mother, "our boy, Joe's conduct was exemplary, very composed and disciplined." He asked the adviser to "observe and guide him over what must be for a young man a terribly difficult period," but not to tell him that his father had made the request. The adviser's response was that Joe IV had made a "fine record" in his first semester and was "certainly off to a good start. One never knows, however, what goes on inside a person who is so apparently self-contained, well-balanced, and mature. I shall make a special effort to keep track of him."[7] Near the end of his second semester Joe IV decided to major in Sanscrit and Indian Studies, which he described as "a religious kind of major." He soon came to dislike it because "I couldn't handle all the languages." These would have included Sanscrit, German, and an Indo-European root language. His father had been supportive, congratulating him for his "intelligent approach to the important decision of your major. If you are free to change your mind and transfer to another discipline, I could see no objection to your present plans."[8] By the middle of the sophomore year, he had changed his mind. He switched to Social Relations, a major composed of courses in sociology, psychology, anthropology, and world religions. More importantly, he had become preoccupied, as had so many of his generation, with the upheaval of Vietnam. "My summation of that whole period is that the social agenda was predominant, much more important at that time than the academic agenda," he explained. "I think it was a very interesting time to be alive and in college. Had it been an agenda like the fifties, who knows if I would have applied myself more assiduously to academic pursuits."

While he was generally opposed to U.S. involvement in Vietnam—the position the *Post-Dispatch* had espoused editorially since 1954—he was not rabid about it. He nevertheless found himself caught up in the drama being played out in the streets and on campuses. "My college years were pretty much interrupted by the agenda of the New Left," he explained. "There were all these strangers hanging around Cambridge. In retrospect, it was a very abnormal student life. I almost resent . . . the fact that it was hard to pursue any serious academic goals."[9] On April 9, 1969, Harvard's Students for a Democratic Society organization occupied University Hall—the administration building—and expelled most of its occupants. Among their demands were that University President Nathan M. Pusey resign,

7. JPIII to Willliam Bentick-Smith, January 15, 1969, and reply, January 20, 1969, JPIII Papers.
8. JPIII to JPIV, May 8, 1969, JPIII Papers.
9. Quoted in Andy Siering, "The Prince of Tucker Boulevard," *The Weekly* (St. Louis), July 26–August 1, 1985, 20.

the Reserve Officer Training Corps (ROTC) program be abolished, and rent controls be set for university-owned student apartments. They also called for a three-day boycott of classes. Police were called after negotiations failed, and 197 students were taken away in police vehicles. Harvard officials called the incident "the most violent and divisive in the school's 330-year history."[10]

In Matthews Hall, Joe IV's dormitory, fire alarms went off at 5:45 that morning, alerting students to the impending confrontation. He watched police in riot gear carrying shields, batons, and tear gas beat and kick demonstrators. To avoid identification, some police officers removed their badges. Joe IV did not take part in the protest—"for me, it was more of a spectacle than anything else"—but he did wear a T-shirt imprinted "On Strike." Shortly after the incident, the *Post-Dispatch* published a "Letter to a Harvard Striker" written by a man identified only as a "St. Louis father to his son at Harvard University." J. P. III sent a copy to his son with the note: "I hope you will think about the letter for discussion when I see you."[11] Had he written the piece himself, it seems likely that he would have said so. In any case, the writer's views on effective persuasion probably reflected his own. Rereading it many years later, Joe IV could not recall what discussion he and his father might have had. The letter called the aims of the strike "laudable," but seizure of the building "a cynical act, contemptuous of the principles of democracy, deliberately employing a standard tactic of groups whose consciences do not extend to means." It continued:

> Great issues, in our system, are not forced quickly, and certainly not by hasty, criminal and irresponsible action. It takes steady, conscientious and responsible pressures to break down reactionary barriers.... In view of the Columbia [University] experience [where a similar episode closed the school and forced the president to resign] it is certainly not unthinkable that Harvard could shut down. I would not regard this as any kind of victory for anyone, and a frustration of your college education is hardly something that you, or your parents, want.
>
> I am also acutely aware that you may be under very unpleasant pressures if you return to class when your classmates may not. But this is not a matter of "solidarity" or majority vote. It is a matter of principle. The majority does not vote your principles into being, and if you follow the majority on such an issue, merely because it is the majority, you would be a conformist of the grossest sort.

10. *New York Times*, April 9 and 10, 1969.
11. JPIII to JPIV, April 23, 1969, with clipping, JPIII Papers.

Events largely overtook whatever impact this might have had on Joe IV. On October 15, 1969, near the start of his sophomore year, there were simultaneous campus demonstrations across the country. He took part in the march from Harvard Square in Cambridge to Boston Common. During the demonstration he met Lynne Steinsieck, who became his wife two years later. The next month, he drove a carload of people from Cambridge to Washington, where 250,000 marched against the war. He took part in the candlelight march around the Treasury building the night before the big rally on November 15, but described himself as simply an observer of the main event. Although he heard nothing from his father on the subject, he assumed his father "probably didn't disapprove" of his participation in the demonstrations because "it was consistent with the newspaper's philosophy." The bombing of Cambodia followed by National Guard shootings of students on the Kent State University campus in the spring of 1970 ignited more protests. Responding to the shootings, Harvard closed spring semester early, before final exams had been given. This was fortuitous for Joe IV, who received grades of "pass" for courses he may have failed had he taken examinations.

Preoccupied with extracurricular events more than his studies in the sophomore year, he was placed on academic probation in early 1970.[12] Determined to improve his grades in his junior year, he moved out of the dormitory and into an apartment off campus with three roommates, including Lynne Steinsieck. "I was out of that Harvard Square street scene and I was able to concentrate and get my work done," he explained. He also joined the Harvard radio station, got his third-class radiotelegraph operator's certificate, and worked two mornings a week as a disc jockey, playing jazz from 6 to 9 a.m. "It was a good introduction to the business and a lot of fun," he recalled. Lynne introduced him to the strictly vegetarian macrobiotic diet that was gaining popularity at the time.

His father got to know Lynne in the summer of 1971 when she and Joe IV drove a Volkswagen to St. Louis for an extended visit. They had been engaged since March, but had told only their parents. To accommodate their diets, J. P. III put Lynne in charge of menu planning, saying he found her to be a "very good cook," although for himself he supplemented the vegetarian fare with some meat. He was further pleased when the young woman decided to take a ceramics course from a potter at Washington University. Joe IV worked for several weeks that summer with a St. Louis

12. Copy of letter to JPIV from tutor Robert A. Ferguson, February 20, 1970, JPIII Papers.

film producer on a documentary about the St. Louis Zoo and helped with a project that showed films outdoors for inner-city young people. After expressing an interest in working in broadcasting, he served as a volunteer script consultant at KMOX-TV—not a Pulitzer property. His father suggested that a job might eventually be arranged with Pulitzer station KOAT-TV in Albuquerque, New Mexico, which the company had recently bought, thus removing him "from too much St. Louis paternalism."[13] However, the idea was dropped after Joe IV decided against television work.

Even though his son was only twenty-one, J. P. III was enthusiastic about his plans to marry. After getting to know Lynne during the summer, he wrote to stepmother Elizabeth Pulitzer and mother-in-law Myra Vauclain:

> I am extremely fond of [Lynne] and believe that both, while young, are devoted to each other and I support their decision. Lynne is a bright, talented girl with interests which are compatible with Joe's—both like the arts, travel, reading, and have inquisitive minds which will lead them into many avenues of interest.... While here they acquired a number of interesting friends whom I did not know previously but who I found stimulating, particularly in the fields of film and television. They are the least materialistic of people and are much more interested in ideas, philosophy (to which Joe comes in part through his studies in anthropology and sociology at Harvard) than in the social scene.[14]

Even though he had not met the in-laws to be, he was disposed to like them. Lynne's father, a surgeon, practiced in the vicinity of Lebanon, New Hampshire, near the family's vacation home in Meridan, where they had moved after Dr. Steinsieck closed his practice of many years in Newton, Massachusetts. "I like their identification with New England, and I share Joe and Lynne's responses to nature against the 'north of Boston' reflections of Thoreau, Emerson, Whitman, Frost and Hawthorne," he wrote. "The young people are aware of this heritage, for which one can be grateful."

The wedding took place on October 23, midway through the autumn semester of the groom's senior year. It was reported modestly in the *Post-Dispatch*, in a story of four paragraphs with a face-only photograph of the bride. This was consistent with the long-standing Pulitzer practice that such events involving the family were handled with reserve. The *New York Times* used the same photo, but gave the story twice as much space. The *Times* story also got the time of the ceremony wrong, a fact error that

13. JPIII to Myra Vauclain, June 10, 1971, JPIII Papers.
14. JPIII to Elizabeth Pulitzer and Myra Vauclain, October 15, 1971, JPIII Papers.

J. P. III noted in a letter he sent his stepmother, mother-in-law, sister Elinor Hempelmann, and Miss Emily Rauh, curator at the St. Louis Art Museum, whom Joe had been dating.[15]

"Joe and Lynne's wedding was marked with such originality and charm that it deserves comment," the letter began. The guest list was limited to twelve so all might be seated at the dining table, "providing an intimacy and warmth which has no precedent in my experience." He described the Steinsieck house in some detail, as "a frame New England cottage which was expanded in the mid-19th century by additions of Greek revival porch and columns.... One of the features of the house I liked was the kitchen, which rather than a service kitchen was an integral part of the family's life situated between the dining room and the pine paneled library.... Attractive export china decorated the walls here and there and the room had the atmosphere of a pleasant, usable living area." He found the Steinsiecks "a charming family, very close, with a talented strain which leans towards the arts," including Lynne's interest in dance and her brother's in sculpting.

The ceremony itself—which the *Times* put at dawn—was actually at 8:30 a.m. in a hillside clearing a short distance from the house where "the vertical birch trees suggested to more than one of us Norman or Gothic architecture." The bride wore a long lavender dress and the others "country clothes, corduroys, sport jackets, etc." A young Episcopalian minister conducted a traditional service. The group returned to the house for breakfast afterward, where the minister toasted the couple "for their devotion to Christian principles. I thought of the courses in philosophy and comparative religion which Joe has taken and how Harvard somehow manages to leave its imprint on its students."

By the time Joe IV graduated from Harvard in June 1972, he and Lynne were the parents of a daughter, Elkhanah, whose name did not appeal to grandfather Pulitzer. "In time," he hoped, "it will be changed or supplanted by a cozy nickname which will not relate to Elk or Elkie."[16] Another major change for Joe IV—though relatively short-lived—was deciding that he was disinclined to become the fourth Joseph Pulitzer to edit and publish the *Post-Dispatch* and superintend the company's holdings in radio, television, and smaller newspapers. A simpler life beckoned, but for a time he feared he might be conscripted for military duty. He had a low number in the lottery system by which young men were being

15. *St. Louis Post-Dispatch* and *New York Times*, October 24, 1971. The letter did not go to Kate Davis, possibly because of strained relations between them that led to the family dispute in 1986. See chapter 10.

16. JPIII to Myra Vauclain, May 24, 1972, JPIII Papers.

drafted, but successfully appealed his 1-A classification. The appeal's basis was a neck injury he had suffered while wrestling at St. Mark's. Although J. P. III never broached the subject, Joe IV said he thought his father was somewhat disappointed that his son, unlike the first three J. P.s, did no military service.

But he sensed no disappointment that he chose not to pursue a career in journalism. Joe IV and Lynne wanted to live in Oregon. He had visited a cousin there and "just loved it." They moved to Portland in September 1972. He got a job tearing down old houses, which he liked, then one as a mason's apprentice, which he did not. He worked for a time as a sheet rock installer. Although keeping their rented home in Portland, the following spring the young Pulitzers bought a farm in the mountains near the small town of Summit, midway between Corvallis and Newport. He hoped to develop what he described as "a productive experimental forest, a sanctuary for trees."[17] He quit his job and spent more than a year improving the house and property, doing most of the work himself.

By 1974, however, he was having second thoughts, as was his father. Joe IV had seen enough of the construction business to know it was not for him. "My activities since acquiring the farm have led me to the decision that I would like to try journalism as a career," he wrote his father.

> I have experienced the pride of conceiving and executing a project successfully within given limits. I have hardened my body and spirit with physical labor, but feel starved in my mind. I have had to deal with people from all walks of life, ranging in background and education from illiterate farmers and loggers to Ph. D. in biology advisors employed by the forest service. I have discovered, rather brutally, that without a trade or field it is impossible to get on in the world, that is, to find a challenging position of employment where you are given the responsibility to exercise some form of judgment affecting the process or product you are working on. I have had an excellent education, but it took two years of living experience out here to find the perspective to want to work, to supply me with the incentive to put that education to good use at an interesting job. . . . I know that my education has given me some of the skills or tools which might make journalism a suitable career for me and am anxious to give it a try.

He would most like to try his hand as a writer and reporter, he explained, believing he could develop a "style suitable for the daily press." He admitted that he was "politically ignorant" and had "hardly ever read a newspaper or watched the news" for the past several years, during which the

17. JPIV to JPIII, April 15, 1974, JPIII Papers.

war had ended and the Watergate scandal had unfolded: "I have remained almost entirely apolitical, regarding with distaste all of the subterfuge and casuistry of political leaders, not interested even in their exposure and flight from justice, essentially a pessimist." But he thought he had matured, and was beginning to better understand himself, making this self-assessment: "What some might regard as a buffer of egotism or selfishness is beginning to break up."

Both he and Lynne were ready to make a change, but did not want to return to St. Louis. He suggested doing an apprenticeship on the *Arizona Daily Star* in Tucson, purchased by the company in 1971. His Uncle Michael was its editor and publisher. Joe IV said he thought it would be better to begin there rather than at the *Post-Dispatch* so that he could "learn the basics of the trade more slowly and more smoothly without the handicap of overcoming initial prejudices or expectations. One thing that bothers me about starting at the *Post-Dispatch* is that I am the founder's offspring and that this gives me an advantage denied all others, in spite of their ability or achievements. I would rather get started in a position where my name carries less implication, for unspoken accusations of nepotism have haunted me all my life, at least until we moved out west." Eventually, he hoped, he could return to St. Louis with his competence as a newspaperman established "so that I may be judged more fairly by the work I do, rather than by my name." He knew his father got his first, although brief, experience at the *San Francisco News* and that Michael worked for nearly four years at the *Louisville Courier-Journal* before joining the *Post-Dispatch* in 1960.

J. P. III liked his son's suggestions. He was not going to push him—in part, most likely, because he had felt some pressure—but was agreeable once Joe IV raised the subject. He agreed that it was not a good idea to begin in St. Louis, and told Michael of his son's wish to move to Tucson. Michael balked. "I think it would be better for him to begin on a paper not part of the 'Pulitzer environment,'"[18] he responded. He saw "a psychological advantage" in Joe IV being "a more or less anonymous member of the staff" who could

> suffer his mistakes and savor his victories without any consideration of family. I know as far as experience goes, the four years in Louisville gave me a professional confidence and perspective that I consider very helpful. . . . While I am flattered that you considered the *Star* for Joe's initial training, I find the responsibility very heavy. Should Joe decide he does not like newspaper work I would feel, rightly or wrongly, some

18. MEP to JPIII, May 17, 1974, JPIII Papers.

responsibility and I would hate to do anything that would cause friction between you and me.... For these reasons I think it would be better for you, me and young Joe if he were given the feeling that he is starting out completely on his own.... I think it would give him a feeling that he was ready, willing and able to organize his own life and not have it organized for him.

This made sense to J. P. III.[19] Michael offered to find a suitable newspaper where Joe IV might start, listing several possibilities. Ultimately, a job was arranged at the *Bulletin* in Bend, Oregon, suggested by retired *Post-Dispatch* editorial page editor Robert Lasch, who knew its owner-editor, Robert W. Chandler, also the proprietor of another daily and several weeklies and biweeklies in eastern Oregon.

The *Bulletin* looked like an ideal choice. The paper was small. Members of the news staff had to become competent in reporting; in writing news, feature, and sports stories as well as editorials; and in editing, page layout, and photography. Joe IV even did a stint on the society section. He liked the work, and Chandler found him "bright and eager to learn." Unaware of Michael's role in the matter, he credited Joe IV for deciding not to start at a Pulitzer paper: "That way he got no special treatment." Chandler thought Joe IV validated his observations across forty years in newspapering "that people with connections in the publishing business are more serious about learning the business." The young man "came here without experience or even very much familiarity with newspapers," he observed, "but he was a hell of a worker. He put in his time and then some, and he learned quickly." He credited Joe IV with developing "a feel for what makes a good story," and for being "a pretty good writer—on occasion a very good writer. He could make the language sing from time to time."[20]

Joe IV sent his father examples of his work, getting favorable responses in return as well as a request that he send "anything that reflects either the success, the failures or the difficulties involved in the work. This would be illuminating to me."[21] Joe IV was not anxious to leave the job, or Oregon, but after slightly less than two years at the *Bulletin*, his father asked him to move back to St. Louis. The reason, although never directly expressed, was that J. P. III was sixty-three in 1976. If his son was to be educated and tested for succession in St. Louis, the time had come, although J. P. III did ponder the possibility of finding his son an interim job on a medium-sized newspaper. He dropped that idea after Joe IV spent several days in

19. JPIII to MEP, May 22, 1974, JPIII Papers.
20. Quoted in Siering, "The Prince of Tucker Boulevard," 20.
21. JPIII to JPIV, December 13, 1974, JPIII Papers.

early 1976 in interviews with senior *Post-Dispatch* editors, not including his father. The editors pronounced him qualified to join the staff.

That settled, J. P. III recorded a pledge in a letter to his son's grandmother Vauclain: "I will keep hands strictly off as I think a young man has to have freedom from parental supervision at such a moment and be unselfconscious and open in discussing the problems and successes of his work."[22] Joe IV's impression was that his father "never wanted to train me himself, the way his father trained him. We didn't really discuss it, but he made it painfully clear. And that was okay, because I don't think I wanted it either. He was content to have surrogates do that, as he was content to have surrogates when I was a little child. Somewhere we kind of ran out of time. It's too bad, because he was really starting, I think, to get excited about my career, and then the family fight came along, and that just really involved all of his attention and energy."

22. JPIII to Myra Vauclain, February 10, 1976, JPIII Papers.

Ten

The Family Fight

The Pulitzer "family fight" and the decision of Ralph Ingersoll II to launch a tabloid competitor in St. Louis occurred one after the other in 1986. Joe had known for more than fifteen years that some minority stockholders were unhappy that the company's voting trust effectively gave him control of the value of their shares and their dividend returns. The most persistent in pressing him about this had been his sister, Kate Davis Quesada, acting on behalf of her sons, Ricardo and Peter, who received stock as male descendants under the terms of the first Joseph Pulitzer's will.[1]

Kate Davis considered artificially low both the stock dividends and the formula at which shares would be bought back from shareholders who wished to sell, which was equal to book value. The company calculated its book value in 1986 at $134 million while market value estimates ranged from $620 million to $855 million. Kate Davis said she and her businessman husband, retired Air Force Lieutenant General Elwood R. "Pete"

---

1. The family dispute became public in April. Ingersoll announced his intention to start a tabloid in 1986. *New York Times,* April 13, 1986; *St. Louis Journalism Review,* July 1986, 4. Some date the family dispute from 1958, when Michael Pulitzer filed a brief challenging a provision of his father's (J. P. II's) will that bequeathed company stock to his daughters, Kate Davis and Elinor, who, as females, were not eligible under the will of J. P. I. The matter was dropped. Following the death of their stepmother, Elizabeth Edgar Pulitzer, in 1974, the women inherited small parcels of stock from her estate. Had the 1958 challenge succeeded, Kate Davis's two sons would have received fewer shares than they did. "I was a young lawyer at the time," Michael said in 1986. "It was a mistake and I did it purely on what I felt was legal interpretation. It never occurred to me that this would cause a family rift, but apparently it has." *Wall Street Journal,* April 11, 1986.

The full names of Kate Davis's children are Thomas Ricardo Quesada and Peter Wickham Quesada. Thomas primarily uses "Rick" or "Ricky," derived from his middle name.

Main sources for this chapter are a collection of documents titled "Pulitzer Publishing Company Recapitalization 1986," JPIII Papers; Papers of David E. Moore given to the author, identified as DEM Papers hereafter; interviews with Michael E. Pulitzer, Joseph Pulitzer IV, Emily Rauh Pulitzer, David E. Moore, Peter J. Repetti, Richard A. Palmer, James M. Snowden, Jr., Kate Davis Pulitzer Quesada, and Peter W. Quesada; *St. Louis Post-Dispatch,* September 30 and October 5, 1986; *Wall Street Journal,* April 11 and May 15, 1986; *New York Times,* April 13, 1986; *Washington Post,* April 27, 1986.

Quesada, wanted to make it possible for their two sons "to be able to sell their shares at a fair value. They were in business and wanted to be able to use their capital to further their careers and not just live on dividends, which were much too low anyway." The Quesadas had opted when their sons were minors not to put the boys' shares into the company's voting trust. This had rankled Joe, because it suggested misgivings about how the company was managed.[2]

A provision of the voting trust required members who wanted to sell shares to offer them first to the company (or, if the company declined to buy, to other shareholders) at the current book value price.[3] This arrangement had maintained close family control for more than one hundred years. However, by not being in the trust, the Quesadas had the option of

2. The book value formula worked for the company because it represented "a fair approximation of what the value of the shares would have been. What really triggered the disgruntlement on behalf of the minority shareholders was the fact that . . . the selling prices of media companies were rising rapidly, and so stocks that used to sell . . . a lot closer to book value were now selling at big multiples above book value." Interview with James M. Snowden, Jr., executive vice president of Huntleigh Securities Corporation, St. Louis, July 30, 1993. Snowden was one of the financial advisers to the company during the shareholder dispute and in 1986 became a company director.

Broadcast Investor estimated the value of the broadcast holdings at $400 million, the *Post-Dispatch* and *Arizona Daily Star* at $320 million and $100 million respectively, for a total of $820 million, and $855 million should revenue growth become higher than projected. *Broadcast Investor*, February 28, 1986, JPIII Papers. The Morgan Stanley Company estimated the company's value "at between $620 million to more than $700 million." *Broadcasting*, April 6, 1986.

"Our point of view was significantly influenced by our father," Peter Quesada said when interviewed. General Quesada was the first head of the Federal Aviation Administration, and president and part owner of the Washington Senators baseball team in the early 1960s. In 1963 he established a development company, L'Enfant Properties in Washington, which built L'Enfant Plaza there. Telephone interview with Peter W. Quesada, July 7, 1995; Elwood R. Quesada obituary, *St. Louis Post-Dispatch*, February 10, 1993; Telephone interview with Mrs. Elwood R. Quesada, October 27, 1987. Her sons owned Fore River Company in Portland, Maine, involved in renovation projects to revitalize that city. Peter was a lawyer on Wall Street before joining his older brother, an architect, in Maine. *SJR*, April 1986, 4.

There are several references in Joe's papers to frosty relations with General Quesada. He wrote in response to a note from Michael in 1971: "I was sorry to learn that Pete Quesada is bothering Kate Davis, but I agree with your assessment that 'it is just another chapter in a continuing annoying situation.'" JPIII to MEP, December 1, 1971, JPIII Papers. Peter W. Quesada said his father and J. P. III clashed when the Quesadas asked to buy some of the shares on behalf of their sons when Herbert "Peter" Pulitzer, Jr., decided to sell some of his stock in 1958. Joe replied that this could not be done. Joe bought most of Herbert Jr.'s shares.

3. The book value per share grew over the years. It was $901.50 in 1949, when the Newspaper Trust established by J. P. I expired and was replaced by the Voting Trust in 1950. As of 1979, it was $12,254 and by 1986, $24,500 per share. JPIII to DEM, June, 13, 1980, DEM Papers; *New York Times*, April 13, 1986.

selling to an interested outsider for more than book value. Although the Quesadas' example had the potential of influencing other shareholders to take their shares out of the voting trust when it was renewed periodically, none ever had. As Michael Pulitzer observed, it was unlikely that any outsider "would offer real money" for a minority interest in a closed corporation because "you have about as many rights as the dog on the street corner." Instead, there was quiet internal lobbying over the years to persuade Joe to establish more generous dividends and share buyout opportunities. Then those who wished to sell could get a "fair" price and those who did not could exercise their right to increase their holdings. Kate Davis made this case regularly, usually when she and Joe would ski together each winter at Vail or Aspen.

"Joe, this is just not right," she said while they were having tea at Vail in the winter of 1970–1971. "Why should my boys be locked into what you want to do with your paper?"[4]

"Well, if you don't like it, why don't you get a buyer?" he replied.

That night Kate Davis made a note of the challenge. She asked for her lawyer's opinion on her position. He advised that a higher stock valuation would be in the interests of her sons and all the other shareholders by his interpretation of Internal Revenue Service estate tax procedures. Joe's advisers took the opposite view, however, and nothing changed. In sending Joe her lawyer's views, Kate Davis emphasized that she did so "in a friendly and affectionate climate which I propose to continue. Above all, I want you to realize that I am a loyal member of the family and not involved in any aggression," adding that she wanted "to find out how I can help—not hurt." A decade later, in 1981, when Peter was twenty-eight and Ricardo thirty-two, Peter told Michael Pulitzer in a telephone conversation that he would like to sell his stock in a few years and "might get nasty" and seek an outside buyer. "I would sum up his call as representing dissatisfaction, but not a threat to take any action in the near future," Michael reported to Joe. Four years later Peter told Michael he thought Pulitzer shares were worth "three times book value, but a selling shareholder would be willing to 'take a haircut' and sell for twice book value." Looking back years later, company chief financial officer Ronald H. Ridgway concluded, "that would have been a bargain."[5] But for Joe, book value

---

4. Interview with KDPQ, April 27 and 28, 1995, Hobe Sound, Florida.

5. Stephen E. Nash to KDPQ, January 11, 1971; "Re: Evaluation of Company Shares" from unidentified source to JPIII, April (day omitted) 1971, disagreed, saying that the conservative valuation benefited shareholders upon their deaths by reducing their estate and inheritance taxes. It also took the position that past practice in selling company stock "would be persuasive evidence" before the IRS "in any tax controversy."

was the limit. "He was not going to give them anything like they thought they were worth. I've sometimes wondered had [Joe] been willing to loosen up there, might we have gotten out cheaper?" Ridgway reflected. "But from an ownership standpoint, I think it was hard for Joe to accept that anyone else owned anything other than him." The history of company stock ownership shows, he said, that Joe had only acquired—never divested—any of his shares. "He wanted to maintain that tradition and family ownership and just did not hold with anyone who did not have that same view."

In fact, the selling prices of media companies were rising rapidly, and tensions escalated at the 1985 shareholders meeting. Joe and Peter exchanged views about implications for the company of the buying "hysteria" for media properties. Joe thought the frenzy made little sense, remarking that "it would take years" to justify the recent sale of the *Des Moines Register* for $200 million. He added that he felt Pulitzer Publishing Company had been "on the right track" for years and saw no need to change its method of stock valuation. Peter called for "a discussion as a family on the best way to maximize the wealth of the shareholders by finding a way to take advantage of the buying frenzy that was pushing values substantially higher than the book value shareholders currently could get for their company shares." When Ricardo Quesada suggested consulting an investment banker, Joe responded that investment bankers "are suspect" because they work for fees and "their motives may involve making money for themselves." Shortly thereafter, the Quesadas hired investment banker Felix Rohaytn of Lazard Freres and Company to help them find an outside buyer.[6]

Rohatyn found A. Alfred Taubman, a Michigan real estate and shopping center developer who also owned Woodward and Lothrop department stores, the A & W fast food chain, a United States Football League team, and later Sotheby's, the English art auction house. He had once owned stock in two radio stations. In early 1986, a coalition of nine minority stockholders offered their combined 43 percent stake in the company

JPIII Papers. Michael Pulitzer observed in an interview that the lower value would also benefit the company, because it "would have to pay less if a shareholder died, to buy back the shares." He added that the younger shareholders, however, who were not yet thinking about estate planning and might want to sell their shares, would mostly likely favor a higher valuation. KDPQ to JPIII, January 27, 1971, JPIII Papers; MEP to JPIII, July 23, 1981, JPIII Papers; MEP, memorandum for file, April 25, 1985; Interview with Ronald H. Ridgway, February 27, 1995, St. Louis.

6. Annual meeting of shareholders, April 23, 1985, DEM Papers. Rohatyn was a major figure in the investment banking business and was considered "Wall Street's premier advisor on takeovers." He was appointed U.S. Ambassador to France in 1997. *New York Times,* January 26, 1996, and May 23, 1997.

to Taubman on the condition that he would offer to buy the entire company, not just the minority share. Taubman agreed, paying the minority $10 million for an option on their shares. The company was an attractive prospect, especially with its seven lucrative television stations. Michael recalled that the minority had proposed at one point that they be given "a couple of the television stations" in return for their shares, but "that didn't get very far" because it would have meant splitting up the company. Peter Quesada disputed Michael's recollection as "an amateurish distortion of what happened," although the minority did propose a spin-off of some assets to those who wanted out of the company, and some of those could have been television properties. That having failed, Taubman offered $500 million and then $625 million for all of the stock. A broadcast industry analysis that put the company's value at least $200 million higher than the second bid concluded: "If we owned [the company] we'd expect to sell it at a premium, not a discount."[7] Joe called the offer "inadequate from a financial point of view."

For that reason plus their desire to keep the company whole and their conviction that selling to Taubman would amount to destroying the company, the majority stockholders—Joe, Michael, and their cousin, David E. Moore, all grandsons of the founder—took the dimmest possible view of

7. *Editor & Publisher,* March 1, 1986, 19. Taubman was convicted in 2001 of price-fixing as the head of Sotheby's for conspiring with rival auction house Christie's to fix fees charged auction house sellers. The scheme cost customers more than $100 million. He was sentenced in 2002 to a year and a day in prison and fined $7.5 million. *New York Times,* December 6, 2001, and April 23, 2002.

The minority stockholder coalition included Clement C. Moore II, a descendant of Edith Pulitzer Moore; Kenward G. Elmslie, Gordon C. Weir, William E. Weir, James R. Weir, descendants of Constance Pulitzer Elmslie; Kate Davis Pulitzer Quesada, Elinor Pulitzer Hempelmann, T. Ricardo Quesada, and Peter W. Quesada, descendants of Joseph Pulitzer II. The *Post-Dispatch* had an operating profit in the 1980s of 5 percent when the industry standard for papers of its size was 15 percent. The company's profits from television were nearly 40 percent. *St. Louis Post-Dispatch,* April 13, 1986. Peter Quesada said the minority proposed to the majority: "We will put on a piece of paper all the company's assets. We will agree on the book value of each asset. We want you to offer each shareholder in this company, whether they are in the voting trust [or not] the opportunity to take their pro rata share of book value in terms of assets. If the group is 10 percent, 20 percent, 30 percent, 40 percent, the group will spin off 10, 20, 30, 40 and they will merrily go on their way with a tax-free spinoff, selling those shares. You will be left with the rest, and we don't have to argue if book value is right." The so-called "Quesada group" had approximately 20 percent of company shares, including those of Ricardo and Peter Quesada, their mother, Kate Davis Quesada and aunt, Elinor Hempelmann. The two women had inherited a small number of shares from their stepmother, Elizabeth Edgar Pulitzer. None of this was in the company's Voting Trust. The other minority shareholders sought release from the trust in a suit—ultimately dropped—asserting that the majority had misrepresented book value as the fair value of their shares. *Broadcast Investor,* February 28, 1986.

Taubman's overture and signed a pact not to consider any offer for at least a year. Together, they held 57 percent of the shares. "That really was an awfully important thing in the battle," said James M. Snowden, Jr., a financial adviser who had worked with the company for several years and recommended that the three band together.[8] If Michael and David had not allied with Joe, he said, "Joe would not have prevailed in keeping the company in Pulitzer hands." And they might have balked, because Joe had for years treated them almost as outsiders, essentially the same as he had those who formed the minority group. "One of the biggest frustrations that everybody had was that Joe took a very imperious approach toward all of the shareholders. He was not very nice to them," Snowden commented. "I always sort of thought that Joe felt that because of the voting trust, it was sort of like his castle, and at night he could go back across the drawbridge and pull the drawbridge up and he was in his fortress and nobody could get across the moat." What made the pact possible nevertheless, he believed, was that like Joe, both Michael and David felt a very strong sense of family, and did not want to see the company "sold out for a quick profit, which is what the minority shareholders wanted."[9] The minority had tried to persuade David to defect and add his 15 percent to the minority's 43 percent. "I really resented that," he said. He had agreed to meet Ricardo Quesada for breakfast at the Harvard Club in New York, and felt ambushed when Ricardo brought along two people from Lazard Freres. They told him they had a buyer for the company, but would not reveal his name.

Still, even with their majority and "even though we would prefer that the company remain private," the grandsons decided they had to do something. They first proposed a limited public offering "that would give those who wanted to sell some liquidity." The proposal also had provisions designed "to forestall takeover attempts" and keep current management in control. The minority rejected it because, as Peter Quesada put it, "We

8. Joe, Michael, and David held 54 percent among them, to which 3 percent held by their children or by trusts for their children was added. "Information Statement," Pulitzer Publishing Company, March 20, 1986, 2–3, DEM Papers. Telephone interview with James M. Snowden, July 30, 2003. Snowden started working with the company in 1976, when he was with Lehman Brothers Kuhn Loeb in New York. In 1984, he became a vice president of A. G. Edwards and Sons in St. Louis, and in 1995 joined Huntleigh Securities Corporation, also in St. Louis, as executive vice president.

9. David in particular felt "a very strong obligation to maintain the Pulitzer traditions," while Michael felt somewhat less so. What most appealed to Michael, Snowden said, was that the agreement "could give him common ground with Joe and David to now get a united front against the dissident shareholders." Telephone interview with Snowden, July 30, 2003.

think every shareholder ought to be able to sell stock to whom they want when they want, without restriction on that transfer."[10]

The majority then offered to buy back all the minority's shares for a total of $185.9 million if Taubman would relinquish his option and his suit to gain full control of the company. Taubman resisted at first, and then, convinced that the majority would not budge, sold the option back to the minority for $16 million, $6 million more than he had paid eight months earlier. The company repurchased the minority shares for $79,000 apiece, more than three times the $25,000 book value price. To help finance the buyout, the majority stockholders took the company public on December 11, 1986. Suits that had been filed by both sides were voluntarily dismissed.[11]

Although the so-called "family fight" ended before the year was out, the filing of suits indicated that it might be prolonged. "And Now the Pulitzers Go to War," said a *New York Times* headline in mid-April.[12] The story referred to Joe as "the staunch guardian of the Pulitzer heritage, particularly the *Post-Dispatch*, the family's flagship." Joe described himself as "very, very interested in retaining the independence, liberality and character of the *Post-Dispatch*," and those who wanted to sell as having "no emotional investment in journalism. To them it would be just like selling a matchbook factory." He had long seen his role as perpetuating

10. *St. Louis Post-Dispatch*, April 3, 5, and 18, 1986; *SJR*, April 1986, 5. The proposal would have amended the voting trust limitations on shareholder selling. In a letter to shareholders, Joe and Michael explained that "implementation of this plan will involve a shareholder vote on a number of complex matters" and that "of necessity, these documents will be long and complicated." Even though limited, "subsequent registered public offerings" could take place. JPIII and MEP to Holders of Common Stock and Voting Trust Certificates, March 19, 1986, JPIII Papers.

11. As James Snowden explained it, minority shareholders have fewer rights in a private company than majority shareholders because in selling their shares, they cannot "deliver control" of the company as can a majority. The $185.9 million the minority finally accepted "was equivalent of putting a value on the whole company of $440 million." Taubman's offer of at least $625 million, rejected by the majority, indicated his willingness to pay a premium for control of the company. "The majority shareholders decided it was more important for them to keep the company in family control and they were willing to forego the difference between $440 million and $625 million," Snowden said. Because the buyback price was "equivalent of the full public company value" of the shares, the minority "got a good deal," he added. JMS interview, July 30, 2003.

In one suit, the company sought the ouster of Peter Quesada from the board of directors, charging that he had given secret company data to Lazard Freres. He denied the allegation. In another, the dissidents charged Joe, Michael, and David with abuse of authority in order to get a "permanent stranglehold over the affairs of the company" by agreeing in 1986 not to sell any of their shares for at least a year. *Post-Dispatch*, April 1 and 5, 1986. JMS to Alfred J. Pastore, December 1, 1986, DEM Papers, summarizes the chain of events.

12. *New York Times*, April 13, 1986.

the "continuity and stability of policy" carried out by his father and grand-father "with minimum interference of shareholders."[13] Peter Quesada, who became spokesman for the dissidents, believed Joe saw them as "sort of ungrateful beneficiaries of a family tradition [who] didn't appreciate the importance of the tradition. He'd worked his whole life to make the company valuable and do public service ... and we just stood there with our hands out and didn't appreciate that he was working in our best interests." But to Peter, involving Taubman simply meant the minority was "just trying to get out and move on. The stock was paying almost no dividends as a percentage of book, let alone of market [value]" and so was "pretty close to worthless. As a general observation, I would say that it is probably bad tactics to back an opponent with nothing to lose into a corner unless you are very certain that you hold all the cards. We thought we had nothing to lose, and we felt there were no avenues of escape left because we had very carefully documented the company's response to each one proposed." Those he characterized as "lots of vague talk about all kinds of things for twenty years."

The *Wall Street Journal,* among others, compared the Pulitzer dispute to three others that had recently ended with sales of the companies, the most acrimonious of which involved the *Courier-Journal* and *Louisville Times* and other properties owned by the Binghams of Louisville, Kentucky— Michael's former employer. However, the Pulitzer differences centered on the issue of control over liquidity and were personal only in the sense that resentments had grown against Joe, as Michael expressed it, for running the company "as a personal fiefdom." One disclosure the minority made was that in 1982 Joe's $952,000 salary and bonus as chairman was only slightly less than the total dividends being paid shareholders. The dividends subsequently were increased and Joe's compensation decreased to $800,000. Still, such criticism was nowhere near the "tale of scandal and suspense" that got extensive public attention for the Binghams, including several books. As two Bingham biographers saw it, that family's newspapers and other media holdings "were far more than income producing assets. They were the passports under which they traveled the world beyond Kentucky, and were the reason why the Binghams were not simply rich people but were The Binghams of Louisville." The Pulitzers, by contrast, were not as closely identified with St. Louis. Only some of the descendants of Joseph Pulitzer II lived and worked there, and they kept a certain distance from civic and social involvements so as to maintain their newspaper's editorial independence. The other family members were scat-

13. JPIII to author, July 30, 1985.

tered and generally unconcerned about St. Louis. Peter Quesada, for example, was a lawyer and his brother Ricardo an architect. They became partners in an urban renovation company in Portland, Maine. Over the years, other heirs cashed in some or all of their shares, enabling some remaining stockholders—especially Joe—to increase their voting control.[14]

Joe was the most committed of the majority shareholders to the belief that only tight family voting control could maintain the company's journalistic integrity. Unlike his brother and cousin, he dismissed the idea of public ownership because it would invade the privacy of the company's business affairs. Also, according to both Michael and David, Joe could not imagine that disaffected family members ever would attempt to dismantle the company for their benefit. Accordingly, he opposed the idea of going public whenever it came up. In 1972 Joe told Michael, "I would find it extremely distasteful to be required to report to a group of security analysts." Two years later he wrote his brother (then in Tucson) that he had "very strong feelings against" public ownership because of "the almost unique privilege of publishing a family-owned, independent, liberal, distinctive newspaper without the necessity of having the 'bottom line' given precedence over all other elements of character, personality, individuality. I think the Pulitzer tradition should withstand this temptation and enjoy the protection it has as a private concern." Without disagreeing directly, Michael replied that it was "a source of some frustration" to him to have most of his estate in not readily redeemable Pulitzer stock. Michael reflected

14. Besides the Binghams, family disputes led to sales of the Des Moines Register and Tribune Company by the Cowles family and the *Detroit News* by the Scripps family in the mid-1980s. *Wall Street Journal,* April 11, 1986. Michael said the Binghams, all of whom he knew, made some "crazy decisions." It made no sense to him "for young Barry to go off to Smith College for a year when all this turmoil was going around and to appoint an editor to run the paper over his general manager.... I think we approached this much more rationally than they did." MEP Interview, January 19, 1995; *New York Times,* April 13, 1986. Michael's salary as company president was $250,240. By company standards, both the $952,000 and $800,000 compensation figures were below earlier norms. Joe's father received $407,603 in 1954—$1,387,338 in 1982 dollars. Income from other sources, including company stock, is not included in these sums. "Information Statement" for April 17, 1986, Pulitzer Publishing Company Shareholders' Meeting, DEM Papers; Pfaff, *Joseph Pulitzer II,* 345; Inflation Calculator, *www.westegg .com/inflation.* David Leon Chandler, *The Binghams of Louisville,* book jacket. See also Tifft and Jones, *The Patriarch;* Sallie Bingham, *Passion and Prejudice;* Marie Brenner, *House of Dreams.* Sellers at the book value rate were: William E.Weir, 21 shares; Clement C. Moore II, 16 shares; Kenward G. Elmslie, 226 shares; Michael E. Pulitzer, 244 shares, and smaller amounts by Gordon C. and James R. Weir and the estate of Adrian P. Moore. *SJR,* May 1986, 4. Herbert Pulitzer, Jr., sold all his remaining 375 shares at book value in 1970. A. Rick D'Archangelo (accountant for DEM) to William N. Packard, Jr., February 25, 1970, DEM Papers; JPIII to Harry Wilensky, October 28, 1970, JPIII Papers.

years later that Joe mistakenly believed that "the fortress of the voting trust was absolutely impregnable" when in fact "the voting trust is not going to prevent litigation . . . and when there's litigation . . . the landscape changes."[15]

The company's lawyers—Robert Thrun and his successors, Peter Repetti and Richard Palmer—frankly considered public ownership desirable. "But you couldn't push it because Joe was against it," Repetti recalled, even though "once you have public shares, you've really got a safety valve with anybody else in the future who wants to get out." Thrun suggested that minority shareholders had a point in the early 1970s in asking that shares be redeemable at two or three times book value or be put in the public market, but got nowhere with Joe.[16] "We also had to tell him that once you're public, Joe, you've got all the scrutiny in the world with the SEC [Securities and Exchange Commission] and all that," Repetti said. "Well, he didn't like that. I think he talked to people who made it sound a lot worse than it is. It's not very pleasant, but it's not that bad, either."

Both Joe IV—who by this time was the company's vice president for administration and agreed with his father but took no active role in the dispute—and Kate Davis said that J. P. III never imagined the possibility of a shareholder revolt. Joe IV recalled hearing his father say many times, "A minority shareholder is the loneliest person in the world." An attitude close to indifference is suggested in a 1971 memorandum from Joe to general manager Alexander T. Primm: "A matter to be 'dusted off' before the annual meeting is my sister's, Mrs. Quesada's, questioning of the fairness of the formula for market value of PD stock. We need not have final answers but should report what we are doing." He showed more concern after seeing statistics showing the net income of eleven publicly owned newspapers in 1971 at 22 percent against 8 percent for the *Post-Dispatch*. "An unfavorable comparison . . . over an extended period would, I am sure, result in shareholder dissatisfaction," he told managing editor Evarts Graham. "To head off such dissatisfaction we have adopted severe cost-cutting measures and are securing new revenues," he added. By 1974 he had concluded "that large metropolitan newspapers can survive and prosper only to the extent that subsidiary operations provide diversification and earnings support. Sound operations rather than speculative situations merit our attention and investigation." He was confident that this approach

15. JPIII to MEP, July 31, 1972, MEP to JPIII, July 22, 1974, JPIII Papers; MEP interview, January 19, 1995.

16. The family-owned New York Times Company recognized this in 1957, as did the Washington Post Company in 1971. Tifft and Jones, *The Trust,* 322; Katharine Graham, *Personal History,* 441–42.

would satisfy most shareholders: "The voting trust is secure in its control without the Quesadas." Joe IV recalled that his father did not respond with concern eleven years later, in 1985, when he told Joe III that a cousin, Clement C. "Chips" Moore II, had visited him at his home in St. Louis and "was very critical of my father's neglect of outside shareholders."[17]

However, Kate Davis got his attention the following year. He was visibly shaken when she told her brother in his office in January 1986 that she was with the minority stockholders in their intention to sell the option to Taubman. "He was totally surprised when I told him what I was doing," she said. "He just thought a bomb had dropped." She asked if he remembered his remark about finding a buyer over tea at Vail one year, "and of course he didn't remember it at all. He remembered going to this little teahouse and having a conversation, but he didn't remember that. And I said, 'Well, I have a record of it, so in case you've forgotten, it was your idea, not mine.'"

Joe had worked to keep control within the family by following his father's practice of taking only a few family members (in his case his brother, Michael, and his son, Joe IV) into the company, and only after they had served apprenticeships elsewhere. When Herbert "Peter" Pulitzer, Jr., of Palm Beach, Florida, applied for a job in 1953, J. P. II discouraged him: "I think you should realize that you would have to go through not less than five years of not too exciting and often dull and dreary work as a reporter before you could prove any aptitude for the purely journalistic side of newspaper work." He advised his nephew to put in "five years or so on some other good newspaper" before applying to the *Post-Dispatch*, and offered to try to arrange an apprenticeship for him. He reminded Herbert Jr. that J. P. III "has a head start on you" and emphasized that "there absolutely cannot be two men running one newspaper. Many, many newspapers have been ruined by just this." By 1970, Herbert Jr. had sold all his stock and was pursuing a career in orange groves, restaurants, hotels, and other ventures. He was involved in a sensationalized divorce from his second wife, Roxanne Pulitzer, in 1982, which the *Post-Dispatch*— but not the *Globe-Democrat*—virtually ignored.[18]

---

17. JPIII to ATP, March 15, 1971, JPIII to EAG, August 10, 1972, JPIII to ATP and GAC, May 3, 1974, JPIII to ATP, August 12, 1974, JPIII Papers; Telephone interview with JPIV, March 28, 2000.

18. The case involved charges of cocaine use and sexual excess. After their divorce, his former wife published a book about it *(The Prize Pulitzer)* that became a television movie. His first wife designed the highly successful Lilly Pulitzer line of clothing. *St. Louis Post-Dispatch,* January 26, 1976; Larissa MacFarquhar, "Everything Lilly," *New Yorker,* September 4, 2000, 36.

When David Moore asked Joe for a position in 1958, Joe quoted his father's letter to Herbert Jr. in response, adding that Michael currently was apprenticing at the *Courier-Journal.* Determined to have a career in publishing, David worked for and then invested in newspapers and eventually operated business publications in the Northeast for many years. He also maintained an active interest in the family company and was a member of the voting trust. He considered being a trustee "no doubt legally important, but substantially of no great significance." He asked Joe in 1977 to get him a seat on the board of directors "as a significant stockholder and as someone with both interest and experience in the field" so that he could play "a more constructive role" in the company.[19] But he did not get a seat until the family fight erupted and he demanded board membership as one of the three majority shareholders. Michael did not agree with Joe's treatment of David. "He stiffed David for years," he said. Ronald Ridgway, one of whose duties was preparing periodic financial reports to the family shareholders, confirmed that. Joe always carefully reviewed Ridgway's drafts of the reports, and often cautioned him not to be too frank in them. David, however, was one to ask questions, and would ask Ridgway for further explanation and detail, something Joe did not like. "Joe gave me pretty much the impression that I wasn't supposed to be forthright with David, and so when he would call, I would hedge a bit. David would start to come on hard with me. I wasn't too fond of being in the middle." He suggested to Joe that he be more open with David, but got nowhere. "I still don't know why Joe kind of wanted to keep David out there on this limb. My gosh, he was a huge shareholder, and as it turned out, we very much needed his support." To Ridgway, David seemed "a very nice person who once you explain to him your views on whatever it is that he's challenging, it's fine." But Joe preferred being remote. "I think Joe kind of felt like David should just take whatever we gave him and just go his merry way," Ridgway concluded. Despite his difficulties with Joe, David rallied to the cause. One of the first things he did as a board member was to join Michael in an unsuccessful effort to get dissidents Clement Moore II and Kenward Elmslie to join the majority.

19. JPII to Herbert Pulitzer, Jr., December 16, 1953, JPIII to David E. Moore, June 6, 1958, JPIII Papers. David Moore, whose mother was the former Edith Pulitzer, was the only other grandchild of the founder who had a career in journalism. He worked as a reporter for both weekly and daily newspapers, owned a Westchester County, New York, weekly for several years, and spent many years as an editor, executive, and owner of business publications. He ended his career as editorial director and chairman of *International Business* magazine, which he sold in 1995. DEM interview, August 8, 1995; DEM to JPIII, April 24, 1977, DEM Papers.

For Joe IV, the shareholder challenge marked the moment when his prospects for advancement evaporated. It was a major turning point in his life, which, after a period of deep disappointment, he came to accept with more understanding than criticism. He remembered being informed of his father's decision to shed the titles of editor and publisher and concentrate on his role as chairman of the board of directors. (Joe IV assumed this was a result of the challenge, but in fact Joe first told William Woo in 1984 that he was considering stepping down from the *Post-Dispatch* positions.)

"I remember that it was [the Friday before] Super Bowl weekend," Joe IV said. "And my dad called me up to his office about four-thirty and he handed me a press release. He said, 'This will appear in the Sunday paper.'

"It talked about how he was stepping down and Nicholas Penniman would be made publisher and Bill Woo would be named editor,[20] positions traditionally held by our family. I was stunned. I was just devastated.

"And I said, 'How can you do this?'

"And he just said, 'I have to. There are not going to be any arguments. I just want you to know, and you're not going to tell a soul because it's going to be in the Sunday paper.'

"Well, I kind of felt . . . that I'm probably never going to realize the kind of stewardship that he enjoyed or his father or his father before him. So I was pretty devastated. I guess in retrospect, it probably was the right thing for him to do. He was carrying a lot of responsibility. He was almost seventy-three years old, and he knew already that he had a major fight coming. So I'm trying to be mature and take the long view. I don't think he felt he had a choice."

In the release, J. P. III described stepping down as editor and publisher after more than thirty years in those positions as "an orderly transition toward retirement." Penniman told the *St. Louis Journalism Review*, speaking of J. P. IV: "His education continues. He is a relatively young man and I think it's a distinct possibility that I'm keeping this chair warm for him or for someone else in the family. My own opinion is that there always has to be a Pulitzer at the head of this company. It's a very important element in the way we are controlled. Part of the transition we are in, which will take a while, will see Mike Pulitzer emerge as the top family member in the company."[21] Even though he knew his uncle was ahead of him in the line of succession, Joe IV, like everyone else in the company, was thrown off balance by how suddenly things had changed. He was especially upset

20. At the time, Penniman was general manager of the *Post-Dispatch* and William F. Woo was editor of the editorial page. *St. Louis Post-Dispatch*, January 26, 1986.

21. *St. Louis Post-Dispatch*, January 26, 1986; Roland Klose, "Pulitzer Retires, Appoints Penniman, Woo," *SJR*, February 1986, 6.

because the name of the man in charge of the *Post-Dispatch* was not Joseph Pulitzer for the first time in the paper's 108-year history.

Michael confirmed that the takeover attempt changed history for the fourth J. P. Before it happened, Joe had promised to get his son a seat on the board of directors. But public ownership altered the board's composition. As a private entity, the company had been governed primarily by *Post-Dispatch* executives led by Joe and, among others, the general manager, certain editors, and the advertising and circulation managers. Because "the symmetry of the board was very important," once the company was public, the three major shareholders agreed that as an unwritten "rule of thumb" there should be one seat for each of them. That ended Joe IV's chance at a seat, because if his father wanted to add his son, Michael and David might insist on the same prerogative. The new board was organized to be "as close as possible" to what the investment community would understand. James M. Snowden, Jr., became its first member from outside the company in 1986.[22] As with other public company boards, its purpose was to elect company officers, oversee business operations, and represent the shareholders.

A *Post-Dispatch* article summarizing the dispute observed that Joe's "commitment to this newspaper transcends money. It is philosophical. Mike's commitment is almost as deep, and David Moore's commitment also is philosophical." Joe's comment was similarly terse: "I think everyone's pleased that it's over. I don't think there is any happiness, but we can move forward."[23] Looking back in 1995, Michael said the main difference between himself and his brother was that "Joe's financial interest and the journalistic rhetoric were absolutely the same," while Michael took a broader view: "I liked my job. I liked what I was doing, and I thought that financially it was better to stick with the company." But for Joe, "by being private, he could also get the big salary, the perks, the low dividends and all that, and really run the company as a personal fiefdom. And I don't think he understood that, but I did, and I could understand where [the dissidents] were coming from." Also, Joe "was the main target, and I'm sure it was not very comfortable to have his whole career questioned

22. The others were the three grandsons, board vice chairman Glenn A. Christopher, the senior vice presidents of finance, broadcasting, and newspapers respectively—Ronald H. Ridgway, Ken J. Elkins, and Nicholas G. Penniman IV—and legal adviser Peter J. Repetti, a senior partner with Fulbright and Jaworski, New York. The second outside director was Alice B. Hayes, provost of St. Louis University, who replaced Glenn A. Christopher after his retirement in 1993.
23. *St. Louis Post-Dispatch*, October 5, 1986.

that way. But to me, that's litigation. I wasn't the guy taking the heat like he was. Everybody won, I think, from a financial standpoint. The loss was in family relationships, [although for most of those involved] there wasn't any relationship there or wasn't much to begin with."

Michael came into the foreground during the conflict by assuming overall management of the company's position. Nicholas Penniman marked Michael's rise to leadership as happening in "a defining moment in the company's history" during a conference at the Bryan Cave law firm in St. Louis in the summer of 1986. There, company executives—minus Joe, who was in Europe at the time—met with lawyers, investment bankers, and other business advisers to decide the company's strategy. At first, there was general indecision about "how we're going to go," Penniman recalled. "And Michael put them all on the starting line. He said: 'Now we'll march down this road together, and here's how we're going to do it.' It was the moment I think that Michael clearly asserted himself and assumed a position of leadership. It hadn't been conferred yet, but it was clearly there." Penniman suspected Joe had deliberately decided to be away at the time. "I think he did it exactly just to see. It would be like Joe to do that.... When Joe got back, he realized ... that the process now was Michael's." As Emily Pulitzer saw it: "It was Joe testing Michael's ability before making him CEO, and he passed with flying colors."[24]

From then on, Joe stayed abreast of everything, but Michael and company vice chairman Glenn A. Christopher attended to the travel, many meetings, and day-to-day developments. Michael, then company president, shortly began to take on functions of chief executive officer, although he did not have that title until later on. "At the time of the takeover [attempt], my legal training came back and I generally understood what was going on," he said. Soon he was interpreting legal language for Joe and David. The experience was "exhilarating in a way," he told the *Washington Post*. "I've learned a lot about investment banking and the hot-shot merger and acquisition business."[25] Recalling the traditional party after the public offering of stock, Michael said: "My line there was that it was

24. NGP interview, February 2, 1995; ERP interview, July 1, 2004.
25. Michael went through a series of titles after reaching higher administration. He held the title of president from 1979 to 1984, before becoming vice chairman. In 1986 he again assumed the presidency and became CEO, and Christopher—who had been CEO—assumed the title of vice chairman, which he held until 1993. GAC to author, March 18, 2002; *St. Louis Post-Dispatch*, April 15, 1986. Michael Pulitzer became chairman, president, and CEO of the company following his brother's death in 1993. *St. Louis Post-Dispatch*, March 30, 2001. He is quoted in the *Washington Post*, April 26, 1986.

like being back in law school again, only I was paying everybody's tuition. And if the lawyers flunk, then I get expelled." Yet at the same time, he knew he had Joe's support. "I could criticize him and say, 'Why did he do this and that?' but I also had the luxury of knowing he was there up to the end." After 1986, "it was a lot different and I was making most of the business decisions." It was easier for him to break with the past. "I think [Joe's] opinions were fine for his time," he said, "but we're looking at survival in an electronic age with a lot of competition around." Michael often remarked that "change is inevitable," and after Joe's death he hired consultants who would ask questions about the company's basic assumptions. That "never could have happened" under Joe, Michael said, because the consultant "makes you think about things you probably don't want to think about."

After the dispute ended, Michael remarked, "If Taubman hadn't come along, we would have had to invent him," because his offer "set the market" and forced an agreement on share price. Without "some kind of outside pressure," Michael said, "we never would have agreed." To him, the dispute was "the kind of fight in a family company that's not limited to the newspaper business. I'm philosophical enough to think it comes at some time in the history of all family companies." He recalled being introduced at a wedding to Felix Rohatyn of Lazard Freres. "I don't know whether I should thank you or not," he said to Rohatyn. "You should thank me," Rohatyn replied, adding, "the Quesadas don't, though." Michael knew that the dissidents told Taubman that either Michael or David "would crack," and he would get more than half the shares from one or the other. "Well, we didn't...and he was furious because they did represent that this was going to be a walk in the park." (A story circulated in Pulitzer headquarters that when Peter Quesada visited Taubman to tell him the deal was off, Taubman "ousted him, bodily, out of his office." On hearing that, Joe asked: "By window or by door? And they didn't know.")[26] Peter, the most forceful advocate for his side during the dispute, afterward expressed regret that it became so divisive. "I have no ill feelings and never had," he said in late 1986. "This was a business decision on our part, and I think it was a business and family decision on [Joe's] part.... Those kinds of situations are situations where people say things maybe they wish they hadn't said. That is more true on average for someone who is thirty-two than for someone who is seventy-two." He was willing to make an apology, he said at the time, if his uncle thought one was due.[27]

26. JPIII to author (by telephone), November 9, 1987.
27. *St. Louis Post-Dispatch*, October 5, 1986.

Peter was keenly aware of the strain the fight created on the close ties between his mother and uncle, both past seventy when the dispute ended. Even so, Kate Davis said nearly a decade later, "We never lost our love for each other," despite being "on absolutely opposite sides of the fence." She recalled that "Joe and I had so much fun together for so many years. You know, that didn't last very long, that horror. It was hard for him to forgive me, I imagine, but I think he just hoped to pass some of it over to Pete [her husband] rather than me" because the two men had "totally different personalities." She described General Quesada (who died in 1993) as "a very direct person, and an accomplisher. Whatever he was doing, he would think of a new way to get it done faster or better and then he would do it. He wouldn't think hard about it, and sometimes he was not thoughtful enough about things, but . . . it would usually work because he had this terrific personality to push it on and make it happen." She agreed with the observations of others that when it came to business, Joe was cautious, deliberative, and, among other things, especially cautious about deficit spending. "But it actually ended up being a rather good fault," she said. "He had good consultants. He was a darn good runner of things, in a different style, I think. Pete was more brash. . . . He had a lot of grit, and I think Joe did too, but in an entirely different way. You weren't going to walk over Joe, either. No one ever tried it, I think."

Joe and Kate Davis never discussed the takeover episode after it ended. "Once it was over, that was it," she said. "No dwelling on it." But it did leave some scars. In light of Joe's long-ago challenge to "find a buyer," Kate Davis believed the dispute "was bound to happen" because it was the "only threat I had." She wished a different prospective buyer than Taubman had been found. "He [didn't] know anything about running a newspaper. He was a terrible choice, but he was the choice they came up with, and we were moving on." Besides, she added, she knew the takeover "was never going to happen anyway. I knew darn well they'd never put up with it." She also believed that Joe "was selfish" because he did not think about the rest of the family. "He just didn't think about it. He wasn't being vicious or anything. He was just self-centered. And I wasn't going to let that get in the way of loving him. But I did think he was wrong."

Although Joe received numerous accolades for holding the company together, he was adamant that thwarting the takeover was not "the most significant thing . . . in my career," as was widely proclaimed. His two most widely quoted statements in the wake of the challenge were: "I was not trained by my father to liquidate this company," and "I will not trade my heritage for a pot of gold." Later, he remarked that his real contribution was "the leadership of the company over a long period of time and the preservation of its ideals while at the same time enhancing its value as a business."[28] Even so, the fight may have been the most stressful time of his professional life. As Emily Pulitzer saw it, there was no question that the strain took a toll on him. "On the business side, he didn't give up," she said. "I think a lot of people would have taken the money and run, particularly at his stage in life, during the family fight." Although no one knew for sure, it seemed to her that the strain could have hastened his physical decline; in any case, "he never was the same."

28. JPIII to author (by telephone), November 4, 1987; *New York Times*, April 13, 1986, and *Missouri Press News*, July 20, 1993; JPIII to author (by telephone), November 4, 1987.

Evarts Graham, Jr., managing editor from 1968 to 1979.

George Hall, editorial page editor from 1971 to 1974.

U.S. Senator Thomas F. Eagleton, left, *Post-Dispatch* Washington Bureau chief
Richard Dudman, and U.S. District Judge Thomas J. Sirica, conversing in 1973.
Judge Sirica ordered public disclosure of the White House tape recordings that
led to the resignation of President Richard Nixon in 1974. Eagleton, a Democrat
and longtime friend of Joe's, became a *Post-Dispatch* columnist after leaving the
Senate in 1987.

Joe in 1973, his eighteenth year as *Post-Dispatch* editor and publisher.

Joe speaking before the Foreign Correspondents' Club, Hong Kong, 1976.
Editorial page editor William Woo is to his immediate right; his wife, Emily
Rauh Pulitzer, is to his left. Courtesy of William F. Woo.

Joe and half-brother Michael Edgar Pulitzer in 1980. After becoming associate editor of the *Post-Dispatch* in 1977, Michael gradually assumed the major business leadership role in the company.

David Lipman, managing editor from 1979 to 1982.

The sixty-sixth meeting of the Pulitzer Prize board at Columbia University in 1982. Seated, from left: Hannah H. Gray, president, University of Chicago; Joseph Pulitzer III, editor and publisher, *St. Louis Post-Dispatch,* board chairman; Lee Hills, editorial chairman emeritus, Knight-Ridder Newspapers; Michael I. Sovern, president, Columbia University; Robert C. Christopher, Pulitzer Prize administrator and board secretary. Standing, from left: John Cowles, Jr., president, Cowles Media Company; William J. Raspberry, columnist, *Washington Post;* Osborn Elliot, dean, Columbia University Graduate School of Journalism; Richard H. Leonard, editor and senior vice president, *Milwaukee Journal;* Howard H. Hayes, Jr., editor and publisher, *Riverside Press Enterprise;* Eugene C. Patterson, editor and president, *St. Petersburg Times;* Warren H. Phillips, chairman and chief executive officer, Dow Jones and Company; Thomas Winship, editor, *Boston Globe;* David A. Laventhol, publisher and chief executive officer, *Newsday* and group vice president, Times Mirror Company; William F. McIlwain, editor, *Arkansas Gazette;* Charlotte Saikowski, chief editorial writer, *Christian Science Monitor;* Roger W. Wilkins, senior fellow, Joint Center for Political Studies.

Portrait of Joe by Lucian Freud, grandson of the founder of psychoanalysis. Joe sat for Freud in London in 1990. Emily Pulitzer described the likeness as of "a very tired old man [with] a lot of strength and character."

Joe in 1986, with the 1905 John Singer Sargent portrait of his grandfather, Joseph Pulitzer.

Across forty-three years, Glenn A. Christopher rose from payroll clerk to vice chairman. He and Michael Pulitzer were the dominant company strategists during the "family fight" in 1986.

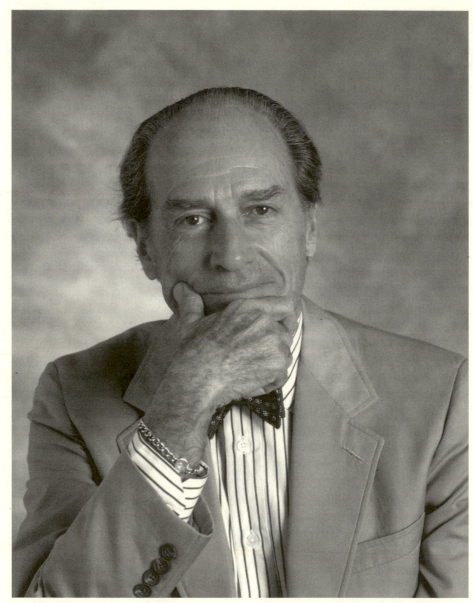

Joe in 1987, at age seventy-four, as company chairman and chief executive officer after appointing William Woo and Nicholas Penniman to succeed him as editor and publisher in 1986.

William F. Woo, editorial page editor from 1974 to 1986; *Post-Dispatch* editor from 1986 to 1996.

Sally Bixby Defty, one of several women Joe added to the newsroom staff who became successful journalists.

Relaxing in Zermatt, Switzerland. From right: Joe, Emily, and Joe's ski instructor, Germann Kronig.

Board of directors, Pulitzer Publishing Company, 1988. From left: Ken J. Elkins, senior vice president, broadcasting operations; Ronald Ridgway, senior vice president, finance; Glenn A. Christopher, board vice chairman; Joseph Pulitzer III, chairman; Nicholas G. Penniman IV, senior vice president, newspaper operations; Michael E. Pulitzer, president and chief executive officer; Peter J. Repetti, legal counsel and senior partner, Fulbright Jaworski and Reavis McGrath, New York; James M. Snowden, Jr., vice president and director, A. G. Edwards and Sons, Inc.; David E. Moore, president and executive editor, Northeast International Business.

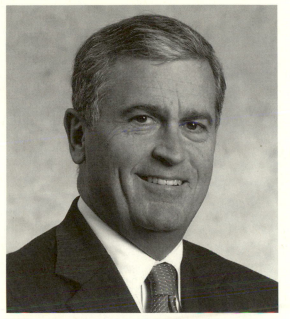

William Bush, a company legal adviser and director.

James V. Maloney, company secretary and director of shareholder relations.

George McCue, arts and urban design critic, edited
the music and art page Joe established in 1956.

Popular *Post-Dispatch* columnist Bill McClellan,
whose work occasionally upset Joe, but he kept
his job.

Peter J. Repetti and Richard A. Palmer of the New York law firm Fulbright Jaworski advised Joe on such key matters as the Pulitzer-Newhouse joint operating arrangement and the "family fight" of 1986.

Robert C. Woodworth became Pulitzer Inc. president and chief executive officer after Michael Pulitzer retired from those positions.

Foster Davis, managing editor from 1992 to 1996. He and editor William Woo clashed.

Joe and Emily, about 1988.

Joe in Italy in 1990 with granddaughters Elkhanah, left, and Bianca.

World-renowned sculptor and artist Richard Serra titled this torqued spiral in weathered steel *Joe*, in homage to Joseph Pulitzer III. It stands in an open area of the Pulitzer Foundation for the Arts in St. Louis.

Eleven

J. P. IV: "There Are No Dynasties"

Joseph Pulitzer IV moved through more than a dozen starting to midlevel positions at the *Post-Dispatch* during the decade before the 1986 shareholder confrontation. His first job was as a general assignment reporter, working nights. He liked the work, but he found his family's living arrangements less than ideal. There was now a second daughter, Bianca, not yet two. Their rented house in St. Louis belonged to a professor who used it in the summers, but taught abroad during the academic year. So the four young Pulitzers became temporary lodgers for their first two summers at J. P. III's residence in Ladue. There are two homes on the property, formerly part of Lone Tree Farm, where J. P. III lived as a child. Joe IV and family lived in a house that had been converted from a stable. His father and stepmother, Emily Rauh Pulitzer, who had been married in 1973, lived a short distance away in a summer house with a pool that Joe and Lulu had built in the late 1940s. Joe IV's work schedule kept him out until 4 or 5 a.m. and he would sleep during the day, which sometimes was difficult with two small children around. The marriage foundered during that time, and he and Lynne divorced in September 1978. Lynne and the children continued to live in St. Louis for a while afterward.

Joe IV worked nights for two-and-a-half years. He had twice moved to daytime shifts, but both times missed the less bureaucratic atmosphere of night work and returned. The uncomplicated chain of command at night suited him better than dealing with the array of editors and managers who worked days. His daytime work consisted of rewriting stories between editions but relatively little reporting. He found the night shift lively, with frequent reporting assignments outside the office. "It was just a lot more fun,"[1] he recalled. "It was a lot less supervision and a lot more responsibility." But at the same time, he confessed, he probably put satisfaction at night ahead of the need to work his way up through the ranks from assistant city editor to assistant managing editor on the day shift: "Career

1. Unless otherwise noted, material in this chapter about Joseph Pulitzer IV comes from the author's interviews with him between October 27, 1994, and May 7, 2001.

advancement in the newsroom was not going to occur unless I stayed on days and moved through this complex bureaucracy."

On both of his short-lived departures to the day-side, the night staff gave him a party in the newsroom with beer and wine—long since forbidden. After his second return, he felt obliged to give them a party. Yet even though it was a companionable group, Joe IV was as subject to criticism as any staff member. After he had been on the job only a few months, Harry Levins, one of his night-side supervisors, was told that some fact errors had been found in one of Joe IV's stories, and reluctantly informed him. Levins knew that Joe IV would take it too seriously: "He gets unbelievably penitent and tends to slip into a melancholy funk, as if he has betrayed his ancestors."[2] On the whole, Levins thought Joe IV was doing well: "He is a good kid—uncomplaining, hard-working, eager to learn, totally silent about The Connection and—to my amazement—is beginning to show more than a touch of brightness in his writing. I suspect that even as I am typing this (at 3:27 a.m.), he is awake in bed, still blushing over his errors of Tuesday. One could have worse traits. Or worse reporters." Joe Whittington, night city editor when Joe IV came to the newsroom, found him to be unpretentious, caring, and thoughtful, and willing to take on any task given him: "He had none of the trappings of wealth."[3]

Others periodically sent complimentary reports, either to the managing editor or to J. P. III himself, who thought it best not to pass these on to his son. He so seldom commented directly to Joe IV on his work that it left a lasting impression when he did. "One of the few times he ever complimented me," Joe IV remembered seventeen years afterward, was when his dad sent a letter to his home—not to the newsroom, presumably to maintain privacy. After a heavy snowstorm hit the area in January 1977, Joe IV produced a feature story about riding with a snowplow driver. "Your snowplow piece was a classic and you deserve cordial congratulations for it," the letter began. "It was a very informative article, well-written, tightly edited and with good quotes and atmosphere. I was pleased to note it ran through all editions." Joe IV recalled that his father liked the story so much that he gave him a two-hundred-dollar cash bonus for it. The letter also said: "Good reports have come in from your superiors recently, which I must treat with some reservations to protect both you and them, but we will talk about this in general terms when we next get together."[4] J. P. III did not talk to his son about his missing work three days later

2. EAG to JP III (quoting Levins), September 30, 1976, JPIII Papers.
3. Telephone interview with Joe M. Whittington, July 24, 2004.
4. JPIII to JPIV, January 13, 1977, JPIII Papers.

because his car broke down. Instead, he asked executive city editor Sally Bixby Defty to handle the matter and dictated a memo for his file with a notation that its content had been given orally to Defty:

> From the grapevine I learned that Joe IV did not report to work last night because his car would not start. Because of my relationship, I would prefer that a reprimand go out from his immediate superior without any reference to me.
>
> He must understand that failure to report, except in some extreme emergency, is a serious offense to his employer, his colleagues, to his professional responsibility and to his self-respect.
>
> Recently, I had the nice occasion to commend Joe on his good work and on the warm approval of two of his superiors. Irresponsibility and youth seem to go hand in hand, I guess.
>
> Thanks, Sally.

Defty made clear to Joe IV that car trouble was "an annoyance only," not a reason to miss work: "Take a cab, lean on a friend for a ride, hitchhike (I've done it twice), but get there."[5]

His father received a commendation from an outside source on one phase of his son's work. Walter C. Ploeser, an acquaintance of J. P. III, wrote him about a series by Joe IV about apparent misuse of public school funds in the city. "You must be very proud to have a son who has the courage and ability to ferret out such public misappropriation," Ploeser wrote. "I am sure there are those who have written because their corns have been stepped on to tell you how badly he has performed. Let me tell you a great majority of this community believe he has performed as a Pulitzer should."[6]

J. P. IV became something of a specialist on the teachers' strike in the 1978–1979 school year, covering it virtually full time for three months. This tired him out, and he complained, not to his father or to anyone with whom he worked, but to one of his godfathers, Perry Rathbone, who had moved from St. Louis to become director of the Boston Museum of Fine Arts. (Julius Polk was the other godfather.) He thought he had made just an "off hand comment that I was really sick of this teacher's strike," but somehow the word traveled, and as soon as the strike was settled, managing editor David Lipman offered Joe IV a job in the paper's state capital bureau in Jefferson City. He took it eagerly and became the second full-time correspondent there. The other man was Terry Ganey, who became a

5. JPIII "Memo to the File," SBD to JPIV, January 17, 1977, JPIII Papers.
6. Walter C. Ploeser to JPIII, May 2, 1978, JPIII Papers.

constructively critical mentor and good friend. When Ganey was detailed to the paper's Washington bureau for six weeks during the summer of 1979, Joe IV ran the state bureau on his own. During that time three of his stories appeared with his byline on the front page of the first edition, which, he thought, may have been a first—and last—for the *Post-Dispatch*. He was cut to two bylines in subsequent editions, because editors did not like the same person getting more than one front-page byline, not to mention three.

He was covering the teachers' strike when a walkout by members of the *Post-Dispatch* pressmen's union halted publication of both the *Post* and *Globe*. The dispute was over management's plan to eliminate several "featherbed" pressmen's jobs by attrition. The paper's ten other craft unions honored the picket lines, but members of the news staffs—most unionized themselves—were unsympathetic. Three strike tabloids were launched to keep St. Louis abreast of local events, but provided no wire service coverage of national and international news. Joe IV readily signed on as a reporter for the *St. Louis News*, established by Charles L. Klotzer, editor of the *St. Louis Journalism Review*, a move not likely to have pleased his father. The strike lasted fifty-four days.

On returning to St. Louis from Jefferson City in April 1979 for a Pulitzer Publishing Company shareholders' meeting, Joe IV was surprised to find that the shareholders were prepared to vote on consolidation of all business operations of the *Post-Dispatch* and *Globe-Democrat* and to revise the profit-sharing arrangement between the Pulitzer and Newhouse companies (see chapter 8). Joe IV had no advance notice of this, and voted against it, joined by cousin Peter W. Quesada, a son of his aunt Kate Davis. He attributed being left out of the loop prior to the meeting as an oversight, not a personal slight, but his negative vote nevertheless surprised the other shareholders and annoyed his father. "My father will try to show me I was wrong,"[7] he told the *St. Louis Journalism Review*. Recalling the episode years later, he said his father "looked at me, . . . obviously upset, and he said 'I will prove you wrong.' And did. . . . I'm still not sure I would change my vote, but financially I understand it a lot better now." He had opposed the changes, he said at the time of the vote, because the business consolidation would mean "the end of any real competition between the *Post* and the *Globe*. I think it will deprive St. Louis of something, something intangible. In other agency cities,[8] I can't think of one paper I would call first-rate. There's something lacking."

7. Clipping from *SJR*, August/September 1979, JPIII Papers. See also Charles Klotzer, "Drastic Changes at the Post-Dispatch," *SJR*, March 1999, 4.
8. There were at the time some twenty-six similar mergers in the country.

He saw his disagreement as a difference of opinion, not as an act of defiance against his father. He told the *Review* that he expected eventually to become publisher and planned to become increasingly involved in management matters. He spoke confidently of the line of succession: "It's going to be my uncle [Michael], then me." There is no written record of succession having been discussed specifically at this point, but it did fit with past practice, and was widely regarded as the likely course of events.

Although there was no invitation for the young man to move into management, Joe IV did not mind. After he had been in Jefferson City a year, he was asked to move to the Washington bureau and was "thrilled" at the opportunity. His beat included the Department of Defense and the Department of the Interior. His tour in Washington was almost two years, from May 1980 to March 1982, including the transition of presidents from Carter to Reagan and the assassination attempt on Reagan in 1981. He was one of three out-of-town reporters selected by lottery to be at the first courtroom appearance of would-be assassin John W. Hinckley, Jr. He remembered his time in Washington as continually interesting. "My mother always told me I would like Washington," he recalled, and this proved true: "It was a very happy time in my life." He earned the respect of his bureau coworkers. "Our senior people . . . all are unstinted in praising his efforts in Washington," managing editor David Lipman reported to J. P. III. "He has turned out to be an intelligent and damn good reporter. His recent efforts demonstrated a real hunger for news and the ability to develop complex and exclusive stories."[9]

He was detached from his Washington responsibilities for six weeks in early 1982 to gather information with photographer Larry Williams for a series on refugees in several African countries to be produced on their return.[10] They went to Chad, the Sudan, Somalia, Djibouti, Ethiopia (illegally, not having visas), and briefly into Cameroon. They finished up in Kenya, where Joe IV interviewed members of the United Nations High Commission for Refugees. On his return to Washington, he interviewed State Department and resettlement agency officials and some resettled Africans. The series won a runner-up award from the Overseas Press Club and favorable notice in some journalism reviews.

On his return to St. Louis, he resumed night work, with a step up in responsibility. He became an overnight city editor, handling copy, and got a seventy-dollar-a-week pay raise— equivalent to his Washington housing allowance. He kept this job for about two years and then moved rapidly

9. DL to JPIII, November 2, 1981, JPIII Papers.
10. The series ran March 21 to 28, 1982, in the *Post-Dispatch.*

through several positions. He spent four weeks in the financial section, three in features, and one each in the sports, wire desk (where he had previous experience), arts, photo, and reference departments. He then did two weeks each on the layout and makeup desks and about six months as news editor.

In the spring of 1984 he spent about eight weeks on the editorial page, with great success in the opinions of William Woo, editor of the page, and James Lawrence, second in command. "In a word, Joe's performance was splendid. Jim awards him an A, and I concur,"[11] Woo wrote J. P. III when the assignment ended and Joe IV was to move to business office assignments on the building's sixth floor. Woo said Joe IV's editorials never required more than light editing, that he participated actively in editorial conferences, and "comported himself professionally" when others disputed his positions. "I was most impressed with the earnestness with which he approached his new duties," he added. "He did not advocate positions inconsistent with *Post-Dispatch* policies; indeed his views were informed by a liberal point of view. I think that bodes well for the paper."

Woo, probably closer than anyone else on the paper to the editor-publisher, felt he could be direct with JP III about his son's future. "It seems to me that Joe needs foremost to establish himself as a serious figure in this institution," he wrote. "My sense of your son is that he wants—and needs—to establish himself in a position of significant responsibility. I think he is ready for this." Woo urged J. P. III to send a definite signal as to the plan for the future of his son, and to tighten the timetable: "My feeling is that the quicker Joe gets set into a position from which he can begin truly building his career, the better it will be for him and for the institution. He is old enough to get started; he is professionally mature enough to handle the responsibility; he is intelligent and thoughtful enough to prosecute whatever new assignment comes to him. The danger, . . . is not the possibility that he may be pushed ahead too quickly, but that he may be held in the wings too long."

Woo knew that Joe IV's casual dress and informal demeanor in his dealings with coworkers—in sharp contrast with his father—had raised some eyebrows and could be an issue in the executive suite. Such things as "punctuality, appearance and overall demeanor" were likely to count for more in the business offices, he observed, "than they do in the more informal environments of the news and editorial departments." Woo said he planned to make these points to Joe IV in a private conversation, which he did,

---

11. WW to JPIII, April 20, 1984, JPIII Papers.

implying that J. P. III might reinforce them. This did not happen, but as to Woo's advice Joe IV later reflected: "I failed to take it seriously enough, I think."

Woo thought that Joe IV needed only a short tour through the business side: "He must, of course, gain a sense of the overall operations of the institution, but so long as he is perceived as the publisher's son, floating from department to department, the more difficult it will be for him to so establish himself." Following his personal inclination to rank news and editorial functions above those of the business office, Woo predicted that the thirty-five-year-old could pick up the essentials of the nonjournalistic departments in a short time: "What he does not learn about these operations in a few weeks, he is unlikely to learn in a year."[12]

Joe IV's business-side mentor took virtually the opposite view. Nicholas G. Penniman, *Post-Dispatch* general manager at the time, respected the younger Pulitzer's intellect and ability, but was not about to send him through an abbreviated crash course on business management. He prescribed an indefinite apprenticeship that ultimately lasted a decade, until Joe IV decided to leave the company. Penniman established a methodical curriculum in business matters. For the balance of 1984, he put Joe IV on "a strict schedule of rotation from department to department with follow-up visits if necessary."[13] The memorandum Penniman wrote to J. P. III at the end of the year made plain that he believed it would take considerably longer than Woo had predicted for J. P. IV to understand business matters. He mentioned no timetable, only that various rough edges would have to be smoothed out.

Joe IV's progress was a standing topic in luncheon conversations between Penniman and J. P. III.[14] Looking back on that time, Penniman confessed, "is very tough stuff for me." On one hand, he knew that J. P. III "took great pride—not openly—but I knew he had some pride in his son's success. He was always very objective about his problems." But on the other hand, Joe IV "was given a more tender treatment than others were," in instances of absenteeism or missing meetings, for example. Penniman

---

12. Joe IV thought Woo's remarks might have influenced his father to offer him the editorship of the Lerner Newspapers, a chain of weeklies serving the Chicago suburbs that Pulitzer Publishing bought for $9.1 million in 1985. "That might have been my dad trying to foreshorten the business cycle," he reflected years afterward. But because he wished to stay at the *Post-Dispatch*, "I was just not prepared to accept that." See also *St. Louis Post-Dispatch*, December 24, 1994.

13. NGP to JPIII, December 18, 1984, JPIII Papers.

14. Interview with Nicholas G. Penniman IV, February 2, 1995, St. Louis.

took responsibility for this lapse: "I didn't sit him down and say, 'Look, you gotta be there. It's time for you to shape up. If you don't want to be there, let me know, but basically, you're supposed to get it done.'" Instead, Penniman said, he saw his role with J. P. IV as "trying to bring him along—not wanting to create any particular controversy. Plus, by nature, he's a very stubborn person. So he was not easy to take to task. There was not the evaluative aspect of his career."

Penniman's memorandums, however, do contain some evaluation. Joe IV spent his first months on the business floor in the office of treasurer Ronald H. Ridgway. He did whatever he was asked, including working "days, nights, weekends and holidays without a word of complaint," Penniman reported. He was largely an observer, much as his father had been many years before. He also attended out-of-town conferences to meet people and learn more about other newspapers. In late summer he asked to be included in management discussions and decisions. Accordingly, he took part in deliberations on the 1985 budget, an advertising boycott by the Home Builders Association, and some demands by the newspaper's carriers. He attended grievance, labor-management, and many other meetings, and was made a member of the Management Economy and Marketing committees. Using the nickname derived from the "J. Pulitzer" byline Joe IV had used as a journalist, Penniman offered a tempered assessment of praise:

> Jay has matured considerably during the year. Initially, he was eager to express his opinions, asked for or not, with practically no regard for his situation at the *Post-Dispatch*. On the other hand, he showed a degree of candor and naïveté that disarmed his coworkers and won their confidence. He is uniformly liked by everyone he comes in contact with. I have yet to hear an unkind or negative remark about Jay's approach and I think most employees welcome the presence of another generation in their midst, particularly a fellow as friendly and engaging as your son.
>
> Jay has a quick mind. He is bright, opinionated and full of perceptive questions. He is fiercely loyal to the *Post-Dispatch*, thus tends to dismiss attitudes and events that somehow contradict his own values. Yet despite this, I think he has learned a need for discretion in that what he says is said by a Pulitzer. It is not easy for Jay, who is an unmitigated egalitarian, to reconcile personal values with the responsibilities he may ultimately face. We have talked about this on occasion and he describes his future role as that of "caretaker," whereupon he may be called to preserve the assets of the family. I think he is excited by the intellectual opportunity but, as yet, fails to comprehend the dimension of the task.

To deal with this, Penniman recommended that Joe IV be put in a production position in charge of the mail room and loading dock. There, he would come in close contact with union issues in two mechanical departments. The job would allow him "to make his own decisions and mistakes" and to show himself and others "that he is capable of managing in a complex, possibly hostile, set of circumstances." The potential hazard was "that Jay might be placed in the position of being 'used.' He may make mistakes; he may say or do something that will haunt him in the years to come." But the reward would be the chance "to apply what he has learned and see the effects of sound, thoughtful strategies applied within the world of everyday management."

Joe IV worked for a year in production, at the end of which Penniman concluded that his maturity had advanced "greatly."[15] In particular, he singled out his work as chair of two production committees as "commendable." But, "that is not to say that everything is perfect. Jay still has a tendency to 'shoot from the hip.' He sometimes forgets that he is a Pulitzer and that employees attach special importance to what he says. Being a gregarious person by nature, it's hard for him to avoid making comments, however venial, in the course of conversation. Also, Jay tends to quickly and openly sympathize with employee gripes before taking time to examine both sides of a question." When shown these comments, J. P. IV said, "Nick was right about those things." Penniman thought it best that he be moved out of production because "the company is expecting a serious confrontation with [its] unions in order to remain competitive." If a strike resulted, he explained, it would be "a serious mistake for Jay to perform any work normally within union jurisdiction. He might be branded as a 'scab' or 'strikebreaker,' which would jeopardize his effectiveness in the future."

Joe IV requested a shift to marketing and became marketing manager of the *Post-Dispatch* in January 1986, just weeks before the family shareholder dispute erupted. He also had expressed interest in moving to the company's Tucson paper, the *Arizona Daily Star*, Penniman reported, "although he realizes it is not a likely possibility." And he wanted to become a member of the company's board of directors. "I kept on my dad about this," Joe IV said, after his father told him in 1984 that he wanted to get him a seat on the board. That never happened, but he was allowed to attend board meetings.

Like his Uncle Michael, Joe IV was candid in explaining his relationship with J. P. III. He knew that his grandfather and father had gotten

15. NGP to JPIII, September 18, 1985, JPIII Papers.

more paternal attention than he as they moved into the company. But any blame, he conceded, was shared. "I wish I'd had more chance to train with my father directly," he said, "but I don't think that was any more his fault than it was mine. I probably didn't give him the respect he deserved, or vice versa. I should have advanced further under his leadership." But, he concluded, "I don't think either one of us wanted to work closely together."

Some family friends and those in the company's top management knew that there was not a close relationship, working or otherwise, between father and son. Longtime employees were aware of the contrast with the first two generations. The first and second J. P.s often clashed, with the father finally changing his will so his namesake son would get only a 10 percent share of *World* and *Post-Dispatch* dividends, against 20 percent for Ralph and 60 percent for Herbert (later amicably adjusted by the sons.)[16] But amazingly, changing the will did not break the familial bond between the founder and J. P. II. This was largely because both understood that as J. P. I grew older and his health declined, he was prone to lash out irrationally—for which he sometimes even would apologize. Almost certainly reacting against his father's harshness, J. P. II assumed the role of encouraging and supportive mentor in dealing with his own son. He frequently asked that "Jody," as he called him, be summoned to his office when important matters were being discussed, and as previously noted, from 1937 on saw that J. P. III got copies of all his father's memorandums.[17] They also spent time together, mostly duck shooting, which both enjoyed.

Joe III and Joe IV each found more congenial company than each other's, although they did occasionally travel, ski, and shoot together. Michael Pulitzer recalled a friend saying to him that "Joe and Lulu wanted to have a baby, or maybe Joe wanted to have an heir . . . and Lulu had trouble conceiving and so forth, and so they finally had the baby and what did they do with him? They put him in the attic with the nurse." While "this is a little bit unkind," Michael said, "there's an awful lot of truth to that." But it was just as true, he added, that—as was the case with Joe and himself—the upbringing of Joe IV reflected the fact "that wealthy families did not have much contact with their children."[18]

Euretta Rathbone, the wife of one of Joe IV's godfathers, said the lack of paternal interest began in the boy's infancy. Lulu was "the biggest carer"

16. "That was adjusted by giving my father [J. P. II] a big salary and bonus. The dividends themselves were not adjusted, but the total compensation was adjusted so that the salary and bonus that he took got him up to them." MEP interview, July 28, 2003.

17. Pfaff, *Joseph Pulitzer II*, 379, 384.

18. MEP interview, June 14, 1995.

when it came to Joe IV, she said, while his father was mostly otherwise occupied. She also saw Lulu as one who put her husband's wishes first. "Lulu protected Joe and didn't sit him down and say 'This is your son, too, and you need to pay more attention to him,'" she explained. "She often would come up to St. Mark's alone to see their son. Joe wouldn't come along."[19] Lulu stayed with the Rathbones, by then living in Boston, on those trips. When told that Joe IV had said of his mother: "My life would have been completely different had she lived," Mrs. Rathbone agreed, with the caveat that she did not think J. P. III was deliberately distant from his son. "I think he wanted to try, but I don't think he had the understanding that Lulu had of his son. And that's what Joe missed—understanding—I think."

Evarts Graham, Jr., who was managing editor when J. P. IV, then nearly thirty, was first working in the newsroom, also observed this. Graham recalled being summoned to the home of J. P. III and second wife Emily and being asked to keep an eye on Joe IV while they were away,

> which was a chore that Pulitzers from time immemorial have pushed off on their senior assistants. . . . So it was not really unthinkable for a Pulitzer to ask a managing editor to keep an eye on his son while he was out of town, but it was unthinkable to me. I had no idea what the hell I was supposed to do. I knew that little Joe was carousing around the Central West End, which is what worried Joe and Emmy—that he might get drunk and end up dishonoring the family name. And I knew that I would never know that he had, or what to do about it if it did come to pass.[20]

Joe IV labeled one family episode "archetypical of the kind of incident that maybe troubled our relationship." In 1990, his father and Emily asked Joe IV, his second wife, Jennifer Williams, and Joe IV's eldest daughters, Elkhanah and Bianca, to be their guests for a week at a country house they had rented in Umbria, Italy. At the end of the week the four guests planned to depart to visit Florence, Sienna, and other sites. But Joe IV wanted to leave alone two days earlier so he could visit a St. Mark's classmate who lived in Italy, and then rejoin his family in Florence. "And this became somehow a gigantic conflict that pitted [my father's] will against mine," he said, "although he never said 'I don't want you to do this, will you please stay?' Emmy said it, Jennifer said it, Elkhanah said it. . . . Well, I went, and it caused a lot of friction." Joe IV "saw absolutely nothing

19. Interview with Mrs. Perry Rathbone, July 17, 1999, Cambridge, Massachusetts.
20. Interview with Evarts A. Graham, Jr., August 20, 1993, St. Louis.

wrong with what I was doing and I made it clear to everybody at the out-set." But Jennifer told him she thought he was "extremely rude, disrespect-ful, bullheaded, stubborn, in that it really upset my dad and Emmy." For them, it was a matter of his failure to recognize his primary responsibility, Emily said, because "it was his time to be with his wife and daughters," and inconsiderate for him to leave Jennifer to supervise the girls.

An important corporate reality also affected the father-son relationship: the company's growth through acquisitions outside of St. Louis during Joe IV's apprenticeship. In itself this meant that the training of the fourth generation would differ from that of the third. In 1985, J. P. III first offered his son an opportunity that may have positioned him for major advance-ment as the company expanded. He tried to get Joe IV to take on the edi-torship of Lerner Newspapers, a chain of small weeklies in the northern Chicago suburbs bought by Pulitzer that year. Joe IV refused: "I just didn't want to go into community journalism. I wasn't interested in that....I turned them down pretty much cold." He had moved over to the business side only the year before and wanted to get more experience there rather than move back into journalism. He got his wish to stay in St. Louis.

He was named vice president for administration in April 1986, just three months after becoming marketing manager. He was one of four execu-tives elevated to vice president as the company reorganized in the wake of the shareholder challenge. In confidential memorandums to J. P. III, Pen-niman gave him generally high marks as a vice president. The job encom-passed marketing, administration services, and quality assurance in the areas of promotion, public affairs, communications, research, buildings and grounds, purchasing, security, and insurance. "There has been a noticeable change in J. P. IV this past year,"[21] Penniman wrote J. P. III in January 1987. "Election as a vice president has given Jay a new sense of responsibility. No longer just the boss's son, he had a chance to perform without direct supervision" and "did a credible job of organizing his department. His chief subordinates neatly mesh and tend not to fall over each other's responsibilities." Penniman also noted that Joe IV was run-ning two miles a week and had lost weight. This undoubtedly pleased his father, who scrupulously kept his own six-foot frame at 162 pounds. Pen-niman reported that Joe IV now showed open loyalty to the company and its top management, "a major milestone." All this, he concluded, "por-tends a good future for your son."

At the end of 1987, Penniman reported further change for the better. Joe IV had shown "vigorous interest in the company's operations outside

21. NGP to JPIII, January 27, 1987, JPIII Papers.

St. Louis" and had made "aggressive inquiry into the affairs of the *Post-Dispatch* beyond matters pertaining to administrative services."[22] The publisher interpreted this as "heightened appreciation for his future in the company and a desire to increase his span of management."

One key area needed work: "sensitivity to the need for confidentiality. The vice president of administration still lacks discrimination in disclosing sensitive business information." That this was "still" a concern reveals that this matter vital to J. P. III had been a standing topic of discussion. Penniman suggested that assigning J. P. IV to labor relations or giving him "direct profit and loss responsibility for a subsidiary operation" should sharpen his focus on the need for confidentiality. Recently hired general manager Thomas M. Tallarico opposed the idea, Joe IV said, and he got neither assignment.

When Tallarico left in 1989 to become publisher of the short-lived *St. Louis Sun*, Joe IV asked to be appointed general manager while having lunch at his father's Pershing Place home.

"Isn't there something else you can do first?" J. P. III asked.

"Yes, but that's the position I've trained for, you know," Joe IV replied. "That's the position that will offer me the best springboard into top management." He thought he was ready for it, but his father put him off. "My dad told me he thought I should have some intermediate steps," Joe IV recalled, "and one of those steps occurred in '92—it took a few years— when I was given responsibility for some of our electronic subsidiaries." These included Post Link, an on-line service to readers and databases; the Wednesday magazine, and Sports Stats, a provider of sports results for media clients. At Joe IV's insistence, but against Penniman's wishes, these were added to his existing *Post-Dispatch* responsibilities, several of which Penniman wanted to reassign. "I said no, I will take those on in addition, but I will not give up my responsibilities at the paper." As soon as he got the additional responsibilities, "he shot off memos to the heads of each of the operations he oversees," the *St. Louis Business Journal* reported. The memos demanded "his approval on all invoices as well as written approval for all capital expenditures," including payroll and hiring and firing, and "a crackdown on spending at the company."[23] Such authority closely matches that of a general manager.

In 1989, the same year he was denied the general managership, he rejected an offer to become news director at WDSU-TV in New Orleans, which the company had just acquired. "I didn't want to do that," he said,

22. NGP to JPIII, December 16, 1987, JPIII Papers.
23. *SLBJ*, March 30–April 5, 1992.

even though journalism still interested him. While his only background in broadcasting consisted of his stint as a radio disk jockey at college, print journalists with editorial credentials such as his commonly move handily into broadcast positions. Both by his own and colleagues' assessments, Joe IV knew how to manage news operations. When he was *Post-Dispatch* overnight city editor, he handled as many as sixty stories a night from wire services and staff writers. "It was a tremendous job, and I enjoyed it. I was fast at the computers, which were in their first generation," he recalled, because he found ways around the machines' slow, balky capabilities.

Joe IV saw his insistence on having wider control at the *Post-Dispatch* as souring what had been a good working relationship with Penniman. In J. P. IV's opinion, while his father considered Penniman to be his stand-in as mentor to his son, "that never really occurred, not to any practical extent. Nick gave me just enough responsibility to think that I was advancing." Yet in fact his responsibilities diminished over the next few years. Post Link and Sports Stats were put under the purview of another vice president in 1993, when the electronic subsidiary was expanded. "So that was disappointing," he reflected. "I never felt I had a chance to do much with it."

Looking back, he said his father's most likely hope for his future was for Pulitzer Publishing to achieve a presence in Chicago that Joe IV could direct. After buying the Lerner weeklies for $9.1 million, the company spent another $40 million to acquire the *Southtown Economist* newspaper and printing properties that became Pulitzer Community Newspapers (PCN). Joe IV was appointed to the PCN board of directors. This subsidiary interested him, especially PCN's strong printing operation, which included contracts with the *New York Times, Christian Science Monitor,* and other newspapers. He rethought his earlier rejection of working in Chicago and told both his father and Penniman that he would like to be put in charge of PCN. However, the job went to Thomas Jackson, another company executive, who had worked in both Tucson and St. Louis. As it turned out, the company's ambitions were not realized, Michael explained: "We thought we could ring Chicago with suburban papers, like the *Suburban Journals* did in St. Louis, but we were not able to do that." The properties were sold in 1992 at a loss.[24]

24. The buyer was the *Chicago Sun-Times*, its main competitor. The selling price was $31.9 million, representing a substantial loss. The daily *Southtown Economist* newspaper and a free-distribution "shopper" also were sold. Another factor, Michael Pulitzer said, was that "the *New York Times* was going to color, so to keep that [printing] contract, we would have had to put in very expensive color printing presses. We had put a lot of money into Chicago, and to put in more just to keep that contract would not

The explanation Joe IV gave for being reduced to a "diminished capacity" was that his father "had Nick [Penniman] and Michael [Pulitzer] on him all the time about not promoting me or promoting me too fast... dogged, dogged resistance.... I know that because I've talked to Nick. He said 'Your dad was always trying to ask for more responsibilities for you.' And I said, 'Well, he wasn't doing it fast enough as far as I was concerned.'"

Michael saw it somewhat differently. The primary reason J. P. III did not advance his son, he said, was that both Michael and Penniman advised him that Joe IV was not willing to sublimate his personal desires and put the needs of the company ahead of his wish to move ahead. His and Penniman's performance evaluation sessions with Joe IV got nowhere, Michael said. "We emphasized to him that he was not a team player. And I guess that he just didn't have any idea of what being a team player means. It's 'My way or the highway,' I guess." He thought Joe IV believed that the top position in the company was his by birthright and admitted that he once believed that himself. During his first years in newspaper work, back in the 1960s, he recalled, he viewed his situation in terms of the cliché about military service: "If you're around long enough and keep your nose clean, you automatically get promoted." In time, he discovered that "business doesn't work that way," and that he would advance only on merit.[25] As much as he wished Joe IV would come to the same conclusion, he concluded that the odds were against it.

There was one other negative development for Joe IV, of which he became aware in the fall of 1990. After undertaking a major revision of his will, scaling it down to bequests of relatively minor size, Joe took his son to lunch to explain what was going to happen. To preserve privacy, most of his estate and art collection—including all his class B company stock with ten times the voting power of the common stock available to the public—would go into a trust. This followed the practice of many wealthy individuals who use trusts rather than wills. Trusts, unlike wills, do not have to be filed in courts and their details are thereby kept from public and press. The *St. Louis Business Journal* noted the irony of J. P. III establishing a secret trust "despite his fortune being made from the sweat of prying reporters."[26]

---

have been a wise thing to do." Annual Report, Pulitzer Publishing Company, 1993, 1994; *St. Louis Post-Dispatch,* December 24, 1994; Pulitzer Publishing Company news release, December 23, 1994; MEP interview.

25. Interviews with MEP, January 19 and June 14, 1995, St. Louis.
26. "Questions Surround Fate of Pulitzer Legacy," *SLBJ,* June 14, 1993.

The most significant feature of his father's estate plan so far as the fourth Joseph Pulitzer was concerned was that his stepmother, Emily Rauh Pulitzer, would inherit and become the voting trustee of his father's 43 percent portion of company stock. She, David Moore, and Michael Pulitzer—the two surviving grandsons of the founder who held 50 percent of the stock between them—thus controlled more than 93 percent of the class B shares.[27] Moore and J. P. IV both said J. P. III offered no explanation for naming his wife rather than his son as trustee of his shares. However, he did tell his son, "There are no dynasties."

Initially, Joe IV said, "I thought that was rather hypocritical of him, because he was the successor to his father, and even built his summer house on his father's land. He trained under his father, got his position from his father...but maybe he's right, there are no dynasties, and maybe it's time for me to do something else." In April 1995, convinced that after nineteen years with the company he almost certainly would not rise to the top, he resigned as vice president for administration to become an independent media consultant. He agreed to become a consultant to Pulitzer Publishing for the next ten years. He was forty-five years old. In August he moved with his second wife, the former Jennifer Williams of St. Louis, and their children Joseph V ("Whistler") and Elinor ("Poppy") to Big Horn, Wyoming. In October 1998, he and Jennifer separated. They were divorced in February 1999. Both remained in the Big Horn area. He was married for the third time in 2001, to Patricia Turner in Casper, Wyoming.

Joseph Pulitzer IV left the company feeling a range of emotions from understanding and acceptance to pain and bitterness. Viewing things logically, he could make sense of the progression of events. The bitterness faded with time. After living for six years in Big Horn and being self-employed as a consultant to several businesses, he was reflective. "I take responsibility for my own actions or inactions," he said, "and over time I've come to realize that there were lots of things I did wrong and it was probably a good decision to leave when I did. It was hard, but I can't really say that I haven't been happier these last six years. It's been a rewarding experience for the most part." He said he was probably at least as well off financially as if he had stayed with the company.

Looking back, he appreciated his stepmother, his Uncle Michael, and Penniman all urging him not to resign in October of 1994, when he first raised the subject. "I'll do whatever is necessary to make this work for the company and me," he told them then. But six months later, sensing that further advancement was unlikely, he notified Michael that he would take

27. *St. Louis Post-Dispatch,* June 9 and August 8, 1993.

early retirement. Michael agreed that Joe IV's advancement had stalled. "That's a sad story," he said shortly before the resignation was announced. "I would say that he just has not shown the leadership or executive ability, up to now, to really go much beyond where he is."

Joe IV also had to deal with the concern Michael had faced: that he was drinking excessively. Michael offered to discuss his own treatment for alcoholism with his nephew. "I tried to keep it light," Michael recalled. "I said: It would be very remarkable if you didn't have some family issues given your mother's family and our family. . . . And he raised up and said 'I'm not an alcoholic!' So that was kind of the end of the conversation." The topic came up between father and son in 1992 because of behavior on his part that Joe IV admitted "really was bad. I ended up with a black eye and I missed an event that is very important every year for the *Post*." His father recommended that he see a counselor about his drinking. Joe IV thought this unnecessary and did not take the advice.

Joe IV retired with what he considered a generous severance package including health insurance for life and the ten-year consultancy agreement. He harbored no ill feeling toward his stepmother after she inherited control of stock that might have gone to him. One reason was that his late mother had known and liked her. He also agreed with his father as to her intelligence and saw her as a humane person who had educated herself about the business and had taken an interest in company issues. "I respect Emmy," he said. "I've tried to work on my relationship with her. I think that part has been a success."

Nor did he fault his Uncle Michael or Nicholas Penniman. "They did their best by their own lights," he said. While Penniman and he had disagreed, he said, "Nick did a hell of a lot for that company." He recalled that Penniman "locked all the mechanical unions and the [Newspaper] Guild into ten-year contracts that saved us tens of millions in operating costs and made us competitive for a decade, and he put in place a number of other improvements. . . . Obviously, Michael is not going to interfere with that. . . . I wouldn't either. You know, you can't upset the apple cart for one personnel case. Michael told me that many times. Michael was very forthright in his advice to me. And we are still friends."

Twelve

Managing Editors

If he had had his way, Joseph Pulitzer III would have served primarily as editor of the *Post-Dispatch* during his tenure as editor and publisher from 1955 to 1986. He kept regular watch on the news operation, working with four successive managing editors. When they met, it usually was just the two of them in his office or over lunch; he seldom entered the newsroom. All four men rose to the managing editorship from within the *Post-Dispatch* news staff. Each had his own ideas about how the position should be handled, and Joe allowed them considerable autonomy—but all knew he had the last word. One who observed the supervisory style of both the second and third J. P.s remembered J. P. II as "a terrier. To convince [him] that he was wrong was very, very difficult, whereas J. P. [III] would listen to reason. But he still didn't let himself get popped off."[1]

It is not surprising that Joe's greatest interest as editor-publisher was the journalistic content of the *Post-Dispatch*. News and editorials were the guts of the enterprise and the source of the paper's distinction. As his father and grandfather had been, Joe was usually an after-the-fact critic of the daily journalistic output. For a number of years "he wanted reports on all the major local stories—how they originated, who suggested them, who wrote them," one of his city editors recalled.[2] His numerous memoran-

1. Telephone interview with EAG, December 1, 1987. The four managing editors were Raymond L. Crowley, Arthur R. Bertelson, Evarts A. Graham, Jr., and David Lipman. All but Crowley, who died in 1981, were interviewed by the author.

2. Joe's memorandums to Crowley, for example, show that he read the range of the paper, including sports and the *Everyday Magazine*, though those less closely than others. He commented most often on national and international affairs, art and culture, editorials, and columnists—especially James Reston and other syndicated writers. JPIII correspondence with RLC, 1955 to 1962, JPIII Papers. Interview with Selwyn Pepper, May 26, 1995. Hereafter, material from interviews will not be cited after the first instance when the source is identified in the text. These include interviews with Arthur R. Bertelson, August 19, 1993; Evarts A. Graham, Jr., December 1, 1987, August 20, 1993, and September 5, 1994; David Lipman, January 11 and February 15, 1995; James Fox, June 16, 1995; Selwyn Pepper and Harry Wilensky, both May 26, 1995, all in St. Louis, and Irving Dilliard, April 24, 1984, and October 7, 1994, in Collinsville, Illinois.

dums covered events worldwide, writing style, page design, personnel matters, competitive pressures, and more. He also paid attention to features and to a lesser extent sports, frequently in terms of their circulation-building appeal.

Joe did not appoint his first managing editor. He inherited Raymond L. Crowley, who had been appointed by his father in 1951. Crowley joined the paper as a copy editor in 1922, and impressed legendary managing editor Oliver Kirby Bovard, described both as a "stuffy, high-hat, supercilious, cold-blooded, know-it-all type of executive" and as the man who "built the reputation of the paper as a hard-hitting, honest paper." Crowley became assistant city editor in 1924 and city editor in 1938. As city editor, Crowley directed three Pulitzer Prize–winning public service campaigns. As managing editor, he assumed Bovard's tough demeanor, following the lead of Bovard's successor, Benjamin H. Reese, the city editor who in 1938 succeeded to the chair Bovard had held since 1910. However, while most Bovard "reprimands were pronounced calmly,"[3] both Crowley and Reese were shouters. This made for a tense newsroom, but Harry Wilensky, Selwyn Pepper, and James Fox, all longtime staff members, believed it had a beneficial effect. "I think the paper was best when it was mean," Wilensky said. He recalled that when reporter Rufus Jarman came in one morning, Crowley—angered because the most vital information had been placed too low in a story—called him over and sat him down. "'The lead is in the third paragraph!'" he said, and "bawled the hell out of him" for doing sloppy work. "He concluded by saying: 'I know you didn't write this story, but the guy who did is off today. A little lecture never hurt anybody.' Bawled him out at the top of his voice. That was typical of Crowley." When Wilensky was sent to Illinois to interview a woman, Crowley called him within an hour of his arrival, demanding the story. "Look, I just got here," Wilensky answered. "She's out in the country." Crowley replied that he was "not interested in the difficulties in the field." Wilensky understood. The office "never cared whether you hired a car or rented a mule," he explained. "They didn't balk about expenses. Invariably they asked, 'What were your instructions? What did you do?' . . . Frequently they were

3. SP interview; Markham, *Bovard,* 63. The three Pulitzer Prizes were awarded in 1947 for coverage of the Centralia, Illinois, mine explosion disaster and efforts that improved mine safety laws in that state; in 1949 for disclosing that fifty-one Illinois editors and publishers were on state payrolls; and in 1951 for exposing widespread corruption in the Internal Revenue Bureau. Wilensky, *Story of the St. Louis Post-Dispatch,* 52; *Editor & Publisher,* April 21, 1951, 90. Bovard resigned in 1938 after disagreeing with J. P. II over Bovard's belief that the *Post-Dispatch* should advocate socialism as the way to cure the ills of the Great Depression. Pfaff, *Joseph Pulitzer II,* 200–218; Markham, *Bovard,* 63.

unreasonable, but they got results."[4] Fox agreed, saying he found Crowley "brutally harsh," but "basically fair" and even cordial when not on duty: "When he had his say, that was the end of the discussion. You could see him the next day and he might greet you affably on the elevator."

Crowley's superior attitude extended to Joe, as had Bovard's. Both thought him poorly equipped to be the paper's editor. Crowley's disdain is evident in memorandums he began filing in the 1950s, after Joe, as associate editor, sometimes overruled Crowley. He simmered over his typewriter when Joe began giving orders that Crowley thought should have come only from J. P. II. One memorandum recorded his annoyance when Joe sided with a reporter and rescinded changes Crowley had made in the reporter's copy. Another disputed Joe's direction to develop two stories Crowley considered worthless. He was insulted when Joe reminded him to do something Crowley considered normal procedure: "I told him that if I didn't do on my own initiative what he had suggested . . . I would quit my job on the *Post-Dispatch*."[5] When he was city editor under Crowley, Evarts Graham, Jr., recalled, he was summoned to Crowley's desk after Crowley had emerged from Joe's office. Having lost his argument against starting a Sunday arts page, he told Graham: "When you become managing editor of this newspaper, don't let that young man destroy it by making it an artists' sheet." Graham said Crowley believed the arts page "would be the entering wedge for the destruction of the *Post-Dispatch* by getting a lot of hoity-toity, artsy-crafty, homosexual probably, material."

While still associate editor, Joe pressed Crowley about the coverage of

---

4. Evarts Graham, Jr., recalled that when he was assistant city editor under Crowley, the *Globe* scooped the *Post* in reporting a grand jury's decision not to indict a police officer suspected of shooting a black man while the man was sitting in an alley eating watermelon. The officer said the man had pulled a knife on him. Crowley, even though racially prejudiced, doubted that, ordered continuous follow-up coverage, and called for a grand jury investigation. The *Globe* gave the story less attention. It happened that the grand jury's foreman, Mildred Shaneen, released the jury's decision nearest to the morning *Globe*'s publication deadline. Both Crowley and Reese thought the release time should have favored the evening *Post-Dispatch* because of its intensive coverage. Characteristically, the two editors sought a staff member to blame, and found her in Mrs. Shaneen's daughter, Marylee, a *Post-Dispatch* society reporter at the time. "So Crowley first bawled the hell out of Marylee for letting this appear first in the *Globe-Democrat*," Graham said. "She didn't have any control over her mother; it was ridiculous." Then managing editor Reese "repeated the bawling out process, only doubled, yelling at the top of his voice, of course reducing her to tears. So this was the way the *Post-Dispatch* operated in those days. . . . There were many more such." However unpleasant, "you got used to them." EAG interview, August 20, 1993.

5. RLC, items labeled "Memorandum," June 18 and 19, 1953, and June 14, 1954, JPIII Papers.

racial prejudice, including rethinking the paper's practice of identifying any black in a news story as a "Negro." He knew Crowley was racially biased.[6] He also understood that Crowley's attitudes reflected the ingrained prejudices of most white St. Louisans of his time. Race relations in St. Louis from Reconstruction to the early 1940s were at most a marginal public issue. For decades, blacks made up about 6 percent of the population, and the attitude of whites, it was said, was "one of patient endurance toward an inferior but necessary creature." Legal separation of the races prevailed, but was somewhat random. Schools, but not libraries, were segregated; blacks could not enter white hotels or restaurants, but could sit where they liked on streetcars although "most whites would rather stand than sit by them." As racial integration emerged as a national issue in the 1940s, J. P. II grew interested in the topic, but gave conflicting messages about where he stood. The editorial page expressed support of racial equality, but not the news columns under Reese and Crowley. J. P. II came close in 1947 to forcing the issue in the news department when he drafted a memorandum to Reese suggesting that a black columnist be hired.[7] But he decided the time was not right and filed the memorandum.

Joe was not as cautious. "He defended liberal causes very substantially," a subsequent managing editor recalled, "and really was much more ahead of the curve than his father had been." However, his father did not interfere when Joe began suggesting that Crowley give readers more information on racial issues. When the *Toledo Blade* published a sixteen-part series in 1951 about race relations in twenty-seven states, Joe asked Crowley to consider printing some of the articles. Crowley vetoed the idea, saying the articles contained nothing new, were "obviously slanted toward the Negro viewpoint," and if published, "could easily lead to a race riot." Joe did not dispute that. He knew that the city was unsuccessful in attempting to desegregate its swimming pools in 1949 after disturbances broke

6. Irving Dilliard, who rose from reporter to editorial page editor during his *Post-Dispatch* career and was regarded by the staff as the paper's leading liberal (and Crowley as its leading conservative), recalled an incident from his reporting days. Dilliard notified Crowley, then assistant city editor, that lightning had killed a man in largely poor, black, East St. Louis, Illinois, while he was standing at a window during a storm. Crowley ruled the death trivial, telling Dilliard that if anything, it might get a sentence in a story about the storm because the victim was a Negro, and "an East St. Louis Negro at that!" Interviews with EAG, June 21, 1995, and ID, April 28, 1984.

7. "How, may I ask, without the rankest hypocrisy can we preach tolerance on the editorial page and then deny a qualified Negro . . . an opportunity to speak for the Negro? Sooner or later we must face this issue. Why not now?" he asked. JPII to BHR, February 5, 1947 (marked "not sent"), JPII files stored at the *Post-Dispatch*. See also Pfaff, *Joseph Pulitzer II*, 232–39; Primm, *Lion of the Valley*, 435–36, 332–36.

out at several pools, and that his father and Crowley had decided against reporting lunch counter sit-ins in St. Louis in the belief that publicity would encourage the protestors and harm downtown businesses.[8]

Racial identifications in news stories troubled him especially. He urged Crowley in 1955 to consider a proposition quoted in a news story: "There is no more dangerous or immoral or absurd idea than the idea of any policy grouping based on color as such. This would mean, in the deepest sense, giving up all human freedom in our time."[9] Crowley did not respond in writing, if at all. He had informed Joe two years earlier that "after considering all the arguments for and against this form of identification, we remain convinced it is necessary for the information of the reader.... It really comes down to a question of whether we ought to identify Negroes as Negroes when they are involved in news stories which don't reflect credit on their race. Our position is that to suppress this information in some stories and emphasize it in others would not constitute an ethical journalistic practice." He also thought it "would be remiss" of the paper not to identify as "Negro" distinguished individuals such as George Washington Carver and Ralph Bunche.[10]

Undeterred, Joe objected to the identification beneath a photograph showing an obviously black boy playing in a chess tournament with two white girls as "Victor Bennett, Negro," telling Crowley that this should not happen again "in similar cases." In 1955, the *Globe-Democrat* discontinued the practice in routine stories such as automobile accidents and "ordinary robberies," winning praise from the city's two black newspapers, the *St. Louis Argus* and the *St. Louis American.* "The *Globe-Democrat* has put into practical application what many other so-called 'liberal' newspapers preach on their editorial pages," the *Argus* commented. Annoyed by this, Joe asked Crowley to bring him examples for discussion from the *Post* and *Globe.*[11]

To reduce the chance of disturbances, the *Post-Dispatch* was careful in handling the issue of school integration. At Joe's suggestion, a story was run in the paper's Sunday magazine rather than the news columns about the voluntary integration of some St. Louis schools and universities. As public schools began to integrate following the 1954 Supreme Court desegregation decision, the *Post-Dispatch* initially placed only short stories

8. EAG interview, August 20, 1993, RLC to JPIII, December 1, 1951, Sam B. Armstrong to JPIII, June 23, 1949, JPIII Papers; EAG interview.

9. JPIII to RLC, April 20, 1955, with partial clipping attached, JPIII Papers.

10. RLC to JPIII, July 15, 1953, JPIII Papers.

11. *St. Louis Post-Dispatch,* August 2, 1955; JPIII to RLC, August 18, 1955, JPIII Papers; *St. Louis Argus,* March 17 and 18, 1955, JPII Papers; JPIII to RLC, March 26, 1955.

on inside pages "pointing out that things are going well in the schools that have been integrated so far." The advertising department also was cautious. Faced with requests that the paper abolish the "Real Estate Available for Colored" classification and thus promote neighborhood integration, advertising manager Fred Rowden pointed out the strong backlash from property owners when black realtors tried to get listings in a white neighborhood: "At the moment . . . this apparently is not the solution to the problem. In fact, we feel that it might further aggravate it."[12]

In 1957, the *Post-Dispatch* adopted a racial identification policy "in order to avoid unfair discrimination in the identification of Negroes in news stories,"[13] ending practices dating from the paper's earliest days. It specified that race was not to be used in minor crime stories "where race is neither essential nor required for clarity." In stories about major crimes, racial incidents, or racial group activities, racial identification was deemed "essential." Well-known blacks were not to be labeled by race, nor were articles to contain the label after the first story about anyone—such as soprano Marian Anderson—whose accomplishments "reflect credit on the Negro race."

Crowley resigned at age sixty-six in 1961 after a decade as managing editor. He was succeeded by Arthur R. Bertelson, fifty-five, whom Crowley recommended. Had the usual practice of promoting the city editor been followed, Evarts A. Graham, Jr., forty-one, would have been appointed. Instead, Graham was promoted to assistant managing editor and had to wait another five years to move up. He was not surprised at being denied the managing editorship. "I displeased [Crowley] in several ways," Graham said, perhaps most of all because the two were at opposite ends of the political spectrum: "There were lots of things that Crowley believed in that I didn't." Crowley knew that Graham was a friend of Irving Dilliard, a dedicated liberal who had moved to the editorial page staff and with whom Crowley frequently clashed. Also, Graham's standing with Crowley had declined "several notches" after Crowley somehow found out that in a personal letter Graham had criticized him for placing on the front page a story about a benefactor of Washington University who had a criminal conviction in his past. Graham would not have publicized the conviction. Joe's early mentor, Marquis W. Childs of the paper's Washington bureau who wrote a nationally syndicated column, also aspired to succeed Crowley. "I think he was very disappointed when I got the job he wanted,"

12. JPIII to JHK Klyman, June 7, 1954, EAG to JPII, December 21, 1954, FFR to Reverend A. Malcolm MacMillan, September 8, 1955, JPIII Papers.
13. Untitled policy, August 6, 1957, JPIII Papers.

Bertelson said. Childs had the consolation of becoming the paper's Washington bureau chief in 1962.[14]

Bertelson had spent most of his twenty years at the *Post-Dispatch* on the copy desk, gaining a reputation as a strict grammarian during stints as makeup editor, picture editor, night editor, and news editor. As Crowley approached retirement age, Bertelson told him, "I want to be managing editor." He also "was writing all kinds of memos, going over the city editor's head, making suggestions about improvements, and I think they impressed Pulitzer," Harry Wilensky recalled. Crowley and Joe worked out the transition to Bertelson in 1960, promoting him to assistant managing that year in order to give him a year as Crowley's second-in-command.[15]

Bertelson was an unpopular choice in the minds of many staff members who wanted Graham instead. Some disliked him because he corrected subordinates "with a bluntness that assured that his instructions would not soon be forgotten." Selwyn Pepper viewed Bertelson's term as "kind of disastrous" because his experience was almost all on the copy desk and "he had very limited experience as a reporter." James K. Lawrence, an editorial writer for many years, viewed Bertelson as "a kind of 1890s thinker. He didn't seem to have the breadth of view necessary for a paper going after major stories, which is what you want." In 1966 Joe indirectly agreed with that assessment in criticizing what he saw as Bertelson's failure to urge Pepper more forcefully to improve local coverage.[16] Citing dates on which certain issues had been discussed, he reminded Bertelson that he had been displeased with the city desk since 1962 for not being "up to the exacting standards of the P. D." He complained that after four years of memorandums and meetings about doing better, the paper was still producing halfhearted initiative and investigative stories that exposed problems but proposed no reforms. He wanted more stories reflecting "energy, resourcefulness, tenacity, inquisitiveness, imagination and skepticism." And he was annoyed that the *Globe* had gained a reputation "as a lively local paper," thereby cutting into the *Post*'s more than fifty thousand

---

14. Childs won the 1970 Pulitzer Prize for distinguished commentary on Vietnam during 1969. ARB interview; Childs obituary, *St. Louis Post-Dispatch,* July 1, 1990; 1970 Archives, Pulitzer Prizes Web site: www.pulitzer.org. The story for which Graham criticized Crowley was about Frank Prince, head of Universal Match Company, who had made a large contribution to the university. Years before, Prince had been convicted of financial wrongdoing. The letter was to John Winship, Graham's Harvard roommate, who had read the story and asked Graham about it. EAG interview.

15. RLC to JPIII, July 27, 1960, JPIII Papers.

16. "Arthur R. Bertelson" (editorial), *St. Louis Post-Dispatch,* July 6, 1996; JKL interview, September 13, 1994, St. Louis; JPIII to ARB, April 22, 1966, marked "Confidential," JPIII Papers.

daily circulation lead by some four thousand copies since 1962. Therefore, he decided, "a change on the city desk was necessary" and appointed Sam Shelton, Jr., city editor and assigned Pepper to be features editor. "I reproach myself and take responsibility for not cutting the Gordian knot sooner," he said.

Bertelson sensed another dissatisfaction: "I do believe that Joe felt that the managing editor should be getting him Pulitzer Prizes. I didn't get him one, so my days were numbered." However, in 1968 he was pushed up—not out—to become the paper's first-ever executive editor, charged with "long range planning and development of news coverage and procedures."[17] Graham, forty-seven, became managing editor. Bertelson appreciated Joe's generosity in creating the job for him, but found the post so undemanding that "I spent most of my time taking days off to play golf and things like that." He also grew disgusted with how the paper under Graham was handling anti-establishment and counterculture issues of the day such as sexual liberation, communal living, marijuana use, and rock music. His efforts "to suggest restraint and utter words of caution" were "either summarily rejected or coldly ignored," he told Joe in 1971. He objected to use of "the clap" for "gonorrhea," "condoms" for "prophylactics," and criticized the church page for being "aimed more at the aberrant than the errant. Is this the place for a discussion of the worship habits of the Gay Liberation Front?" He had "rationalized the situation," he explained, by characterizing himself "as an old square and a relic of a vanishing journalistic era." However,

> when ... such poor judgment is exercised that the *Post-Dispatch* prints a story saying that the Virgin Mary "was knocked up, knocked down with no clues ... impregnated and left alone to suffer," it is time, I think, for me to speak up. It is one thing to be "hip" or "with it." It is another to be tasteless and crude, to present propaganda as news, to abandon standards of objectivity for "relevancy" or to permit the endless flogging of moribund horses by writers who are more advocate than reporter. . . .
>
> There is, of course, much in journalism that should be jettisoned, but, I believe, there is much more worthy of saving. Among those ... are unquestioned honesty, a strong degree of objectivity, a modicum of taste, and a liberal sprinkling of skepticism—in other words, the qualities on which rest the foundation of the great *Post-Dispatch*.[18]

Joe agreed that certain references should have been omitted, especially the quotation about the Virgin Mary. But he was comfortable overall where

17. ARB interview, August 19, 1993; *St. Louis Post-Dispatch*, July 11, 1968.
18. ARB to JPIII, May 5, 1971, JPIII Papers.

Bertelson was not. For example, he found the Associated Press story on homosexual church congregations, used with a local sidebar article, to be "straightforward coverage of a subject on which there seems to be an open season—no longer a taboo on discussion in civilized society of homosexuality. A borderline case, but acceptable by the standards of uncompromising realism."[19]

The executive editor position was a mistake, Graham concluded. He was not told in advance that the position was being created. As soon as he became managing editor, he objected to the job descriptions of the executive and managing editors prepared by Bertelson and approved by Joe. They gave responsibilities to Bertelson that Graham believed were his. "I need to have the authority to hire, to fire, to raise salaries, and do these things," he told Joe. "That's the way I discipline [and] control the staff." He and Bertelson tried for a year to work out separate zones of authority, but their differences in outlook and machinations by subordinates defeated their efforts. If Graham rejected a staff member's request for a raise or a plum assignment, for example, the individual would take his or her case to Bertelson. "I finally convinced [Joe] that this was an impossible system," Graham said, and he "began chipping away" Bertelson's responsibilities until "eventually there wasn't anything left to do." Bertelson retired in 1972 at age sixty-five.

Graham, like Joe, was a Harvard graduate and the son of an important St. Louisan. His father, for whom he was named, was a distinguished physician and head of the surgery department of the Washington University School of Medicine. His mother was a professor of pharmacology at the university, and his brother became a physician. But Graham, not interested in medicine or science, earned his degree in 1941 in the history and literature of Germany. He developed a strong interest in international affairs. He was hired by the *Post-Dispatch* shortly after graduation, and did police and other general assignment reporting for a year until he was drafted and served as an Army intelligence officer in Europe for four years.

Their Harvard connection, similar war experience, and the fact that both regularly attended St. Louis Symphony concerts suggest that Graham had more in common with Joe than any previous managing editor. His other assets were a reputation as a talented writer with a deft touch and his attraction to the *Post-Dispatch* because of its liberal outlook. He had moved through more positions at the paper than had any former managing editor, and his extensive reporting experience included a stint in the Wash-

19. JPIII to ARB, May 19, 1971, JPIII Papers.

ington bureau. When he was offered a job by *Time* magazine in 1948, he rejected it "because I didn't like the place and I didn't want to work for Henry Luce," whom he considered reactionary. Irving Dilliard invited him to join the editorial page in 1949, where he worked for about three years, writing mostly foreign affairs editorials and becoming disenchanted. "Nobody gave a damn what the editorial page was saying," he concluded. "It was a dumb way to waste your life. So I got back to the news department, where the action was." He began at the copy desk, moved up to news editor, then makeup editor, and, in 1956, to city editor.[20]

Compared with his predecessors, Graham was a relaxed administrator with an "approachable, easy-going nature." No one feared calling him "Ev" rather than "Mr. Graham." But that did not mean he was dependably agreeable. For some time, he had believed that the staff was in a rut, mainly because too many were old hands who had passed their peak. He first took his concern to Joe in 1958, saying he thought the paper was "losing some of its energy" because of the advanced age of some of its staff. He said he was pondering resignation.[21] Joe cautioned against "overemphasizing the age problem" and suggested that Graham stop thinking about resigning. He said he was satisfied with his performance "with one reservation" and considered him a prospect for eventual promotion to managing editor. Graham replied that he was "very honored" by that expression of confidence, but disputed Joe's reservation: that he might lack "sufficient determination to uncover crime and corruption." (Although Joe did not say so, this likely related to his ambition to win public service Pulitzer Prizes.) In disputing Joe's reservation, Graham cited examples of recent exposés. When he became managing editor in 1968, he still felt the staff needed more energetic and imaginative individuals "who had some ideas about aspects of newspapers that were not necessarily derived from what the *Post-Dispatch* did in 1902." Joe had no objection to that. As a gesture of confidence in his performance and potential, Joe raised his pay in 1969 to forty thousand dollars a year.[22]

Graham and Joe agreed that the *Post-Dispatch* must give the black civil rights movement generous coverage as the demands for equality increased. They worked harmoniously toward that goal, with Graham's memorandums suggesting that he was somewhat more impatient for change than Joe. Blacks made up 41 percent of the city's population by

20. *St. Louis Post-Dispatch*, January 3, 1962.

21. Graham obituary, *St. Louis Post-Dispatch*, March 8, 1996; EAG to RLC (with copy to JPIII), May 17, 1958, JPIII Papers.

22. JPIII to EAG, June 6, 1969, JPIII Papers.

1970, and "housing segregation" kept most blacks on the north side, where planners had located most public housing.[23] There was racial strife in cities nationwide. For the *Post-Dispatch*, there were challenges at every turn, including doing the obvious: printing more news about blacks. As coverage increased, Joe heard complaints: "Many white readers are turned off by the number of stories devoted to Negro problems," he told Graham, suggesting that they discuss the volume of coverage. Graham did not think they were overdoing it. He had been pondering publication of a city zone edition "concentrating on news of the black community," but the idea proved unfeasible because there were concentrations of both blacks and whites in the city. He was disappointed but not deterred by "infighting in the Negro community for power, prestige and money." He told Joe about a local NAACP official "whose constant complaining about our racial coverage really boils down to a feeling that we don't give him enough publicity." The paper should not be manipulated by such individuals, he believed, but on the bigger issue, he advocated giving racial issues close attention in light of U.S. Civil Rights Commission reports "that there has been virtually no progress toward eliminating racism" throughout the country. "It isn't necessary to accept all the commission's arguments to agree that blacks are still a discriminated-against minority in St. Louis as well as the United States."[24]

Among other places, there was discrimination in the paper's own newsroom, as at many metropolitan newspapers, where blacks typically were employed as janitors or security guards, but not as journalists. John Hicks, from East St. Louis and a new graduate of the University of Illinois journalism school, broke the *Post-Dispatch* newsroom color line in 1949. He was hired as a reporter assigned primarily to cover the black community on the assumption that he would be better received than a white reporter. The managing editors during Hicks's twelve-year tenure were Reese and then Crowley, neither one a nurturer, and both racists. Whites often refused to be interviewed by Hicks and, Harry Wilensky recalled, he ended up doing more weather stories than anything else. He resigned in 1961 to begin a long career in the U.S. Foreign Service.[25]

Finding qualified blacks was difficult, but by 1969 the newsroom employed five—three reporters (one a woman) and two photographers—and expected to get three more. By 1972, this group had formed a caucus

23. Primm, *Lion of the Valley*, 513–14.
24. JPIII to EAG and response, October 12, 1970, JPIII Papers.
25. *St. Louis Post-Dispatch*, February 12, 1980.

to raise awareness of racial issues at the *Post-Dispatch*. The caucus called it an insult to blacks when the *Post-Dispatch* address was changed that year to Twelfth Street, the location of the building's main entrance. It had been Martin Luther King Drive, the location of a side entrance. The change was not reversed, but Graham met with the caucus about that and other issues. "I think we are in for a very difficult time in . . . our relations with our own black employees in general for the next ten or fifteen years," he told Joe. In an effort to increase the pool of qualified black journalists, Pulitzer Publishing Company established an annual four-year scholarship at the University of Missouri with preference given to black high school graduates interested in journalism careers. The paper hired several who earned degrees, and found, Graham reported in 1976, that they were performing as well as other hires and that the scholarship program "produces enormous good will for us among middle class blacks here."[26] There was less good will in the newsroom, according to Harry Wilensky, who said many blacks resented "not getting enough plum jobs. . . . They [didn't] know that it takes ten years to make a city editor and twenty years to make a hell of a good managing editor who knows every run by heart and who knows when and where and what. . . . We had black reporters who would work six months and go on television and complain about the discrimination in the industry."

There also was discontent among women. At the height of the women's liberation movement, Graham said, "the news department was beset with complaints of discrimination against women staff members. There were a whole series of them." One was by Pamela Meyer, a business reporter, whose complaint to the Equal Employment Opportunity Commission almost instantly opened the door for the hiring of women directly into newsroom jobs. Martha Shirk, who became the first woman directly hired to the news desk, attributed her hiring to Meyer's complaint, which eventually was dismissed. "I think the *Post-Dispatch* came very reluctantly to equal opportunity," she said. "It was very much a departure from how hiring was done before." The newsroom had been virtually a male fortress for ninety-seven years when Shirk was hired, with women limited to the society page or feature writing. Indirectly, Joe helped breach the barrier in the 1960s by hiring a few women he knew to do "women's interest" reporting. One of them was Sally Bixby Defty, whom Joe hired for the society

26. EAG to JPIII, September 22, 1969, JPIII Papers. Twelfth Street eventually became North Tucker Boulevard, named after former Mayor Raymond Tucker. EAG to JPIII, November 27, 1972, JPIII Papers; Wilensky, *The Story of the St. Louis Post-Dispatch*, 48; *St. Louis Post-Dispatch*, October 8, 1976.

section in 1964. She was a granddaughter of prominent St. Louis industrialist, banker, and art collector William K. Bixby, whose fortune did not
survive the Depression. She knew St. Louis, having grown up there, and
had lived in England for several years after her marriage to Eric Defty, an
architect. They returned to St. Louis in the late 1950s, where she first ran
an art gallery and then opened a restaurant. She got to know Joe and Lulu
through St. Louis architect William Bernoudy and his wife, Gertrude.[27]

After she tired of running the restaurant, Joe offered Defty the job at
the *Post-Dispatch*. Her writing experience was mostly in preparing menus,
and she thought Joe was going "way out on a limb" in hiring her. But he
was optimistic, telling her that he had admired her grandfather and that
"blood will tell."[28] His hunch proved correct. She learned the job quickly
and was women's editor eighteen months after being hired. Two years
later she asked to move to the "real news staff," worked under Marquis
Childs at the Washington bureau for a summer, and returned to St. Louis
to write local news and features for eight years. In 1976, Graham insisted
that she take the position of executive city editor, for which she felt un-
qualified, but agreed to try. She was unhappy in the job, quit after a year
to resume reporting, and eventually moved to the copy desk. Joe took a
similar chance on Patricia Degener, a trained artist whom he and Lulu
knew socially for years. She was hired to write about design and eventually became an art critic. Joe liked her work so well that he often sent her
to review art shows in New York and other cities. On a few occasions

27. Interview with Martha Shirk, June 1, 1995, St. Louis, and telephone interview,
October 2, 2003. Graham told Shirk she was not a viable candidate when she first
sought a job there even though she had degrees from Swarthmore and the University
of Chicago, and had worked for the *Philadelphia Bulletin* and *Boston Globe* and for a
year on a paper in Durbin, South Africa. About two weeks later—after Meyer had
filed her complaint—he called Shirk in for an interview. "I got the job on the spot,"
she said, "and a series of young women were hired in the months after that." She
spent more than two years at the Washington bureau starting in 1978, and then returned to St. Louis. She eventually married William Woo while he was editor of the
editorial page.
    Even Virginia Irwin, who achieved high praise for being the first American reporter
to reach Berlin after the fall of Germany in 1945, had been hired as a "women's angle"
reporter and feature writer, and was returned to writing the paper's "Martha Carr"
advice column after the war. When she retired in 1963 after working thirty-two years
for the paper, she wrote Joe: "The first 30 years were wonderful; the last two, during
which I have been required to perform the horrible, stultifying task of writing Martha
Carr, are years I would like to forget." Joe replied warmly and commended her for the
"large volume of correspondence" she had built for the Carr feature. Virginia Irwin to
JPIII and reply, September 13, 1963, JPIII Papers. *St. Louis Post-Dispatch*, October 29,
1931; EAG interview, June 21, 1995.
    28. SBD interviews, October 27 and December 12, 1994, St. Louis.

when she thought "somebody was pushing me around" in handling her copy and illustrations, she objected via memorandum to Joe, who came to her defense.[29]

For the most part, Joe appreciated Graham's work, and frequently congratulated him on specific stories or overall performance. But he did not grant him any more leeway than his predecessors. The first thing Joe had him do when he was appointed was to sign an undated letter of resignation, a long-standing Pulitzer practice. "Whew! If you could think of a better way to deflate pride or ego or whatever, I would recommend it," Graham remarked. Even so, he might challenge Joe on a criticism even though unlikely to prevail. When Joe censured him for placing a light feature item at the top of a front page filled with news of international calamity and domestic racial conflict, Graham answered that J. P. II had favored a bright page one item to counter the gloom. "Irrespective of any past practices," Joe replied, "I do not like trivia and inconsequentiality above the fold on page 1 unless the subject is so unusual or remarkable that to place it elsewhere would be inexplicable by any standards of competent news judgment."[30] Joe "was determined to do things differently from his father," Graham said, "so he announced and continued to announce throughout his term that there were no 'J. P. [III] Musts,'" which he believed characterized his father's top-down style of administration. In fact, both father and son said they did not issue "must" commands, but subordinates soon learned to take their suggestions as such. "I knew damn well there were J. P. [III] musts, and even if I disagreed with something I would damn well do it," Graham said. Joe might discard some of his father's practices, he added, "but don't do anything different in the existing system if it was something J. P. [III] happened to like. So it wasn't always so easy."

Joe also kept Graham off balance because "I never knew... which staff members he was seeing, who he was getting his information from. He obviously kept himself very well informed of what was going on in the office. He had several close friends who were staff members on the intellectual side—people who were interested in the arts, for example." He often told Graham which of them had raised certain concerns. For Graham, these behind-the-scenes assessments of his performance "made for uncertainty of position" and "insecurity in the job." He considered this intentional on Joe's part, but understandable. "He knew how to handle news, what news was, what news wasn't, and aside from being a Pulitzer and having this

29. Interview with Patricia Degener, May 13, 1995, St. Louis.
30. JPIII to EAG, June 18, 1963, EAG to JPIII, June 17, 1963, JPIII Papers.

riding-the-tail-of-your-executives habit that all Pulitzers had, there was nothing wrong with him . . . as far as I could see."

One of Joe's newsroom sources, Graham assumed, was Sally Defty, who saw Joe at dinners and parties. Another was William Woo of the editorial page.[31] Graham watched him and Joe become closer, especially after Woo became editor of the page. He felt sure that they were discussing the paper's future, and that Woo, who had worked at the *Kansas City Star* and had done lengthy special assignment pieces at the *Post-Dispatch* before moving to the editorial page, had different ideas than Graham about the handling of news. "I prefer *New York Times* style, . . . and that was what I was given to believe J. P. III wanted too, but I'm not so sure that he really did," he said. He was inclined to think that Woo wanted the paper to shed some of its decorum and become more like "all the newspaper chains in the United States." In any case, he read the friendship between Woo and Joe as "handwriting on the wall" that his term as managing editor was coming to a close.

There were more tangible signs in the pressures throughout Graham's term to make the *Post-Dispatch* both more reader-friendly and cost-effective. Graham described himself as disappointed but ultimately understanding when faced with budgetary restrictions. "That's a good idea, Ev, I wish we could do that," Joe would say to proposals Graham made to improve news coverage, such as hiring more reporters, "but we just can't afford it now." Eventually, once the paper is "back on its feet financially . . . we'll do what the rich papers do." Graham argued over certain constraints with general manager Alex T. Primm, but knew that Primm "was really doing a faithful job as Joe's representative on the money side," to keep spending in check.

At the same time, however, Graham was a firm believer in the tradition of strict separation of the news and business operations, and had been mostly absent from management-economy meetings where representatives from both departments discussed money matters. Finally, Joe pressed him to take part. "The separation of departments which existed for many years was one of the paper's greatest weaknesses," he told Graham in 1973, asking him to meet as often as possible with the management-economy committee. He now considered the teamwork of news and busi-

31. Both Defty and Woo said Joe did not use them as sources. "I was really surprised that Ev Graham imagined that I was sort of an agent of [Joe's], but that's how he must have felt," Woo said of Graham's assertion. Telephone interview with WW, October 2, 2003. Defty said Joe "never, ever" made her feel that she was "being used" and that although she never asked him a question about the paper, "occasionally he would ask a question," though never anything about specific newsroom personnel "or how people related or any of that." Telephone interview with SBD, June 25, 1995.

ness executives "one of the present strengths" of the newspaper, and wanted the managing editor "to be approachable and informed on the business affairs of the company."[32] This was not Graham's style. He was "thunderstruck" when Joe did not object in 1975 to arrangements for the management-economy group to discuss readers' objections to vulgarities in some sports stories and the paper's handling of such topics as abortion and gun control. "In the best interests of myself, my successor, and the editor of the editorial page," he told Joe, "I do not believe the business office should be permitted, much less invited, to discuss the news content of the Post-Dispatch in the managing editor's presence. It is a matter of fundamental principle to me that the managing editor and the editor of the editorial page report directly to you, not to the business office. I believe business office 'guidance' of the news content of the Post-Dispatch would destroy this newspaper." Joe removed that item from the agenda.[33] When the Frank Magid readership survey company proposed a redesign of the paper in 1977 in line with reader preferences, Graham exploded again: "I must oppose as strenuously as I can Magid's thesis that the *Post-Dispatch* should be dedicated to making money and should abandon coverage and analysis of important and significant news. His proposal . . . would result in the installment of a counting house as the only motivation of our being. I would rather kill the *Post-Dispatch* first."[34]

In an important way, Graham initiated modernization. Among the first things he did as managing editor was to make thirty-seven-year-old assistant sports editor David Lipman—in Graham's opinion "one of the few really self-starters on the paper"—his "principal assistant" with the title of news editor. Lipman, knowledgeable about the role of graphics and display in attracting readers, proceeded to update the look of the newspaper. The most significant change was the paper's conversion to computer-based "cold type" photocomposition and offset printing in 1969. The *Post-Dispatch* was the first metropolitan paper in the country to drop the then standard "hot type" letterpress method which used molten lead to cast type and printing forms. The new process was much faster and less labor intensive. It also increased page layout possibilities and sharpened photo reproduction.[35] Lipman served as Graham's "ambassador" to the circulation,

32. JPIII to EAG, June 1, 1973, JPIII Papers.
33. EAG to JPIII and reply, June 2, 1975, William Bransted to EAG, May 27, 1975, JPIII Papers.
34. EAG to JPIII, July 8, 1977, JPIII Papers.
35. It eliminated many jobs in newspapers' mechanical departments and led to stressful union disputes. *St. Louis Post-Dispatch*, July 13, 1975; Katharine Graham, *Personal History*, 515–30.

business, and mechanical departments, where he discussed matters of mutual interest and probably gained the broadest understanding of the entire operation of anyone in the newsroom.

In October 1977, Graham got the signal that he was on his way out. He was detached from his usual duties—with Lipman sitting in for him—to prepare a special edition for the one hundredth anniversary of the founding of the *Post-Dispatch* on December 12, 1978.[36] This varied from earlier transitions between managing editors, when the sitting editor would be sent on a months-long cruise so that his probable successor could have a trial period. Graham thought Lipman likely would be selected. As a backup, he suggested assistant managing editor and former Washington correspondent James C. Millstone.[37] Known for his high standards and thoroughness, Millstone also had a quality that drew staffers to him for guidance and, Graham said, "was much loved by all levels at the *Post-Dispatch*."

Lipman, however, had the edge. The financial pressures at the time and his familiarity with the business and mechanical departments favored his selection. He almost certainly was the best-qualified person in the news department to deal with the interplay of news and business issues, and had no fear in taking them on. Joe appreciated those qualities, commenting on his "untiring efforts and initiative."[38] Graham's *Post-Dispatch* obituary in 1996 attributed the end of his editorship to the rapid pace of change: "Mr. Graham brought to the job a heritage of conservative graphics, lengthy analytical stories and an emphasis on national and international news. But in an era of shortened attention spans, that approach encountered problems. He searched for answers—splashier graphics, feature stories on page one, an infusion of women and blacks in a newsroom that had been largely male and almost totally white. Circulation turned downward as readers here, as elsewhere, abandoned afternoon newspapers. Most of the papers died."[39]

36. The issue was not published until March 25, 1979, because a strike closed the newspaper on December 12, 1978.

37. A passionate civil libertarian, Millstone covered the civil rights struggle in the South in the mid-1960s, including the demonstrations in Selma, Alabama, in 1965 that led to passage of the federal Voting Rights Act. When at the Washington bureau, he covered the U.S. Supreme Court. He died at sixty-two in 1992. *St. Louis Post-Dispatch,* June 26 and 29, 1992.

38. JPIII to DL, June 25, 1976. The previous year, he congratulated Lipman for his "tenacious, persistent, dogged, you name it," contract negotiations with the Associated Press and United Press International that both saved money and improved service. He granted him a ten-thousand-dollar bonus for 1982 as "recognition of exceptional achievement." JPIII to DL, December 12, 1975, December 21, 1981, JPIII Papers.

39. *St. Louis Post-Dispatch,* March 8, 1996.

Of course, Graham had known all this. In 1978 a longtime reader complained about the decline in hard news content by comparing front pages in 1956 and 1978—the latter giving 41 percent of its space to a story about a Rolling Stones concert. "The *Post-Dispatch* of 1956 could not survive in the world of 1978," Graham replied, but "must change as the public changes." He noted that television was now the public's main news source, that newspaper readership was in a "continuing decline," and that people were reading less—especially those under thirty. This favored story choices likely to interest "the greatest number of readers," and making the rock concert "by all odds the most important event that day." His personal view was that this could be carried too far. He would have no interest in being associated with the paper if it were to "err on the side of supplying only the froth," he declared. For his part, Joe was ready to move boldly ahead as Lipman took over. "There should be no taboos, no sacred cows, no untouchable past or current practice, no sacred myth which cannot be examined," he notified the new managing editor.[40]

Lipman was ready to handle the challenges. "You never wanted for a decision from me, whether I was in a decision making position or not," he remarked. Thirty years before he got the job, he told his eighth grade teacher that he wanted to become "managing editor of the *St. Louis Post-Dispatch*." He earned a journalism degree from the University of Missouri in 1953, and worked for three Missouri newspapers,[41] starting in sports and then moving to news. He pestered the *Post-Dispatch* for a job until he was hired as a sportswriter in 1960 and rose to assistant sports editor— although he would have preferred a job in news. In 1968 he leapt at Graham's invitation to become city editor.

In June 1971, Graham appointed Lipman to be his substitute while he traveled to St. Lucia in the Windward Islands. Soon after Graham left, the *New York Times, Washington Post,* and *Boston Globe* began publishing sections of the classified "Pentagon Papers" history of the Vietnam War. This was followed by government action to halt their publication. Joe was away too, cruising in the Aegean Sea. Because neither he nor Graham could be

40. EAG to Mrs. Ronice E. Branding, July 21, 1978, Mrs. Branding to James Fox (*Post-Dispatch* reader's advocate), July 19, 1978, JPIII to GAC, MEP, DL, August 24, 1979, JPIII Papers.

41. All in Missouri: the *Jefferson City Post-Tribune, Springfield Daily News, Springfield News and Press,* and *Kansas City Star,* where he became assistant city editor. He served as an Air Force officer in Europe between 1954 and 1956. He joined a Kansas City advertising agency in 1956, but quit to become a general assignment reporter back in Springfield. "I was not suited for any job in which I had to be nice to people, so I went back to newspapers, where I didn't have to," he said.

reached easily by telephone, Lipman became the chief decision maker. The *Post-Dispatch* entered the fray just as the governmental restraint-of-publication issue was to be argued before the U.S. Supreme Court. It published a story from the Washington bureau on Friday, June 25, reporting that the paper had obtained several hundred pages of the Pentagon Papers. Lipman planned to start publishing them Sunday so they would reach the paper's maximum circulation. When asked by a U.S. attorney on Friday whether more stories were forthcoming, Lipman replied that nothing was planned for the Saturday paper, although the *Post-Dispatch* would not agree not to publish the Pentagon Papers. He said nothing about Sunday. The Justice Department interpreted Lipman's response to mean that the *Post-Dispatch* would hold off pending the court's ruling, and announced that as a fact.

Lipman and other company executives considered that tantamount to saying the paper had accepted a prior restraint. He shifted publication to Saturday. "We took the principal part of the installment for Sunday and put it in Saturday's paper," he explained. "We got part of the run off Sunday before they served us with an injunction and we had to shut down. We then joined the *New York Times* and *Washington Post* before the Supreme Court." Marquis Childs initially favored defying the injunction and continuing to publish the material, but, out-voted, changed his mind.[42] Joe had only intermittent contact with the office during these developments. Afterward, he and Lipman talked by telephone. "He praised me for what I had done," Lipman recalled, and then gave him a "battlefield commission" as assistant managing editor.

Although the two men worked well together, Lipman came to regard Graham as too backward-looking, especially "when he tried to create a bigger gulf between himself and the money men." Lipman was convinced

42. DL interview, January 11, 1995. See also Unger, *The Papers and the Papers*, 188–89; Emery and Emery, *The Press and America*, 5th ed., 598. Childs had two telephone conversations with Joe, in which he argued that the paper could do a "heroic thing" by violating the injunction and continuing publication, as a gesture "for freedom of the press . . . in the *Post-Dispatch* tradition." Joe replied that company lawyers opposed defiance because major legal repercussions could result, such as a shutdown of the paper, a large fine, and criminal prosecution of company executives. All the other senior executives endorsed that position, and Childs shortly told Joe that he had changed his mind. "It might have meant two or three days of national kudos on the free press issue, but I think we might have subsequently paid heavily for it." JPIII quoting Childs to EAG and others, July 15, 1971, JPIII Papers. Washington correspondent Richard Dudman, who, like Childs, thought the paper should defy the injunction, said conjecture at the bureau was that the company feared losing its television license if it were to do so. Telephone interview with RD, September 21, 1994.

that in order to strengthen the *Post-Dispatch*, the time had come to forge alliances previously unheard of, both internally and in the community. The wiser course, he believed, was to get to know business people and take part in some civic activities; he could handle hostility if necessary: "I figured I could out-argue them.... But we were a part of the same factory. We were one seamless production line when it came down to it.... We were the motor in the car, but we needed the rest of the car. I tried to understand their problems, and I made them aware of ours." He thought he and J. P. III made a good team in these conditions. "My personality and Joe's were dramatically different," he said. "I'm a street fighter and he's a sophisticate. I was Patton to his Dwight Eisenhower. I only lacked the pearl-handled pistols.[43] I was a battler."

Throughout his tenure as managing editor, a portion of the staff always resented Lipman because of what they viewed as his coziness with business leaders. They also considered him a poor listener and brusque in dealing with them as subordinates. They described him as "a son of a bitch, or hardheaded or without feeling," he admitted. "I was not necessarily known as a touchy-feely editor." Rather, "I'm what people call a 'hands-on' editor, and a lot of other names as well."[44] As for his ties with business leaders: "Frankly, I think I had a better sense of business" and "was a better businessman than most journalists.... I felt you have to know your enemy. You have to know the fabric and the principal players in the community.... There were a hell of a lot of business stories we wrote because I had the entrée." Even though business leaders might dislike the paper's editorial philosophy, he added, they "knew my face and knew I would at least talk to them and hear their side." In all of this, he said, he had "Joe's full encouragement." Joe Whittington, who as of 2004 had worked twenty-eight years at the *Post-Dispatch* and served as city editor under Lipman, also appreciated him. "City editor's tough," he said, "but when you've got a guy who's as fire-breathing as Dave, that makes it tougher. But at least you know you're going to get news and hard stories."[45]

Rumors circulated among the staff during the early 1980s about the

---

43. U.S. Army General George S. Patton, who wore ivory-handled pistols as sidearms, was a tough-minded subordinate of Supreme Allied Commander Eisenhower during World War II.

44. Quoted in the *St. Louis Jewish Light*, October 8, 1996, 2. While acting managing editor in 1978, he commented to Joe: "Journalists have always been our most old-fashioned class—all too damn busy with the news of the day to put aside mental habits of 25 years before." DL to JPIII, June 29, 1978, JPIII Papers.

45. Telephone interview with Joe M. Whittington, July 24, 2004.

imminent sale of the paper to this or that newspaper chain, Newhouse's being one of them. Lipman dismissed the rumors, and believed the joint operating arrangement with Newhouse strengthened the *Post-Dispatch* even though some agency decisions "had an impact on what I did." News decisions "were always made based on the best editorial judgment that we could make, within the business limits: How much space I could have. How much staff I could hire." There were times, however, when he protested Joe's desire to reduce newsroom costs: "I was not adverse to throwing myself on his floor and kicking and screaming and having a tantrum to get my way."

After Lipman's appointment, Graham was named contributing editor. Graham's concept of the job, he had told Joe, was to be a planning administrator reporting directly to Joe with "cross-departmental" responsibilities. Joe rejected the idea: "Your forte is journalistic." He said that the company already had "considerable talent" in planning, and that Graham's value lay in his "demonstrated congeniality" among journalists rather than administrators, business executives, and technology specialists.[46] Until his retirement in 1985, Graham wrote a column, part of the time from the Washington bureau, where he was assigned, he believed, "to get me out of Dave's way so he could do his thing without having me interfere."

One of the bigger controversies during Lipman's tenure developed in 1986, two months after Joe transferred his titles as editor and publisher to William Woo and Nicholas Penniman respectively. On May 5 the *Post-Dispatch* published the first installment of "The Mayor's Money Machine," a six-part, front-page series. It was based on evidence gathered during an eight-month investigation showing that city contracts had been awarded to contributors to the election campaigns of St. Louis Mayor Vincent C. Schoemehl, Jr. It did not allege criminal behavior. The mayor demanded and got an unedited page one reply on Sunday, May 11, over objections from the three reporters involved,[47] and—via petition—more than fifty staff members. Executive city editor Richard K. Weil, Jr., who directed the series, opposed running the reply on page one. Woo placed two conditions on allowing it: readers would be told it was not a retraction, and the paper could rebut in a separate article any factual assertions it disputed. He also limited its length to "about 2,700 words," to be submitted by Friday noon.

Because Woo had to be away, Lipman was in charge when the reply was submitted late, too long, and, in the view of Lipman and others, substantively in error. Still, they decided to go ahead. "After a lengthy meet-

46. EAG to JPIII and reply, December 18, 1978, JPIII papers.
47. Michael Sorkin, Edward H. Kohn, and Robert Koenig.

ing with the reporters involved and most of our editors, we decided that we had nothing to gain by being picky about it," Lipman said.[48] A non-bylined *Post-Dispatch* rebuttal of the mayor's reply was published with it, the three reporters having refused to write one on grounds that the series spoke for itself. Lipman defended running the reply, both at the time and later. "I have never had a problem with giving space to critics of the *Post-Dispatch*," he said in 1995, pointing out that it was nothing new for the paper to do. Schoemehl's reply rated front page space because of his position, he said, and also because "there were very ample reasons in what is a changing view of the role of the media in the public. I think there was a new public responsibility, public challenge, that we had to meet." Some critics of the decision, he suggested, were unhappy because "we would now indeed not close our doors to discussions with leaders of industry and business any more than we would close our doors to . . . minority groups, poverty groups, or political groups."

A *St. Louis Journalism Review* article by *Post-Dispatch* feature writer Eliot F. Porter, Jr., saw the matter differently. The series was badly handled, he argued, because it was played as a major exposé when its disclosures, while interesting, were relatively commonplace. Perhaps, he suggested, this reflected "the *Post*'s split personality. On one hand was the old *Post*, courageous, but serious-minded and distant, dedicated to progress and reform, but a little fretful, sometimes stimulating but as often irritating, easy to respect, but hard to love. On the other hand is the new *Post*, the cheerful, colorful, pictorial, sometimes frivolous, celebrity-watching celebrator of upward mobility that emerged in the circulation-seeking desperation of the 1970s. It has been a curious and inconvenient marriage."[49]

Lipman, however, did not see how the paper had evolved as either curious or inconvenient. For him, the changes made were in line with new conditions, and did not compromise the paper's central mission of providing hard news content. During his term, he contended, the *Post-Dispatch* became "almost a totally recreated paper from what it was when I became managing editor." While softer fare had its place, he said, "the business we're in is reporting the news, not running features on how to buy better tomatoes." He put more emphasis on local news than on national and international: "I like to think I sold the paper and kept St. Louis informed." The *Post-Dispatch* won prizes during this time, he observed, "except Pulitzers." "We put out a paper that got readers, and that's the business we're in. Yes, we must put out a hell of a news product, but we're not writing it

48. Quoted in Staci Kramer, "The Post vs. the Mayor," *SJR*, June 1986, 13 and passim.
49. Eliot F. Porter, Jr., "Good Material, Poor Presentation—Porter," *SJR*, June 1986, 16.

for our colleagues or our peers—we're writing it for the public." (Reflecting on the Schoemehl incident a decade afterward, Woo said the mayor's reply should have been run inside the paper, not on page one.)[50]

Lipman was managing editor for thirteen years, the last six after Woo became editor. Following Woo's appointment, new lines of authority were slowly established, producing strains similar to those during the executive editor–managing editor combination of Bertelson and Graham. Even though Woo was Lipman's superior within the organizational hierarchy, Lipman preferred to continue reporting to Joe, who did not discourage him. Because *Post-Dispatch* journalism formed the company's core in Joe's mind, he was not able to fully abdicate editorship. His role diminished gradually, however, and Woo was able to hire his own managing editor in 1992. Lipman agreed that year to head newly created "Pulitzer 2000" to assess future opportunities, particularly new technologies, for all Pulitzer properties.[51] He held the job until his retirement at age sixty-five in 1996.

50. *SJR*, July–August 1996, 17.
51. *St. Louis Post-Dispatch*, May 3, 1992.

Thirteen

The Page

At 11 a.m. on Tuesday, October 1, 1957, Joe met in his office with Irving Dilliard and fired him as editor of the editorial page.[1] It was the first time he had fired anyone. "It was terrible," he recalled in 1984. "I was young and it's awful when you have to fire somebody, but it was done as humanely as possible, and he didn't question it."[2] Dilliard did express shock, but as Joe saw it, the dismissal was virtually inevitable: "almost a legacy from my father." About a year before he died in 1955, J. P. II told Joe that he was "going to have a great deal of trouble" with Dilliard, and "don't be afraid to let him go." Joe understood why. Both his father and he wanted the page to be a voice of "independent liberalism," loyal to no hard-and-fast ideology. But as Joe saw it, "Dilliard just got very excessive. He just wouldn't recognize any deviation from the left, and I think my father did recognize it, and was unhappy about [editorial treatment] of certain Supreme Court decisions. It was a very unpleasant era, and I think Dilliard was much too . . . doctrinaire, dogmatic, austere and unbending." Joe knew his father was ready to seek a new editorial page editor at the time of his death.

The trouble with Dilliard started in 1949, almost as soon as he became editor of the page. He succeeded Ralph Coghlan, a brilliant editorialist who developed a severe drinking problem and was retired early by J. P. II. Dilliard, a graduate of the University of Illinois who had done graduate work at Harvard, had been on the editorial page staff for nearly twenty years when he was promoted. He was an expert in constitutional law and history,[3] specializing in civil rights and liberties issues, particularly the

1. JPIII, "Memo for file," October 1, 1957, JPIII Papers.
2. Interview with J. P. III, July 17, 1984, St. Louis. He was forty-four years old when he dismissed Dilliard, and had been editor-publisher for two-and-a-half years. Dilliard had been on the page since 1930, and its editor for seven years. *St. Louis Post-Dispatch*, October 8, 1978.
3. Dilliard's series on the secret Constitutional Convention of 1787, "Building the Constitution," was published in the *Post-Dispatch* in 1937, and reprinted in 1987. Some 850,000 copies in pamphlet form for free distribution were in print as of 2002. When

free expression guarantees of the First Amendment. He saw these as total prohibitions against governmental interference with the expression of ideas, however perilous they might seem to some. J. P. II believed advocating force or violence to overthrow the government crossed the "clear and present danger" line between protected and unprotected speech, the doctrine endorsed by a majority of the U.S. Supreme Court at the time. Dilliard supported the minority "absolutist" view that the First Amendment protects all speech, including threatening and inflammatory language.

Aware of their differing views, Dilliard nevertheless published an editorial in 1949, while J. P. II was away, denouncing as unconstitutional the convictions by a federal district court of eleven Communists under a 1940 law (called "hysterical" in the editorial) forbidding advocacy of force or violence to overthrow the government.[4] J. P. II had no forewarning about the editorial, and was angry when it came out. He was even more upset in 1951, when Dilliard—again without first consulting him—lambasted the six-member Supreme Court majority that upheld the convictions. "Six Men Amend the Constitution,"[5] the headline declared. "Never before has such a restriction been placed on the right to hold opinions and express them in the United States of America," Dilliard wrote. J. P. II, summering at Bar Harbor, ordered him to run an editorial reversing his stand within a week, but Dilliard persuaded him to delay such a major change until they could first confer in person. This took place when J. P. II returned from Bar Harbor at the end of the summer, with Joe present. Dilliard came armed with a stack of law journals containing articles supporting his point of view. Joe said he was impressed by the legal commentary, Dilliard recalled in 1994. "He didn't just come head on at his father. He didn't say 'I'm dead against you' or anything like that." But he did say that the legal scholars were "people the *Post-Dispatch* could respect and be influenced by."[6]

Although J. P. II was still annoyed and believed he was right, he let the editorial stand, but remained distrustful of Dilliard. He got him to promise "in future to take a sterner attitude toward domestic Communism," but Dilliard did not do so. "It was this failure to keep agreements and

---

asked in 1975 which journalists knew the U.S. Supreme Court best, Justice William O. Douglas, who shared Dilliard's First Amendment views, replied: "There is only one. His name is Irving Dilliard." *St. Louis Post-Dispatch,* November 13, 1994; Dilliard obituary, *St. Louis Post-Dispatch,* October 10, 2002.

4. *St. Louis Post-Dispatch,* October 10, 1949. The law was the Alien Registration Act of 1940, known as the Smith Act. The district court's ruling was upheld by the U.S. Supreme Court in *Dennis v. United States,* 341 U.S. 494 (1951). See also Pfaff, *Joseph Pulitzer II,* 301–22.

5. *St. Louis Post-Dispatch,* June 5, 1951.

6. Interview with ID, October 10, 1994, Collinsville, Illinois.

reach clear understandings with [J. P. II and III] that persuaded them both to fire him," Dilliard's successor Robert Lasch concluded.[7] He also suspected that J. P. II "felt there was a question as to whether he or Irving was running the paper," similar to the conflict he had in the 1930s with managing editor Oliver K. Bovard, whose obstinate rejection of the editor-publisher's authority resulted in Bovard's retirement. "Irving was a devout admirer" of Bovard, Lasch said.[8] Joe, aware of this background, was not.

Dilliard's rebelliousness grew out of his cocksure interpretation of the *Post-Dispatch* platform. "Never tolerate injustice" was his favorite clause.[9] He considered his reading of the platform to be pitch-perfect, the same as his reading of the First Amendment, placing him above any other authority, including the paper's owner and editor-publisher. "I yield to no one in my attachment to the principles in our founder's platform," he told J. P. II in 1951. "The conduct of the page should not be and has not been out of any desire to please you as such. It has been to apply the platform.... If [an idea] tests out by the platform, fine. If it does not, then I should say to you why I think it does not."[10] He also, it seemed to J. P. II, arrogantly assumed the *Post-Dispatch* was superior to other newspapers, sometimes criticizing them in editorials for not understanding certain events as well as the *Post-Dispatch* did. "I must ask you to leave it to others to do the lecturing," J. P. II told him, "for after all the P-D is not always THE PERFECT NEWSPAPER, either in its own news columns or on its editorial page."[11]

Dilliard grated on the editor-publisher in other ways. The paper was accused of bias when Illinois Governor Adlai E. Stevenson was being urged to enter the 1952 presidential race against General Dwight Eisenhower, and Dilliard—a good friend of Stevenson's—ran positive articles about Stevenson and negative pieces about Eisenhower well before J. P. II had decided the *Post-Dispatch* would endorse Stevenson.[12] J. P. II became exasperated with Dilliard for the page's unceasing criticism of Communist-hunting Wisconsin Senator Joseph R. McCarthy in the mid-1950s, even

7. Lasch was hired as a *Post-Dispatch* editorial writer in 1950. He was assistant editor of the page when Dilliard stepped down. RL, "For the file," October 12, 1957. Given by RL to author.

8. RL to author, May 18, 1985; Pfaff, *Joseph Pulitzer II*, 195–218.

9. "[T]here would be a great hole in the platform without it. I think it is significant that our founder put it immediately after 'always fight for progress and reform.'" ID to JPII, April 5, 1951, JPII Papers, reel 56, frame 492.

10. ID to JPII, April 5, 1951, JPII Papers, reel 56, frame 492.

11. For example, when Dilliard editorially denounced Roy Cohn, Senator McCarthy's legal adviser, as a draft-dodger, he also criticized the press generally for not doing the same. JPII to ID, December 14, 1954, JPII Papers, reel 55, frame 220.

12. SS to JPIII, January 2, 1957, JPIII Papers; RL, "Memo for the record," October 1, 1957, given by RL to author.

though he also detested McCarthy. After Dilliard ignored his instructions to cut back on the subject, he ordered him not to mention the man for a week. He also thought Dilliard, who spent much time with office visitors and writing letters, did an inadequate job of supervising the editorial page staff, resulting in mistakes. And he was annoyed when Dilliard stopped wearing socks at work—one of several eccentricities—and ordered him to do so.[13]

No one, including Joe and his father, doubted Dilliard's intelligence and dedication. When Coghlan was editor of the page, he wrote this description of him for J. P. II in 1939:

> Dilliard is a native of Illinois and still lives in the small town of Collinsville across the [Mississippi] river. He apparently stems from the same stock that produced Abraham Lincoln, Clark McAdams [a former *Post-Dispatch* editorial page editor], and Elijah Lovejoy. Lovejoy, as you undoubtedly recall, is the editor who suffered martyrdom for his belief in the abolition cause. Dilliard's culture is of a fine homespun variety, lacking worldly sophistication and based on the old principle of plain living and high thinking. He is...of a somewhat religious turn of mind, Protestant, of course. He is a person of exemplary habits. He has been known to go to bibulous parties and take possibly a single drink, but he is more himself when he is working in his garden at home, reading books, attending sessions of the Collinsville library board, of which he is a member, or engaging in college fraternity activities.[14]

Coghlan portrayed him as one who hates "all human injustice" and can be "extremely persistent in his pursuit of objectives, sometimes boringly so." Foreshadowing the difficulties J. P. II and III would have with him, Coghlan observed: "Dilliard tends to give the impression of being a professional liberal, accepting with apparent lack of skepticism all so-called liberal causes. . . . I believe, in general, that Dilliard, for all his fine qualities, is a long time in maturing. There is something still of the ardent school-

---

13. JPII to ID, December 31, 1949, and March 17, 1950; JPII to SS, February 2, 1954; SS to JPII, July 2, 1954, and SS to JPIII, July 5, 1956, and January 2, 1957, in JPIII Papers contain details on Dilliard's difficulties with both editor-publishers. See also Pfaff, *Joseph Pulitzer II*, 301–2. Among Dilliard's other eccentric behaviors, when greeting others, he shook both their hands. He saved paper by reusing correspondence and envelopes he had received. He relaced the shoes of many people he met (including the author), so that the laces did not criss-cross, often telling them "it could change your life" by making them walk straighter. There is no evidence that he tried this on any Pulitzer. Interview with James K. Lawrence, September 13, 1994; *St. Louis Post-Dispatch*, March 25, 2001.

14. RC to JPII, December 9, 1939, JPII Papers, reel 44, frames 5–9.

boy about him. Lovable in itself, but a quality that is not always able to cope with the tough facts in a tough world." He added that Dilliard was "a sort of collector of celebrities" with whom he "carries on an interminable correspondence." One was Harvard law professor and Supreme Court Justice Felix Frankfurter, whose Cambridge home he rented after Frankfurter joined the court in 1939 and Dilliard was in the Nieman Fellows program for professional journalists at Harvard.[15]

James K. Lawrence, an editorial staff member for many years, watched a parade of luminaries stop at the *Post-Dispatch* when in St. Louis. "Most of Dilliard's visitors were pretty high blown people," he recalled.[16] Dilliard often invited Lawrence and other staff members to take senators, Supreme Court justices, and other notables to nearby Lucas Park to eat sandwiches and "shoot the breeze. Even people like [Carl] Sandburg, the poet. Twice we took him over to the park and sat around and looked at pretty girls on a warm day and ate sandwiches. I got to know Adlai Stevenson that way." In addition, Lawrence said, Dilliard knew more people in the community than the rest of the staff combined. Joe did not get involved with the office visitors "unless they were awfully big, and it kind of had to be made into a state affair. I may be wrong, but I don't think he liked [meeting with visitors] very much."

Dilliard could not get enough of meeting people. He was known in Illinois from the governor on down, was a trustee of the University of Illinois, and belonged to numerous organizations. "He was a glad-hander," Lawrence said. "He knew everybody, talked to everybody, and went around making speeches—endless speeches, and some of them were not the world's greatest speeches. He went to my university, Kansas, started out the speech with all the great people in Kansas—including me—and he asked me to read it in advance. I said, 'This thing's going to take an hour; cut out all that crap.' But he wouldn't do it. It wasn't his nature."

Lawrence believed Dilliard's stubbornness damaged his working relationships with both Pulitzers, especially Joe: "The two just didn't quite get along." To Dilliard, Joe was a Harvard boy, interested in art at least as much as he was in the *Post-Dispatch*. Joe "wanted sophistication," Lawrence said, "and he wasn't getting the appearance of it from Dilliard," who might on first impression seem "a country bumpkin." What Joe failed to appreciate, Lawrence suggested, was that if "you dig a little under Dilliard, you find quite a fellow...who knew more about more damn

---

15. Others were historian Charles A. Beard, *Nation* editor Oswald Garrison Villard, and theologian Reinhold Niebuhr.
16. JKL interview.

things than just about anybody I ever ran into." He thought he knew more about the *Post-Dispatch* than Joe, "and he probably did; the journalistic side of it, I'm sure he did." But he was no diplomat. "Well, I've got to go in and educate the young man," Lawrence recalled Dilliard saying of Joe. "Now Joe was a very proud guy all his life... and Dilliard was absolutely wrong to take that attitude. He may have needed educating, but [Dilliard] had to do it in a much subtler way; show a little more respect. After all, Joe owned the newspaper. So they rubbed each other the wrong way, and I think up to the end did, although I think Joe, as he got older and mellower, was probably much more forgiving."

Probably Dilliard's greatest achievement was writing a series of editorials in 1954—strongly supported by J. P. II—opposing U.S. involvement in the war in Indochina that became the Vietnam War. At the time, the *Post-Dispatch* was alone among major newspapers in doing so. "The risks that go with entering this war are limitless," Dilliard wrote. "At their worst they include atomic warfare and the destruction of the civilized world. Those are risks to be run if the United States is attacked or if we are required to go to war to defend allied forces in Europe. But they are not risks to be indulged in to support a discredited [French] colonial regime in the jungles of Indochina. We state it as our profound conviction that the Indochina War is a war to stay out of."[17] That editorial and two others he wrote on the subject were nominated for a Pulitzer Prize, but did not win. Dilliard thought J. P. II had stage-managed him out of the editorial competition shortly before he died by influencing the Pulitzer Prize Advisory Board, which he chaired, to give the cartoon award to *Post-Dispatch* editorial cartoonist Daniel R. Fitzpatrick for an anti-war cartoon based on Dilliard's editorials: "The fact that the cartoon appeared enabled him to recognize the value of the subject matter but at the same time not to give it to me, who had been involved in the [Communist convictions] matter that had never been cleared up for him." Even though board members excused themselves during deliberations on submissions from their own newspapers, Dilliard's rocky relationship with J. P. II could support his theory of what happened.[18]

17. *St. Louis Post-Dispatch*, May 5, 1954. See also Robert W. Tabscott, "Irving Dilliard: Sage of the Midwest," *SJR*, July 1987, 2.

18. ID interview, October 7, 1994; *St. Louis Post-Dispatch*, June 8, 1954. The cartoon "depicted Uncle Sam... pondering whether to wade into a black swamp marked 'French mistakes in Indochina'" with the cutline: "How Would Another Mistake Help?" The 1955 awards for achievements in 1954 were made shortly after J. P. II died. The Advisory Board, now headed by Joe, was told—by whom is not recorded—that

Something else also likely worked against Dilliard's winning. In the spring of 1954, after difficult negotiations with him, J. P. II established a "guidance" or "tutelage" system under which Sam Shelton, his trusted assistant, would oversee Dilliard's work. Shelton, formerly an outstanding reporter, had a reputation for integrity and fairness throughout the *Post-Dispatch*. Shelton and Dilliard were to discuss each day's editorials to be sure they were not out of line with J. P. II's views. While he and Dilliard more often than not found common ground, Dilliard—who it was understood had the final say—sometimes published material Shelton could not approve.[19]

Just five days before J. P. II died in March 1955, he told Joe and Shelton that they should start searching for Dilliard's replacement. However, on succeeding his father, Joe continued the "guidance" for more than two years before deciding to let Dilliard go. In 1957 he asked Lasch, whom his father had hired as an editorial writer in 1950, to take the editorship, with no one watching over him. Joe told Lasch he considered the guidance system "an anomaly" under which the page could not run efficiently. Lasch strongly agreed. With Dilliard in charge, Joe explained, he "had no feeling of security when he was away from the office lest I. D. by some serious error of judgment should embarrass the paper," and this finally forced him to act. Dilliard was gracious in stepping down. In a memorandum to the staff, he said that after much thought, he was "disposed to agree" with Joe's decision to make a change, and praised his successor. He stayed on as an editorial writer until 1960, when he resigned from the *Post-Dispatch*. He lectured and taught for the next fifteen years, retiring in 1975 at seventy-one. He died in 2002 at the age of ninety-seven, the recipient of

---

as a last wish, J. P. II wanted Fitzpatrick's cartoon to win the cartoon prize. The cartoon jury had recommended a different winner, but the advisory board exercised its prerogative to disregard a jury's selection. The prize also recognized the body of Fitzpatrick's work across more than forty years. "P-D Notebook," May 1955, 1. Hohenberg, *The Pulitzer Diaries*, 25 and 315. An editorial by Royce Howes of the *Detroit Free Press* about an unauthorized strike against the Chrysler Corporation won the editorial prize. *www.pulitzer.org*.

19. SS to JP, April 2, 1954, JPIII Papers. Frustrated after three weeks of negotiations on the mechanics, Shelton told J. P. II he was convinced that the plan would fail: "I. D. is so satisfied . . . that he is right and you and I are wrong in my opinion he cannot enter into the plan in the spirit necessary for success," but the publisher wanted to keep trying, and the system began on April 12. SS to JP, April 2, 1954, ID to JPIII, May 25, 1954, JP III Papers.

Shelton started as a *Post-Dispatch* reporter in 1913 and earned wide respect for his integrity in leading some of the paper's most important reform efforts. Shelton obituary, *St. Louis Post-Dispatch*, August 29, 1976.

awards and recognitions dating from his newspaper days to the end of his life.[20]

Dilliard had recommended hiring Lasch, an editorial writer at the *Chicago Sun-Times*, in 1949. After earning a philosophy degree from the University of Nebraska, Lasch spent three years as a Rhodes Scholar at Oxford University. He returned from Britain in 1931 and worked for ten years as a reporter for the *Omaha World Herald*. He won a Nieman Fellowship at Harvard in 1941, and in 1942 joined the *Chicago Sun*, which became the *Sun-Times*. After Lasch expressed "mild interest" in joining the *Post-Dispatch*, Shelton went to Chicago, and "urged me to join the P-D. I first said 'no,' but Sam called and urged that I see J. P. [II] at least. I did, and was hired." Before the interview, he was asked to provide written answers to eight questions, one of which asked his "opinion of the conviction of the Communists in New York." He replied that "the prosecution of the Communists was unwise" and that the Supreme Court should declare the law under which they were convicted unconstitutional: "I do not see how genuine concern for free speech can be squared with the motives and outcome of this trial. Communists do not believe in civil liberties, but in a democracy they should nevertheless be permitted to enjoy them within the limits of the 'clear and present danger' doctrine."[21] His acceptance of the danger doctrine undoubtedly pleased J. P. II.

In offering Lasch the editorship, Joe said he had been impressed by his direction of the page during Dilliard's absences because it showed "maturity, balanced judgment, urbanity and sensitivity to good writing style." He stressed the need for "not going off half-cocked, being liberal but sound, persuasive but not hortatory, commanding respect even though

---

20. SS to JPIII, January 2, 1957, JPIII Papers. Shelton continued in the assignment until his retirement at the end of 1956. Joe then asked Lasch, technically Dilliard's subordinate, to take over. "I was terribly embarrassed, but agreed," he said, because Dilliard was a friend. "[Dilliard and I] were uncomfortable, but managed to go along." He told Joe he would not have taken the editorship if the "guidance" continued. Joe assured him that it would not. RL to JPIII, October 3, 1957; RL "Memo for the record," October 1, 1957, given by RL to author; RL to author, May 18, 1985; ID, "To the staff," October 13, 1957, given by RL to the author. After leaving the *Post-Dispatch*, he was first a lecturer at an American Studies seminar in Salzburg, Austria. He held an endowed professorship in journalism at Princeton University from 1963 to 1973, and then headed the Illinois Department on Aging in 1974–1975, after which he retired. ID obituary, *St. Louis Post-Dispatch*, October 10, 2002. See also *St. Louis Post-Dispatch*, October 8, 1978, and March 25, 2001.

21. RL to author, August 20, 1987, with enclosures: "J. P. II Questions for RL," December 8, 1949, and excerpt from answers to J. P. II questionnaire, December 1949. The last sentence of his answer was: "People who believe in democracy should fight Communists by contesting their control of union movements, political parties and governments, not by suppression."

we might not obtain agreement from all our readers." Lasch noted that "he came back to 'urbanity' several times," and once told him he was preferred over Dilliard because he was "urbane." William Woo saw Lasch as a perfect fit for Joe: a "really towering intellect" with "great moral conviction. He had all of the elements that Joe really liked and wanted in his editors."[22]

Lasch and Joe worked harmoniously from the start. Joe "was determined to keep the paper on a moderate liberal course in accordance with its tradition. But he was also afraid of being too extreme or intolerant of other views," Lasch said. They had "a close relationship, but seldom on a personal level. When he was in St. Louis, he had a habit of calling me for lunch and we walked to the Statler Hotel discussing events of the day and how to handle them editorially. He almost never tried to impose his own views on mine. If we disagreed, which was seldom, we papered over the difference with compromise." That did not happen, however, after President Kennedy's assassination in 1963, Lasch recalled. "When Kennedy was killed, I wrote a hasty piece on the theme that he had never quite fulfilled hopes that he would be a great president. As a passionate admirer of Kennedy,[23] who invited him to the White House several times, J. P. [III] was more displeased than I had ever seen him, and ordered me, in effect, to rewrite the editorial. I crept away and did as bid, but the editorial, of course, was a failure."

That incident aside, Joe clearly saw Lasch as a great asset. Their compatibility rested on a common understanding of how the concept of liberalism meshed with the paper's platform. "However it may be defined," Lasch wrote in 1965,

> liberalism has one essential element and that is being alien to power. Subscribers to the faith do on occasion come into public office, but at the highest levels of decision and administration their influence is bound to be evanescent. Often they cease to be liberals, or the national mood ceases to be receptive to their proposals. . . .

22. RL, "Memo for the record," October 1, 1957; RL to author, and March 18, 1985, and November 5, 1994; Interview with William Woo, who granted ten interviews between October 12, 1994, and June 20, 1995, in St. Louis. These interviews constitute a continuous body of information and reflection about a range of related subjects. Because they contain cross-references to numerous items, they are not cited here or subsequently by specific date, but as "WW interviews."
23. After his election in 1960, Kennedy telephoned Joe to thank the newspaper for its endorsement of his candidacy. Joe told him that he was "glad . . . that he felt our editorials had been helpful." In other memorandums he encouraged strong support of the administration. JPIII to GH, November 20, 1960, June 21 and 22, 1961, JPIII Papers.

Liberalism as a faith, a body of ideas...must content itself by and large with being on the outside looking in. The reigning politician concerns himself with consensus; liberalism, as one of the social vectors whose tension and interplay compose the consensus, cannot hope to dominate the stage for long, and should not try. Its function is one of long-range education and conscience. If after 30 years of struggle the principle of social insurance for medical care has been embodied in the American statutes, the liberal's attention no longer centers on that but on the next frontier of social advance.[24]

Joe frequently complimented Lasch. "You are a hell of a good editor," he said in thanking him for help in preparing a talk for the paper's labor unions. "It is fine to have your strong right arm to lean on." When going out of town, he wrote: "Thank God I can go to New York on trustees business with confidence that the editor of the editorial page will reach judgments which are fair, impartial, measured and sound." He told Lasch that he thought several of his editorials worthy of Pulitzer Prizes, including one opposing U.S. policy in Vietnam that won. "The Containment of Ideas,"[25] published in 1965, received the 1966 editorial prize that also recognized the body of Lasch's work. After his death thirty-three years later, in 1998, the *Post-Dispatch* remarked on his powerful foresight in that editorial: "How—from the vantage point of 1965...could he see so clearly what was invisible to the accumulated wise men of Washington? That the Vietnam War promised a 'profound psychological shock.' That America had neither the right nor power to interfere with other people's self-determination. That the natural aspirations of Eastern Europe would melt the Iron Curtain. That the idea of Communism would be contained only by the better idea of freedom."[26]

One of Joe's concerns in the page's handling of Vietnam was that it should convey its anti-war position unemotionally. After reading two editorials that struck him as having a "sarcastic, perhaps a bit sneering, condescending tone," he cautioned Lasch against "any display of emotion which might be misread as disgruntlement, disgust or exasperation in view of the controversial, immensely complicated situation." He advised Lasch to "play it cool," and "present the logic of our arguments with icy

---

24. Robert Lasch, "Liberalism and the American Mission," *St. Louis Post-Dispatch* (special supplement: "Challenges and Choices: The State of Man In An Anxious Era"), September 26, 1965, 32. Jacques Barzun, Gunnar Myrdal, J. William Fulbright, and R. Buckminster Fuller were among the other contributors.

25. JPIII to RL, May 24, 1963, May 28, 1970, JPIII Papers; JPIII to RL, October 26, 1961, January 9, 1963; January 7, 1967; *St. Louis Post-Dispatch*, January 17, 1965.

26. *St. Louis Post-Dispatch*, April 8, 1998.

detachment." Lasch agreed: "You have a sharp ear for nuance. If I sounded disgruntled, disgusted and exasperated it is only because I am disgruntled, disgusted and exasperated. But you are right as usual. From now on, 'cool, man, cool,' it is."

Even so, the anti-war editorials did not sit well with some. President Johnson sent Secretary of State Dean Rusk to St. Louis to turn the editorial page around, but he got nowhere and the White House canceled its subscription to the *Post-Dispatch*.[27] Lasch had a low regard for Johnson. After hearing the president speak at a Washington dinner in 1965, he gave Joe his analysis: "Altogether I got the impression of a tense man, highly strung, harboring a lot of resentments and some sense of insecurity; a man of action rather than reflection, whose compulsive verbosity substitutes for thought. He seems to have little regard for foreign policy except as it shapes the forces that will have a bearing on the next election. . . . He was clearly putting on a performance in order to convey the desired picture of himself as strong, decisive and farsighted. He was not in the slightest interested in the views of anybody else, or in two-way conversation." While he agreed as to Johnson's foreign policy record, Joe cautioned Lasch not to be "down on Johnson" when "at home he is compiling an impressive record which, if it were not overshadowed by the ominous events in Vietnam, would stand out as a major achievement." He mentioned aid to education, the Medicare and domestic Peace Corps programs, and his civil rights record as examples.[28]

Predictably, the paper's anti-war position angered some subscribers. One carrier reported that fourteen who canceled said its Vietnam editorials proved the paper was pro-Communist. The charge had been heard before, particularly during the McCarthy era. Joe was not concerned: "We would be a bland, innocuous and dull newspaper if we tried to compromise and accommodate such opposition. The paper has not yielded to pressure during other periods of tension and I have no intention of

---

27. Lasch obituary, *St. Louis Post-Dispatch*, April 8, 1998; undated clipping with RL to JPIII, February 16, 1968, JPIII Papers.

28. RL to JPIII, May 21, 1965, JPIII Papers. The following year, he dissuaded Lasch from shifting editorial support from some Democratic congressional candidates to some anti-war Republicans contrary to Lasch's theory that "Johnson responds only to political leverage." Lasch thought endorsing those against the war "would deny L. B. J. the claim of all-out support for his Asian policy and could influence him to moderate it." Joe's position was "that the P. D. should avoid the appearance of turning its back on candidates who had supported the liberal programs we have endorsed." He also doubted that the election of "selected Republican candidates (doves) . . . could restrain or deter Johnson from his war buildup." JPIII to RL, July 26, 1965, JPIII, "Memo for file," July 15, 1966, JPIII Papers.

soft-pedaling our opinions merely for the sake of making circulation easier to achieve." He called it "a compliment" to be criticized because "it indicates that the paper's vigor and independence are recognized." Lasch felt the same, but admitted that it was not easy to go against the views of the *New York Times* and other highly respected newspapers; it was only later that these papers became disillusioned with American policy. At the same time, others recognized the paper's foreign policy commentary as significant. Historian Henry Steele Commager proposed in 1968 that a book of *Post-Dispatch* foreign policy editorials be published, but Lasch said he could not compile it when asked by a publisher.[29]

Work done out of the paper's Washington bureau bolstered its editorial policy on Southeast Asia. Richard Dudman, who joined the bureau in 1954 and became its chief correspondent in 1969, was a specialist on the region. He had handled assignments in Central and South American hot spots before going to Vietnam in the early 1960s, when only American "advisers" were serving in Vietnam. He made another trip in 1970, and with two other journalists—one of whom spoke Vietnamese—traveled on May 7 from Saigon into neighboring Cambodia, where they were captured by guerrilla fighters and held for forty days. To no avail, "we three captives made no secret of our personal belief that the U.S. intervention in Vietnam was a mistake," Dudman recalled. The reporters had planned to cover the "incursion" into Cambodia ordered by President Richard Nixon to dismantle staging centers from which Communist soldiers were entering South Vietnam. A Viet Cong general, Bay Cao, arranged their release after satisfying higher-ups that they were international journalists, not Central Intelligence Agency spies. While detained, Dudman wrote managing editor Evarts Graham: "I am anxious to begin writing for publication as soon as possible about this accidental opportunity to tell about the other side of the war that Nixon is now widening to include all Indochina." In

---

29. JPIII to RL and EAG, November 19, 1970. Lasch thought it was wrong to blame editorial policy for circulation declines. He noted that only three in a survey of twenty-three "stops" gave editorial policy as the reason. Most said they did not have time to read the paper, reflecting the general decline in reading. With tongue in cheek, he observed: "It just goes to demonstrate Lasch's law, developed from long experience, which is: All circulation gains are attributable to incredible sales effort of the circulation department, and all circulation losses are attributable to the editorial page or misguided news policies." SP to JFH, October 27, 1965; RL to JPIII, November 19, 1969, and March 11, 1970. General manager Alexander T. Primm tied circulation losses of the period to circulation price increases, difficult economic times, social unrest, and greater competition from television. ATP to JPIII, May 28, 1970, JPIII Papers; *Arizona Daily Star,* September 10, 1981. Joe liked the book idea, believing "the book would have promotional value, handled with discretion and restraint." Harper and Row was the interested publisher. JPIII to RL and response, January 11 and 23, 1968, JPIII Papers.

a dispatch, he reported that the incursion was a failure because it only increased resistance and convinced Cambodians that the United States was "waging unprovoked colonialist war" and "as a would-be successor to the French, trying to turn back the clock of history in the face of a swelling spirit of Asia for Asians." (In 1994, twenty-four years later, Dudman returned to Vietnam for a reunion with General Cao, who told him: "You were lucky you met me.")[30]

When the war ended in 1975, after Lasch had retired, he wrote Joe: "In retrospect we were taken in by Johnson's and Nixon's assorted peace offensives, but then so was everybody else." He complimented Joe for the "independence of mind" that sustained the long campaign against the war, especially "in the face of the overwhelming public opinion that was initially against us."[31]

Joe hired Bill Mauldin on Lasch's strong recommendation when veteran editorial cartoonist Daniel Fitzpatrick retired in 1958. Mauldin had won fame and a 1945 Pulitzer Prize for his World War II cartoons featuring infantrymen Willie and Joe in the military newspaper *Stars and Stripes*. He won a second Pulitzer in 1959 for a *Post-Dispatch* cartoon. It depicted two prisoners laboring in Siberia. "I won the Nobel Prize for Literature," one said to the other. "What was your crime?"[32] "The *Post-Dispatch* has a strong tradition of independence for its staff," Mauldin said when he was hired. "I have a reputation for raising hell in cartoons, and there are not many newspapers that will stand for that." His contract had a provision that he would not be required to draw cartoons opposed to his conscientious convictions. However, his association with the paper ended when he and Joe could not agree on contract renewal terms in 1962, and he moved to the *Chicago Sun-Times*. Joe had offered Mauldin a twenty-three-thousand-dollar salary and 70 percent of the proceeds from syndication of his work, but Mauldin wanted twenty-five thousand and all of the syndication income. His work was published in 141 papers at the time. "The P-D has been very good to me, and it will be a real wrench to leave," Mauldin said when he quit. "I'm not going out of here mad." Joe called his departure "a source of real regret."[33] His successor was Tom Engelhardt, who held the

30. Dudman, *Forty Days with the Enemy*, 60–70; *St. Louis Post-Dispatch*, April 10, 1994. Elizabeth Pond of the *Christian Science Monitor* and Michael Morrow of Dispatch News Service International were the other captives.

31. RL to JPIII, May 6, 1975, JPIII Papers.

32. *St. Louis Post-Dispatch*, October 30, 1958.

33. A year later, Lasch told Joe that "Mauldin misses the stimulation and criticism" of the *Post-Dispatch*, and might eventually want to return. But nothing came of it when he approached Lasch in 1969 about returning because the *Star-Times* was becoming "too much of a soul-less corporation," and he regretted leaving the *Post-Dispatch* over

post for thirty-five years. Joe was dissatisfied at first with Engelhardt's drawing style, especially his caricatures. In one, he thought President Kennedy "appeared to have rouge on his lips and a wooden, unlifelike appearance." Lasch recommended that Engelhardt take art classes at Washington University. Within months, Joe found his work "markedly improved," because "subjects are treated with more authority, are more three-dimensional, and show a better grasp of perspective and form."[34]

Lasch retired at age sixty-four in 1971, twenty-one years after joining the *Post-Dispatch*, and two years before the last American soldiers left Vietnam. He had been editor of the page for more than thirteen years—longer than any predecessor but George Johns, who worked under the founding J. P.[35] He thanked Joe for giving him "a degree of freedom and confidence that any editor would be grateful for" and said he could not imagine a better way to have spent the last two decades than on the paper's editorial staff.

George H. Hall succeeded Lasch. Hall was a native St. Louisan who had known Joe since 1934, when they met at Kate Davis's debut party. He joined the *Post-Dispatch* as a reporter in 1942 and served in the Washington bureau from 1945 until Joe made him assistant editorial page editor in 1959. Having specialized in national politics and international affairs as a Washington correspondent,[36] he was versed in many issues, but never had written an editorial. Hall told Joe he didn't know if he could do it, but would try. He quickly succeeded, enjoyed the job, and worked comfortably with Joe. "I understood him pretty well," Hall said. "I knew his background as well as some personal points. I understood how he felt about things . . . and it just happened to coincide with the way I did. So we never had a problem." Although they never discussed it, Hall shared Joe's dislike of Dilliard's "super moralist, didactic" style of editorship. He favored talking with those with whom the page disagreed in hopes of changing their minds rather than "just sitting there and praising or blaming people." In picking Hall as Lasch's successor, Joe cited his "good judgment, calm

money. *Time,* April 28, 1958, 66; *Newsweek,* June 18, 1962, 82; JPIII to Mauldin, June 1, 1962, Mauldin to CJH, April 25, 1962, RL to JPIII, May 15, 1963, and September 10, 1969, JPIII Papers.

34. *St. Louis Post-Dispatch,* November 25, 1997, JPIII to RL, September 23, 1963, and May 14, 1964, JPIII Papers.

35. Johns served for thirty-one years, 1897 to 1928, under J. P. I and II. RL to JPIII, April 22, 1970, JPIII Papers.

36. Had illness not intervened, Hall might have become the paper's primary Asian expert. He was assigned by Joe's father to investigate colonial overthrows there after World War II. He contracted a nearly fatal case of hepatitis, wrote one article, and never returned. Interview with George H. Hall, August 25, 1994, St. Louis.

temperament, reasonableness and cooperative attitude in accepting suggestions or instructions."[37]

However respectful of Joe, Hall never felt he had to check every decision with him, and took a few chances at overstepping. One was when there were calls for the replacement of Missouri Senator Thomas F. Eagleton as the Democratic vice presidential candidate in 1972 because Eagleton had received electroshock treatments for depression. Without consulting Joe, Hall ran an angry editorial, "Mr. Eagleton Should Stay," critical of those who wanted him off the ticket. However, Joe liked the piece, calling it "exactly to the point, and including a phrase I like—'medieval attitudes about nervous ailments.'"[38] Hall also thought Joe might object to his strong endorsement of legalized abortion in several editorials following the Supreme Court's 1973 *Roe v. Wade* decision, which outraged the Catholic community and many others in St. Louis, but Joe never mentioned it: "He left it all to me, so he must have agreed. I felt so strongly about this that if he wanted me to stop it, I would have left."

Hall directed the page for three years. He was sixty-two when he was named editor, and chose to retire in 1974, at sixty-five. His replacement was at hand. William F. Woo, whose Chinese father and American mother were divorced when he was young, had a degree in English literature from the University of Kansas. His interest in classical literature was nurtured by his mother, who took him to meetings of the Great Books Foundation in Kansas City, which she headed. Aristotelian ethics was the topic at the first session he attended, at age twelve. He was hired by the *Post-Dispatch* in 1959 at age twenty-five by Harry Wilensky, editor of the paper's *Everyday Magazine*. Wilensky became interested in him after asking a friend at the *Kansas City Star* to have a *Star* reporter do a story for the *Post-Dispatch* when St. Louis Symphony conductor Vladimir Golschmann guest-conducted in Kansas City. The friend selected Woo, a *Star* reporter since 1957. His story "just sparkled," Wilensky recalled. "He wrote about Golschmann losing his pants. They didn't come in on the plane, and he borrowed a pair of pants and conducted." Wilensky had to persuade cost-conscious managing editor Arthur Bertelson to let him hire Woo. "What in the name of God has he got that so electrifies you?" Bertelson asked. "He's got a

---

37. Interview with George Hall, August 25, 1994, St. Louis; *St. Louis Post-Dispatch*, May 2, 1971. Many opponents of *Post-Dispatch* editorial policy were from old St. Louis families, whom he knew. "Most of my friends were on the other side, and most of them hated the paper," he said, but they heard him out. JPIII, "Memo for file," July 31, 1968, identifying Hall as the likely successor to Lasch, JPIII Papers.

38. JPIII to GH, August 1, 1972, JPIII Papers. Eagleton was replaced on the ticket by R. Sargent Shriver.

quality of writing that we at this paper badly need," Wilensky replied. He thought Woo would bring a "sprightly, energetic" style to the magazine, whose feature stories he considered "too stiff, too dull, and too long."[39]

Joe began watching Woo's work when a series he wrote about computers displayed his reportorial and writing abilities. In 1966, Woo followed Dilliard and Lasch in winning a Nieman fellowship at Harvard. While there, he got word that Joe wanted him to go to the Soviet Union to report on the fiftieth anniversary of the Russian Revolution. The result was a thirteen-part series and a sixty-four-page Sunday magazine article based on research guided by a Harvard expert and followed by two months in the Soviet Union. When he returned, he became a largely self-directed correspondent assigned to do in-depth series that took several months to develop. He knew this was Joe's idea, appreciated the assignment, and wanted thereafter to produce journalism that "would not disappoint him." Woo conceived of his articles "essentially as Harvard term papers turned into journalism: unemployment in the black community, America's housing problems, explicit sex in the cinema ([Joe] may actually have suggested that one), and campus rebellion," among others. He did a series about privacy in 1968. Woo was confident that even though he could find professors knowledgeable on that subject at nearby Southern Illinois and St. Louis Universities, he could find privacy experts at Berkeley or Harvard, and that the editor-publisher "would prefer to have his *Post-Dispatch* represented" by the bigger-name universities as a way of enhancing the paper's prestige. His series all began with information-gathering tours to centers of thought—among them universities in California, Chicago, Boston, and New York and governmental offices in Washington. "It was on the strength of these things that I think Bob Lasch invited me to join the editorial page," he said. "And I loved it."[40]

He first worked on the page in 1969, while another writer was away. Lasch told Joe he liked Woo, mentioning his "zest and judgment" in producing editorials on his own, and remarking that all editorial page staff members "are pleased with his work." Lasch said he wished Woo's assignment could become permanent, but hadn't mentioned the possibility to him.[41] Within a year, he was transferred from news to replace a writer who retired. Almost simultaneously, he was offered positions by *Newsweek*, to be a correspondent in either Hong Kong or Russia, and by the *New York Times* to be a civil rights correspondent in Atlanta. "I wanted to make a

39. HW interview, May 26, 1995.

40. Biographical material is from the *St. Louis Post-Dispatch*, July 6 and 7, 1996, and WW interviews.

41. RL to JPIII, February 12 and 20 and March 17, 1969, JPIII Papers.

great mark in journalism," he said, "and I figured that great mark probably would be made somewhere else." But after both Joe and Lasch let him know they wanted him to stay at the *Post-Dispatch*, he did. Joe shortly made him assistant editor of the page and Hall's likely successor.

Woo's presence gave Joe the opportunity to personally mentor an editorial writer with potential to lead the page. In a relatively short time, he developed a closer friendship with Woo than had been the case with any other of his editorial page or managing editors. Woo attributed this to the fact that, unlike the others, he was from a younger generation and came to the paper after Joe was its editor rather than its editor-in-waiting. As a result, he probably felt a greater regard for Joe than had older subordinates who "knew him when." When he was appointed editor, Woo asked for Lasch's advice on how to establish a working relationship with Joe. It "will develop naturally enough," Lasch replied. "The important thing is to gain his confidence. Once you have that, you can just about write your own ticket." Lasch told him that Joe "read every line and questioned a lot of them" during his first year as editor, but then the questions "tapered off." He emphasized that "major issues must be discussed with him and he must not be surprised by sudden departures." Two months after Woo took over, Joe sent him a note full of praise, concluding: "My grandfather is reported to have said, 'Every reporter a hope, every editor a disappointment.' This, happily, does not apply in your case."[42] Nor was Joe a disappointment to Woo. While managing editor Crowley and Dilliard had viewed Joe's art interest as a disqualifier for editorship, Woo saw it positively. He sensed "that if J. P. [III] were a collector and connoisseur of art, he might be a collector of intellectual viewpoints as well." Over time, he found that they both had a "deep respect for the notion of intellectual attainment as an end in itself" with a common concept of editorials as "explanation and creative imagination guided by the power of reason." Both Emily Pulitzer and Woo's wife, Martha Shirk—as well as others— compared the relationship of Joe and Woo to that of father and son. "I certainly know how Bill felt about him," Shirk said. "He was kind of like the father he never had."[43]

Following established custom, Joe and Woo had many of their discussions about editorial matters over lunch, frequently at the Shanghai Inn or another Chinese restaurant, where, Shirk recalled, Bill found that Joe was a stingy tipper, and eventually bought him a laminated tipping card to consult when paying, which he used thereafter. Woo said Joe always

42. Quoted in WW to JPIII, May 8, 1974, JPIII to WW, August 5, 1974, JPIII Papers.
43. Interview with Martha Shirk, June 1, 1995, St. Louis.

drove to the restaurant, often remarking during the ride "that he could not drive and talk at the same time. And he was right about that." Joe usually ordered a spicy Bloody Mary to start and Woo had a beer. The ninety-minute sessions were mainly business, following an agenda Joe had prepared. Woo found the meetings "very engaging and enjoyable" but "never confused them with purely social events." Because Joe was "a stickler for tone," that topic often arose. There "was almost nothing on issues that [the page] could not express," Woo observed, "but it was quite important that we express these things properly," and not be flippant, smart-alecky, sarcastic, or arrogant. At the same time, he added, Joe "thought indignation was very important for a newspaper that took public issues seriously. How to be indignant without being disrespectful was not always easy."

Woo once arranged a meeting of Joe with members of the editorial page staff. They gathered for lunch at the Shanghai Inn, where Joe commended the staff for its fidelity to the paper's platform. He then discussed examples of editorials that exemplified its ten mandates, from "always fight for progress and reform" to "never be afraid to attack wrong, whether by predatory plutocracy or predatory poverty." He and Woo had developed the examples. "Well, we got to . . . predatory poverty and frankly didn't know what the hell it really meant," Woo recalled. After pondering the matter across several weeks, Woo came up with: "Poverty itself was the predator and poverty stalked the lives of these unfortunate men and women," but Joe rejected it. "No, I think Grandfather meant the rabble," he said. In the end, Woo said, they recognized that neither interpretation defined the term, and "wound up sort of finessing 'predatory poverty.'"

Woo's tenure as editor of the page coincided with the company's circulation, advertising, and profit declines of the 1970s and 1980s. While Joe emphasized his commitment to "the independence and integrity of the editorial page," he also admitted his "preoccupation with economy." Sometimes financial concerns collided with editorial positions. In 1975 he established a policy to deal with this after Woo complained that a company telegram to legislators opposing possible increases in unemployment compensation benefits went against the page's support of "reasonable" unemployment compensation. The policy required that when statements by company management about business matters might be at odds with an editorial position, they were to be discussed in advance with the editor of the page, and as a last resort with the editor-publisher. Joe also used his authority in less formal ways. For example, when the automobile industry criticized editorials favoring pollution controls and safety improvements as being hostile toward their businesses, Joe asked for "moderation toward these sensitive issues."[44] Over time, Woo became aware of Joe's inclinations on certain topics. He knew, for example, that on "matters of taxation, bond issues, significant public expenditures, significant electoral offices," Joe wanted the final say. "But in certain areas it never would have occurred to me to seek his permission." Among these were the freedom of speech, the Bill of Rights, and abuses of human, economic, or political rights: "On human rights issues, we were in accord."

Joe disagreed with only three of Woo's editorial positions during his eleven years as editor of the page, Woo said. He attributed this to "the tremendous rapport that we had and being on the same wave length. Someone less kindly inclined toward me might suggest that I had tailored my opinions to fit. I think the record doesn't bear that out." One of the disagreements was with Woo's wish to oppose the federal government's financial bailout of Chrysler Corporation in 1979. Woo recalled being "appalled at the impending rescue of failing capitalism,"[45] but could tell after discussions with Joe that he wanted to approve the bailout. Since Woo had already run several editorials leaning toward disapproval, they had to find, he said, "a rational way to get out of the box." They settled on justifying the rescue so as to avoid damage to the economy and the loss of many jobs. During their conversations, Woo also sensed another element in Joe's calculation: "Chrysler was an old company... with a proud name and a proud history. At this very time our company was undergoing a lot of stress and [was] not doing well. The argument that the current managers of this proud and old and venerable company with the great name should be compelled to pay the price for mismanagement, to pay the price for poor performance, was one that he just did not want to embrace."

44. Among the issues were the costs of mandating air bags, emissions controls, and safety equipment in vehicles. One complaint was against a cartoon criticizing the House of Representatives for favoring less stringent automobile pollution regulations that made it appear that cars were killing people. WW to JPIII, February 12, 1975, and JPIII to ATP, February 14, 1975, JPIII to EAG, July 2, 1976, JPIII to WW, September 8, 1976, WW to JPIII, June 1, 1977. In 1977 Joe assigned his assistant, Bob Broeg, the paper's popular former sports editor, to call on people in the business community to "sound off" against the paper "in the hope that we can improve our image in this sector." JPIII to WW and EAG, June 2, 1977, JPIII Papers.

45. In a by-lined column, Woo wrote: "If the notion of a free enterprise economy is not to become wholly fictional, we must begin by saying that the assistance of the taxpayers should be invoked only if the private sector cannot provide the jobs and investment income that are associated with Chrysler. Never mind that tax dollars have and are being used to prop up other concerns. If the principle is sound, there is no need to repeat previous mistakes—and certainly not to the tune of $1 billion." *St. Louis Post-Dispatch,* August 8, 1979.

Woo expressed respectful dissent when he did not see eye-to-eye with Joe on the second editorial, published the day after eight U.S. servicemen died on April 24, 1980, in a failed attempt to rescue fifty-two hostages held by Iran. It questioned whether President Jimmy Carter took "rash action" in authorizing the mission. Joe considered this an inappropriate reaction so close to the event. In his opinion, he explained to Woo, the page's first duty was to "sympathize with the valor, the courage, the devotion to national interest and the audacity represented in the abortive rescue mission. . . . let the dust settle." He also advised remaining "aware of the 70 percent popular support for Carter's rescue attempt and when possible . . . tilt toward this public opinion." Woo agreed that the page "should not be insensitive to public opinion," but added: "At the same time, a vigorous editorial page cannot take its lead from the public opinion polls." After mulling it over, however, he decided it was he himself who had been rash and that Joe was "absolutely right." Days later, he published a column complimenting Carter for assuming "full responsibility" for the disaster. "In a democracy that is more than rhetoric, for what the president did was make himself accountable to the people," he wrote. "More details will emerge; more information will become available for the public to make its judgment. A tragedy has revealed the strength of the system."[46] In the third instance, Joe decided in 1982 not to accept the page's recommendation for editorial endorsement of Democrat Betty Van Uum for St. Louis County Council. She was the incumbent, and was endorsed by the paper in the previous election. Instead, he selected her opponent, Republican Ellen Conant, a woman active in community and social service whom he knew personally. Both candidates were qualified, Woo said, but he and the editorial staff considered Van Uum "closest to the *Post-Dispatch* platform."[47]

A matter on which Joe and Woo differed for years was whether the paper should have an opinion and editorial ("op-ed") page where columnists and others could air varying views. Joe opposed it even after the *New York Times* and other newspapers had such pages, Woo said, because he had a "strong aversion to the paper seeming to be at odds with itself."

---

46. He also advised: "Support the goal of national unity and unity among the U.S. and its allies; let the wounds heal; call for steadiness and restraint by the White House until the fallout from the Iran tragedy can be analyzed in a calmer atmosphere by government, press and public. We would not abstain, of course, from sharing in press evaluations." JPIII to WW, April 29, 1980; WW to JPIII, April 30, 1980; *St. Louis Post-Dispatch,* April 25 and May 2, 1980; WW interviews.
47. *St. Louis Post-Dispatch,* October 25, 1982; WW interviews. Woo said Joe ordinarily simply accepted the editorial staff's recommendations for local offices.

In his opinion, the *Times* damaged its credibility by publishing pro and con arguments on the Vietnam War. "I never saw the *Times* engaged in an act of self-destruction," Woo said, "but to him, a cacophony of voices, contradictory opinion, would diminish the authority of the editorial page." Joe altered his stance after the *Globe-Democrat* failed, virtually closing the marketplace of ideas in St. Louis. He then agreed with Woo that being the city's only daily made it "incumbent on us" to have an op-ed page with some conservative points of view.

About 1984, Woo became aware that Joe was thinking of retiring as editor-publisher and was considering candidates from outside the *Post-Dispatch* to succeed him.[48] Woo suggested to Joe that he consider Nicholas Penniman for publisher and himself for editor because both knew the operation better than would an outsider. Joe, embroiled behind the scenes in the family shareholder dispute at the time, did not respond immediately, but agreed when public ownership became inevitable in 1986. Although unsure of what Joe's response to his self-nomination might be, Woo speculated that he wanted a successor who "would do justice to the Pulitzer tradition." He was on firmer ground on that score than he assumed. Company vice chairman Glenn Christopher recalled Joe telling him "that Bill Woo embodies the philosophy of the *Post-Dispatch*. He was the one man who really understood Joe's feelings about what the *Post-Dispatch* should be editorially. That made him the obvious choice to succeed Joe, and nobody wanted to quarrel with that. We knew that Bill was not a clone of Joe, but certainly very sympathetic."[49]

Still, his transition into the paper's editorship was difficult. "I found myself with . . . all the authority in the world and not one single function," he said in 1995. "I had to create a function and I'm still trying to create it." Joe proposed in 1985, as he was stepping down, that Woo and managing editor David Lipman share his former functions and Joe would arbitrate differences between the two.[50] "I think what he wanted to do," Woo said,

---

48. Among them were two of Joe's Pulitzer Prize Board colleagues, James F. Hoge, publisher of the *Chicago Sun-Times,* and David A. Laventhal, a vice president (and later president) of the Times-Mirror Company. Two others were Byron Campbell, publisher of the *Bergen County* (N.J.) *Record,* and Charles H. Everill, president of Harte Hanks direct marketing. Negotiations with all four were unsuccessful. WW, NGP, and ERP interviews.

49. GAC interview, May 19, 1995.

50. Woo wrote: "Structurally, whatever its virtues may be, a duumvirate leadership (with deadlocks arbitrated by a third party, who by role is distant from the details and dynamics of the argument) is a formula for (1) debilitating rivalry; (2) institutional leadership marked by compromise instead of decisive judgment (controversial or unpopular as that might be) and (3) bitterness on the part of the one who fails to be the arbitrator. I cannot think of a successful and distinguished news organization that

"was to give me the job as keeper of the flame and maybe of the past, but to leave David intact as day-to-day executive for the paper." Instead, Woo told Joe he thought "that to make it work, you have to build up the new person." Joe accepted that and assigned Woo chief responsibility for the news and editorial operations, but at the same time did not fully step aside. Woo recalled him referring to "being on a glide path toward retirement," which he interpreted as "unwillingness to surrender... central and ultimate authority." Joe also hoped that by keeping his hand in, he could foster a harmonious working relationship between Woo and Lipman, whose personalities differed. One of the things he liked about Lipman, Woo said, was his "decisiveness, a certain willingness to get things done that were in the public interest even if you sort of had to cut the corners. And of course I was always raising the objection, waving the Constitution and due process." Nor did Joe want the paper to be "at war with itself" as had happened when fissures developed at the *New York Times* over such things as the handling of the Pentagon Papers and the Vietnam War. "He said that many times," Woo said, "and I think his analysis was faulty,... but nonetheless it made a profound impression on him." Woo also saw industry conditions working against Joe's outlook for the future: "I know he wanted this paper always to be coherent. It was his fate, his misfortune, I think, to be presiding over a newspaper in an era in which perfect coherency was swiftly becoming impossible."

---

deliberately substitutes committee leadership for individual command." Draft memorandum by WW to JPIII, October 8, 1985, given to author by WW.

Fourteen

*R*unning *the* *B*usiness

"Please try to avoid the word 'publisher' in identifying me," Joe advised the city desk in 1956. "Of the various hats I wear, the editor's hat is the one I like." No one in the company ever doubted that, but as related earlier, he often was obliged to wear the hats of publisher and CEO as one business challenge after another came his way. Ken J. Elkins, a company senior broadcasting executive under Joe, described him as a "very conservative" businessman who "may have retarded the growth of the company, but never put it at risk. He was in my opinion a very, very prudent businessman. He was not a person who was going to take huge risks or . . . even marginal risks that caused the company exposure." Another executive agreed, adding that those in management under Joe "all pretty much [had] a conservative bent on financial matters."[1]

For Joe, the best way to minimize risk was to personally superintend business operations. During most of his career, "certainly before we became a public company, Joe was very much involved in the day-to-day financial details," said Ronald H. Ridgway, the company's vice president for finance. He, as did Michael and others, considered Joe to be a micromanager who involved himself in lower-level concerns that others might delegate. "He watched those purse strings a lot," Ridgway commented, adding that he was surprised to find the company president and chairman "involved in $25,000 capital expenditures." Both Ridgway and Nicholas G. Penniman IV, Joe's successor as publisher, agreed that Joe gave much more business attention to the *Post-Dispatch* than to the company's other properties. "There was a great thoroughness to the way he approached the management of this newspaper," Penniman said.[2] Rival *Globe-Democrat* publisher G. Duncan Bauman agreed: "Joe was not a dumb man. Oh, no. He ran that paper with an iron hand. . . . If I had a problem relative to my production facilities, and Joe was out of town, I couldn't get any answers. . . .

---

1. JPIII to EAG, February 8, 1956, JPIII Papers; Interview with Ken J. Elkins, Senior Vice President, Broadcasting Operations, Pulitzer Publishing Company, March 10, 1995, St. Louis; Interview with RHR, February 27, 1995, St. Louis.
2. Interview with NGP, February 2, 1995, St. Louis.

Joe would say to the public, 'I didn't do that, my staff did.' Why that's a lot of bunkum."[3]

This did not happen instantaneously. When Joe first assumed leadership, company vice chairman Glenn Christopher recalled, turf battles and jealousies led to "a great deal of dissension among the main executives." To deal with this, Joe arranged for daily luncheons at a downtown hotel and invited all the executives. They attended, Christopher said—"oh yes, free lunch"—but the luncheons failed to make them "better acquainted or friendlier toward one another" and were discontinued. Charles Hentschell, Christopher's predecessor as general manager, initiated a procedure that helped to quell infighting: any executive could send a memorandum on any subject directly to Joe as long as Hentschell got a copy. Before, Christopher said, "it was very difficult for Joe to get the real facts or details of situations. Charley wouldn't know anything about" the issue, and "things were sugarcoated to put [them] in the best light."

Joe dealt with most business matters during group meetings in his office, where everyone followed his custom and wore a coat. "A few of us assumed we could call him 'Joe,'" Christopher said, "but most still called him 'Mr. Pulitzer.'" He sat at his desk, Ridgway recalled, with the others in chairs facing him: "Joe always treated you with the utmost of respect. He never embarrassed you in front of a group. He was never direct. If he were delivering a reprimand, or what you might call a reprimand in a group, it would always be very subtle...you had to read it. I never saw him take off on anybody. You never had that tension in a meeting where you thought he was going to raise his voice." Even so, he added: "To earn your stripes with Joe—as Glenn Christopher used to refer to it—it took a long time for him to trust you.... He held you out there, a bit aloof I guess is the word." Christopher recalled that during his tenure as the newspaper's general manager, "everything was my fault if it went wrong because people knew that the buck stops here. If people accepted responsibility for what happened, [Joe] appreciated that." Joe's trust of Christopher included having him prepare his personal income tax forms.

All his business lieutenants quickly learned that Joe expected to be kept fully informed. Ridgway, who became a company senior vice president, recalled that when he was hired as assistant treasurer in 1978, "I was told that Joe didn't like bad news." Accordingly, he sent Joe a report known as the "Gray Book," from which he extracted fifteen examples showing *Post-Dispatch* performance to be superior to that of seven other newspapers. "The items you enumerated were indeed favorable and to

3. GDB interview, May 15, 1995.

the credit of our management people," Joe responded. "However, there were serious unfavorable comparisons elsewhere in the book, particularly in production data. The point is that, like a politician, a treasurer should be able to 'point with pride or view with alarm.' Such a balanced approach would be more helpful in the future."[4] Ridgway "never made that mistake again." It was possible to disagree with Joe, if "you were careful in the way you did it," he said. In fact, he found Joe easier to deal with than some of the other executives. In discussions with Joe "you got the feeling when you were finished that he understood it almost as well or maybe better than you did.... He would keep pounding at it until he understood it.... I did not find him difficult to work with on complicated things if you understood it yourself. But you better understand it yourself."[5] His executives also found that he had an "elephantine memory," and that they were expected to be historically consistent when presenting information.[6] Because he wanted all sides aired in discussion, Joe sometimes played devil's advocate and listened carefully to arguments with which he disagreed, Penniman recalled. "Never once, when someone was intellectually honest and opposed Joe did I ever see him exert anything other than his own intellectual force. He never preempted arguments by position, by authority."

Penniman thought Joe's style improved his effectiveness as a leader. He said he often told him, approvingly, that he saw "a little ruthlessness in his character," and Joe would deny it. But Penniman and others got "a glimpse every now and then. Everybody knew it was there. You could get on Joe's best side and you stayed there for a while. And you could do something, and he could flash at you. I think that was very important to how Joe ran this company—that everybody had a slight bit of fear of him."

Joe's business training, like that in journalism, followed the established pattern of observing and then working with the company's business executives. He also had an early mentor outside the company in Robert Brookings Smith, nine years older than Joe, whose father's St. Louis brokerage firm, Smith, Moore and Company, handled some of the Pulitzer family's investments. Smith, who attended but did not graduate from Princeton, joined his father's firm in 1928, and over time gravitated toward venture capital work and away from trading stocks and bonds. He became involved in the early 1930s with a group of young St. Louisans—Joe among

4. JPIII to RHR, July 3, 1978, JPIII Papers.
5. RHR interview.
6. NGP interview.

them, "and of course a bunch of girls"—who were interested in music and the arts generally, Smith recalled. In 1934 the group founded the St. Louis Little Symphony, which presented summer concerts.[7] Smith was its first president—"because I was the fat cat"—and Joe its second. He was impressed by Joe's art collection, and considered him "entirely artistic" when he first knew him. In due course, it became clear to him that Joe expected to become publisher of the *Post-Dispatch*, and "was being trained for a job which required good judgment and understanding of some business principles."

In the years before both men entered the Navy in World War II, Joe and Smith often lunched together. "We used to talk business a lot, and I think Joe had great confidence in me and the ethics and standards that I impressed on him in business. He was just a great learner," with a natural aptitude for business responsibility, Smith said. "I was just delighted to see a man with the artistic temperament he had become a very, very capable business leader."[8]

Smith was asked by Joe's father to arrange the financing for the *Star-Times* purchase in 1951, a deal Joe and business manager Charles Hentschell completed. "In those days they wanted absolute secrecy, oh God, have it so secret," Smith said. "And it's all so silly, but still, that's the way it was." Smith became vice chairman of the Mercantile Trust Company in St. Louis about the time Joe took charge of Pulitzer Publishing. He consulted Smith on acquisitions and other business matters over the years, in the course of which Smith found Joe to be much less of a risk taker than he. "I'm an entrepreneur, basically, a promoter," Smith said, while Joe was "very cautious." He spoke highly of the business staff Joe inherited from his father, especially Hentschell, whom he described as being like "a chief bosun's mate in the Navy that kept we green officers from making mistakes" and "the most loyal employee I ever saw in my life." Hentschell was company vice president when he retired in 1970.

Even though Hentschell succeeded somewhat in easing Joe's reluctance to put pressure on labor unions when the company faced adverse business conditions, Smith was disappointed that Joe was unwilling to do more "to keep the unions from encroaching too much." So was *Globe-*

7. Wells and McIntosh, *Symphony and Song*, 66. The Little Symphony provided work for some St. Louis Symphony Orchestra musicians during the off-season.

8. Interview with RBS, December 12, 1994, St. Louis; *St. Louis Post-Dispatch*, May 27, 1993; Smith obituary, *Post-Dispatch*, January 5, 2003. Smith advised Pulitzer Publishing on various matters into the 1980s. He left the family firm in 1956 to join the Mercantile Trust Company. He left Mercantile Trust in 1968, but was involved in business ventures into his nineties. He died at ninety-nine in 2002.

Democrat publisher Bauman, who recalled that during an electricians' strike, he and Joe and their advisers met at the Jefferson Hotel to discuss strategy. "Joe was walking up and down the room explaining in his princely way that the *Post* is not a bottomless pit of money [and that] we will never give in to these demands. . . . And I said to Joe: 'You are ruining these two newspapers; one of these papers is going to go. . . . We ought to stay down six months or a year.'" To which Joe replied: "Oh, Duncan, I can't do that." When Bauman asked why, Joe's answer was: "Because as long as this paper makes money, we're going to favor unions. And when it quits making money, we won't favor the unions." To Bauman, "that was a highly suspect moral position."[9]

Others understood Joe's reluctance to face down the unions. As had his father, he disliked strikes, in part because the *Post-Dispatch* supported collective bargaining editorially. There were strikes lasting forty-six and fifty-three days respectively in 1973 and 1979, the latter closing both the *Post* and *Globe* during the year-end holiday season. More often, there were settlements to avoid strikes. As Ridgway saw it, given the advertising competition with the nonunion, free weekly *Suburban Journals* and other media, the company was in no position to make tough demands on its eleven unions. For that reason primarily, he said, "the unions in this company, up until about 1990, pretty well had the company where they wanted it. You were kind of between the devil and the deep blue sea because they could shut you down. Your alternative was to take a strike, which would just be devastating in those days." He recalled that there were labor negotiations about the time the company was considering public ownership. Investment bankers and underwriters advised settling because going public would not be possible "with a very unsettled labor situation at your largest property." Penniman said Michael took the lead in labor relations decisions after the company became public, "because I think [Joe] knew it was going to get rough." In 1989 Michael decided, with Joe's concurrence, that the company would "continue to conduct negotiations at a high level—civil but serious," but if a union struck, "we'd publish and we'd replace them."[10]

Penniman began his newspaper career as a laborer, a pressman. He described himself as a competitor who "loves conflict," as in tennis, where there is always a winner and a loser: "That's why I'm a good negotiator. . . .

9. Interview with GDB. "The immorality [of Joe's position]," he said, "is that as long as he was making money he was going to be pro-union. Where the hell's the principle in that?" Asked if the *Globe* was "not necessarily pro-union," he replied: "No, we were not pro-union. We weren't anti-union, either. Absolutely not."
10. NGP interview.

Negotiations are what interest me." By 1991, when the company was financially stronger, it negotiated favorable contracts in which the unions accepted no-strike clauses and decreased health care costs, besides making other concessions. Recognizing that the *Post-Dispatch,* as the city's only daily newspaper, had the upper hand, the unions also agreed to give up at least 130 positions by 1993, representing 12 percent of the newspaper's workforce and an estimated $5.4 million in annual savings.[11] Under those conditions, Joe had no quarrel with the result, Ridgway said, but earlier, "when he knew he wasn't in a position of strength, he was cautious." Some might "throw stones at him" for not standing firm earlier, he observed, "but I have a tough time doing that."

All the company's managers knew that from the first years of his tenure, Joe pushed for *Post-Dispatch* self-sufficiency. "Every tub on its own bottom," he was often heard to say. "Unsatisfactory operating results make it imperative to reduce expenses," he told his executives in 1959, when the newspaper's net income before taxes dropped more than $1 million—to $116,018—from 1958. Joe blamed "the steady climb" of costs and called for "a relentless economy program to restore earnings to a safe margin of profit" and "a satisfactory return on investment."[12] Despite seventeen million dollars in revenue, the paper was returning a "dangerously low" one-half of a percent of that in profit. Five months later, Hentschell told the Newspaper Guild, representing news and editorial employees, that "the management is confronted by terrific problems" even with *Post-Dispatch* circulation, advertising volume, and revenue at the highest levels ever. He calculated that every one-hundred-dollar reduction in spending equaled approximately twenty-five hundred dollars in revenue.[13]

To promote savings, a management-economy committee involving all departments was established in 1960 and continued into the 1980s. The strategy was to bolster earnings through savings while the newspaper's growth was virtually stagnant. Although Joe seldom attended the meetings, detailed minutes provided a record of the economy initiatives implemented or under consideration. He regularly wrote memorandums pointing up business concerns, but went back and forth on the extent to which business should prevail over journalism. In 1962 he criticized the

11. Within the first quarter of 1991, twenty-two mailers left their jobs, and twenty-eight paper handlers were laid off an hour after the contract was signed. An analyst for A. G. Edwards Company called the contracts "among the best ... in the country." *St. Louis Journalism Review,* June 1991, 6; NGP interview.

12. JPIII to CJH, FFR, DBS, RLC, HOG, August 13, 1959; "Schedule Showing Newspaper Net Income Before Federal Income Taxes," 1950–1967, JPIII Papers.

13. CJH to JPIII, January 20, 1960, JPIII Papers.

publication of a story based on Securities and Exchange Commission reports disclosing St. Louis corporate executives' salaries because it lacked a "newspeg to make the story newsworthy." The story "might well be resented by businessmen," he explained, because "certainly the majority prefer to minimize the publicity on their compensation." He also had in mind his own strong personal desire for privacy in speculating that the executives identified were likely to resent the absence of the Pulitzer Publishing Company from the list, even though it was "a closely-held, unlisted company" not required to submit compensation data to shareholders or the Securities and Exchange Commission. In another case, he suggested sending notes of regret to those who submitted photos to the society section that were not published. He thought the gesture might "avoid alienating potential readers . . . when we are using every known device to increase circulation." Certain "devices," however, were unacceptable. He vetoed a suggestion to "exploit the assassination" of President John F. Kennedy in a special section about a month after the event "in the hope of attracting readers and souvenir hunters" even though "I like circulation as well as the next man." He also favored ending handgun and mail-order gun advertising in the wake of Senator Robert F. Kennedy's assassination in 1968. He supported banning both print and broadcast cigarette advertising for nearly three years, until statistics showed that cigarette consumption in the circulation area went up rather than down during the ban. The company did achieve a large savings when it sold its Grumman Gulfstream III corporate jet in 1972 for $2.6 million. Joe considered maintaining and operating a plane—a holdover from his father's day—an unnecessary extravagance.[14]

The company's growth—particularly into television—accelerated after 1970. Even though the *Post-Dispatch* remained Joe's primary interest, he knew the company had to keep pace in an evolving industry. "We are a growth company . . . and will be in the market to the extent financing can be secured to make investments in the communications media," he said in 1971. "In other words, we are not remaining static."[15]

Even so, Joe wanted the *Post-Dispatch* to pay its own way and not be supported by the company's other enterprises. Achieving that goal was

14. JPIII to ARB, May 23, 1962, JPIII to ARB, November 2, 1960, JPIII to FFR, December 13, 1963, JPIII to ATP, September 26, 1968, ATP to JPIII, September 8, 1972, JPIII Papers. *Editor & Publisher*, October 26, 1974, 19; telephone interview with PJR and RAP, April 13, 1995. He also canceled use of the helicopter used by the company's St. Louis station, KSD-TV, to save sixty to eighty thousand dollars, because "everybody knows the traffic patterns during the rush hours." JPIII to HOG, January 6, 1971.
15. JPIII to HOG, August 8, 1971, JPIII Papers.

easier said than done, and not fully achieved in the views of at least two executives. "I think that was more idealistic than real," Elkins said. "I think 'every tub on its own bottom' other than the *Post-Dispatch* would be my sense." Penniman agreed: "The television stations really kept this company afloat for many years." The 1970s had been difficult for the city of St. Louis, with a huge drop in population and sharp economic decline as businesses and jobs migrated away.[16] Even so, there was potential for regeneration, among them promises of such major employers as Anheuser-Busch and the Ralston Purina Company to stay in town. Pulitzer Publishing Company made a like commitment when it bought and occupied the *Globe-Democrat* building in 1959–1960.

Elkins appreciated Joe's devotion to the city and the company's flagship. There was no doubt that the *Post-Dispatch* was "the center of the universe," he said in 1995. "We have benefited substantially from that dedication and heritage. Even Pulitzer Broadcasting has a level of expectation . . . that is above the norm, because of the heritage of this company. There is an element of integrity and professionalism and class that relates to the name." He believed this weighed favorably with sellers of broadcast stations who believed Pulitzer Publishing would better serve their communities than some other potential buyers.[17]

16. The problem facing the company, in its agency agreement with Newhouse, Penniman explained, was how to make the *Post* and *Globe* profitable. "We would be bouncing around these little losses of a few million here, a little profit of a few million there, but were still net in the red." The reason, he said, was that contrary to what most outsiders thought, the *Post* and *Globe* were the first and third papers in St. Louis, not the first and second. The *Suburban Journal* free shopper papers were in second place, and the *Globe* was third. In rough figures, he explained, the *Post*'s advertising revenue was $125 million, the *Journals*' $80 million, and the *Globe*'s $30 million. "And here we were in a market trying to keep the first and third paper going. Had it been the first and second paper, I think we might have financially been able to swing it." NGP interview, February 2, 1995.

The city's population dropped 27 percent during the 1970s, from 622,000 to 453,000, a greater percentage loss than any other U.S. city, with negative consequences for newspaper circulation and advertising, among other things. "The people left in St. Louis proper are, to a large extent, the poor, the elderly, and the unemployed," *Time* magazine reported in 1981. More than 16 percent of its residents were on welfare, 18 percent were sixty-five and older, 8 percent were unemployed, and the city was "starkly segregated"—90 percent black on the north side and 95 percent white on the south side. *Time*, May 4, 1981, 30. However, company director James M. Snowden, Jr., pointed out that the wider St. Louis metropolitan area was generally prosperous and growing while the downtown declined: "There was a big migration out of the city itself, but not out of the immediate geographic territory" as businesses moved to the city's suburbs, where, among other things, their employees would have easier commutes and not be subject the city's employment tax. Telephone interview with JMS, September 2, 2003.

17. KJE interview.

The ever-present tug of institutional history, however, did not change the fact that economic constraints forced changes in how the paper was operated. As never before, the publisher faced choices about whether spending or economizing was the prudent course to take. Joe's father had not had as challenging a time during the Great Depression.[18] Twenty years later, in the 1960s, the longstanding prohibition against business office interference with the news and editorial departments, including advertising department requests for stories favorable to advertisers and "business office must" demands began to erode. Gone were the days when the managing editor could kill advertisements to make more space for news.[19] Increasingly, employees were obliged to think about the whole operation rather than its parts. As related previously, the move toward greater cooperation between the news-editorial and business sides intensified in the 1970s, despite objections from managing editor Evarts Graham and others who considered this contrary to the paper's philosophy.

Yet while greater attentiveness of editors to business realities increased the likelihood of influencing their judgments, Joe also strove to maintain the paper's reputation for news and editorial independence. Outside Joe's own domain, Penniman said, he "was one of the most misunderstood people in St. Louis from a business perspective," in part because he "chose to live his life as independently as he did." He recalled Joe telling him more than once to "beware of the establishment." Of course, he knew many business leaders by serving with them on art museum and symphony boards, but did not interact with them in other ways, such as belonging to business or civic organizations. It seemed to Penniman that in Joe's mind, "the *Post-Dispatch* had its own identity, and life out there had a different identity, and the two weren't related."

Such a perception is suggested in the way Joe reacted in 1975, when he refused to meet with Zane E. Barnes, president of Southwestern Bell Telephone Company, a major advertiser. Barnes requested the meeting after the *Post-Dispatch* refused to print in full a Southwestern Bell rebuttal to articles and editorials it had published criticizing the company. The paper charged that Southwestern Bell was operating a political contribution fund

18. When the paper's advertising linage declined more than 40 percent, in part because J. P. II established an advertising censorship office at the *Post-Dispatch* in 1929 that rejected hundreds of thousands of dollars worth of advertising deemed false, misleading, and distasteful during the Depression decade. See Pfaff, "Joseph Pulitzer II and Advertising Censorship."

19. "In an emergency and when you consider it vitally necessary, please consider yourself authorized to inform the advertising manager that he will have to kill advertisements to give you the space you need." JPII to BHR, November 14, 1942, in Wilensky, *The Story of the St. Louis Post-Dispatch*, 17.

in violation of Missouri law and that it had provided hunting trips and other favors to a member of the Missouri Public Service Commission, which set utility rates. Barnes contended that the deletions the paper made in the rebuttal distorted the company's response and that the *Post-Dispatch* had betrayed its agreement by accepting and then altering it. William Woo, editorial page editor at the time, disagreed. "I'll present myself to heaven on the fairness of that editing job," he reflected years later. Even so, Woo was surprised that Joe would not see Barnes: "This is the chairman of Southwestern Bell, and Joe Pulitzer wouldn't see him." Instead, Woo recalled, Joe curtly dismissed the request, saying Barnes could "send a letter or something." Barnes's response was to cancel Southwestern Bell advertising in the *Post-Dispatch* for the remaining fifteen years of his tenure as president, a loss to the newspaper somewhere in the millions. A Southwestern Bell public relations man denied that this was an attempt to influence editorial policy, asserting instead that his company believed critical news and editorials would diminish reader response to its advertising.[20]

When a similar situation *not* involving news and editorials developed in 1991, a different resolution resulted. Southwestern Bell had just resumed *Post-Dispatch* advertising under Barnes's successor, Edward Whitacre, Jr., when Bill McClellan, the paper's best-read columnist, wrote a column cynically describing a high-society Southwestern Bell Christmas party to raise money for the Salvation Army. By this time, Joe was company chairman and Woo had been the *Post-Dispatch*'s editor for five years. Joe wanted Woo to fire McClellan. Woo agreed that the column was a "cheap shot," but contended that if any individual were to be penalized, it should be someone in the chain of editorial command because writers do not decide

20. *St. Louis Post-Dispatch*, February 5 and 7, August 15 and 18, December 12 and 22, 1975, April 15 and 19, 1976; James V. Maloney to J. P. III, September 23, 1991; WW interview, January 20, 1995; WW interviews, 1994–1995; NGP interview, February 2, 1995. When the company resumed advertising in 1991, it was scheduled to spend five hundred thousand dollars that year. Receipts during Southwestern Bell's boycott would almost surely have been lower because of lower advertising rates during that time, but still several million dollars. Barnes told Penniman that Joe also refused to return two telephone calls from Barnes. Penniman tried without success to get Barnes to resume advertising in 1986. EAG to JPIII, June 12, 1975, JPIII Papers. To the dismay of consumer advocates, the Missouri Public Service Commission in 1976 exonerated Southwestern Bell of the allegations that it had contributed company funds to politicians. It also decided to take no action to determine whether the company paid for hunting trips of former commissioner William R. Clark, who resigned after the *Post-Dispatch* story was published. However, the commission was reorganized after this incident and began holding open rather than closed meetings. *St. Louis Post-Dispatch*, April 15 and 19, 1976.

what gets published: "Some editor up to me puts it in the paper." No one was dismissed, but for some time afterward McClellan's column carried the title "On My Own," to indicate that views expressed in the column were his, not necessarily those of the *Post-Dispatch*. On *his* own, Joe sent a handwritten letter of apology to Whitacre. It said the column "should never have been printed" and that the editor on duty at the time "had a disastrous lapse in judgment" in approving publication. Whitacre was gracious about it: "Mistakes happen in all our businesses."[21]

Always interested in how the paper looked, Joe believed that spending money to modernize its appearance would help build circulation. He disliked the somber, gray typography of his father's tenure, and considered the paper's illustrations far behind the times.[22] "I do not believe the . . . *Post-Dispatch* is static and so we evolve and find new solutions to reporting and interpreting the affairs of man," he said in 1969. "If you compare the *Post-Dispatch* of today with the same newspaper fifty or even twenty-five years ago, you will find a journal more attuned to the tempo of life today with more emphasis on presentation, style, brevity and with more latitude for interpretation and expression of color and the human equation. The fundamentals of the newspaper's platform are unchanged— only the techniques are modified."[23]

All three Joseph Pulitzers were so keenly interested in technological advances that they typically were among the first to experiment with or adopt, among other innovations, larger and faster presses, facsimile publication (which failed to catch on), and offset printing. Joe's interest dated to at least 1937, when the potential of the photoelectric cell to set type from typewritten copy was being discussed. "The invention certainly warrants attention," Joe told his father.[24] Three decades later, as soon as large-scale photo composition became feasible, Joe led the way in adopting the technology. "It would be stupid not to avail ourselves of the electronic advantages which science and technology have developed," he told David Lipman in 1972. "How to reconcile the electronic capabilities with human and union resistance will be a challenge which I believe we will devise ways to meet."[25]

He believed so strongly in the potential of color that he wanted the *Post-Dispatch* to be among the first newspapers in the country to print color

21. JPIII to Edward Whitacre, Jr., December 17, 1991, Whitacre to JPIII, December 24, 1991, JPIII Papers.
22. JPIII to WW and DL, April 14, 1987, JPIII Papers.
23. JPIII to Friedrich Strusch, June 3, 1969, JPIII Papers.
24. JPIII to JPII, July 20, 1937, JPII Papers, reel 88, frames 16–17.
25. JPIII to DL, November 28, 1972, JPIII Papers.

photographs. The paper's first attempts in the 1960s were disappointing, Harry Wilensky remembered: "The red lips would end up on the forehead, and the whole thing was blurred and lousy." When Joe was told that the best color printing in a newspaper was to be found in a German newspaper, the *Hamburger Abendblatt*, he sent a ten-member *Post-Dispatch* delegation to Hamburg to study the paper's process. The team returned with inks, cameras, and the *Abendblatt*'s head photographer as a temporary consultant. *Post-Dispatch* color reproduction improved steadily thereafter. Former managing editor Bertelson did not believe Joe's artistic interest influenced his desire for better color printing: "I think it was his awareness that competition was going to come from TV and not from other newspapers."[26]

As much as he wanted quality reproduction, Joe also wanted the paper to remain dignified in keeping with its primary intention of being serious and thoughtful. Despite the prospect of savings, he believed the mandate to be "drastically independent" could be compromised if the *Post-Dispatch* joined news and feature pools with other newspapers. He feared this would contribute "to the standardization, equality, banality and loss of individualism which are criticisms of much of the press." He was willing to join if the paper could "reserve the right to withhold at our whim whatever feature, story or picture we wished as exclusive and in the P. D. tradition." He rejected proposed graphics changes in 1986 as being "almost indistinguishable from *USA Today*, which does not represent the character, personality or image of the *Post-Dispatch*."[27]

Even though Joe gave less comprehensive attention to the company's broadcast stations, he appreciated their financial vitality, especially that of television. He rejected the idea of "disparaging television" when *Post-Dispatch* advertising manager Fred Rowden asked his opinion in 1966 of promoting the newspaper as a news medium superior to television: "I think it would be most unwise for this company to engage in such a self-destructive campaign." Otherwise, his interest in television was tempered. "I have ambivalent feelings about the tube inasmuch as it does meet payrolls very conveniently, but the social and philosophical implications of the medium are something else again,"[28] he remarked in 1971. However, his files show an active interest in broadcast programming while Pulitzer Publishing owned stations in St. Louis.

26. ARB interview, August 19, 1993.
27. JPIII to ARB, July 9, 1970, JPIII to DL, January 31, 1986, JPIII Papers.
28. JPIII to FFR, November 11, 1967, JPIII to Clarence Olson, *Post-Dispatch* book editor, April 20, 1971, JPIII Papers.

The company was the first to introduce radio and television to the St. Louis area, in 1922 and 1947 respectively. Both his father and Joe considered the stations "subsidiaries" of the *Post-Dispatch,* and news broadcasting their most important purpose. Joe became annoyed in 1956 when KSD-TV chose to carry a sponsored program rather than a live broadcast of Democratic presidential candidate Adlai Stevenson's visit to St. Louis. "The *Post-Dispatch* and its radio and television stations have, justifiably, the reputation of being the first news institution in the city," he reminded broadcasting general manager George M. Burbach. "When news of paramount importance is made in St. Louis, we must strive to maintain our reputation, even in the face of serious commercial penalties."[29] With that in mind, Joe gave regular attention to the stations. As had his father, he had limited tolerance for frivolous banter and off-color insinuations on the air. Joe considered it "quite offensive" when a KSD disc jockey told a story during a morning program in 1971 about a fish being caught in a boy's pants. "The unsuitability of the story, even though relative to a kid but with overtones that were unmistakable, disgrace the character of KSD," he told Harold Grams, the company's recently appointed vice president for broadcasting. "I wish somehow we could instill the recognition that KSD is a metropolitan station, not a small town ham operation." After watching two newscasters introduce a KSD-TV news program with what seemed to him "an inept attempt at humor," he told Grams that he disliked the station's "lack of appreciation of hard news, with overemphasis on feature material, much of which is trivial and not worth including." He asked Grams to restore the newscasts "to responsibility, sobriety, and a genuine responsiveness to hard news with some degree of dignity and authority in the manner of delivery." He did not outlaw all humor, but cautioned that "it must be treated with discrimination and some sophistication. Corny humor, heavy-handed or sophomoric, can only damage the character of the station."[30]

Although he had never liked editorials on radio,[31] he briefly gave KSD-TV broad permission in 1969 to experiment with them "without direction from the *Post-Dispatch,*" assuring Grams that "no control will be exercised over the KSD-TV decisions." He hoped that the station's editorials would not "depart radically" from the newspaper's opinions. A day later

29. The station's management feared an advertising boycott by the scheduled program's sponsor, the Ford Motor Company. JPIII to GMB, September 28, 1956, JPIII Papers.
30. JPIII to HOG, October 21, 1971, and January 28, 1975, JPIII Papers.
31. JPIII to HOG, November 5, 1965 and October 21, 1971, JPIII Papers.

he tightened the rule in a confidential memorandum to Grams "emphasizing the importance of the paper's platform and traditions as guides
for television editorials. We must not have a babble of conflicting voices
which could make the *Post-Dispatch* editorial page suspect as to its convictions and, likewise, by embarrassing the owners. We certainly do not want
to diminish respect for the hard hitting editorial policy of the P. D."[32]

There was no such problem, of course, with the stations it owned in
other states, but the company did pay attention to more than the business
credentials of the cities in which it invested. The decision to buy KOAT-TV
in Albuquerque, New Mexico, in 1969, for example, was based in part on
a positive report on the city's progressive character and potential from
Harry Wilensky, then the paper's national correspondent. The station,
which was losing money when purchased, proved to be "a gold mine,"
Grams later told Wilensky. Joe encouraged Grams, in whom he had great
trust, to scout for other possibilities through his industry contacts. This
continued after Elkins succeeded Grams. The company's number of out-
of-state television stations grew to five over the next thirteen years with
purchases in Nebraska, Pennsylvania, North Carolina, and South Carolina,
and to nine after acquisitions in Florida, Iowa, Kentucky, and Louisiana
by 1993. In the process, KSD radio and renamed KSDK television were
traded for out-of-state stations in 1978 and 1983 respectively.[33]

"Joe got comfortable with TV as a business," Ridgway said, but there
was tension in 1993 when company directors proposed buying stations in
Des Moines, Iowa, and Orlando, Florida. This would be "the largest acquisition by a multiple of three times than we had ever done at one time,"
Ridgway said. Joe "thought it was too much debt," and almost withheld
his support, but finally voted to make an offer. Ridgway felt sure Joe, seriously ill at that time, would have been "happiest" just paying off the debt
on the 1986 shareholder buy-back, rather than taking on more. Once the
vote was taken, however, "there were no sour grapes" on Joe's part. "You'll
never hear from me, 'I told you so,' or anything like that," Ridgway recalled
him saying.

Ken Elkins came to St. Louis in 1980, in the midst of the company's
growth in television. He found that Joe "didn't take that big an interest in
broadcasting personally." He did not think Joe respected broadcasting,

32. JPIII to HOG, August 7 and 8, 1969, JPIII Papers. Grams, a long-time Pulitzer
employee, was broadcasting vice president from 1967 to 1979.
33. Changes in Federal Communications Commission rules also figured in this,
including those against cross-media ownership of newspapers and television stations
in the same city and those raising the limit on the number of television stations a
company could own in other markets.

"particularly the news side," but saw it financially—as had Joe's father—as "a very good business." It also seemed to Elkins that when it came to television and radio, Joe "was not particularly comfortable because he didn't know precisely what we were doing," while "he knew how the newspaper functions work together." Elkins could not recall Joe ever making an official visit to meet with people in any of the company's out-of-state stations.[34] He said he never received a memorandum from Joe, and other than some interaction with him at board of directors meetings, he and Joe had few direct dealings. For the most part, Elkins worked with Michael Pulitzer, who developed a serious interest in broadcasting, and company vice president Glenn Christopher. Elkins said it was Joe's decision to geographically diversify the company across a number of markets in the expectation that there would be business fluctuations in all, but seldom all at the same time, thereby minimizing risk. Much like Ridgway's reading of Joe, Elkins found him to be a "terrific listener," but could never tell how what he heard affected his judgment. "People like Mr. Pulitzer, who are very polite, would always give you the courtesy of listening," he said, but "he wasn't a yes or no person. You had to read between the lines. When people come into my office, it's yes or no," but Joe operated differently. "He would make inferences that, 'I don't think this is the right way to go,' but ... would not be as decisive as I would be."

Although he never discussed broadcast content issues with Joe, Elkins said he was able, even without specific instructions from him, "to ascertain what he would want." He recalled that when he made a comment during a directors' meeting about a station's public service activity, Joe asked "did I give away the store? I said no, I wouldn't let you do that." He concluded from the exchange that Joe "was a very astute businessman," but also committed to community responsibility: "He wanted his television stations to do the same as his newspapers." Elkins also believed that "if what I wanted was different from what he wanted, I would have a lot of trouble with that," but there never was a conflict.

Their similarity of purpose was evident in Elkins's handling of public service issues. In one instance, the Albuquerque television station produced a ten-part series about automobile odometer rollbacks by car dealers.

---

34. Interview with KJE, March 10, 1995, St. Louis. Joe was attracted by the business potential of television earlier than his father, who saw the advent of television as "the death of radio." But by 1952, it was clear that newspapers were affected most of all, with some St. Louis advertisers spending three dollars in broadcast advertising for every one in the *Post-Dispatch*. "We should consider ourselves very fortunate to have under our roof KSD and KSD-TV," J.P. II remarked. JPII to CJH, May 9, 1952, JPII Papers, reel 88, frame 554; Pfaff, *Joseph Pulitzer II*, 334–36.

Although he seldom previewed programs, Elkins did this one, pronounced it "brilliantly done," and approved its broadcast. The station did a follow-up six months later, found that odometers were still being tampered with, and ran the story again. "Just for some perspective, automobile advertising represents about 30 percent of our money, so it's a huge category," Elkins explained. He said the station temporarily lost some automobile advertising, but got it back: "We have never compromised in any way, shape, or form the editorial content of our programming or our product for commercial purposes. Nobody in the newspaper would ever come within a mile of believing that. They think we'd sell our mother, but we wouldn't."

In another case, Elkins assembled a panel of people from churches, law enforcement, and other community groups to preview a program about guns that had been offered to one of its stations. The program "had 'motherfucker' in it twelve times," Elkins said, "so I didn't like that program." After the panel viewed it, Elkins was "astounded" to hear that he was the only one who was bothered by the language. His view was that the word had never been spoken in at least 90 percent of American homes, but he took the panel's guidance and ran the show after removing its commercials and adding content disclaimers. The process, he felt sure, was "very much what Mr. Pulitzer would want us to do."

Though not as readily as his brother and Christopher, Joe grew to appreciate Elkins's skills in acquiring and operating television stations. While a student at the University of Nebraska, Elkins worked at Omaha station KETV. He did not finish college, but by 1975 was the station's general manager. Pulitzer Publishing bought the station the next year, and asked Elkins to continue as general manager. He doubled the Omaha station's profits in the next five years and was promoted to general manager of renamed KSDK-TV in St. Louis in 1980. Two years later, Multimedia Incorporated asked Elkins to continue managing KSDK after Pulitzer agreed to trade it for two Multimedia stations in North and South Carolina. Elkins preferred to stay with Pulitzer, but decided to take Multimedia's attractive salary offer. Joe, described by Christopher as "not the most generous of people when it comes to compensating his people," had offered Elkins the title of operating officer for Pulitzer Broadcasting and a few shares of Pulitzer stock, but no increase in his salary of about $120,000. Disappointed, Elkins telephoned Michael to tell him he was accepting Multimedia's $150,000 offer. "So Mike and Joe and I got together," Christopher recalled. "We did not want to lose this man." Joe told them to meet with Elkins and "see what we could do." After a long talk over lunch, Christopher wrote "175" on a piece of paper and showed it to Michael, who "kind of winked" and offered Elkins $175,000 to stay with Pulitzer. He accepted. Joe had given them no authority to name a figure, but approved the deal. "I think Joe realized he had made a mistake in underestimating Ken," Christopher said.[35]

Elkins shortly became president and chief executive officer of Pulitzer Broadcasting. He had opportunities to leave the company for much more money, he said in 1995, but chose to stay because he thought highly of Michael and was "very happy" in his job. He regretted not getting to know Joe better. "I've always been disappointed about that," he said. "I think we probably could have learned a little from each other. There's talk about his shortcomings. I think probably his biggest misjudgment was the significance of the minority shareholders. The most positive is that he guided the company through some very difficult times and was able to survive them all and was able to have ongoing growth from them all. And he did it with style."

35. Interviews with GAC, May 19; MEP, June 14; and KJE (by telephone), June 16, 1995.

Fifteen
Patron of the Arts

A typical recollection among those who spent time with Joe was that they got to know as much about him as he wanted them to. "Joe was approachable, and yet there was always something of a gulf and one was held back from presuming to cross over it too quickly," former St. Louis Art Museum Director Charles E. Buckley commented. "He never minded if almost perfect strangers addressed him as 'Joe.' But I think that if that person who didn't know him very well had suddenly called him 'Joe' and also slapped him on the back in a jovial kind of way, that would not have gone down." Buckley described Joe as a "rather old-fashioned person" in some respects, influenced by his family heritage and the formality of upper-tier St. Louis society. "Heavens, he always dressed the part. You never saw Joe running around in blue jeans. He wasn't a hail sort of fellow at all."[1]

Throughout his adult years, Joe lived largely within the boundaries of his varied activities: editor-publisher and chief executive, Pulitzer Prize board chairman, art collector and advocate for the arts, and social and recreational diversions both in and outside of St. Louis. In the company, "Joe separated everyone's personal life from the corporate life very carefully," Nicholas Penniman said. There were no country club or golf club memberships, no company cars, automobile allowances, or other perquisites of the corporate world "because in Joe's opinion, that's part of another life that you have. And when you work for the company, we're not going to get into those things. He always had a very rigid policy about those, which is fine. I think it sort of goes back to his own personality, where he clearly had separate lives."

Adam Aronson, founder and chairman emeritus of Mark Twain Bank in St. Louis, who got to know Joe through their mutual interest in the arts, saw him as inhabiting "different worlds," though not rigidly separating them. He observed, for example, that rather than setting the conversational agenda at dinner parties, Joe would discuss whatever subject another per-

1. Telephone interview with Charles E. Buckley, April 18, 1995.

son might raise, including politics, business, the arts, charities and endowments, as well as trivialities. "He was as good a dilettante as any in town" because he knew who was who and what was going on in the city. "But if you wanted to talk to him about the newspaper or the television station, he was delighted to do so and was infinitely more interesting, and immediately became a different personality," Aronson explained. "If you wanted to have a very engaging conversation with him at dinner, that's what you talked about." The person to whom he was talking also made a difference. "He very seldom talked about the newspaper business to me," said Walter W. Barker, Jr., an art professor, artist, and friend who lived and worked in St. Louis for a number of years and whose work Joe liked and bought. "And when he did talk about it, I didn't get the impression that he was as enthusiastic about the newspaper business as he was about art."[2]

In reality there was a porous boundary between Joe's art "avocation" and his work in journalism, although he reminded the news staff periodically that he should not be identified as the source of story suggestions, especially those about the arts, and wanted his name in print as seldom as possible. Yet he was not entirely truthful in saying to a magazine interviewer in 1978: "I have been able to divide myself clearly between my vocation and my avocation. I have been very scrupulous about not having my personal interest in art infringe on the paper's positions. In fact, I have kept 'hands off' strictly *because* of my involvement with the museum."[3] Actually, from the time he was associate editor, it seemed natural to him for the *Post-Dispatch* to cultivate appreciation of the arts in St. Louis and beyond. He tended to be low-key about it, offering editors ideas and tips that "might be looked into." However, these advisories "came down as Mosaic law," no matter how tentatively expressed, William Woo said. Joe queried managing editor Crowley in 1951: "May there not be a news story in the difficulties the Museum is encountering in its restricted quarters as

2. Interviews with Adam Aronson, May 30, 1995, and Walter W. Barker, February 8, 1995.

3. "St. Louis' Modern Medicis," *St. Louis Commerce*, June 1978, 46. In 1960 he jotted down some ideas that might be assigned to *Post-Dispatch* art critic George McCue, who was going on an assignment to Baltimore, Washington, Boston, and Minneapolis—cities comparable to St. Louis in size with more than one art center—to investigate the degree of cooperation or competition between the art institutions in those cities as compared to St. Louis: "Any joint financing? Any joint exhibitions, lectures, publications? Has the Boston Arts Center harmonized the interests of the area museums? Purpose of a three or four installment report would be to inform the art interested public of the dangers as well as the benefits of diversified art activities." JPIII "Memo for File," December 28, 1960, JPIII Papers.

reported in the annual report? I happen to be interested in the Museum and to like [museum director Perry T.] Rathbone personally and so I leave to your judgment whether this inquiry is newsworthy. I suspect it is."[4] He was more direct in later years. "I would like the paper to become more concerned with preventing horrors like the La Chateau development, the Saks Fifth Avenue complex at Lindbergh and Clayton, the Breckenridge motel on Lindbergh and Westport," he notified managing editor Graham in 1974. "These may be popular expressions of uninformed attitudes toward architecture and entertainment, but they would win no confidence from [*New York Times* architecture critic] Ada Louise Huxtable." He recommended taking "a lively interest in heading off ostentatious and vulgar eyesores."[5]

An eyesore was exactly what many thought was inflicted on the city in the form of a huge, weathered steel sculpture in downtown St. Louis in 1982, supported by, among others, Joe and Emily Pulitzer. Had critics of the work known of Joe's memorandum, they might have turned it back on him. The piece, named *Twain*, for which $290,000 was raised through foundation grants and donations, was designed by Richard Serra, a prominent sculptor with works in other cities and a brilliant future ahead of him.[6] Joe had commissioned Serra in 1971 to install an environmental sculpture in steel set into the landscape of the grounds of his summer residence in Ladue, and Emily had invited him to speak at the St. Louis Art Museum while she was a curator there.

She was a member in 1973 of the jury appointed by the National Endowment for the Arts to select an artist for the downtown space, and became perhaps the most publicly visible advocate of the work. "I realized after the jury was over and Serra had been chosen unanimously that there wasn't anybody to carry it through," she said, so she organized a group of people who raised the money and made it happen. Joe, she added, had no part in the project other than giving her moral support. There were protests against "Twain" from the time of its approval in 1973 to several years after its installation in 1982 on park land ten blocks from the city's Gateway Arch. The most incessant critic was the *Globe-Democrat*, which made plain its opposition to what one of its editorial writers considered "ultra-modern

4. JPIII to RLC, October 4, 1951, JPIII Papers.
5. JPIII to EAG, July 15, 1974, JPIII Papers.
6. The funds came from the National Foundation for the Arts, the Missouri Arts Council, and thirty-five corporations and individuals. *Riverfront Times*, December 5, 2001. Serra "is one of those rare artists whose careers seem to have had no weak or fallow periods . . . Just about every major museum in the world now owns at least one Serra." Calvin Tompkins, "Man of Steel," *New Yorker*, August 5, 2002, 61.

abstract crap."[7] But as she and relatively few others knew, Emily said, the *Globe* had supported the project by joining with the *Post-Dispatch* in providing half of a twenty-five-thousand-dollar donation for the project.

Twain consists of eight wall-high panels of weathering steel arranged in a triangular shape. Three-foot openings between panels allow people to walk through and around it. As a *Post-Dispatch* art critic described it, the sculpture "depends on human activity within its walls, the open slots offering up varying views of the surrounding cityscape. Like much of Serra's art, it's a tough piece both physically and conceptually, a combination not often conducive of wide appeal." Emily's advocacy for "Twain" "caused her to be looked at askance by a lot of people," said George R. McCue, *Post-Dispatch* art and urban design critic from 1956 to 1975. "Actually, the piece is not at best advantage downtown, taking up a whole block in an area that needs people circulation. It kind of pushes people back." He said he thought the sculpture would have been better placed "somewhere else. I have no idea where." Joe, however, liked it right where it was. "It's a great celebration of 20th century architecture," he commented in 1988. "It's just a wonderful expression of the weight, the balance, the texture, the presence, the power, the grandeur that can be made out of steel. It complements the [surrounding] architecture." The reporter noted that he added with a wry grin: "Of course, it's much better than the architecture."[8]

Even if Joe had divorced himself from the paper's arts coverage, there can be little doubt that his active involvement was widely assumed, since

7. Robert H. Orchard headed a foundation established by St. Louis Mayor Alphonso J. Cervantes to raise funds for the sculpture. Under terms of the largest grant, fifty thousand dollars, from the National Endowment for the Arts, the artist had to be "an American artist of international stature," Orchard said, and Serra, one of "only about a half dozen that fitted that paradigm," was chosen unanimously by the selection committee. Interview with Mr. and Mrs. Robert H. Orchard, April 19, 1995, St. Louis; Interview with ERP, July 1, 2004, St. Louis. The Gateway Arch was designed by architect Eero Saarinen and completed in 1965. It was derided during its construction in the 1960s as a "big hairpin" and "giant croquet wicket," but was a popular success and major attraction once completed. Primm, *Lion of the Valley*, 482–86. The *Globe*'s criticism of Serra's sculpture was made plain in a conversation with Orchard, after which the newspaper attacked Orchard editorially. Orchard interview.

8. *St. Louis Post-Dispatch*, October 7, 2001. Regional disparities in the appreciation of modern art were mentioned in 1957 by *New York Times* art critic [and wife of the Gateway Arch's architect] Aline Saarinen, in an assessment of Joe's collection at that time: "The most advanced painters in the collection may be fashionable and sophisticated in New York, but they represent a very avant garde taste in the Midwest." *New York Times*, April 7, 1957. Agnes Mongan, "Richard Serra," in *Modern Painting, Drawing and Sculpture Collected by Louise and Joseph Pulitzer Jr.*, vol. 3, 538; *St. Louis Post-Dispatch*, July 24, 1981, September 18, 1994, and October 7, 2001; undated (probably 1982) brochure, "Richard Serra's Steel Sculpture: A New Landmark for St. Louis"; interview with George McCue, February 3, 1995, St. Louis; *St. Louis Post-Dispatch*, April 24, 1988.

his interest in the arts was no more secret than his editorship. Moreover, there are passages in several things he wrote indicating parallel conceptions in his thinking about art and journalism. This shows up in language he used in two art lectures, and is implied in his Harvard thesis on Picasso.[9] Speaking in Kansas City in 1956, he used terminology much like that found in his memorandums to and about reporters and editors: "The private collector's concern . . . is in the exercise of his capacity for recognition and discovery, the employment of maximum judgment, discernment, and taste in his search for works of art as valid interpretations of contemporary life." In remarks at the opening of an exhibit of his collection at the St. Louis Art Museum in 1968, several references seem to echo language in the *Post-Dispatch* platform:

> What endows a work with significance, I submit, is the degree to which it heightens the spectator's awareness, illuminates a hitherto unseen idea, intensifies the perception of man's predicament, or provides a sign or symbol for a deeper understanding of human affairs. It is the power and authority of the symbol accordingly which makes compatible works from styles as dissimilar as nineteenth century realism and post-impressionism . . . and later styles. The key, I believe to be the degree of revelation, that is, the eloquence with which the image or metaphor communicates.[10]

Shortly after succeeding his father in 1955, he started planning for a *Post-Dispatch* music and art page and a book page. The next year he tapped George McCue to handle coverage of art and urban design and to edit the Sunday music and arts page. Only a few major newspapers at the time seriously covered these subjects.[11] McCue's résumé included a wide variety of reporting, writing, and editing experience, both on the *Post-Dispatch* since 1943 and in earlier jobs with three smaller papers and the Associated Press. "I sort of gravitated toward writing about art and architecture when those matters came up," he said. Joe liked McCue's writing and told

9. See chapter 2.
10. JPIII, "The Challenge in Collecting Modern Art," William Rockhill Nelson Gallery of Art, May 10, 1956; "Image and Metaphor in Modern Art," lecture at the opening of an exhibition of his art collection, January 25, 1968, JPIII Papers. A closely related point is made in this comment about his art collection: "The collector of these works bears a name internationally respected for its high standards of journalism. Clearly his inheritance has indicated to him that he should keep himself alert, informed, and sympathetic to new developments in the arts as in all other fields." Agnes Mongan in *Modern Painting*, vol. 3, 334.
11. *St. Louis Post-Dispatch,* June 1, 1975.

Crowley to offer him the art and music page, which he accepted instantly. "It was the best thing that ever happened to me," he said. McCue recalled getting "the vibration from Crowley and some others in the newsroom that sort of indicated that young Joe liked the idea of [having an arts page] and they were going to do everything they could to make it work and back him up. Between the lines, the vibration was 'and then he'll be out of our hair so we can keep on running the paper.'" The ploy failed, McCue said, as Joe continued to involve himself in the full spectrum of news coverage, making clear "that he was to be reckoned with. He was not to be indulged." Joe and McCue worked compatibly, with Joe offering many story ideas. He read McCue's work closely, commenting on one story, for example: "In discussing Paul Klee you observed that he was 'an artist who has grown constantly in stature.' Surely you mean it is recognition of Klee's stature which has grown. This seems like a rather picayunish complaint and it is sent in good humor. Klee has always been, in my humble opinion, one of the giants of 20th century art."[12]

Memorandums back and forth were McCue's only contact with Joe for some time after the music and art page was established. McCue described their relationship as professional and "mostly in writing. . . . We were not buddies or anything like that." They met in person when Joe invited him to his office to ask him to go to New York to visit galleries and see art dealers and others in the field, with Joe arranging introductions as needed. This shortly grew into an annual eastern tour, with Boston, Philadelphia, Baltimore, and Washington, D.C., included in the itinerary. One trip, for example, yielded seven stories and background material and ideas for several others.[13]

McCue—who was largely self-taught in art and architecture—soon began winning prizes for his work. One of the earliest was first place in the American Institute of Architects' architectural journalism competition. After reading one of McCue's critiques, Joe wrote him: "This thoroughly urbane, informed, perceptive account, both scholarly and witty, would rank with any art criticism in the metropolitan press." He told him to assume the title of *Post-Dispatch* art critic and use it "whenever an appropriate occasion calls for identification."[14] McCue often observed Joe at art show openings, where, he recalled, "he wouldn't put up with any nonsense. Some of the artists sort of tried to capture him, and he would edge

12. JPIII to GRM, October 21, 1964, JPIII Papers.
13. GRM to JPIII, April and May 1961 (no days given), JPIII Papers.
14. JPIII to GRM, January 17, 1961, JPIII Papers.

off. If they didn't overstep or move in on him too fast, they had good possibilities," but "when he started walking away from you, you knew you were being walked away from."

St. Louisans interested in art knew that Joe had a close but unofficial involvement with the art museum, including as a donor and lender of major works from his collection. For nearly thirty years, however, he kept the relationship informal by refusing requests to assume a more official role. In 1972 he finally decided to do so, and joined the museum's board of commissioners.[15] Charles Buckley, the museum's director from 1965 to 1975, could not explain what made Joe decide to take the position: "I think everything just worked itself out in Joe's mind. I don't think anybody put anything in his mind that he didn't want there." He chose a low profile for years, Buckley said, because "he felt the *Post-Dispatch* would be able to comment editorially without feeling that punches had to be pulled or compliments paid to the museum because Joe was on the board." Part of his role as a trustee was chairing the acquisitions committee. In that position, he promoted the view that the museum's collections and activities should be broad and avoid promoting any single point of view. "He was always willing to consider as acquisitions works of art of many different kinds, even though they were sometimes far removed from his own sphere of interest as a collector," Buckley said. "And by being the strong person he was, he was very helpful in keeping an opinionated and perhaps interfering trustee from causing needless trouble. Joe was good at that. The curatorial staff greatly enjoyed seeing Joe at acquisitions meetings.... It's kind of hard to resist someone called Joseph Pulitzer... when he has an idea that something should happen."[16]

Over the years, Joe served in St. Louis as a commissioner and trustee of the art museum, a member of the board of directors as well as the executive and music committees of the St. Louis Symphony, a member and chairman of the Washington University visiting committee on the arts, and a member of the board of the Grand Center arts redevelopment project in midtown. To Woo these were "awkward associations" incongruent with Joe's refusal "to be a party to Civic Progress or to other things such as that" and inconsistent with *Post-Dispatch* canon that community affiliations endangered the paper's journalistic integrity and independence.

15. The first time he met the Pulitzers at their home after he was hired as director, Buckley said, Joe told him they were giving their great painting "Bathers with a Turtle" by Henri Matisse rather than just allowing it to remain at the museum as a loan. "What a splendid demonstration of support for an incoming regime," Buckley said. CEB interview; JPIII to ARB, January 15, 1965, JPIII Papers.

16. CEB interview April 18, 1995; letter to author, April 15, 1995.

(He kept to that standard in part, Buckley thought, in avoiding "close encounters with the St. Louis business world, or at least that's how it struck me.") Without success, Woo offered some "very respectful suggestions" that Joe give up his official ties with the symphony and the art museum, but never pressed the issue: "I always did know when to stop." Joe also served for many years on the visiting committee of Harvard's Fine Arts Department and Fogg Art Museum.[17]

"Once upon a time," *New York Times* art critic John Russell wrote in 1988, "there were collectors who did not follow fashion, never resold or traded what they had bought, preferred the difficult and the taxing to the easy and ingratiating and never, ever, used the word 'I' when discussing the art that they owned. The very idea of ownership made them feel uneasy, and quite often they gave it to a museum in their lifetime." He identified Joseph Pulitzer III as one of very few such collectors remaining. Russell's comments came in connection with the exhibition of eighty-six paintings, drawings, and sculptures collected during the past fifty years by Joe and his wives Louise and Emily. The works were on display first at the Fogg Art Museum and then at the St. Louis Art Museum, to both of which, and to the Washington University Gallery of Art, the Pulitzers had made substantial gifts of art. "Obviously, this is one of the great private collections of America," the *Boston Globe* commented.[18]

Concurrent with the exhibit's run in St. Louis, the *Riverfront Times*, a St. Louis free weekly newspaper, published a mean-spirited attack against Joe and Emily Pulitzer that fell flat. The story was about "loan backs," the Pulitzers' practice of borrowing back for their temporary use items from their collection that they had donated to the St. Louis Art Museum. The story reported that since 1970 they had loaned the museum 375 items and donated fifty-one. Museum records showed that on a number of occasions they had been allowed to borrow eighteen of the donated works for display in their homes. Museum policy allowed this, considering it "reciprocity" for the donors' generosity. Museum director James Burke said legal counsel had confirmed that "we're not doing anything wrong." Joe said the gifts "are unconditional," adding: "The loan of art works to the museum is up to the museum. I ask for them back in compliance with their policy.

17. He also served on Harvard's Board of Overseers from 1976 to 1982, and was a member of the visiting committee to the Harvard University Press in 1951.
18. *New York Times,* April 24, 1988. The Pulitzers also made donations to the Boston Museum of Fine Arts, the Smith College Museum of Art, and in New York to the Museum of Modern Art and the Guggenheim Museum. JPIII to John G. Jackson, January 7, 1959, JPIII Papers; JPIII obituary, *St. Louis Post-Dispatch,* May 27, 1993; *Boston Globe,* April 24, 1988.

The practice of loans back and forth is widespread."[19] Nothing came of the article's allegations of impropriety, and several readers sharply criticized the attempted smear. "We should all be found guilty of committing such a community minded act," said one. Another accused the paper of "stretching to find controversy—or shall we say, create controversy." A third observed that because of its loan policy, the museum "gets masterpieces before anyone has to die and the Pulitzers get to have a few well-loved works around once in a while," adding that without their generosity, "the rest of us would be that much worse off."[20]

So would they have been without Pulitzer benefactions to the St. Louis Symphony, which dated back to the first J. P. Joe's concern about the symphony's financing began during his Little Symphony days in the 1930s. "The indifference and laissez-faire attitude of citizens and industry in St. Louis toward the symphony is characteristic of the lack of leadership which has resulted in much decay and not much progress in civic affairs," Joe told his father in 1953. J. P. II had asked his opinion about giving the symphony fifty thousand dollars a year for ten years. Joe proposed that instead the *Post-Dispatch* offer a lesser but "generous gift over a pledged period contingent on X number of large firms doing likewise" in the hope of establishing ongoing support and "a very real service to St. Louis."[21] Whether or not that approach was tried, company support was substantial. A symphony executive thanked Joe in 1990 for deciding to recommend continuation of a one-million-dollar Pulitzer Publishing Company Foundation commitment for several years into the future. The record of his personal philanthropies was never disclosed, but Adam Aronson said he and others involved in the arts felt sure that Joe gave large anonymous gifts to the art museum and the symphony. Quiet philanthropy was his preference. "He didn't do it to get name recognition," Emily said. She was surprised when he put his name on the chair in modern art he gave to Harvard in 1978 "because it was so unlike his usual way of doing things." Robert H. Orchard, who served with Joe on the symphony's executive committee for a num-

19. Robert H. Orchard, who was on the museum board at the time, recalled that Joe "was very outspoken about it. He said, 'I see nothing wrong with this.' . . . He wasn't feeling embarrassed or feeling guilty about anything. He figured it was his right. . . . He was very generous to the museum. That's not saying he didn't make money on it too—tax deduction. He bought a picture for $10,000 and donated it to the museum for [its currently appraised] value of $100,000. But there was nothing wrong with that." Emily Pulitzer said "one of the major ways [Joe] funded his art buying" was to donate works that had appreciated in value and then use the tax savings to acquire more art. Interviews with Orchard, April 18, 1995, and ERP, June 5, 1995.

20. *RFTs*, July 27, 1, 8, 10; August 3, 2; and August 10, 2, all 1988.

21. JPIII to JPII, March 3, 1953, JPIII Papers.

ber of years, said he heard that on at least one occasion he "stepped in and sort of pulled things out of the fire" for the symphony. His importance to the symphony was recognized in his selection in 1989 as one of six lifetime members of the symphony's board of directors.[22]

Music and art blended in Joe's long friendship with Vladimir Golschmann, who conducted the symphony for twenty-seven years starting in 1931. Golschmann, born in France of Russian parents, was a musical prodigy. He began studying the piano at age four and the violin at five, became a member of the Paris Conservatoire Orchestra in 1918, and was a guest conductor with several European orchestras before joining the St. Louis Symphony. He also built a collection of French modern paintings and etchings, ancient bronzes, and African art. Most of his paintings were by Picasso, whom he knew. Joe was enthusiastic when Golschmann's collection was to be shown at Washington University in 1958, as the conductor was ending his tenure in St. Louis. He recommended a color page on the exhibition, "with emphasis on the little-known and strikingly pictorial African art," adding: "I would if necessary clear a color ad page as there should be no advertising to mar the display of this collection."[23]

Later that year, when Golschmann and his wife, Odette, were living in Paris as usual during the summer, Golschmann sent Joe a playful letter in which a domestic encounter and the art collection played a part. He reported spending a few days on the Rivera

> with a nephew who knows more about politics than anyone I ever met. I made the trip just in order to learn about politics; I learned a lot.... We visited Picasso and my nephew lectured him about communism, and the master learned a lot, also. My nephew learned much also about the great man, who looks better than ever and whose recent paintings are simply on the formidably formidable side.
>
> Odette and my mother-in-law stayed in Paris because our private lives ... have recently been quite shaky. Madame Odette Golschmann ... having decided that [because] the Paris apartment had to be "fixed," I had to choose between keeping the collection intact or selling half of it in order to fulfill Mrs. Golschmann's wishes about what had to be done as far as interior decorating goes....
>
> Frankly, the idea of divorcing, we discussed. I offered Odette to settle for a half and half proposition, to which she agreed. Then I added: "You

22. Wells and McIntosh, *Symphony and Song*, 237–38; Aronson and Orchard interviews.

23. Golschmann obituaries, *St. Louis Post-Dispatch* and *St. Louis Globe-Democrat*, March 2, 1972. In 1950 his twenty-seven Picassos ranked as "the largest private collection in the world" of the artist's work. *Globe-Democrat*, March 3, 1950; JPIII to RLC, February 4, 1958, JPIII Papers.

get all the etchings and lithographs and I get all the paintings." Then
she disagreed and her counter proposal was: "You (meaning me) keep
the whole collection save a few things, the four big Picassos, the four
Braques, the Modigliani and the three Picasso landscapes and the bronzes.
The Africans are yours."

I talked things over with a famous international lawyer who advised
me to keep the collection and also my wife.

He closed the letter with "fond and affectionate regards" from himself
and Odette, "with whom I am today on speaking terms." Joe replied that
he would forgo an answer except to say that when he and Lulu came to
Europe soon for several weeks, they hoped to see the Golschmanns. He
suggested a reunion in Venice.[24]

Joe's own collecting, of course, went on nonstop. Between 1957 and 1988,
the Fogg Museum at Harvard published four volumes with illustrations
cataloguing 315 works in the Pulitzer collection.[25] "I buy only what I like
and what I consider significant," he told *Time* magazine in 1957. "Otherwise, my collection would have neither character nor individuality." He
never thought of it as an investment. "When I was educated at Harvard,
art history was concerned with the intrinsic values of art, esthetic considerations, historic context and scholarship," he told the paper's *Everyday
Magazine* editor in 1965. "Very rarely did our instruction involve monetary values. Today the fashion is to gossip about the monetary values and
to ignore the significance of art as a revelation of the age which produced
it. I find this trend abhorrent, and I would much prefer to see the *Post-
Dispatch* concern itself with scholarship than with speculation. The way to
do that would be to keep in touch with the young scholars, Harvard
trained, who have greatly strengthened the art community." In 1988 he
described his approach to collecting as "leisurely and cautious in a sense,
often waiting for new forms to be developed and settle down and become
kind of accepted. . . . I guess there's a sort of classical sense, the examples
are pretty definitive . . . they've come to rest." That had not always been
the case, as he recalled in 1954: "When I bought my first Picasso in 1936,
his pictures were highly controversial and not then regarded as 'financially
safe.' Quite the contrary, I was then regarded as an eccentric."[26]

24. Golschmann to JPIII, June 3, 1958 (some punctuation added), JPIII to Golschmann, June 17, 1958, JPIII Papers.
25. *Modern Painting, Drawing and Sculpture: Collected by Louise and Joseph Pulitzer Jr.*,
vols. 1–3, and Rudenstine, *Modern Painting, Drawing and Sculpture: Collected by Emily
and Joseph Pulitzer Jr.*, vol. 4.
26. *Time*, April 15, 1957, 98; *St. Louis Post-Dispatch*, April 24, 1988; JPIII to HW, January 19, 1965, JPIII to Howard Derrickson, December 20, 1954, JPIII Papers.

As he grew older, however, he continued to buy works of contemporary artists. His marriage in 1973 to curator Emily Rauh, who had art history degrees from Bryn Mawr and Harvard, figured in his willingness to do so. "My present wife has had obviously a very strong influence in opening my eyes to art which was newer for me than for her because of her being younger and also being very much involved in the art immediately being produced. Whereas . . . my tendency has been to wait until the dust has settled," he said in 1988. Commented *Post-Dispatch* critic Harper Barnes: "It is possible that the dust falls from the air more quickly for Joseph Pulitzer than it does for the rest of us." Emily thought Joe gave her too much credit for selecting more recent works: "Yes, I did open some doors, but I think that his response was his own, and I think that before I came into his life, he looked at contemporary art over a considerable period of time. So you can't really say he became venturesome after I came into his life."[27]

Among the duties of one of Joe's secretaries was to maintain the collection's records, including the history of each item and its whereabouts. Parts of it were frequently on the move to and from exhibitions in the United States or abroad. "He could give you some odd requests," said Joan M. McSalley, who was the art collection secretary for twelve years. "He wanted me to take a Degas, I think it was, to New York, via plane, drop it off at a gallery and fly back the same day." Her parents and brother "had a fit," she said, fearing that she might be "accosted along the way or something with a valuable painting." But there was no incident, and by having her do the errand, "it saved him courier fees."[28]

Sally Defty, a friend of Joe's before becoming a writer and editor at the *Post-Dispatch*, recalled once having the experience of seeing Joe at work as a collector. She and her husband, Eric—an architect who did some work for Joe—were in New York one time when Joe was, and he invited them to go with him to see a portrait by Alberto Giacometti he thought he might buy, and ultimately did. They watched him look at the work for half an hour. "There were no layers of anything between his appreciation and pleasure in that painting, and it was a thrilling thing to watch it," she said. "I just remember feeling the way you feel when you are in the presence of the real thing."[29]

---

27. *St. Louis Post-Dispatch*, April 24, 1988; ERP interview, March 29, 1995, St. Louis.
29. Interview with Joan M. McSalley, March 20, 1995, St. Louis.
29. SBD interview, December 12, 1994, St. Louis.

Sixteen
Prizes and Principles

Joe had been chairman of the Advisory Board on the Pulitzer Prizes for eleven years when he presided at the fiftieth anniversary celebration of the country's most prestigious awards in journalism, letters,[1] and music. Some six hundred guests—including 189 of the 300 then-living Pulitzer Prize winners—attended the black-tie dinner on May 10, 1966, at the Plaza Hotel in New York City. Others did most of the talking. "While any system of awards may be open to improvement—and the Pulitzer Prizes undoubtedly form no exception—I note no reluctance on the part of authors or publishers to submit their products to our juries," said Grayson Kirk, president of Columbia University where the prizes endowed by the first Joseph Pulitzer had been awarded since 1917. "I am a believer in human fallibility," he observed, "but as I look over this magnificent audience tonight I am confident that each of approximately 200 of our guests, plus their wives or husbands, know that in at least one instance the judges exercised impeccable and flawless judgment."[2]

At the outset of the celebration, Joe had said, "this is like a large family gathering." *Post-Dispatch* reporter Sally Defty wrote: "Like any large family party, it had its embarrassing incidents as well as its moments of heart-warming solidarity." There was an awkward moment when the *Boston Globe* was awarded the 1966 Pulitzer Prize gold medal for public service for its campaign to block the appointment of Francis X. Morrissey to a federal judgeship in Massachusetts. The politically powerful Kennedy family had supported Morrissey, and Mrs. Joseph P. Kennedy and U.S. Senator Robert F. Kennedy, whose late son and brother, President John F. Kennedy,

1. This category includes biography, drama, history, poetry, fiction, and general nonfiction.
2. *St. Louis Post-Dispatch*, May 11, 1966. The paper carried two articles about the event that day, both of which contributed to this account.
The first deadline for submissions was February 1, 1917, for works published or performed the previous year. John Hohenberg, *The Pulitzer Prizes*, 24. Hohenberg's *The Pulitzer Diaries* brings the history of the prizes up to 1997. Hohenberg was Pulitzer Prize administrator from 1954 to 1975.

won the 1957 biography prize for *Profiles in Courage,* were seated directly in front of the head table. They "stared intently at their menus" during the presentation, Defty reported.[3] On a warmer note, many there were glad to have the chance to thank the indefatigable crusader for social justice—Upton Sinclair, then eighty-seven—for his impact on their lives. He had won the 1943 fiction prize.[4] Mrs. Sinclair said being at the dinner was "the crowning achievement of his life."

There were remarks by five Pulitzer Prize winners on the importance and meaning of the awards: composer Aaron Copeland, historian and biographer Arthur M. Schlesinger, Jr., *New York Times* reporter James B. Reston, novelist and poet Robert Penn Warren, and poet and dramatist Archibald MacLeish.[5] "We do not all of us have the courage, and we certainly do not have the reasons which made it possible for Keats to say, at the loneliest moment of his life, that he knew he would be among the English poets at his death," MacLeish said. "We need, most of us, not a sign of recognition of our ultimate worth as poets—only poetry itself can give that—but recognition that we exist, that we are there among those who went before and those who will come after."

Joe had hastily assumed the position of Advisory Board chairman in April 1955, barely a month after his father's death on March 30. J. P. II knew Joe was interested in being on the board, and had been discussing with Columbia's journalism school dean the possibility of getting him on relatively soon, although he was concerned about what became a moot point: that others on the board might object to having two Pulitzers as members. Even without a gradual introduction to what his father termed "the difficult business of awarding Pulitzer Prizes," Joe quickly adapted to the chairmanship. The board formally elected him on April 29, and his first meeting proceeded, board secretary John Hohenberg recorded, with "no speeches, no hoopla. It was strictly business from then on."[6] He held the position for thirty-one years, until 1986.

---

3. *St. Louis Post-Dispatch*, May 11, 1966.

4. For *Dragon's Teeth,* about the rise of Nazism. The work that made him famous was *The Jungle* (1906), a novel about exploitation of workers in the meatpacking industry at the turn of the twentieth century.

5. Copeland won for music in 1945; Schlesinger for history in 1946 and biography in 1965; Reston for national reporting in 1947 and 1957; Warren for fiction in 1947 and poetry in 1958; and MacLeish for poetry in 1933 and drama in 1959. Hohenberg, *The Pulitzer Prizes,* 358–78.

6. JPII to Carl W. Ackerman, January 13 and 18, 1954, JPII to Grayson Kirk, March 10, 1955, JPIII to JPII, March 8, 1955, JPII Papers, reel 137, frames 234–39. Hohenberg, *The Pulitzer Diaries,* 24; Hohenberg to JPIII October 17, 1973, JPIII Papers.

In 1974, his nineteenth year as board chairman, Joe complimented managing editor Evarts Graham on the quality of *Post-Dispatch* entries for the year: "It seems more important to me to have competitive material to submit for the prizes than the accident of winning one, which, under the hit or miss methods of selection, are highly subjective and accidental. I claim that winning a Pulitzer Prize is something like roulette, where the ball may bound all around the winning number before it settles down." Prior to that point in Joe's tenure as editor-publisher, the *Post-Dispatch* had won three prizes: for a Bill Mauldin editorial cartoon in 1958, a group of editorials by Robert Lasch in 1965, and commentary by Marquis Childs in 1969. It received a fourth for music criticism by Frank Peters, Jr., in 1972. The paper never won in the most coveted "meritorious public service" category while Joe was editor-publisher. In contrast, the *Post-Dispatch* won an unprecedented five such awards in a span of fifteen years during his father's forty-three-year career.[7]

Joe knew, of course, that others had made much the same assessment as he about the unpredictability of winning a prize. The three-step judging process got the most criticism. First, a jury of four to six people for each field winnowed the entries to a list of recommendations for the advisory board's consideration. Each jury was to follow prescribed criteria in selecting its nominees, such as "giving prime consideration to initiative, resourcefulness, research, and high quality of writing" in judging investigative reporting. Second, using the jury nominations, the advisory board members—almost all newspaper editors and publishers—picked a slate of recommended winners. After serving on the national reporting jury in 1966, Robert Lasch told Joe that they found none of the recommendations "exciting," but made four recommendations. Most, he said, were "long and rather tedious series on such pig-iron subjects as civil rights, water pollution, education reform, and poverty." Having their selections second-guessed sometimes angered jurors—particularly those on drama, music, and literature juries who considered themselves better qualified in those areas than journalists. Third—until 1975—the advisory board's choices went to the university's Board of Trustees for ratification or veto—another opportunity for second-guessing. However, the trustees used their veto power just once, in 1962, when they rejected the advisory board's unani-

---

7. JPIII to EAG, January 22, 1974, JPIII Papers. As per standing practice, Joe took no part in board deliberations on nominations from his newspapers. JPIII to Frank Peters, May 2, 1972, JPIII Papers. *St. Louis Post-Dispatch*, March 25, 1979; *Kansas City Times*, April 23, 1981; Harris, "The Gold-Medal Crusade Years," 5 ff.

mous selection of W. A. Swanberg's life of controversial media mogul William Randolph Hearst for the biography award.[8]

Joe "certainly had no objection to giving the prize to a biography of his grandfather's old foe," Hohenberg recorded. The board found the work "impressively detailed" and "based upon massive research." As for his role as a newspaperman, it concluded: "Hearst may have exercised a lamentable influence on American journalism. Nevertheless, he cut a wide swath across American life." It also applauded the work for providing "much insight into a now vanished social era." Nevertheless, the trustees decided that *Citizen Hearst* did not meet the terms of the biography award as "a distinguished American biography or autobiography teaching patriotic and unselfish services to the people, illustrated by an eminent example,"[9] and there was no biography prize that year.

As publicity about the rejection boosted sales of the biography, Swanberg remarked that it was a "high distinction to be the only man in history to be turned down for a Pulitzer Prize by Columbia's trustees." Even though William Randolph Hearst, Jr., did not like Swanberg's treatment of his father, he thought the Pulitzer Prize was appropriate. "After all, everything my Pop learned about journalism came right from old man Pulitzer," he said.[10] Swanberg's life of prize founder Joseph Pulitzer came out in 1967, but did not attract an award. Six years later, in 1973, his biography of Henry Luce, *Luce and His Empire*, did win, with unanimous support of the jurors, advisory board, and trustees.

In 1975 the trustees relinquished their role in awarding Pulitzer Prizes and delegated the responsibility for final approval to the university president, an arrangement much more to Joe's liking. The change grew out of

8. Juror John McCormally, "Memo from Mac," *The Hawk-Eye*, Burlington, Iowa, March 10, 1971; RL to JPIII, March 11, 1966, JPIII Papers. Joe sometimes shared in negative views of juror qualifications, writing Hohenberg in 1972 that he agreed with critics that the 1971 fiction award winner, *Angle of Repose* by Wallace Stegner, was a "dull, acceptable but not distinguished book. . . . Somehow we must breathe life into the jurors by increasing their number with younger, non-establishment literary lights . . . to bring about more imaginative and bolder recommendations in the letters field." JPIII to Hohenberg, May 31, 1972, JPIII Papers. On Hearst, see Swanberg, *Citizen Hearst* (1961) and David Nasaw, *The Chief* (2000). Nasaw's book goes further into Hearst's personal life than does Swanberg's, especially his thirty-six-year relationship with his mistress, performer and actress Marion Davies.

9. The terms of the award were subsequently changed to read: "For a distinguished biography or autobiography by an American author published during the year, preferably on an American subject." "The Pulitzer Prizes Plan of Award," Columbia University, June 1972, JPIII Papers.

10. Quoted in Hohenberg, *The Pulitzer Diaries*, 109.

the divisiveness of the war in Vietnam and events leading to the resignation of President Richard Nixon on August 8, 1974, resulting in another
difference of opinion between the advisory board and trustees. Hohenberg
described the disagreement as "the last stand of President Nixon's loyal
supporters among the trustees against...reporters who were helping
bring about his downfall."[11] The background was that meritorious public
service Pulitzers had been awarded to the *New York Times* in 1972 for publishing the Pentagon Papers, and to the *Washington Post* in 1973 for un-
raveling the Watergate conspiracy. Nixon attacked the prizes in a speech
in March 1974, saying: "People don't win Pulitzer Prizes for being for,
they usually win them for being against."[12] The next month, a number of
the Columbia trustees objected to the advisory board's recommendation
that a national reporting prize be given to reporter Jack White of the *Provi-
dence* [Rhode Island] *Journal-Bulletin* for a story based on an Internal Revenue Service leak of Nixon's income tax payments for 1970 and 1971. Columbia President William J. McGill agreed with the opposing trustees: "I
don't believe you should get any award for violating the law. The newspaper profession has to discipline itself. I don't think the profession pays
enough attention to matters of repercussions—they are a very hard-bitten
type of people."[13] However, there was no effort to overturn the advisory
board, and the award stood.

Several weeks later Joe had what he described as "an intensive two-
hour conversation" with McGill. Afterward, he told Hohenberg that "the
awards will eventually be announced by the President, rather than by the
University trustees, to relieve them of any responsibility for the decisions
of the advisory board." In 1979 it became the "Pulitzer Prize Board," the
word "advisory" having been removed, and as a note in Joe's files recorded:
"no longer advisory to anybody." The note also said that henceforth jurors
would be designated "nominating jurors" and that "juries are not the final
decision makers."[14]

11. Ibid., 276.
12. Quoted in ibid., 273.
13. *Columbia Spectator,* October 17, 1974, JPIII Papers. The award was shared by
White for his income tax disclosures and James R. Polk of the *Washington Star-News*
for his story about financing irregularities in Nixon's 1972 reelection campaign.
14. JPIII to JH, November 25, 1974, JPIII Papers. See also Hohenberg, *The Pulitzer
Diaries*, 273–75. McGill almost always was an ally of the advisory board. On becoming
president he said he would not interfere with selection of Pulitzer Prizes and would
not tolerate attempts by others to do so. "It was a pledge that he kept with considerable cost to himself," Hohenberg recorded. *The Pulitzer Prizes*, 296. Unsigned, undated
note, approximately 1975; administrative changes noted in Pulitzer Prize files of JPIII,
JPIII Papers.

The jury issue—again involving Vietnam and with Joe not surprisingly on the side of the jury—was at the core of a widely publicized dispute about a 1967 award that put him at odds with six other advisory board members. Four of the five international reporting jurors recommended that the prize go to *New York Times* reporter Harrison Salisbury for a series of dispatches from Hanoi, North Vietnam. The advisory board voted six to five against Salisbury and picked the jury's second choice. Joe voted with the minority, going against his past practice of being "scrupulously careful not to comment in public on the work and judgment of my colleagues on the board."[15] Instead, the *Post-Dispatch* reported that during the board's deliberations, Joe made "an eloquent plea for preserving the integrity of the awards" by giving the prize to Salisbury. In an editorial, the paper argued that the board "made a serious mistake in overturning the professional jury's recommendation," and called the dispatches "a distinguished example of independent reporting by a correspondent of unassailable integrity, on matters of vital import to the American people." It commended the jurors for evaluating the work "strictly on professional grounds and without regard to government attitudes either in Hanoi or Washington." And it said the vote of the board majority "raises a question of whether the decision was affected by personal viewpoints toward the Vietnam war, or by the Johnson Administration's reactions to the Salisbury dispatches and its attempt to discredit them. In an award for journalistic excellence these considerations ought, of course, to play no part."[16]

The *Globe-Democrat*, as supportive of the war as the *Post-Dispatch* was against it, editorially applauded the majority "for vetoing the unthinkable recommendation" of the jury. It denounced Salisbury for "using false 'facts' from enemy territory" and his newspaper for lacking "the wisdom to recognize the dispatches for what they were." It scoffed at Joe's references to "journalistic merit" and "integrity" in describing Salisbury's work:

15. The jury's second choice was R. John Hughes of the *Christian Science Monitor* for articles from Indonesia. Hohenberg, *The Pulitzer Diaries*, 176. Joe's "past practice" was demonstrated when he was on the losing side of a 6 to 5 vote in 1963 overturning the drama jury's recommendation that the award go to *Who's Afraid of Virginia Woolf?* by Edward Albee. Privately, he commended *Post-Dispatch* reviewer Myles Standish for his review of the work as produced in a movie in 1966: "As one of the minority of five who voted to award it a Pulitzer Prize, I was greatly impressed by your perception and your ability to convey in a short space the substance of this remarkable work." JPIII to Standish, July 20, 1966, JPIII Papers. Albee won the award in 1967 for *A Delicate Balance*. "I privately think of this as my second Pulitzer Prize," Albee commented. *St. Louis Post-Dispatch*, May 3, 1967; JPIII to HW, May 13, 1963, JPIII Papers. Juries were asked not to rank-order their nominations, but some did so anyway.

16. Hohenberg, *The Pulitzer Prizes*, 296–99; *St. Louis Post-Dispatch*, May 1 and 2, 1967; *Newsweek*, May 17, 1967, 89, and May 13, 1968, 86; *Nation*, May 15, 1967, 613.

"Journalistic integrity indeed. A true reporter is one who seeks out the truth for himself and from credible sources, not one who takes even his own nation's handouts, much less enemy propaganda, and spreads it on the record as gospel." Even so, it added, "It probably doesn't make much difference anyway, the Pulitzer Prizes being what they are these days."[17] Joe sent copies of both editorials to Salisbury, who thanked him for sending "the fine editorial of the PD and the unfine editorial of the GD." For his part, Joe saw publicity value in the dispute, writing Herbert Brucker of the Stanford University communication department: "I don't believe controversy hurts the Pulitzer Prizes as an institution and, in fact, it may help by creating lively discussion . . . and thereby stirring up public interest in them. Controversy has long surrounded these awards so that in this perspective the furor this year isn't so terrible after all."[18]

Joe received many expressions of respect and admiration for his work as chairman of the Prize Board. After the 1979 session closed, board member Richard Leonard, editor of the *Milwaukee Journal*, wrote him: "I thought you ran the meeting beautifully, as usual, skillfully guiding the group through the customary tempests." Even rambunctious member Benjamin Bradlee of the *Washington Post*, in a letter to Joe stating his case against awarding the 1972 public service prize solely to the *New York Times* for the Pentagon Papers series, did so with humility: "If you feel I am out of order in writing you this, please tear it up." Bradlee's argument—which he admitted might be seen as "the sourest of grapes"—was that no paper should get the award "based on anything hand-delivered by a single source to a newspaper."[19] He proposed instead that the *New York Times* and *Washington Post* should receive special Pulitzer citations "for their noble fight" in successfully challenging the government's effort to block publication of the Papers in the federal courts. However, the *Times* got the prize, Hohenberg recorded, as "in effect, recognition of the dominant responsibility of the *Times*'s publisher, Arthur Ochs Sulzberger, in the decision to disclose the hitherto secret Pentagon file."[20]

17. *St. Louis Globe-Democrat*, May 3, 1967.

18. Harrison Salisbury to JPIII, May 5, 1967, JPIII to Herbert Brucker, May 23, 1967, JPIII Papers.

19. Benjamin C. Bradlee to JPIII, January 24, 1972, JPIII Papers. The "single source" was Daniel Ellsberg, a researcher with the Rand Corporation of Santa Monica, California, who had served in the Marines and worked for the U.S. Defense and State departments. He leaked the Pentagon Papers to *New York Times* reporter Neil Sheehan. Unger, *The Papers*, 15, 85–86; "It's Time to Take Risks," December 2, 2002, The Guardian Unlimited (Web site: www.guardian.co.uk), December 2, 2002.

20. Richard H. Leonard to JPIII, April 18, 1979, JPIII Papers; Hohenberg, *The Pulitzer Prizes*, 309; telephone interview with Bradlee, March 31, 1999.

Bradlee remained unhappy about what he saw as the prize board's preferential treatment of the *New York Times*. In his autobiography, published in 1995, he indirectly disputed a statement Joe made in 1986, when he was quoted as saying: "The integrity of the board's procedures, devoid of politics and lobbying is not challenged. Free, open and unhurried discussions are the rule."[21] As Bradlee, who served on the board from 1969 to 1978, saw it: "As a standard of excellence, the Pulitzer Prizes are overrated and suspect.... In my experience, the best entries don't win prizes more than half the time. Votes are subtly, if not openly, traded between advisory board members, and while lobbying is frowned upon, the crime is lobbying and losing." He emphasized in an interview in 1999 that "Joe, to his credit, wasn't involved. I'm not even sure [of] the detail to which he knew it was going on." Nevertheless, he said, "the back door deals and the subtle lobbying" were "enough to curl your hair." He saw the majority of the board as "establishmentarian" and himself as a "maverick. I think a lot of times people wished I would go away. And Joe, he kind of loved that." He recalled that when he joined the board, "I really wanted to take them on on every issue. Joe would say, with a smile on his face: 'Now we'll hear from Mr. Bradlee,' with warmth and humor. He liked me, and I liked him.... He was just such a decent guy. His instincts were always on the side of fairness and quality journalism."[22]

A Pulitzer Prize Special Citation recognizing his board service and his accomplishments as editor and publisher of the *Post-Dispatch* was awarded to Joe when he retired from the prize board in late 1986. "You have been awarding Pulitzer Prizes for so long that it is only reasonable that you be on the receiving end," a friend remarked. In accepting, Joe said he would "treasure the citation as a remembrance of a splendid experience over the years." In response to one of many notes of appreciation, he wrote: "I call my present status 'an orderly transition toward retirement' but [at Pulitzer Publishing Company] I remain chairman, chairman of the executive committee, voting trustee, and member of the long range planning committee, so I wonder how many positions to drop before I do, in fact, retire." Former board secretary Hohenberg expressed his gratitude for the rapport between them: "It is rare in a lifetime that a relationship of perfect confidence and perfect trust exists between two people for more than two decades without a harsh word, or even a question, passing between them."[23]

21. *St. Louis Post-Dispatch,* November 7, 1986.
22. Bradlee, *A Good Life,* 365–66; Bradlee to JPIII, January 24, 1972, JPIII Papers; Bradlee interview.
23. Hohenberg was succeeded when he retired in 1975 as board administrator by Columbia journalism professor Richard T. Baker, who served until 1981. Robert C.

There is no record of Joe's having harsh words with anyone in doing Prize Board business. While he did not care for coarse or suggestive language in the *Post-Dispatch*, he did not let that influence his judgment in certain board decisions. From the beginning of his tenure on the Prize Board, he had no hesitation in voting for works in the drama category containing sexually explicit subject matter to which some board members objected.[24] Plays with uplifting themes and purer content that matched the moral attitudes of the majority of jury and board members had long had a strong advantage, to the distress of some critics who thought other plays should have won. This began to change at midcentury. During his first season as chairman, Joe voted for *Cat on a Hot Tin Roof* by Tennessee Williams, of which a wire service critic said: "There is more and rougher dialogue of a sexual nature—a lot more and a lot rougher—than in any other American play ever produced on Broadway. Much of it is completely unnecessary." However, the major New York critics praised the work. Brooks Atkinson of the *Times* said it was "stunning" drama, and Walter Kerr of the *Herald-Tribune* called it "beautifully written." Joe agreed, Hohenberg recorded: "He had little patience with the arguments against its extravagant language and unpleasant sexual themes, but based himself entirely on its effectiveness as a piece of realistic theater." The board endorsed his view, and Williams won his second drama prize.[25] He did not prevail eight years later, though, when the board denied the award to Edward Albee's uncompromising *Who's Afraid of Virginia Woolf* by a margin of one vote, Joe being with the five-member minority. Two members of the unanimous jury resigned in protest.

Joe's liberal attitude about uncompromising language in drama did not carry over to the tone he believed the *Post-Dispatch* should take. He was fond of the aphorism that newspapers should "comfort the afflicted and

---

Christopher, formerly of the *New York Daily News*, succeeded Baker and was the last board secretary to serve with J. P. III. Minutes of Fall Meeting of Pulitzer Prize Board, November 21, 1986, JPIII to Columbia President Michael I. Sovern, November 5, 1986, and April 30, 1987, Sovern to JPIII, April 16, 1987, JPIII to James H. Ottaway, December 23, 1986, JH to JPIII, November 17, 1986, JPIII Papers.

24. Emily Pulitzer said "a large spectrum of theater really did interest him—virtually the whole range of things, from experimental works to performances of the Black Rep Theatre and classical plays." Friend Richard Gaddes, founder of the Opera Theatre of St. Louis in 1975, agreed: "Some of these shows were very thought provoking" on subjects such as AIDS. "He had a very curious mind and he enjoyed them." ERP to author, April 6, 2005; Interview with Richard Gaddes, May 24, 1994, St. Louis.

25. Jack Graver of United Press International and JPIII quoted in Hohenberg, *The Pulitzer Prizes*, 260–61. Williams's first prize was in 1948 for *A Streetcar Named Desire*.

afflict the comfortable,"[26] seeing it as appropriate to his newspaper's dedication to civic betterment, but he did not treat it as an endorsement of crude, irreverent, or flippant references in news or editorials. This was not necessarily inconsistent with his acceptance of frank expression in other forums, such as novels and plays, whose approaches to communication were different. As editor, he strove to keep the paper within boundaries his grandfather, the self-reformed yellow journalist, dictated in 1911: "Now about this matter of sensationalism. A newspaper should be scrupulously clean, it should avoid everything salacious or suggestive, everything that could offend good taste or lower the moral tone of its readers; but within these limits it is the duty of a newspaper to print the news."[27] It proved a harder task than he might have expected to apply those norms, although it was somewhat easier during the first decade of his editorship than after, when issues of sexual freedom and women's liberation gained wide attention.

He had inherited a paper whose female domain was the society page, reigned over for forty-one years by society editor Margaret Ruhl. Olivia Skinner, who became the paper's first women's page editor in 1965, described the *Post-Dispatch* as "suspicious of women. I was patted on the head and told to write weddings and garden parties."[28] Harper Barnes, who was hired as a reporter the same year, described the newsroom of that day as a scene from the 1931 film *The Front Page*, complete with spittoons, clattering manual typewriters, and "guys in white shirts with their sleeves rolled up.... It was a very macho business. There were very few women. Everybody smoked." Things began to change during the year Skinner served as women's editor before shifting to feature writing, which she preferred to editing. "She helped kill the society page," said a story on her retirement in 1975. "The society department was destructive to the city," she argued. "It did not give recognition to the thousands of women who did things for St. Louis, but did not belong to society." She renamed the page "Today's Woman," stopped running stories about debutante parties and other society functions, and forecast the demise of women's pages. "I did not see the new section as permanent," she said. "Women were coming on so strong that they no longer needed sections like that."[29]

26. Often mistakenly attributed to his grandfather rather than its author, early-twentieth-century Chicago newspaper editor and wit Peter Finley Dunne (1867–1936). JPIII speech, Harvard Club of St. Louis, October 22, 1982.

27. Quoted in JPIII to EAG, July 9, 1969, JPIII Papers.

28. *St. Louis Post-Dispatch*, April 6, 1975; Margaret Ruhl obituary, *Post-Dispatch*, February 19, 1963.

29. *St. Louis Post-Dispatch*, April 6, 1975.

While Joe did not object to Skinner's changes, he was accustomed to the older way of doing things—"a sort of anything below the neck should not get mentioned in the paper" prissiness, Sally Defty called it—and favored maintaining a well-mannered approach toward news by and about women when he became editor.[30] "As a matter of taste, I would like, hereafter, not to print pictures on the society page of pregnant women," he wrote managing editor Crowley in 1960. "News pictures, of course, are quite another matter." He also objected to the use of the phrase, "her daughters by her late husband" in a wedding story, saying it struck him "as related to animal husbandry," and suggested that a "less awkward" alternative be found.[31] When "Today's Woman" was in its early days he told managing editor Bertelson that he did not consider the section suitable for "difficult, unpleasant subjects of an economic or social nature." In particular, he did not think a story about birth control methods should have appeared there.[32]

His attitude changed, however, as it became clear that society was moving in a new direction. "In every field, the emancipated woman is more and more measured by the same criteria which apply to men," he commented in a note to Defty when she succeeded Skinner as women's editor in 1966. "The old-fashioned conception of the frivolous 'society woman' is only a quaint, nostalgic...memory."[33] In a report to Joe after she attended an American Press Institute seminar in 1968, *Everyday Magazine* editor Joan Dames said that while the magazine was "much admired" by seminar participants, "our women's pages were not." They criticized the *Post-Dispatch* for giving only five columns of space each day to women's news, less than any of the thirty other papers represented. "They also thought we were too cowardly and timid about tackling major issues of interest to women: e.g., the emotional results of illegitimate pregnancy on a family, changing morality, or in-depth coverage of the impact of the pill on the modern woman's world. On the basis of this, I suggest that we reexamine the taboo against writing about reproduction and sexuality on the women's pages. Women tend to be more down to earth about these matters than men suspect."[34]

Joe recorded no disagreement with that, but in his opinion, the magazine blatantly overstepped the next year in its description of the film *Midnight Cowboy*. A sentence on its cover page described the main character,

30. SBD interview, December 12, 1994.
31. JPIII to RLC, December 12, 1960, and November 10, 1961, JPIII Papers.
32. JPIII to ARB, February 3, 1966, JPIII Papers.
33. Undated note to Defty with JPIII to EAG, October 24, 1968, JPIII Papers.
34. Joan Dames to JPIII, undated, from EAG files for 1968, JPIII Papers.

portrayed by actor John Voight, as a man who goes to New York "to sell his body to lonely, rich women and finds only men are buying." He instructed managing editor Graham to "hold a clinic" with various editors and "find an acceptable standard of taste regarding sex" using the founder's dictum on sensationalism as guidance. "Although this is a period of uncompromising realism," he explained, "I think it is a mistake for the P. D. to advertise offbeat films on the magazine cover which is read by children." The next day Graham circulated a list of guidelines to be followed. These included: "Eliminate unnecessary details or words that may be offensive to some readers and do not significantly illuminate their understanding of the story."[35]

Although such suggestions may have helped, the fact remained that no formula subject to interpretation could be definitive. Across society, including in legislatures, courts, and editorial offices, people were struggling to establish margins of good taste and morality in expression. Rules and regulations were devised and then challenged on freedom of speech grounds and in turn either modified, replaced, or rejected as new permutations of "offensiveness" appeared. U.S. Supreme Court Justice Potter Stewart memorialized the complexity when he admitted in 1964 that while he could not define obscenity, "I know it when I see it."[36]

Through it all, Joe did what he thought best, paying attention to ethical considerations as well as matters of taste. He had no difficulty agreeing with the news staff's decision to publish a stark photograph showing the bodies of a father, mother, and daughter who had been tied to trees and shot to death in 1973: "Gruesome pictures which would not have been carried a number of years ago seem less shocking today, after years of indoctrination [by] television and film. A part of truth is 'uncompromising realism,' and if brutality exists, it is a part of life which cannot be wished away," he wrote Graham.[37] That said, he did not shrug off certain things that started showing up on television, at least when the local NBC affiliate was company-owned. "I had the misfortune to view the NBC show 'Saturday Night' on October 2,"[38] he notified chief broadcasting executive Harold Grams in 1976. "I regard the show as a disaster or a

35. JPIII to RLC, December 12, 1960, and November 10, 1961, JPIII to EAG, July 9 and 10, 1969, EAG to ARB and others, July 10, 1969, JPIII Papers.

36. In *Jacobellis v. Ohio*, 378 U.S. 184 (1964). With limited success, the Supreme Court began a seemingly never-ending effort in the 1950s to separate "obscene" speech from constitutionally protected forms of expression. Wayne Overbeck, *Major Principles of Media Law*, 336–50.

37. JPIII to EAG, January 18, 1973, JPIII Papers.

38. Usually referred to as *Saturday Night Live*, the program began its twenty-ninth season on NBC on October 4, 2003. www.nbc.com/Saturday;Night;Live.

catastrophe because of its amateurism, lack of taste, lack of finesse, lack of sophistication, heavy-handed vulgarity and absence of charm or wit. . . . I suppose this is a reflection of an industry obsessed with ratings." Grams confirmed the importance of ratings, pointing out that the show had become one of the network's "few recent successes" by targeting "the 18–35 age group." Then he added: "It has had good reviews from the critics. Most people over 35 don't like the style of the show or the material used and they don't tune in. I assume you will join that group."[39]

Joe's distaste for "Saturday Night" was mild compared to his criticism of a feature story in 1981 about a woman psychologist's book on female sexual response titled *Nice Girls Do.* In a memorandum to managing editor Lipman, he called the story "one of the most shocking and disgusting things I have ever read in the *Post-Dispatch.*" He objected to promoting the commercial success of the book, questioned the author's credentials, and declared: "It is not the role of the *Post-Dispatch* to serve as a clinic for sexual therapy." In questioning the failure to apply the paper's existing guidelines, he told Lipman to "report to me that my objections to the story are understood" by staff members and to get assurances that "care will be taken" to avoid a repetition.[40]

He was similarly emphatic in 1984 in objecting to "tasteless and crude" references in a Sunday feature story about middle age. "I demand that you institute a clean-up squad to prevent materials of this nature from appearing in our news or feature columns," he told Lipman. "The *Post-Dispatch* should maintain the same standards of sensitivity and decency as the *New York Times.* I am opposed to the Rupert Murdoch obsession with sex and violence and will not tolerate such methods for attracting circulation."[41] He previously had made clear that KSD-TV would not use sensational subjects to compete for viewer ratings. When a rival station scheduled a series on incest during a ratings period, Grams thought it would be a mistake "to permit Channel 4 to clobber our ratings with this type of news programming," but Joe ruled otherwise: "I do not believe . . . that KSD's integrity and reputation for good taste should be compromised by trying to meet such undeserving competition."[42]

39. JPIII to HOG, October 4, 1976, HOG to JPIII, October 6, 1976, JPIII Papers.
40. JPIII to DL, April 6, 1981, JPIII Papers.
41. JPIII to DL and DL reply, February 14, 1984, JPIII Papers. Lipman agreed that the paper's standards had not been followed and pledged to be more careful.
42. HOG to JPIII, January 22, 1976, JPIII to HOG, January 27, 1976, JPIII Papers.

Seventeen
With Family and Friends

Joe and Lulu Pulitzer lived their private lives largely as they had growing up, in surroundings of status and comfort, often in the company of friends. During their twenty-nine-year marriage, they divided their time in St. Louis between their two residences there. In the colder months they lived on Pershing Place in the city's Central West End. They moved in the spring to the suburb of Ladue, where they owned fifteen acres that had been part of his father's one-hundred-acre estate, Lone Tree Farm. There were two homes on the property, a summer house with a pool and—for spring and fall use—a house converted from a stable that had been part of the former farm. Someone dubbed the house by the pool "the summer palace." The city house was in an area of fashionable homes dating from the 1890s described as an "ambitious effort of the wealthy to wall off the outside world" and—into the 1960s—as "the real heart of St. Louis society." Their home was modest in comparison with others in that section of town. Like Joe's parents, the couple belonged to the St. Louis Country Club, "the most exclusive of the [city's] larger social organizations."[1] They also enjoyed travel, and regularly spent time away from St. Louis with people they knew through art and other connections.

In St. Louis, they were somewhat atypical of most in the city's upper-class establishment. While they enjoyed luxury and sophistication, they were not as exclusive in their friendships as others in their social tier, involving themselves less than most, for example, in St. Louis Country Club activities. Joe did not enjoy such pastimes as golf and tennis, or the banter that went with them. "There are different tribes in a town like this," friend and businessman Nelson Reed said of St. Louis.[2] He described "Joe's tribe" as "the people he grew up with, the movers and shakers in the art world, and I would also say to an extent, [some] in journalism." In deference to journalistic independence, as earlier noted, Joe did not join business-oriented organizations such as Civic Progress. There was, of

1. Primm, *Lion of the Valley,* 366–67; Polk and Curley, *Uncle Polky,* 27.
2. Reed, like J. P. III, was the head of a St. Louis family business, Reed Rubber Products, used primarily in building. Reed interview, February 16, 1995, St. Louis.

course, the gulf in sociopolitical outlook between the *Post-Dispatch* and many of the merchants, manufacturers, bankers, and lawyers who made up the city's commercial elite. Although Joe knew many people in business, these, with a few exceptions, were not close relationships. Sally Bixby Defty, who observed high society behavior as the granddaughter of a powerful St. Louis industrialist and businessman,[3] remembered parties "where there would be a bunch of Country Club types, and one of them would start talking to Joe about the 'commie pinko rag' in the most offensive way." Joe "never got into it," she said. "He didn't turn and walk on his heel. He would just say something rather deft and turn to somebody [else], but it never got under his skin." Once when she asked him how he managed to maintain his civility, he replied: "My father told me I just have to let it, you know, water off a duck's back." (He did remark in a 1988 speech commemorating the paper's 110th anniversary, however, that because of *Post-Dispatch* exposés of corruption involving some of the city's wealthiest individuals, his grandfather "evidently was not a candidate for membership in the St. Louis Country Club."[4])

Joe preferred to keep the social side of his life private. He made clear that the activities of himself and his family were not to appear in the paper's society columns, although those of people they knew sometimes did. In 1961 Joe notified managing editor Crowley that "my wife has heard quite a lot of adverse comment" about a women's page columnist's account of a weekend outing attended by some St. Louisans at exclusive Watch Hill, Rhode Island. "Apparently the affluence and perhaps the dissipation reported were distressing to the participants and close friends." The column had the partiers rushing from cocktails at one place to drinks at another and "then on to a buffet," with barely time to change clothes between engagements. It described the arrival of a couple "and their attractive children" who traveled aboard their "magnificent new sloop" from their summer home in Hyannisport, Massachusetts, "right next door" to President Kennedy's home. The party's hostess "dashed down to the Yacht Club" to meet the sailors and "sent her chauffeur" to meet a guest who came by train. "This again demonstrates the difficulties of a chitchat column," Joe reminded Crowley.[5]

---

3. William K. Bixby was head of the American Car and Foundry Company and a director of several banks, railroads, and other corporations. Obituary, *St. Louis Post-Dispatch*, October 29, 1929.

4. Address at the Newcomen Society Dinner Meeting, St. Louis Club, December 1, 1988, JPIII Papers.

5. JPIII to RLC, September 15, 1961, with *Post-Dispatch* clipping dated September 11, JPIII Papers.

A decade later he asked managing editor Graham to "please tactfully explain that I think it is in poor taste for the Pulitzers to be named in social items." "Frankly, I was very disappointed and dismayed to read that my brother and his wife and I, among others, were to attend a $100 a plate dinner for the [opening of the] Kennedy Center in Washington." His sister, Kate Davis Quesada, was one of the organizers. He criticized the article for being "too long, too effusive, too impressed by the aura of wealth and social pretension of the individuals. . . . We are to be resolute and positive in news evaluation of what is or is not promotion, and when promotion rears its head irrespective of its source, in this case my sister, Mrs. E. R. Quesada, we are to place it in perspective, reducing it to reasonable proportion."[6]

These reactions would not have surprised Joe's longtime friend Julius Polk ("Polky"), who knew Joe admired sophistication but disliked ostentation. "He was pretty sophisticated himself," Polk said, and was "perceptive enough to usually detect pseudo-sophistication. One thing he thought was really horrible was pretension." Said another friend: "He never, never, flaunted what he had."[7] Polk remembered that he and Joe, both interested in the theater, got together occasionally when both were living in St. Louis after college to try to write dialogue for a drawing-room comedy in the style of playwrights S. N. Behrman and Noel Coward. Nothing but their own amusement came of the effort. Their observations of the local social scene nourished their imaginations. Polk recalled, for example, that Mrs. George Niedringhaus, whose husband's family was in the steel business, was once overheard instructing a young lady: "My dear Miss Warfield. I married into commerce and am very happy. I would advise you, Miss Warfield, to do the same."[8] During the same post-college period, Polk said, he, Joe, Kate Davis, and two or three friends congregated weekly at "5 o'clock, the martini hour," in one of their homes as the Monday Martini Society. Only French—in which Joe and Kate Davis were fluent— was spoken during these gatherings.

People who knew Lulu described her warmly. One remembered her as "a grande dame" who was "very elegant, wise, compassionate, generous and beautiful. She had bright, sparkling brown eyes that shone with intelligence and merriment." Another said she "certainly wasn't stuffy." A third complimented her "genius for friendship, for understanding other people's problems, and wanting to help them. Somehow, she was a person

6. JPIII to EAG, May 10, 1971, JPIII Papers.
7. Interview with Helen F. (Wiz) Jones, March 23, 1995, St. Louis.
8. Polk and Curley, *Uncle Polky*, 34.

you could talk to about anything."[9] Joe's artist friend Walter ("Wally") Barker remembered that "she loved partying, but only with certain people that she could feel absolutely confident about. When we were all together in a small group, it was just a howl. We were all really impudent." Barker's former wife, Ruth "Tookie" McClenahan, a fashion illustrator, described her as "like an empress. She would always sit like she was a lady." She also found her playful. She once stooped beside Lulu to ask a question during a party, putting her elbow on the knee of a man sitting beside Lulu. "A lady never puts her elbow on a gentleman's knee," Lulu remarked. Tookie then put her chin on his knee, to which Lulu reacted: "Chin yes, elbow no." Similarly, Wally found Joe to be "very discreet" among people he was not sure of, but when with close friends "he would constantly joke, especially when [former Art Museum Director] Perry Rathbone was in town and we would have a drink or two together... roaring with laughter at some of the silliness of St. Louis aristocracy." Jerry Berger, the writer of a widely read *Globe-Democrat* and then *Post-Dispatch* column about St. Louis movers and shakers and behind-the-scenes goings-on in the city, especially enjoyed his sense of humor. He remembered attending an "A-list" party where Joe introduced him to a woman whose family once owned a large part of the land on which St. Louis University was built. Before making the introduction, Berger said, "he whispered to me: 'Very old money.' And while he's talking, he lifts her necklace, bit into a diamond, and said, 'I love the taste of old money.' He was putting her on. He mocked rich people, and sort of made fun of himself—self-deprecating humor."[10]

One time in the mid-1950s, Wally and Tookie were living on the unfashionable Left Bank in Paris when Joe and Lulu were in the city and asked them out for dinner. They met the Pulitzers at the Ritz Hotel on the other side of the Seine, expecting to be taken to a fine restaurant in that vicinity.

---

9. Sally Defty found Lulu to be especially caring. She remembered how, at a party "when my marriage was in just terrible shape," Lulu took her aside to tell her, "You just don't get divorced. Everybody has these ups and downs, but you just don't." The couple did divorce.

Information about the social lives of Joe and both his wives comes from interviews with Adam Aronson, Walter Barker, Charles Buckley, Patricia Degener, Sally B. Defty, Robert Duffy, Richard Gaddes, James V. Maloney, Ruth McClenahan, Robert and Lois Orchard, William J. Polk, Jr., Elkhanah Pulitzer, Emily Rauh Pulitzer, Joseph Pulitzer IV, Michael E. Pulitzer, Kate Davis Pulitzer Quesada, Euretta Rathbone, Nelson A. Reed, William F. Woo, and the obituary of Louise Vauclain Pulitzer, *St. Louis Post-Dispatch*, December 22, 1968.

10. Berger's column ran for sixteen years in the *Globe*, then moved to the *Post* when the *Globe* closed in 1984. He retired in 2004. Interview with Jerry Berger, February 27, 1995, St. Louis; *St. Louis Post-Dispatch*, March 28, 2004.

To Tookie's disappointment, Joe said he knew of a good place on the Left Bank. "We piled into a small car with Joe driving at a fast clip through very dark streets with no names," she said. "We found a dark storefront with no lights or name or address that Joe decided was the place and he was right. Inside was very elegant; ladies with diamonds flashing and food served under glass. I couldn't get over Joe driving all through Paris on these dark little streets. He knew Paris well. That was Lulu's favorite city." She and Joe celebrated their twenty-fifth wedding anniversary in 1964 at the Paris Ritz, with guests from both America and Europe.

In St. Louis, the Crystal Palace cabaret and theater was a favorite night spot of the Pulitzers in the late fifties and early sixties. It was the center-piece of Gaslight Square, a midtown area of several blocks where second-hand and antique shops had been transformed into restaurants, coffee houses, and nightclubs, creating a bohemian ambience. The area flour-ished for about a decade, then fell into decline. Jay Landesman, who grew up near the Central West End, was the guiding force behind the Crystal Palace, established by him and his brother, Fred. *Post-Dispatch* reporter Robert Duffy described it as the locale for "the best drinking conversa-tions to be found between New York and San Francisco," and "a state of mind created by the Landesmans."[11] It was inspired by places Jay Lan-desman frequented while living in New York's Greenwich Village where he worked as editor of *Neurotica,* a poetry magazine he founded. His circle there included Allen Ginsberg, Jack Kerouac, and other avant-garde poets, writers, and artists of the so-called "Beat Generation."

In addition to "beats," the Crystal Palace attracted business and profes-sional people and socialites. Landesman described its décor, which com-bined crystal chandeliers and stained glass, as "a cross between a church and a movie palace, without the reverence." He brought some emerging talents to the cabaret's stage, including singer Barbra Streisand and come-dians Woody Allen, Mike Nichols and Elaine May, the Smothers Brothers, and Dick Gregory. The night rough-talking comedian Lenny Bruce ap-peared, Joe left "the opening-night audience well before the intermission."[12] In 1959 *The Nervous Set,* a musical satire, opened at the Crystal Palace. Jay Landesman and Theodore J. Flicker wrote it, with lyrics by Jay's wife, Fran, and music by former St. Louisan Tommy Wolfe. The musical mocked both uptight "squares" and rebellious "beats." It got enthusiastic reviews,

11. *St. Louis Post-Dispatch,* April 2, 1973.
12. Jay Landesman Papers, 1937–1997, Web site archives of Western Historical Manu-script Collection, University of Missouri, St. Louis, www.umsl.edu; Ernest Kirschten, *Catfish and Crystal,* 407–10; Joe Pollack, "Rocco Landesman: Gambling on Broadway," *St. Louis* (magazine), March 1998, 42.

including unpublished praise from Joe in a memorandum to editorial page editor Robert Lasch recommending "a short editorial bouquet for the Landesman brothers" for bringing "a breath of fresh air to St. Louis." Joe called the play "a sparkling and provocative musical which I am convinced would be a smash hit on or off Broadway."[13] That may have been wishful thinking because he was one of the production's financial backers. The musical made it to Broadway, but lasted only twenty-one performances. *New York Times* theater critic Brooks Atkinson commented that the show had "an unfortunately wholesome conclusion, . . . but Mr. Landesman's satirical portrait in early scenes of beatnik intellectuals at war with soap, water and respectability deserved a happier time than it had in New York."[14]

Wally and Tookie Barker lived for several years in an apartment in the Gaslight Square area, where he had a studio. After Joe saw some of Wally's paintings at a show, he and Lulu visited the Barkers to see more of his work. During the visit, Lulu asked them if they would stay at the Ladue home while she and Joe took a trip. They accepted, and for several years afterward one or both were house sitters at the city and suburban residences. Joe sometimes stopped by Wally's studio on his way to work. "He enjoyed being in the sort of bohemian atmosphere and casualness, talking about art and making jokes about people we didn't like," Wally said. "He had a wonderfully wry sense of humor. He could look right through anybody and pick a phony just like that. It was low key, but very telling." Tookie remembered attending parties at the Pulitzers' summer home. "I'd never seen things like this," she said. "They would have a huge party and cover the swimming pool to make it into a dance floor, and have an orchestra at one end and tables and waiters. It was wonderful." So, she said, were their dinner parties, held inside with guests seated around tables for eight or ten. Lulu, "very good at putting things together," was the social organizer, Euretta Rathbone said, adding that Joe was glad to let her do it.

Lulu and other women considered Joe remarkably good-looking. "Lulu was very proud of his looks," Euretta Rathbone said. "She thought she was married to the handsomest man." Tookie McClenahan remembered him from a party, probably after he had returned from a trip to Mexico. He was suntanned and wore plaid trousers, a ruffled Mexican shirt, and a tomato-red blazer. "I had never seen anybody so handsome in my life." She would tell him so on occasion, she said, and he would reply, "Oh, I

13. JPIII to RL, March 12, 1959, JPIII Papers.
14. *New York Times*, August 30, 1959.

sure appreciate that. I sure need that." Sally Defty doubted the sincerity of the reaction. "I always thought Joe was just the right amount of vain for an extremely handsome man. It's sort of like when you see a very old woman and something tells you that there's just a little bit of vanity there— a becoming amount."

There were, of course, some social occasions related to Joe's work. He and both his wives attended such gatherings as those of the American Society of Newspaper Editors and the American Newspaper Publishers Association, and were socially friendly with such people as *New York Times* publisher Orville E. Dryfoos, who invited Joe and Lulu to "our annual dancing party" in the city in 1959. That occasion was black-tie, but one some years later was not. Benjamin Bradlee of the *Washington Post* recounted being in San Francisco for a newspaper executives meeting in 1973 with Joe and Emily and him and his future wife, Sally Quinn. At the end of "some deadly dinner," Bradlee proposed going for a drink somewhere. He had already picked the venue—a strip club he had visited a day or two before. En route, he told Joe their destination. Once there, he said, "Joe was just appalled to find himself sitting with his wife and his friend in a strip joint, but he sure as hell had fun."[15]

Joe's biggest recreational passion was snow skiing, which he took up in 1960 at the age of forty-seven. Before that, he and Lulu had been going to Mexico, where he enjoyed water skiing. Joe's sister, Kate Davis, who learned mountain skiing before Joe did, encouraged him to try it. The two of them skied together for a number of years after Joe learned to ski in Europe. It was there that he became an avid practitioner of the sport. The annual routine during most of the 1960s was for him and Lulu to travel to Zermatt, Switzerland, in early January, where he joined his ski instructor and guide, Germann Kronig, for several weeks of skiing between then and April. Joe fractured a small bone in his right leg the first year he skied, but recovered ready to resume.[16] He and Kronig developed a kind of skiing tour, typically starting in Zermatt and following favorable snow conditions to other resorts in the French, Italian, and Austrian alps. There were respites from the skiing, partly because Lulu did not ski. She and Joe took side trips to various European cities, and Lulu usually spent some time alone in Paris, shopping and seeing friends. Joe IV learned to ski the same year as his father and, starting at age ten, flew alone to Switzerland each

15. Telephone interview with Benjamin C. Bradley, March 31, 1999.

16. JPIII to Marshall Field, Jr., publisher of the *Chicago Sun Times* and *Chicago Daily News*, April 8, 1960, declining Field's invitation to the "Young Publishers' Dancing Party," at the American Newspaper Publishers Association meeting that year. JPIII Papers.

year so the two of them could ski together during his spring breaks from school. "That was always a fun thing," he said. During the winter vacation, Joe stayed abreast of office matters by mail, following the same pattern his father had during his annual fishing, bird hunting, and sailing vacations in Maine and Canada. Following his father's practice, he instructed the top editors and managers to send summaries of their activities to wherever he might be. When he was in Zermatt, he would receive a thick envelope of material nearly every day.

In 1967 Joe and Lulu went to Zermatt in December instead of January, taking their son along for the Christmas and New Year's holidays. Lulu had again been diagnosed with cancer, this time of the esophagus. "She made a big effort to keep us all together that holiday," Joe IV said. "I think she knew that by spring, she would not be well." After the holidays, he returned to St. Mark's to finish his senior year while they stayed in Europe so Lulu could have radiation treatments in Edinburgh, Scotland. These were not successful, and they came back to St. Louis in April. From then on she was in and out of the hospital until her death on Joe IV's birthday, December 21.[17]

After she died, Glenn Christopher said, "Joe was a very lonely man. He was adrift and had very little private life without Lulu." Christopher remembered sitting with Joe in his office in January 1969, and sensing that Joe "was feeling low." "Sometimes I think I would like to retire," Joe said to him. Christopher recoiled at the thought. "Oh, Joe, what are you going to do when you retire?" he asked. "Right now you're Joseph Pulitzer, editor, publisher, chairman of the board. You are well recognized and welcome all over the world. If you retire, within a couple of years, you're going to be Joe Pulitzer of Ladue." And he reminded him: "You can't leave the company—not in the shape it's in now."[18]

Obviously, Joe accepted the advice, although it seemed to Christopher that he was "at loose ends" for some time after Lulu died. Eventually, his social interest returned and he began dating. Over a period of two or more years, Joe IV said, his father went out with a number of women, and then "got serious about Emmy." As Emily remembered it: "He had a very mixed group of friends before I came into his life.... When Lulu died, lots of socially prominent women were thrown at him—or leapt for him—and that wasn't what he wanted." Joe had known Emily Rauh, who had degrees in art history from Bryn Mawr and Harvard, since meeting her at the

17. Additional detail in chapter 9.
18. GAC interviews, August 21, 1993, and May 19, 1995, St. Louis.

Fogg Art Museum at Harvard during her tenure there as assistant curator of drawings from 1957 to 1964. As a member of the museum's visiting committee, Joe visited the Fogg regularly. Her father, Frederick Rauh, was the third-generation head of a family insurance agency in Cincinnati, and was active in civic organizations. Her mother, Harriet Rauh, became a travel agent after Emily and her brother, Louis, were grown, and also worked for social reforms such as racial integration.

Emily was hired as the curator of the St. Louis Art Museum in 1964.[19] Joe had nothing to do with her selection, but after she arrived in St. Louis knowing no one, he and Lulu helped her become acquainted. Lulu was particularly thoughtful, she said. "She was really sort of a grande dame in the old fashioned sense—a really kind, lovely, gracious lady." Before long, Emily knew many in the Pulitzers' circle and was one of those Joe and Lulu asked to house-sit for them when they were away. During Emily's nine years as curator, "she presented extraordinary exhibitions, and significant acquisitions were made on her watch," said an article about her in 2001. "Moreover, the collecting base of St. Louis expanded. . . . She tutored a new generation of collectors with the formation of the Contemporary Art Society, which took tours to galleries around the country and brought in important artists to speak."[20]

Joe's courtship of Emily spanned four years, longer than he preferred, but she wanted to take her time. Joe proposed marriage "quite soon" after they started dating, she said, but "I still had Lulu very much in my mind, and thought I couldn't live up to her." Initially, she thought Joe mistakenly believed she would take up Lulu's social role. She described Lulu as "a much more social being than I" and herself as "an active professional, independent, with my own life, and, if you like, a modern woman. [Lulu's] life was very much her husband's." Viewing the prospect of marriage as "a big step for me into a different life and no career," Emily needed time to think it through.

Meanwhile, Joe was persistent. About two years before she agreed to marry him, he tried to give her a large diamond ring. She recalled their dialogue: Emily: "I can't accept this." Joe: "Oh yes you can." Emily: "But it's an engagement ring." Joe: "Oh, just wear it in your belly button." She remained resolute, and he put the ring away "for a couple of years," she said. In 1973 she accepted it, and they were married. She was thirty-nine; he was sixty. Cincinnati Mayor Theodore M. Berry performed the ceremony

19. Then known as the City Art Museum.
20. Eddie Silva, "Emmy Award," *Riverfront Times*, December 5, 2001.

on June 30, 1973, at the home of her parents, before thirty-five members of both families. Joseph Pulitzer IV was the best man.[21] They honeymooned in Guatemala.

After that, Emily said, she "just moved into his routine." New patterns of living gradually replaced old as the couple worked out a mutually agreeable lifestyle. Art, of course, remained her foremost interest, and she became involved in a public art project for St. Louis and privately did some curatorial work. She also belonged to arts organizations outside of St. Louis, and attended their meetings. Joe did not like being left on his own during those trips, she said, but "made enormous adjustments. He was incredibly flexible. His world really changed from dressing for dinner with a butler to me being the cook." She was used to cooking—a friend said she was "an extraordinarily gifted cook"—and told Joe that for the number of nights they were home, she would be glad to do it.[22] On fundamental matters, they found themselves like-minded. "He was very private," Emily said, "and so I think our tastes, our interests, were incredibly compatible—not only what we liked, but what we disliked." Neither was interested in expressionist art, poetry, or spectator sports. Music meant more to Joe than to her, Emily said, "but I was perfectly happy to go along." Harriet Traurig, a friend of both Joe and Emily, described their personalities as opposite in certain respects and yet compatible overall:

> Emmy is so serious and somber, although she does giggle and laugh and she's really funny. But Joe was so playful and she's so serious. And they played that off of each other really well. They had similar eyes in art, and they both knew when something was right and when something wasn't right. There were a lot of times when she got really frustrated with him. He was a big name and a big personality, and it would be "Oh, Joe, come on. Get off it." They were just the perfect marriage, and you would never have thought that. She's much younger and so serious, and such a curator, and he was such a connoisseur.[23]

When it came to making social engagements, it became clear that Joe preferred that she handle them and he would happily go along. "I think in general, Joe was socially lazy," Emily said. "He didn't make any effort

---

21. *New York Times*, July 1, 1973.

22. Joe and Lulu always had a cook, but Lulu did some cooking. She specialized in French, Italian, and Mexican dishes. Joe tried without success to get her to write a cookbook. *St. Louis Post-Dispatch*, December 22, 1968; Lois Orchard, Orchard interview.

23. Silva, "Emmy Award," 24. Ms. Traurig and the Pulitzers became friends after she became the first director of the Forum for Contemporary Art in St. Louis in 1984, now the Museum of Contemporary Art.

to see people," and they gradually stopped seeing some of those he and Lulu had enjoyed. Although he occasionally would make suggestions for social engagements, she said, "most of the social arrangements were made by me, and I suspect were done by Lulu as well." They did not go out socially as often as Joe and Lulu had, although Joe liked parties and having a good time as much as ever. "He was gay in the wonderful old fashioned sense of the word, which has always been difficult for me," she said. "He also was very optimistic—he was always the cup is half full and I was the half empty—and I must say he influenced me a lot to think more positively." Emily described herself as "much more of an activist" than Joe. "He was very happy. It may have been because he had the final say in the company, but there, too, he was not an activist. He did not get out into the newsroom."

Friends Robert and Lois Orchard gave Emily substantial credit for Joe's happiness. "I think Emily really humanized Joe to a great extent," Robert said. "He never knew there was another world out there or people other than this small group that he and Lulu were involved with." Lois remembered Joe telling her about a time he and Emily were part of a group visiting an art museum in another city, and the group was to be transported by bus. He asked Emily if they were to get on the bus: "Emily said, 'Yes, we are all riding on the bus.' And he said, 'Emily, I have never ridden on a bus.' And she said, 'Well, you can ride on the bus or you can have your chauffeur follow the bus. It's up to you, but you might have more fun if you get on the bus.' And he got on the bus," and enjoyed the new experience. His marriage to Emily enlarged Joe's sphere "to an entire community of people with whom he had never consorted before," Lois Orchard added. "He would say to me frequently: 'Life is wonderful. I have a good time.'"

Richard Gaddes, who was the founding general director of the Opera Theatre St. Louis in 1975, was a close friend of Joe and Emily's. He and Joe had well-matched senses of wit, Gaddes said, and repartee between them always was fun: "I really appreciated his sense of humor, and he always knew that I would get it, so he often played to me." He sometimes helped Emily prepare for dinners or parties at one or the other of the Pulitzer homes. Joe's role, Gaddes said, was always to remind Emily and himself of the importance of going out of one's way to be sure that everyone had a good time. "I came to realize that it was sort of grace or hospitality, those ideas that he was raised with," Emily said. He also made himself scarce until after the finishing touches of preparation were complete. When everything was in place just before the guests arrived, the dapper host would appear, looking "as if he had stepped out of the Neiman

Marcus catalog," Gaddes recalled, and ask them: "Is there anything I can do?" Gaddes also recalled that while Joe was an intellectual, "he didn't demand intellectual conversation. He actually loved gossip," and often would say to Gaddes: "Richard, let's be frivolous tonight."

Once the guests had arrived, Martha Shirk, a *Post-Dispatch* reporter married to Bill Woo, found Joe to be "the perfect host. He always remembered what people drank, and that was a constant from one party to the other," she said. Joe could not provide the bitters she asked for in her drink at the first party she attended, but had them thereafter. Often, "there would be an out-of-town person who would be sort of the centerpiece guest," she said, recalling that Mexican novelist Carlos Fuentes was "the most fascinating person I ever met at their home or almost in any social setting." Some of the guests were "old friends from around the world, and anytime they came through they would throw a party." Among Joe's favorite local guests were Walter Metcalfe, a managing partner at Bryan Cave, the largest law firm in St. Louis, and well connected in city affairs, and his wife, Cynthia. Joe enjoyed Walter, Shirk said, because he told "fabulous political stories," and Cynthia because she was both arch and funny and "very unconventional. None of the women he liked were kind of typical society wives." He also made sure guests knew of Emily's behind-the-scenes contributions to the event. For example, whenever herbs or vegetables that she had grown in the garden at the Ladue home were served at dinner parties, he made sure the guests knew that—and, as was often the case, that she had prepared the meal.

Joe encouraged Emily to learn to ski after they were married. Both enjoyed the sport, both in Europe and Colorado. Gaddes had skied a little, took lessons to improve, and accompanied the couple on several trips to Vail. Gaddes remembered Joe as "a very elegant skier," who never seemed to fall: "So there his dignity would remain." His style was "slightly old fashioned," Gaddes thought, "but it was a certain style that he had that was just absolutely correct." He did not ski the moguls—the most demanding slopes—but he could handle some of the minor moguls, Gaddes said. He kept in shape for these by doing exercises, and he regularly walked up the five flights of stairs to his office rather than using the elevator. He showed Nelson Reed a set of exercises he used "that just about kill you" to get Reed ready for a skiing trip. "You put your foot up on the john and then deep knee bend and all these terrible things. I could hardly stand it," Reed said. But after following the regimen for three weeks, he skied with no problems: "It really did a good job."

Dealing with children was another matter. Emily liked them, and wanted to spend time with Joe's two oldest grandchildren, Elkhanah and

Bianca, born in 1972 and 1975, the daughters of Joe IV and his first wife, Lynne Steinsieck. This was not a high priority for Joe, but he understood Emily's feelings because she had grown up in a nurturing family atmosphere. "I was interested in them because I had no children and realized that this was sort of my chance. They needed us because of Joe [IV] and Lynne breaking up in the early years, and I think, based on the way I was raised, you just did things with family. This clearly was not the way [Joe] had lived, and so I planned Christmas" and other activities involving the girls "and he went along with it." He got to know the girls better as they grew up. "I think when the girls got old enough for him to enjoy talking to, he had a chance to be with them in ways I suspect he didn't have much time for with his own son," Emily said. In his later years, "he was more slowed down, and I think he really enjoyed it." Joe IV's son and daughter by his second marriage, Joseph Pulitzer V and Elinor, born in 1983 and 1986, never became as close to Joe and Emily as did the two older girls.

Elkhanah said she did not think her grandfather "understood kids very well," but came to appreciate Emily's "way of incorporating us into their lives in ways that were pleasant for him to see."[24] She remembered getting "Grandpa to talk to me" by asking about various art pieces as they were walking around the house: "He would describe it from his perspective, which was incredibly interesting." As small children, she and her sister had no idea of the importance and value of the art around them. When she was about seven, she said, she and Bianca were jumping on a bed in the summer house directly in front of a large Claude Monet painting of water lilies. "And he just said, 'don't fall and scratch it.'" Gentle as his caution was, she knew it was not to be taken lightly. She had seen his temper flare, usually when he became frustrated "if something wasn't going the way he expected it to go." The girls also were warned against jumping on the bed in the master bedroom, above which hung Andy Warhol's portrait of Elizabeth Taylor. At the same time, they also saw their grandfather's softer side in, among other places, his pleasure in the family's springer spaniel, selected by the girls as a puppy and named Gambai, the Chinese term for "cheers!" or "bottoms up!" "We thought he was a very cheery or bottoms-uppy dog," Emily explained. Gambai became Joe's inseparable friend, and always sat beside his master's chair.

Joe and Emily took several vacations with the girls when they were older, including one to England, two to Italy, another to a Montana dude ranch, and several skiing trips to Vail. When traveling, her grandfather always dressed to fit his surroundings, Elkhanah said. "In Italy he looked

24. Interview with Elkhanah Pulitzer, May 11, 1995, St. Louis.

Italian, in London he looked English. . . . Somehow, he would always throw something together that looked right." He usually brought up the rear when they were sightseeing on foot, she said. "We used to kid him about walking behind because he looked authentic and we didn't." What he really wanted to do, she said, was to take his time and "fit in without feeling like a tourist. He could find out more things that way." The trips were always educational, she said, thanks to Emily's careful pre-planning and "capacity for travel and getting a lot of experiences in." Joe, Emily, and the two granddaughters were Richard Gaddes's guests during part of the English trip at Gaddes's Lake District cottage. Gaddes was born in England, started his career in artistic management there, and bought the cottage after he moved to the United States. He found that as houseguests, the Pulitzers were all easy to please. "Joe and Emmy lived a very unpretentious life," Gaddes said, including living "in that little house of mine. They loved it. Their demands were not great. They were happy with a simple lifestyle."

After stepping down as general director of the Opera Theatre in 1985, Gaddes expected he would soon be leaving St. Louis and decided to sell his home and live in a hotel. When Joe and Emily heard of this plan, they asked him to stay at whichever of their homes they were not using. Every six months, they would rotate residences, an arrangement that continued for ten years after Gaddes accepted the presidency of the city's Grand Center Arts redevelopment project. (He left St. Louis in 1995 to serve as associate general director of the Santa Fe Opera in 1995 and became its general director in 2001.) Joe was less interested in opera than in some other musical forms. Gaddes described him as "a great lover of music" but "very specific in the things he liked." He recalled listening with Joe to a piece by Dmitri Shostakovich. "Tears were running down his cheeks. . . . He certainly loved listening to a symphony orchestra, and he particularly loved the music of George Gershwin," once envisioning a Gershwin "spectacular that the symphony might do." As a young man, he developed an interest in jazz, and for some years afterward played jazz improvisations on the piano. Most years he enjoyed the program of Christmas music at Christ Church Cathedral downtown. Both Emily and Gaddes went with him at various times, and could tell that it was special to him.[25]

As previously noted, even though Joe for the most part kept his social and business lives separate, certain newspaper staff members were per-

25. Joe was a member of St. Michael and St. George's Episcopal Church in the suburb of Clayton, but never went to services there. "He considered himself very much an Episcopalian," Emily said, and when he attended church—usually at Christmas and Easter—went to Christ Church Cathedral, whose dean he knew.

sonal friends as well as employees. Among them were music critic Thomas Sherman, reporters Sally Defty and Florence Shinkle, and art critic Patricia Degener. The women were family friends whose talents, in his opinion, merited hiring them.[26] He and Robert Duffy became friends after being introduced by the Landesmans. Duffy, who studied art history at Washington University, was hired as a feature writer and became *Post-Dispatch* arts editor. Bill Woo and both his first and second wives also became social friends of Joe and Emily. After Woo became editor, his second wife, Martha Shirk, recalled, he began holding an annual Christmas party for the newsroom staff at Blueberry Hill, a restaurant in University City, which Joe and Emily attended. Their willingness to do so, Shirk said, made her believe that "this myth in the office about his remoteness and snobbishness is just a misunderstanding by people who didn't know him. . . . I'm sure Joe Pulitzer had never been to Blueberry Hill in his life. It has a fabulous collection of Elvis memorabilia and fifties toys and it's a real scene. And the party was always in the basement, which smells like beer, and for Joe to come to this party was really something. It meant a lot to the staff." Joe and Emily would stay for about two hours, she said, mingling and talking with people.

This, among other things, made clear to Woo that on a personal level, Joe favored news and editorial people over those in other departments. "Joe was not immaculate in separating friendships and professional decisions," he said. "While he tried hard to separate his private life from his life as an editor, he did not achieve that separation perfectly all the time, and neither has any other editor in the history of journalism. The last thing I would want to convey is a loose reading of 'not immaculate' to mean that this was an everyday occurrence. In the years that I was the editor of the editorial page, only once in an important editorial decision did his personal friendships affect his professional decisions."[27]

Another way his regard for the journalistic staff was evident, Woo said, was when things "would get particularly sticky" during negotiations with the Newspaper Guild, and Joe "would be a source of recourse for the Guild," to the dismay of his business executives. "Joe was determined that the paper should maintain its quality," Woo said. "I'm certain that

26. William Woo said of such hires: "I'm sure there were many people who wished to use their social connection with him toward the end of employment. . . . He was not in the habit of just sending along any person because they bumped into each other at a cocktail party. He did not wish to diminish, prostitute, trivialize this paper with a bunch of social hangers on. These are people in whom he had confidence."

27. This involved endorsement of a local political candidate whose opponent the editorial staff favored as being more compatible with *Post-Dispatch* policy.

one of the reasons that he felt this sympathy was not merely because these were men and women doing the work of journalism for this newspaper," but because he had come to know some of them and to "appreciate their qualities." Woo also observed that when it came to decisions about who among the top editors and managers would get a 1 percent bonus from profits, the majority of those who benefited—because Joe personally approved these—were in news-editorial positions. Over a period of time, Woo observed, "the number of newsroom people on the 1 percent plan relative to advertising, circulation, promotion, etcetera, was way out of balance." (J. P. II had the same bias, once telling Joe that there were two salary scales for *Post-Dispatch* executives, $25,000 for the journalists and $20,000 for the business department heads.)[28]

Because Lulu and Emily were in the *Post-Dispatch* building at times, they became acquainted with some of the staff. Lulu visited Arthur Bertelson in his office shortly after he became managing editor in 1962 and noticed that his desk was a hand-me-down. "Why don't you go to a furniture store and get yourself a new desk and decorate this office and charge it to Joe?" she asked. "He'll pay it." Bertelson chose to keep what he had.[29] His successor, Evarts Graham, sometimes sought Emily's advice when selecting illustrations for certain layouts, especially those dealing with art, because, he said, "I knew nothing about it. She took care of me when I had something to produce."

Some years later, Joe had a less harmonious experience with a portrait artist. Banker and art collector Adam Aronson remembered when he and Joe were having their portraits painted in 1989 by "one of the great neo-realists," Alfred Leslie.[30] Aronson saw Joe's portrait in Leslie's studio before Joe saw it, and discussed it with the artist. Aronson thought it was a telling likeness, because it "makes Joe out to be a very tough, strong, powerful businessman." Joe disliked it. Leslie told Aronson that Joe would not cooperate with his effort to get him to relax while posing by conversing with Leslie or allowing the television to play during sittings. Joe told Leslie that "he needed no outside stimulation" to be himself. Because "a neo-realist paints exactly what is there—an unerring, beat-you-up visibility with no correction whatsoever," Aronson said, the painting "was harsh." Joe expressed his dislike to Leslie in a letter that Aronson read. "I do not look like that," he remembered it saying. "You made me so fierce. You made my upper lip so huge." To Aronson, the painting was truthful: "The

28. Telephone interview with JPIII, June 19, 1986.
29. ARB interview, August 19, 1993.
30. Interview with Adam Aronson, May 30, 1995, St. Louis.

lip is not really the lip the way it was, but it was the way he posed, and I'll bet you it was the way it was when he was about to say 'No.'" He added that "as a banker, I thought it was a Joe Pulitzer that I would be dealing with if he were borrowing money from me." He made his case to Joe: "I don't know why you are denying that picture because it isn't the sweet, charming Joe Pulitzer that you choose to be with all of us socially and in the art world, but it is the tough son-of-a-bitch who built the Pulitzer company from a much smaller thing that your father passed on to you. You put in the television stations, you expanded the newspaper... and that portrait is the absolute Joe Pulitzer who built an empire." Joe was not persuaded. Aronson concluded: "Joe liked other people to do exactly what he wanted—and usually had them do so, I suspect."

Eighteen
Giving Good Measure

The "orderly transition toward retirement" Joe referred to on stepping down as editor and publisher in 1986 was never completed. It was no more in his nature to step out of the action than it had been for his predecessors. He did cut back, however, especially when he finished the transfer of chief executive duties to Michael in April 1988, keeping only the title of chairman of the board. Beyond that, Emily said, "he just didn't want to give up. The idea of retirement just had a horrible sound to him." Even though he passed the titles of editor and publisher to William Woo and Nicholas Penniman in 1986, they and other executives understood "orderly transition" to mean he still expected to be consulted in key *Post-Dispatch* decisions, as he was, for example, in the hiring of new managing editor Foster Davis in 1992.[1] Not counting his four years of naval service in World War II, he was directly involved in the company for fifty-three years, from the autumn of 1936 to the spring of 1993.

He enjoyed good health most of his life. His most frequent complaint was a ragweed allergy, which he treated by leaving St. Louis in late August for what he called "my hay fever vacation," rather than taking shots for it.[2] He kept himself physically fit by exercising and carefully watching his weight. "He loved good food, but he was totally disciplined about his eating," Emily said. "He got on the scale every morning... and if he was up that day, he didn't eat. If he was where he wanted to be, he ate. He never varied more than a half pound in weight. It didn't matter if we were going to the most glamorous dinner party the night he was up. He ate, but very sparingly." His granddaughter, Elkhanah, remembered his target weight as 162 pounds and that "generally part of the conversation every day at breakfast or dinner was, 'Well, I was down, so I can have some more sorbet,' that sort of thing—very much a part of his life. He always used to say the word 'fat' in a really funny way: 'faaaht.'"[3]

1. Woo had the final say in the matter, but Joe met with each of the finalists for the job.
2. JPIII to MWC, May 20, 1970, JPIII Papers.
3. Unless otherwise noted, sources for this chapter are archival, *Post-Dispatch*, or

His conscientiousness about his health was another sign of the orderliness in his life since his school days. It was evident in his attentive but quiet style of administration and his desire to keep attention off himself. For many years, he avoided the public eye by having Joseph Holland, a lawyer and former *Globe-Democrat* reporter, as his envoy to the St. Louis community. Later on Bob Broeg, the widely known sports editor of the *Post-Dispatch*, represented him and the paper at some events. Both were outgoing, respected, and skilled speakers. Joe believed he had little talent for speaking, but those who heard him thought otherwise. As he grew older, he seemed to gain confidence and accepted more speaking invitations, as always drafting his remarks with a broad-tipped pen in his distinctive longhand.

In 1988 he agreed to be both honored and "roasted" by the St. Louis Press Club as its first-ever Media Person of the Year. Some 360 guests paid up to one hundred dollars each to attend the dinner event at the Marriott Pavilion Hotel. The proceeds went for journalism scholarships and a fund to establish a media museum at the city's public library. Former U.S. Senator Thomas F. Eagleton, at the time a *Post-Dispatch* columnist, was master of ceremonies. He referred to Joe's private nature at the outset, quoting a statement he attributed to *Washington Post* board chairwoman Katharine Graham: "Joe has the capacity to walk into an empty room and blend right in." Similarly, his friend Richard Gaddes, a frequent Pulitzer house sitter, remarked: "I thought it was a bit much when I took a call at the house and it was the *Post-Dispatch* wanting to know if Mr. Pulitzer wanted to subscribe." Stanley J. Goodman, former chief executive of the May Company Department Stores headquartered in St. Louis and manager of the company's Famous-Barr stores there before moving into upper management, commented on Joe's dress: "I could not help but admire Joe's unusual shirts, and the beautifully selected ties, the ensemble being elegant if slightly daring, and occasionally verging on the conspicuous. After a time, I began to dress more expressively. He may even have noticed this, because one day he greeted me: 'Now Stanley, you didn't get that jacket at Famous-Barr!' "[4]

Joe did not get to enjoy one "tribute" until after the event. It arrived late from Ben H. Wells, retired chief executive of the Seven-Up Company, and—like Goodman—a former president of the St. Louis Symphony

———
other published sources and interviews with Sally Bixby Defty, George Hall, Richard Gaddes, William J. Polk, Jr., Emily Rauh Pulitzer, Elkhanah Pulitzer, Joseph Pulitzer IV, Kate Davis Pulitzer Quesada, Martha Shirk, and William F. Woo.
    4. Transcription of a videotape of the event by the author.

Society. Wells mixed fact and fiction in an updated version of the *Post-Dispatch* platform:

> You know that your retirement will make no difference in the cardinal principles of the *Post-Dispatch*. That it will always fight for monopoly in the St. Louis market and never tolerate a rival daily newspaper. It will always fight corporations for making a profit and never run one that doesn't. It will always oppose tax relief for those above the poverty level, and will show sympathy for the poor by handouts from the public treasury. It will always be devoted to the welfare of the *Post-Dispatch*— what is good for the *Post* is good for the public. It will never be satisfied with merely printing news—only the news the readers should know, and adjusted to those noble principles of the *Post-Dispatch*. It will never be afraid to attack wrong, whether by predatory competitors or by avaricious take-over tycoons. There'll always be a holy, immaculate, infallible, untouchable *St. Louis Post-Dispatch*.[5]

Although the guests never heard the Wells version, they did hear the real thing when Joe recited it in his closing remarks. But first he explained how he had established himself as an independent voter in national elections. In the first election for which he was eligible—1936—he voted for Democrat Franklin D. Roosevelt, but "in 1940, when Roosevelt was running against Wendell Willkie, I made the one Republican vote in that national election that I've ever made—the one! That established my record as an independent voter." One way he had kept his independence intact, he explained, was to follow his inclination to stay away from country clubs, where "gaggles of Republicans" congregate. "I can't get involved in that," he emphasized. "It would be indiscreet. It would be very bad for my health."

His health was good at that time, and for the next two and a half years. He frequently went to his office, though Michael and others were effectively in charge. In late 1990, his physical condition began a marked decline, although "he clearly was sick before that," Emily said. "We just didn't understand what was going on." He curtailed going downtown and "somehow gave himself permission to stay home and read and do things he enjoyed, and didn't have to pretend that he was still working full time." They took an extensive trip that fall, beginning in London, then traveling to Macao, Hong Kong, Germany, and Hungary, where they visited Mako, the birthplace of Joe's grandfather.[6] While in London, Joe had several sit-

---

5. DL to JPIII, July 26, 1988, with a copy of the Wells "toast," JPIII Papers.
6. Their host was Dr. Andras Csillag, professor of American Studies at the University of Szeged and author of a biography in Hungarian of the first Joseph Pulitzer.

tings for a portrait by renowned artist Lucian Freud—grandson of the founder of psychoanalysis. The sittings were not finished when it was time to travel to the other countries. He was exhausted throughout the trip, Emily said, but as soon as they left London for the other countries, he told her, "I'm going back and get [the portrait] finished." Emily needed to return to St. Louis by that time, so he flew back to London on his own for the remaining sittings before going home. "I felt he knew somehow that it was important to get it done then and not wait, although at that point we didn't know he had cancer," Emily said. He was pleased with the portrait, as was Emily. "It's a very tired old man, but it's got a lot of strength and character," she said. Freud was highly selective in his subjects, but had agreed to meet Joe and then decide whether he would take the commission. "The two of them hit it off extremely well," Emily said. She never asked Joe about this, but speculated that their compatibility may have derived from the fact that "they both were grandsons of very famous men, yet created their own distinguished lives."

Medical tests done in November revealed colon cancer, for which he underwent surgery in early December. By February 1991, he was well enough to travel, and he and Emily went to Mexico. On their return, he began chemotherapy. He experienced minimal side effects, drove himself to and from his treatments, and remained active. "He was pretty strong then," Emily said. However, he had reason to believe that his time was growing short. He and Emily were told shortly after the surgery that there was a small cancerous lesion on his liver. Afterward—with one exception—he never mentioned this finding to his wife. "Unbelievable as it sounds," she said, the only time it came up was when they were driving home after hearing the news. "They did say that it was in the liver, didn't they?" he asked. "Yes," she replied. "And that was sort of it." If he spoke to anyone at the office about it, he did not tell her.

Emily remembered Joe saying to her after the cancer was confirmed: "The hardest thing I ever went through was Lulu's illness." That experience, she concluded, "conditioned how he behaved, because he never discussed [the lesion]. It was almost as if we didn't discuss it, it would be easier on me." He followed the course of treatment prescribed by his oncologist, Dr. Alan P. Lyss of the Missouri Baptist Cancer Center in St. Louis. Joe did not press him for details about the prognosis during appointments where Emily was present. He may have asked questions

Csillag researched the biography in Hungary and, as a Fulbright Scholar, in the United States. Emily Rauh Pulitzer to Mako Mayor Sandor Santa, July 19, 1993, JPIII Papers; author's correspondence with Csillag between 1987 and 2003.

when he saw Lyss alone, she said, but she was privy to no talk of second opinions or other treatment options. "I did witness Lyss giving him some openings, where he could have gotten the bigger truth, and he chose not to follow those," Emily said. "I don't know whether he was doing it for himself or he was doing it for me, but I think he was a man of such self control and such pride that he was going to keep a stiff upper lip and get through this with all the grace he could muster. And did."

They went to Italy in the summer of 1991, where they met friends William and Catherine Curtis, whom they met while he, an architectural historian, was a visiting professor at Washington University. Mrs. Curtis was an architect. The foursome drove to Spoleto just after its annual music festival had ended. The women decided to retrieve their car from some distance away, and on their return were motioned by William to come closer to one of the festival sites, a former church furnished only with a piano. "And there was Joe, sitting at the piano in this church, playing," Emily said. It was a rare sight, because he almost never played the piano in his later years. "I think the reason was that if he couldn't do it well, he wasn't going to do it," she said. "He didn't want to do it poorly," and for the same reason gave up bird shooting. He did continue skiing into 1992, even when taking chemotherapy, and continued attending symphony concerts. They visited Italy again that year, and he took some treatments in Florence. Then a change to a stronger medication caused a severe reaction and the treatments were stopped. Joe took it stoically. "He didn't say anything, didn't complain," Emily said. She remembered Joe's regular physician, Dr. Neville Grant, telling her that "when Joe would come into the office, the nurses and people would kind of perk up and treat him differently" because of his upbeat behavior toward them: "There was a sort of gallantness about him that they responded to."

He never lost that ability as his condition worsened and he spent most of his time at their Pershing Place home. Emily took care of him there during the last months of his life; he was never hospitalized. One of his last outings was a visit to the "period room" his father had donated to the St. Louis Art Museum in memory of his first wife, Joe's mother, Elinor Wickham Pulitzer.[7] He was unable to preside at the Pulitzer Publishing Company's 1993 annual meeting on May 12, for the first time since it went public in 1986. Michael ran the meeting with Joe in attendance by speak-

7. The room was furnished and decorated with items that their mother had especially liked. Later, Joe and his sisters, Kate Davis and Elinor, had the room reconfigured and reinstalled, and Kate Baxter, a daughter of Kate Davis, did needlepoint upholstery for a stool for the room.

erphone from home.[8] Sally Defty, a restaurateur before she became a news-paperwoman, made soups for him. Richard Gaddes lived with the Pulitzers during the last two weeks of Joe's life, helping with his care. May 13, Joe's eightieth birthday, was a busy day for him. In the morning he took a call from Yves-Alain Bois, the Joseph Pulitzer Jr. Professor of Modern Art at Harvard, a specialist in twentieth-century art. Joe endowed the professor-ship in 1978. Then his son, Joe IV, came to the house to give him a picture of the first Joseph Pulitzer's New York mansion on East Seventy-Third Street, designed and built in 1901 by architect Stanford White.[9] "He obvi-ously had made a big effort over that, and I think that pleased Joe," Emily said. In the evening, she invited five close friends for a dinner—Bill Woo and Martha Shirk, Sally Defty, Robert Duffy, and Richard Gaddes. Joe was too tired to get up, so the group went upstairs to his bedroom. There they sang "Happy Birthday," drank a champagne toast, and gave him some gifts. He said something personally to each of them as they left. Martha Shirk told him how important her relationship with him had been. "Keep on flying," he responded. Recalling the experience, she mused: "Whether he meant it the way I took it or not, it was just a wonderful thing to say to someone. . . . It said to me that he saw me as sort of a free spirit who he wanted to soar." Sally Defty said she felt uncomfortable while upstairs, "thinking this must be a terrific strain to kind of muster up that gracious-ness one more time." After the group went downstairs for a small dinner, she said there was a sense of closeness and warmth among them. They were grateful to Emily for bringing them together, and admired her abili-ties as a caregiver. "She was just wonderful through the whole thing."

On the day after his birthday, also in his bedroom, Joe was presented an honorary doctor of laws degree from Washington University. It was especially meaningful to him because his father had received the same recognition. He declined rapidly in the following days, and had some help from hospice caregivers. He died at 2:53 p.m. on May 26, 1993, at home.

Joe had directed the arrangements for his father's funeral at Christ Church Cathedral downtown, but—unlike his father—left no instruc-tions for his own. The cathedral was the obvious choice for his service, too. Emily, Gaddes, and Duffy took care of all the details, working with Bishop Hayes Rockwell and the Very Reverend J. C. Michael Allen, dean of the cathedral where the service was held on May 29. About six hundred

8. *SJR*, May 1993, 5.
9. Swanberg, *Pulitzer*, 280; *Harvard Gazette*, May 10, 1991, 5.

people attended. Emily selected some of the readings, including a Psalm read at Joe's father's funeral, and chose the flowers for the service and for the reception afterward in the Grand Hall of the Grandel Square Theatre, across the street from Powell Hall, home of the symphony. Gaddes planned the music, including some performed by instrumentalists and singers from the St. Louis Symphony and the Opera Theatre of St. Louis.[10] Duffy arranged for the printed materials, coordinated press coverage, and handled final details. The body was to be cremated.

Five people spoke during the service: *Post-Dispatch* editor Woo; William J. Polk, Jr., his friend from childhood; Richard Gaddes; James N. Wood, director of the Art Institute of Chicago and a former director of the St. Louis Art Museum; and Angelica Zander Rudenstine, an art historian, whose husband, Harvard University President Neil L. Rudenstine, was one of the eight pallbearers.[11] Woo spoke of Joe's contribution to the *Post-Dispatch:* "Joseph Pulitzer [III] gave us the one thing which means more than anything to those who are led; and that is a worthy goal, a mission so dignified and so encompassing and so lofty that not one of us could ever say it was done, that the challenge had been put behind, finally."[12] Likewise, those who spoke of his contributions to the arts emphasized their lasting significance. "He was a benefactor of all those who lived in St. Louis, one way or another," an unidentified woman told a television interviewer outside the cathedral after the service. In addition to the *Post-Dispatch* and many St. Louis publications, tributes appeared in newspapers and magazines nationwide and abroad. Of these, Joe may have appreciated as much as any an editorial in the *St. Louis American* observing that it

> and many other local African-American institutions and individuals were the beneficiaries of his influence and quiet support.... Before the ultra-conservative *St. Louis Globe-Democrat* folded in 1983, the *Post-Dispatch*'s coverage helped balance the largely negative portrayal (particularly in the political upheaval of the 1960s) of African-American activists.... Though he and his newspaper were often the targets of bitter criticism, much of it narrow and unwarranted, he never relented and stayed with his convictions.... Mr. Pulitzer, a "liberal aristocrat," helped

10. Among them Christine Brewer, soprano, who subsequently became internationally renowned. Interviews with Richard Gaddes and ERP.

11. The others were: Sally Bixby Defty and Robert W. Duffy of the *Post-Dispatch* staff; Nicholas G. Penniman IV, *Post-Dispatch* publisher; James V. Maloney, secretary of Pulitzer Publishing Company; Ronald K. Greenberg, a St. Louis art dealer; and artists Ellsworth Kelly and Richard Serra.

12. Memorial booklet of the funeral service, privately printed, 1993, pages not numbered.

enrich and improve the quality of life for many. He then helped moderate some of the harsh excesses that were heaped on the less privileged
and less powerful.[13]

As earlier noted, the bulk of Joe's estate was held in trust, where details
of its contents, including its total value, could remain private. The trust
contained 43 percent of the company's family-held stock, with ten times
the voting power of its public stock, and most of his art collection. Emily
was named its beneficiary, and became a company director and trustee
with voting power over the largest portion of family stock.[14] At the time
of his death, Joe's Pulitzer stock was valued at nearly $122 million. He
also had a will, which left art of undisclosed value, the homes in the Central West End and Ladue, and $5 million to Emily. Joe IV also received art,
including the bronze bust of the first Joseph Pulitzer by Auguste Rodin,
and his father's interest in Beechcroft, the family's summer home at Bar
Harbor, Maine. (Sometime afterward, Joe IV sold his interest to his aunt,
Kate Davis, who used the home most often.) Joe's sisters, Elinor Hempelmann and Kate Davis Quesada, received portraits of family members.
Germann Kronig, Joe's ski instructor at Zermatt, Switzerland, received
$25,000.

One of Joe's strongest preoccupations during the last years of his life
was planning for construction of what became the Pulitzer Foundation
for the Arts, a key element in the revitalization of Grand Center in midtown St. Louis, eventually completed almost nine years after his death.
The Grand Center district covers a ten-block area along or close to Grand
Boulevard, where, between the 1920s and 1950s, more than a dozen movie
palaces, major office buildings, shops, restaurants, and three churches
constituted a lively social center. Many of these places closed and the area
fell into neglect after midcentury as people moved to the suburbs. A slow
revival began in 1966, when the St. Louis Theatre, a dilapidated movie
house, was restored and in 1968 became the St. Louis Symphony's home.
In the early 1980s the forty-five-hundred-seat Fox Theater was restored as
a venue for concerts and Broadway productions. These successes led to
the establishment in the mid-eighties of Grand Center, a nonprofit organization of St. Louisans interested in art, education, and entertainment. Their
aim was to restore the boulevard's numerous empty spaces and reestab-
lish it as a cultural center. One project converted a former church into the

13. *St. Louis American*, June 3, 1993.
14. *St. Louis Post-Dispatch*, June 9, June 13, and August 28, 1993. William Bush, a
lawyer with Fulbright and Jaworski, New York, and James V. Maloney, secretary of
Pulitzer Publishing Company, were also named trustees of the Pulitzer Trust.

Grandel Square Theatre, where the Black Repertory Theatre Company established residence.

Richard Gaddes became Grand Center president in 1987, at Joe's urging. "If you will take it, Emmy and I will help," Joe told him. "That's what got me into it," Gaddes said in 2004, "and they were hugely generous on an annual basis. Grand Center would not exist were it not for Joe and Emmy, because they actually provided most of the seed money to get it going, and the success it is beginning to realize today is directly attributable to their ongoing support." Joe served on the Grand Center board of directors, and was, Gaddes said, "very active. . . . He would ask very deep, perceptive questions, particularly if there was lots of friction."[15] The Pulitzer Foundation opened in 2001, and in 2003 the city's Forum for Contemporary Art moved into a new building next door. By then, the city's public television station was in new quarters in Grand Center, and housing, shops, art galleries, and restaurants filled other spaces.[16]

One of Joe's last wishes, expressed to Gaddes shortly before he died, was about the yet-to-be-built Pulitzer Foundation: "Richard, it must be perfect." The privately funded project (the cost was not disclosed) largely took shape under Emily's direction after his death.[17] She and Joe had picked Tadao Ando from Japan, one of the world's most important architects, to design the building. Richard Serra and Ellsworth Kelly, artists whose work they had collected for years, suggested that they look at some of Ando's buildings. As soon as she and Joe saw photographs of several of them in Japan, Emily recalled, "We said with one voice: 'This is the one.'" At the time, they envisioned renovating an old automobile factory into a modest space where larger works from their collection, then in storage, could be shown on the second floor with the ground floor being turned over to public use and run by someone else. However, after Joe's death, Emily went to Japan to see Ando's buildings and realized that "in selecting Tadao Ando as the architect, we had really given Ando the wrong project, and so we embarked on a new building." It was Ando's first major

15. Gaddes interviews, May 24, 1995, and June, 9, 2004.

16. Unless otherwise noted, information about Grand Center and the Pulitzer Foundation for the Arts is from the *St. Louis Post-Dispatch,* March 16 and September 1, 1995, October 27, 2000, January 14, September 9, and October 7, 2001, and May 25, 2003; *New York Times,* January 15, 2001; *RFT,* September 19, 2001; Transcript of "Breakfast at the Arts: Grand Endeavor: The Pulitzer Foundation for the Arts," June 16, 2002, A & E television network; Web sites of City of St. Louis Development Activity, St. Louis Convention and Visitors Commission, and *St. Louis Commerce Magazine,* September 2002, accessed via Web search for Pulitzer Foundation for the Arts, March 4, 2004.

17. Emily donated $12.5 million in stock to the foundation in 2000. *St. Louis Post-Dispatch,* September 9, 2001.

project in the United States, and, she said, "he had a bigger vision than we." Ando said his goal was "to create a place that really makes you feel the possibilities that arise, a promise of moving forward into a new age." The end result was a twenty-seven-thousand-square-foot, three-level gallery of steel, concrete, and glass with both indoor and outdoor spaces, a reflecting pool, and beds of hardy greenery. These elements interact with the ever-changing natural light to create a tranquil experience for visitors. The walls inside and out are of so fine a finish that they also reflect light, and, as a visitor remarked, feel "like satin." The foundation's exhibits change periodically and often include pieces from the Pulitzers' collection. It also houses the Pulitzers' library of resource materials for the study of art.

Whether the Pulitzer Foundation for the Arts is "perfect," as Joe wished it to be, the four-year-long construction process begun in 1996 pressed deliberately toward that ideal. Perhaps the key factor in this was Emily's willingness to give the builders the time to concentrate on the details. "To do a world-class concrete building, well, it just doesn't happen by accident," construction manager Peter Clarkson commented. Steve Morby, the project's general superintendent, added, "It is simplistic construction, and that means that everything has to be perfect—every elevation, creating windows and doors, alignments of walls. It has to be zero tolerance." Carpenter foreman John Pleimann observed that the builders "wanted to do the best work they probably could ever do in their lives, and it shows."

Emily commissioned Serra and Kelly to provide new works for the foundation. Serra considered Joe and Emily's decades-long interest in his work a major factor in the development of his art. He produced a massive 125-ton torqued spiral of two-inch-thick weathered steel approximately forty feet wide, forty-eight feet long, and nearly fourteen feet high through which the viewer walks. The work, which Serra named *Joe*, was assembled in a courtyard beside the foundation building from five 25-ton pieces. Kelly's contribution was *Blue Black (2001),* two vertical monochromatic aluminum panels twenty-eight feet high placed one atop the other under a skylight at the end of the main gallery. Emily described the foundation as "a place where people can see art in a setting that is different from the traditional museum setting. It is another alternative for looking at art.... This building is not like anyone's home, but there are aspects of the way one sees art here that are similar to the opportunities one has at home. The light is not static, it is ever changing, so every day of the year, every period during the day, it is a different experience." She characterized it as "an experimental haven which we hope will encourage new art and architectural experiences." Admission is free, as it is at most of the city's other museums, but open to the public only two days a week. On other days it is used by researchers and for meetings and seminars and hosts concerts, lectures, and discussions. After some initial questioning of the decision to regulate public access, the reasoning for doing so gained acceptance. The *Riverfront Times* spoke of "many jaw-dropping moments the Pulitzer provides," and described the visitor restrictions as "less limitations to the public [than] they are preserving [of] an engagement that is unlike the common museum or gallery experience." The *New Yorker* magazine called the Pulitzer Foundation building the most important in St. Louis since the Wainwright Building, one of the first skyscrapers, was built there in 1891. St. Louisans were readily appreciative of Serra's *Joe,* in contrast to the chilly reception many gave his *Twain* when it was installed downtown nearly two decades earlier.

Post-Dispatch art critic Jeff Daniel observed in an article about the foundation that "what Ando and his team have done is to remind us of the power of order at a time that seems chaotic. This is not a stultifying order, but one that is liberating and deeply restorative. It is about shaping a genuine dialogue between art and architecture, between the natural and the manmade."[18] With little alteration, the same might be said of Pulitzer journalism and of the contributions of Joseph Pulitzer III and his team in perpetuating it.

18. *St. Louis Post-Dispatch,* October 7, 2001.

Epilogue

"Giants rule the media sea," read the headline over a story by *Post-Dispatch* business writer Christopher Carey in the issue of Sunday, November 28, 2004. The accompanying illustration fashioned from newspaper cutouts showed a huge fish about to swallow three smaller ones. The story discussed the possibility of Pulitzer Inc. being sold to one of the larger media companies. Reuters news service was first in disclosing the development on November 19, not naming its sources. Company chief executive Robert Woodworth initially characterized the report as "just speculation," but within days confirmed that New York investment banking firm Goldman, Sachs and Company had been hired "to explore strategic alternatives," including the possibility of selling. He told employees via e-mail that "it is far from certain that any transaction will be reached," and that "the company is simply exploring various possible options to enhance shareholder value." The announcement itself had that effect, almost instantly increasing the share price by 17 percent to $65.25. There were estimates that the company's fourteen daily newspapers and more than sixty-five weeklies, shoppers, and niche publications could sell for as much as $1.5 billion.[1]

This came to pass two months later, on January 30, 2005, when Lee Enterprises of Davenport, Iowa, bought Pulitzer Inc. for the slightly lower figure of $1.46 billion, or $64 a share. Lee, though not a media giant, was about 50 percent larger than Pulitzer, but a tenth the size of the country's largest media group, Gannett Company, which also considered buying the property.[2] Lee's 2004 revenues were $683.3 million with a profit of $86.1 million, against Pulitzer's $444 million in revenue and $44.1 million profit.

---

1. The Reuters announcement was published November 19, 2004, and the next day by the *Post-Dispatch,* which followed the story closely thereafter. *St. Louis Post-Dispatch,* November 20–23, 28, and December 1, 3, 12, and 30, 2004; *SLBJ,* November 26, 2004; *Wall Street Journal,* November 22, 2004.

2. Had its bid been accepted, Gannett faced the prospect of federal regulatory challenges in buying Pulitzer because of its ownership of television station KSDK in St. Louis, and the joint operating agreement between its *Citizen* and Pulitzer's *Daily Star* in Tucson, Arizona. An attempt by a group of *Post-Dispatch* news and editorial employees to buy the company through an Employee Stock Ownership Program was rebuffed by Goldman Sachs.

Family shareholders in both publicly traded companies held most of the voting stock. The top three at Pulitzer—Emily, seventy-one, Michael, seventy-four, and David Moore, eighty—unanimously approved the sale, as did the company's board of directors. With the addition of Pulitzer's fourteen dailies to its forty-four, Lee's holdings grew to fifty-eight dailies in twenty-three states and ranked fourth in the country in the number of daily newspapers owned and seventh in weekday circulation.[3] The *Post-Dispatch* became its largest paper. At the time of the sale, Pulitzer—which financial analysts had been touting as a likely candidate for sale—was the smallest publicly held newspaper chain. Lee and Pulitzer executives agreed that their companies, both based in the Midwest and emphasizing local and regional coverage over national and international, were a companionable fit.

Emily Pulitzer explained the reasoning behind the decision to sell. "The next generation [of Pulitzers] is not involved in the company," she said. "We felt by dealing with issues that face newspapers today, which are very different than eleven years ago when I first joined the board [of directors], we could do a more responsible job than waiting and passing it on to the next generation." Nevertheless, she added, "It's been very emotional. This has not been an easy process or decision." Michael called the sale "absolutely the right way to go," but "a lot harder for me than I thought it was going to be." At the same time, as often observed, it is common after the third generation—or even sooner—for family members to choose other pursuits rather than taking a turn at running the family enterprise. "That's one of the problems of a family-run business, whether it's a family farm or a newspaper company," a financial analyst commented.[4]

Former editor William Woo, publisher Nicholas Penniman, and advertising and marketing director James Cherry all believed that given his devotion to the *Post-Dispatch*, Joe would have opposed the sale. "He never would have countenanced it," Woo said. "It was his birthright. Selling it for a mess of pottage? It would have killed him." Lee chairman and chief executive Mary E. Junck sought, however, to calm concerns that the sale would mean the end of Pulitzer-style journalism. The merger agreement between the companies provided some assurance of that. It stipulated that Lee would retain the *Post-Dispatch* name and its editorial-page plat-

---

3. The total circulation figures were 1.7 million daily and 2 million on Sundays. Unless otherwise noted, information about the sale to Lee is from articles in the *St. Louis Post-Dispatch*, January 31, and February 1 and 2, 2005, and the *Wall Street Journal* and *New York Times*, both February 1, 2005.

4. Barry Lucas, senior research vice president of Gabelli and Company, quoted in *SLBJ*, November 26, 2004.

form statement and keep the news and editorial headquarters in St. Louis for at least five years. Lee's strategy with acquisitions, Junck explained, is to leave news and editorial decision making in local hands, adding that none of Pulitzer's four thousand employees would be laid off.[5] "We're very much a company that believes you can't save your way to good performance. You have to drive revenue." *Post-Dispatch* publisher Terrance Egger agreed: "Lee's overwhelming emphasis . . . is to grow revenues and serve advertisers. And you can't do that if you don't have an audience."[6] Junck did, however, predict that Lee could achieve at least $6 million in cost savings, mostly in administrative overhead.

St. Louis Journalism Review editor Ed Bishop said he was saddened by the loss of the Pulitzer name, but thought it unlikely that *Post-Dispatch* editorial positions would change under Lee ownership. "I see a minnow swallowing a whale, at least from the point of view of journalistic tradition," he said. Bishop suggested two possibilities for the future of the *Post-Dispatch:* "The rosy scenario is that the people at Lee see the *Post* as their premier flag and turn it loose and finance some enterprising journalism. The dark view is that Lee just borrowed a lot of money. Will the pressure be for a smaller news hole, to cut the news budget? We just don't know. I suspect it will be somewhere between."[7]

Others looked beyond the possible impact on the *Post-Dispatch* to wider implications for the newspaper industry. Paul Janensch, editor of the *Louisville Courier-Journal* when the Bingham family sold it to Gannett in 1986, predicted that in time, "we're probably going to end up with three or four companies that own maybe 90 percent of the circulation." A 2001 media watch organization report made a closely related point in noting that six corporations controlled "most media outlets in television, cable, radio, newspapers, magazines, and the internet, and consequently, most information, artistic and cultural expression, and public discussion in the United States." Brian Steffens, executive director of the National Newspaper Association, pointed out that when newspapers were privately

---

5. Securities and Exchange Commission filings, January 29, 2005, PREM 14A, 56, www.pulitzerinc.com; *SLBJ,* May 20, 2005.

6. *Post-Dispatch* senior writer Harry Levins to author, January 21, 2005; WW to author, February 10, 2005; *St. Louis Post-Dispatch,* February 1, 2005. Junck, a journalism graduate of the University of North Carolina, never worked as a journalist, but before joining Lee was publisher of the *St. Paul Pioneer Press* in Minnesota for two years and publisher and chief executive of the *Baltimore Sun* for four years. During her tenure there, the *Sun* grew in both revenue and circulation.

7. This was the largest acquisition in Lee's history. The company borrowed $1.55 billion from Deutsche Bank and SunTrust Bank. Junck replied when asked about the debt: "It won't be a problem." *St. Louis Post-Dispatch,* January 31 and February 1, 2005.

owned, the "stakeholders were the owners, the readers, and the advertisers." On becoming public, shareholders—with "no vested interest in the product other than monetary return"—became a fourth constituency. Washington University professor of business, law, and economics Glenn MacDonald described newspapers as a mature industry: "It's very hard to find a mature industry that doesn't become very consolidated at some point. They all go through periods of rapid consolidation, often associated with a change in technology or some important change in the business."[8]

From a strictly business standpoint, there was no pressing need for Pulitzer to be sold in 2005. Even though *Post-Dispatch* daily and Sunday circulation declined 11 and 18 percent respectively between 1994 and 2004, the company as a whole was financially sound. It earned $106 million in 2003, a profit of nearly 25 percent—a return many other industries might envy—but as *Post-Dispatch* business writer Carey pointed out, was "well below the goals of major media companies," especially those invested in both print and broadcasting. Mario Gabelli, chairman of Gabelli Asset Management, did not see this as a friendly environment for a company as small as Pulitzer. For several years, he had rated its stock a smart buy for investors because of the company's attractiveness as a property for which one of the larger media companies might well pay a premium price. Acting on that belief, Gabelli's company accumulated more than 40 percent of Pulitzer's "nonvoting" public shares.[9] "The costs of being public for a small company are growing enormously," he explained, making their sale to larger companies increasingly likely. Unless a small company makes "a very strong commitment to grow," it likely will sell out, he added. "You can't stay a small company. You either have . . . to grow, or try to take your company private again."[10]

This was hard to dispute as the pace of change in media businesses accelerated after Joe's death. Dominant ownership of the nation's newspapers and other communications outlets by media companies was an

8. The *Courier-Journal* sold for $305 million. Tifft and Jones, *The Patriarch*, 482–86. The other holdings of the Louisville Courier-Journal and Louisville Times Company, including a television station, a printing company, and an electronic data firm, were sold to other buyers for an additional $143 million.

The six large corporations controlling media outlets were AOL Time Warner, Disney–ABC, GE–NBC, Viacom–CBS–Westinghouse, Bertelsman, and Murdoch's News Corporation–Fox. Dorothy Kidd, "Legal Project to Challenge Media Monopoly," *MediaFile*, vol. 20, no. 3, May/June 2001, *www.mediaalliance.org*. Janensch and Steffens quoted in *St. Louis Post-Dispatch*, November 28, 2004; MacDonald quoted in *Post-Dispatch*, February 2, 2005.

9. *SJR*, September 2004, 27. The publicly traded shares actually had one vote while those held by family members had ten votes per share.

10. *St. Louis Post-Dispatch*, November 23, 2004.

accomplished fact by 1993, and certain to continue. The clash of traditional journalistic values with a corporate culture interested primarily in financial growth continued to trouble journalists and others, even though many had witnessed closings and consolidations over the decades and knew that newspaper readership and the amount of space allotted to thought-provoking content had long been declining. In 1930, some 40 million copies of daily newspapers were published for a national population of 122 million; by 1990, only 60 million copies were published for twice as many people. Between 1990 and 2002, circulation dropped by 11 percent, or 1 percent each year. In St. Louis, *Post-Dispatch* circulation began a steady decline after it became the city's sole daily. In the mid-eighties, the daily circulation of the two St. Louis newspapers exceeded 600,000. On its own in 1990, *Post-Dispatch* circulation was 374,000 and falling, destined to drop below 300,000 in 2000.[11] Between 1980 and 2002, the number of newspapers in the United States declined 17 percent, from 1,745 to 1,457, resulting in more single-newspaper towns.

Several things accounted for these developments. One was that network television became dominant in the 1950s and 1960s and, as journalist David Halberstam noted, "killed off many of [its] print competitors and left most major American cities with a de facto monopoly paper."[12] The effects were similar in St. Louis, where only the *Post-Dispatch* survived, in large part because the Pulitzer Publishing Company under Joe had become a media group, ranking about fortieth in size, with holdings mainly in newspapers and network television stations. The competition was stiff. By 1990 there were 135 newspaper groups in the United States—the top three being Gannett, Knight-Ridder, and Newhouse—totaling 1,228 newspapers and constituting 75 percent of all dailies and 81 percent of total daily circulation.[13] Cable television also was in the ascendancy by that time, challenging both newspapers and the major networks by spreading audiences and advertising revenue more thinly across the commercial media. Cable's strategy, Halberstam noted, was "to push a tabloid formula—sex, crime, and a kind of dimwitted celebrity-obsessed journalism."

This resembled competitive practices at the turn of the twentieth century, when the first Joseph Pulitzer, William Randolph Hearst, and others used sensationalistic techniques to battle for circulation and advertising dollars. By the year 2000, Halberstam said his depiction of the public service nature of the print media was sadly dated in his 1979 book, *The Powers*

11. *SLBJ*, March 4, 1996, May 29, 2000, and November 11, 2004.
12. David Halberstam, *The Powers That Be*, xi–xiii.
13. Emery and Emery, *The Press and America*, 538.

That Be. After the purchase in 2000 of the *Los Angeles Times* by the Chicago Tribune Company for $8 billion, Halberstam commented that the deal gave "the feeling of an ownership that has little passion for the profession, and has carefully figured out the precise return on investment needed to keep stockholders happy and adjusted the quality of [its papers] accordingly— that is, journalism adjusted to economic needs, rather than economic needs adjusted to journalistic ones." On rereading his book two decades after it was published, he said, "it seems like something that was written a hundred years ago, not merely twenty years ago."

Looking back on conditions during the 1940s and 1950s, when he was associate editor under his father, Joe might have agreed with Halberstam. But having worked through the following three decades and making some uncomfortable accommodations, he could not ignore the new realities. Despite these new conditions, however, the paper during Joe's leadership continued to buck the establishment despite the consequences in largely conservative St. Louis, in the opinion of former Democratic U.S. Senator Thomas F. Eagleton, a native St. Louisan and friend of Joe's since the mid-1950s. Eagleton believed it remained as true under Joe as it had under his father that there were limits to how far the *Post-Dispatch* would go for the sake of circulation and advertising if this meant compromising the paper's independence. "He knew that the *Post-Dispatch* was running against the grain of this community," Eagleton said, but it remained "light years more liberal . . . in the dinosaur atmosphere" of the late eighties and early nineties, and from the 1930s to the 1960s had been "considerably more liberal than the community consensus." Being "some kind of cheerleader" for St. Louis, Eagleton added, "ran counter to [Joe's] personality and probably counter to what he thought was good journalism."[14]

The nature of journalistic independence had long been at the core of differences of outlook between the *Post-Dispatch* and *Globe-Democrat.* Looking back in 1995 on their rivalry, former *Globe* publisher G. Duncan Bauman described his paper as "conservative, pro-American, determined to serve the people and the community. We talked *with* the people; the *Post* talked *to* the people, and still does. It was our feeling that we were to reflect and serve the needs of the community, not tell the community what its needs were." Bauman and his predecessor, Richard Amberg, kept themselves as much in the *Globe-Democrat* as Joe kept himself out of the *Post-Dispatch.* Stories and photos publicizing the St. Louis–friendly activities of the *Globe* publishers were a fixture in their paper. They belonged to a variety of St. Louis—and other—organizations, and so did "any of our

14. Eagleton interview, May 10, 1995, St. Louis.

staff members who wanted to," Bauman said.[15] To avoid potential conflicts of interest, such affiliations were forbidden at the *Post*—a mistake, in Bauman's opinion. He believed the top people at the *Post*, not just its reporters, should spend time with St. Louis's movers and shakers. "Is firsthand or secondhand knowledge best?" he asked.

By 1995, about eighteen months after taking charge of the company, Michael was pondering questions of a different kind. It was obvious to him that the company had to change. But what shape should it take? He decided to hire a team of media consultants to find ways the company might be improved by restructuring. "I knew something was wrong... but I was raised in the dysfunction, so I didn't know how to get out of it," Michael said. He hired William Boggs, forty-eight, a partner in Synectics, a Cambridge, Massachusetts, business consulting firm, to direct the Odyssey Project. Other newspapers that had retained Boggs and associates had recommended him to Michael. "As implied by the Greek myth to which it refers, our journey will bring us to new places and open new horizons," Michael explained in a letter to all employees. The *American Journalism Review* described the project as "a dramatic, costly effort to revamp Pulitzer so that it might thrive in a fast-changing media environment." It characterized Boggs as "a cigar smoking, earring-wearing former Marine and onetime Methodist minister with a Ph.D. in philosophy." His goal was "to change the decision making process at a company known for its procrastination."[16]

15. GDB interview, May 15, 1995; *St. Louis Post-Dispatch*, April 15, 2003. Bauman's résumé, given to the author, lists more than sixty local, state, and national memberships, the majority of them in St. Louis. In some, he was an officer. Bauman died in 2003.

16. MEP interview, July 26, 2003. When not attributed specifically, material about the Odyssey Project is from *SLBJ*, July 31, 1995, and March 4, 1996; *American Journalism Review*, July-August and September 1996, and May 1998; telephone interviews with MEP, October 31, 2003, and James M. Snowden, Jr., November 4, 2003; MEP to The People of Pulitzer, June 27 and December 15, 1995, and June 27, 1996, provided by MEP. Michael mentioned that Boggs was recommended by the *Raleigh News and Observer*, *Orange County Register,* and *Sacramento Bee*. Synectics, in business for thirty-six years at the time, also had consulted for business and industry clients, including Coca-Cola, Chase Manhattan Bank, and International Business Machines. The *AJR* article reported that "Synectics...charges up to $500,000 for a long-term development project." It also said that Boggs "created a stir" at the *Post-Dispatch* when he showed up on a winter day "in a parka made of the pelts of wolves he'd killed in Alaska after they began tearing apart a black bear he'd bagged." Alicia C. Shepard, "Consultants in the Newsroom," *American Journalism Review*, September 1996, 19–23. Boggs's comment on his goal for the *Post-Dispatch* is from *SLBJ*, March 4, 1996. Said Michael Pulitzer: "One job of a consultant is to push a conservative company that is used to mulling over decisions for long periods of time and frequently not coming to any decision. The job of a consultant is to get us off the dime and start making some decisions. So I think Bill

In a letter introducing the project to employees, Michael noted that the company "has always stood for excellence in print and broadcast journalism," but needed to change in order "to sustain that excellence" and remain profitable "in the face of unprecedented and unrelenting change" in the media industry. "Odyssey is not about fixing what's wrong. It's about preparing for an unpredictable but exciting future. We want to make those preparations while we are healthy and strong, as we are now," he explained, adding that "Synectics believes that nobody knows a client's business better than the client. The answers we seek reside within our own organization." The project took a year, and included some unusual exercises designed to help companies "find untapped reservoirs of creativity and innovation from within."[17] In one, Michael, *Post-Dispatch* editor William Woo, publisher Nicholas Penniman, company finance vice president Ronald Ridgway, and broadcasting vice president Ken Elkins—all dressed casually—got down on a hotel room floor to work together with twenty-five Lego blocks, a children's building toy, for a specified length of time. The purpose of the exercise was "to help them refine their skills" in such areas as "functioning in teams, problem-solving in a new medium, building with limited resources, and thinking unconventionally."

James M. Snowden, Jr., a company board member and financial adviser, did not participate in the Lego exercise, but did discuss the Odyssey project frequently with Michael, and sometimes with Michael and Boggs together. "What Michael was trying to do was to view the company as a business," Snowden said. "When Joe was alive, almost all the focus was on the *Post-Dispatch*. . . . Joe would never have done [the Odyssey project]—not in a million years—developing consensus and team building. I give Michael a lot of credit for taking this on—to shed a lot of baggage, to go through this psychobabble. Joe would have seen this as enormously undignified." Boggs was "not likely to impress someone like Joe," he added. Company legal adviser William Bush agreed: "Mention a consultant to Joe and you almost always got a negative reaction." Emily was certain that Joe "would have found Boggs particularly offensive, as did many other people."[18] Michael, however, considered it essential to understand the entire company in "a much broader scope" than just the *Post-Dispatch*, and no one disagreed with that. The work progressed in steps, from the newsroom—

[Boggs] and I understand each other. The ultimate decision lies with me, but Bill's job is to keep pushing."

17. *SLBJ*, September 23, 1996.

18. Part of Joe's aversion to consultants was their cost, Bush said. Telephone interview with William Bush and Richard A. Palmer, December 5, 2003; ERP interview, July 1, 2004, St. Louis.

where the consensus was that lines of authority were not clear—to the newspaper as a whole, and then to the entire company, except for broadcasting, which was considered to be in good shape. A key piece of the project was a company-wide survey of its thirty-six hundred employees, more than 50 percent of whom responded. The survey identified five "areas of opportunity to improve," including doing "a better job of communicating with each other and cooperating across boundaries."[19]

This meant, Snowden suggested, that the *Post-Dispatch*, dutifully maintained by both Joe and his father as the flagship, could no longer remain at the top of the company pyramid. During the eight years after Michael returned to St. Louis from Tucson in 1977 to understudy Joe, he had concentrated on understanding the company's broadcasting interests, something Joe had never done. It had been evident for some time that broadcasting was overtaking the newspapers as the company's biggest moneymaker. In 1986, the newspapers produced about 50 percent of its cash flow; by 1994, broadcasting was producing 76 percent.[20] This figured, of course, in Odyssey's 1996 recommendation that the company's chain of command be reconfigured vertically, with corporate budgetary control over both the newspaper and broadcasting elements. "Other newspapers have experienced a similar shift in power from the editorial side to the business side as publishers have imposed increasingly tight controls on spending," the *New York Times* observed.[21]

To make the change, "the anomalous management structure" of the *Post-Dispatch*—as the *Times* called it—was abolished. Under Joe, the editor-publisher, CEO, and board chairman were the same person. When he transferred his titles of editor to Woo and publisher to Penniman in 1986, they functioned as coequals reporting to him. Essentially the same arrangement stayed in place after Joe died until early 1996, with the understanding that Michael would act as tiebreaker if Woo and Penniman found themselves at loggerheads. "But the way it worked was that they figured out that if it ever came to me, one of them would lose," Michael said. Consequently, there never was an appeal to Michael, and "a lot of decisions

19. The others were active support of innovation, openness to outside perspectives, breaking down traditional boundaries to foster cooperation among senior leaders and managers, and doing more to achieve productive meetings that can achieve innovative results. MEP to People of Pulitzer, December 19, 1995; JVM to author, June 4, 2004.

20. In 1994 the *Post-Dispatch* and the *Arizona Daily Star*, the company's only newspapers, earned $30.5 million from $305 million in sales. Its nine television stations earned $48 million on $181 million in sales. *New York Times*, April 1, 1996. See also *SLBJ*, April 29, 1996.

21. *New York Times*, April 1, 1996.

were not made." In the post-Odyssey structure, the paper would have an editor-in-chief and a general manager—the latter a position that had been vacant since Thomas Tallarico left in 1989—both reporting to vice president for newspapers and publisher Penniman, and in effect making editor Woo Penniman's subordinate. Furthermore, Michael said as Odyssey neared its end that "a change in leadership was indicated" in the news department.[22]

Woo was vacationing in Europe when Penniman told the newsroom staff on February 23, 1996, that Woo would be replaced. "I came home to find the broadcast media reporting that I had been fired, my minister was on the phone saying he was praying for me, my children were asking, 'Daddy, are you being fired?'" he said. Penniman conceded that the announcement of Woo's fate was poorly handled, but that saving by cost cutting could go on only so long until "you have to go out and get more readers and advertising dollars."[23] In early March Penniman said there would be a nationwide search to replace Woo. Two weeks later, on March 7, managing editor Foster Davis resigned. Woo handed in his resignation on July 5, ending his thirty-four years at the newspaper, the last ten as editor. He said he left "of my own free will when otherwise I might have stayed in a company that itself was undergoing fundamental change, from the values and philosophy that drove Joseph Pulitzer [III], who was my chairman, to something quite different."[24]

Both he and Davis were disillusioned and upset, for different reasons. There had been friction in the newsroom for some time, in large part because the two men did not work well together, even though Woo had considered Davis—like himself, a former Nieman Fellow at Harvard—the best candidate in the search to replace David Lipman in 1992. At least part of the explanation for their incompatibility, Michael said, was that Davis "was a soft news person" and Woo favored hard news. Davis said in a 1995 interview that he thought even before he took the job that "this paper has problems . . . There's a real disconnect between the *Post-Dispatch* and the community that supports it." Yet he decided to take the position, he explained, because "I thought I could contribute something, not because everything is just hunky dory." He found the operation stodgy, based on an O. K. Bovard model of "the omniscient senior editor who knows all."

22. Quoted in ibid.
23. Ibid.
24. *Editor & Publisher,* September 21, 1996, 17; Alicia C. Shepard, "Consultants in the Newsroom," *American Journalism Review,* September 1996, 19–23. Woo became a journalism professor at Stanford University after leaving the *Post-Dispatch* and was still teaching there in 2004.

He thought the platform was "taken too literally as a tablet from the mountain" that "allows you to conceive of yourself as a scourge and a scold and not much more." Instead, he argued, the *Post-Dispatch* "has got to be a newspaper that scares the right people," namely wrongdoers, "but doesn't kind of hit and run the innocent on the way to the big story. It's got to be more attentive to its community."

It did not appear to the staff, however, that Davis himself was sufficiently attentive either to them or to St. Louis. He spent many weekends in Charlotte, North Carolina, where he had been assistant managing editor of the *Charlotte Observer* before joining the *Post-Dispatch*, and he kept his house there. People in the newsroom tagged him "the Charlotte Observer."[25] On his departure from St. Louis, Davis acknowledged that "there were, indeed, some differences between Bill [Woo] and me." He said he saw his role as managing editor as "challenging the old ways of doing things, making the start on the road of creating a culture of confident editors and trying to get the paper to talk levelly to the community, rather than down its nose."[26] He predicted that after things settled, he would "be seen as a transitional figure between the old *Post-Dispatch* and the new *Post-Dispatch*."[27]

Woo, fifty-nine at the time of his departure, said it did not come as a complete surprise, but "was distressing," because his understanding had

25. Interviews with Foster Davis, February 21, 1995, St. Louis, and MEP, October 31, 2003, by telephone.

26. The *Wisconsin State Journal* in Madison and the *San Jose Mercury News* were other papers doing this.

27. After Davis resigned, "reporters castigated his news judgment for being too soft." Woo and Davis had disagreed about the value of reporting about government, Davis arguing that it deserved less space because many stories about government are dull. For Woo this missed a larger point: "Six men and six women sitting two hours in a dull room saying dull things will do more to affect the lives of people than any number of school children wearing funny masks. . . . Do you say this is inherently dull and old ladies exercising in spandex are not inherently dull? I don't think so." Furthermore, "if you wish to do investigative reporting, it does not fall out of the sky into your lap. Investigative reporting grows out of the coverage of institutions. Investigative reporting lives off of the abuses of power. Institutions have power. Unless you cover [them] . . . day in and day out, so that you have sources who will call you, you will not do investigative reporting. Investigative reporting will wither and die. You can sit around the office and say, 'by God we need investigative reporting but we're not covering the school board,' and you won't get it." *SLBJ*, April 29, 1996; Woo quoted in *SJR*, July-August 1996, 17.

Davis died of cancer in 2001 at sixty-one. In his obituary, Laszlo Domjan, the paper's executive city editor, described Davis in terms almost identical to those used to describe his predecessor, David Lipman: "He wasn't much of a diplomat, which sometimes got him in trouble. What you got from him was straight talk and bluntness." *St. Louis Post-Dispatch*, May 21, 2001. Davis was succeeded by assistant managing editor Richard K. Weil, Jr., who joined the paper as a reporter in 1973 and rose through the ranks. *St. Louis Post-Dispatch*, March 8, 1996.

been that he would be involved in the eventual transition to a new editor: "It was not news to me that there was going to be a succession and that I would have a role in the identification of that person." Emily Pulitzer thought he should have a role, but knew Michael had misgivings. She said in a memorandum to Michael in December 1995 that even though she knew he was concerned that Woo might "interfere with the effective functioning" of the new editor, she thought otherwise. She recommended that Michael's and Joe's self-appointed successors as editor and publisher, Woo and Penniman, lead the search. "I feel quite certain that if [Woo] is part of the selection process, agrees with the choice and sees this person as a potential successor. . . . he will work hard for success. He wants nothing more than to be able to turn the *Post-Dispatch* over to good hands for a healthy future." However, Woo was not asked on his return from vacation to take part in the search, but only to run the paper until a new editor was hired and then remain in some serious role in line with his experience. He chose not to accept this role and resigned in July. Neither he nor Michael would discuss the matter beyond Woo saying his continuation at the newspaper "had been foreclosed," and Michael citing "differences in operating style" with no elaboration. Their comments were interpreted to mean that Woo was "forced out" while the search for his replacement— who did not arrive until October 7—was still in progress.[28]

Consistent with his noncombative nature, Woo was inclined to be understanding about the turn of events. "I think everybody is in a difficult situation," he told an interviewer for the *American Journalism Review*. "I've been in difficult situations which did not produce the result that hindsight would have led me to produce. Nobody's perfect." Furthermore, he added, "the issue of an ownership wishing to change the editor is entirely legitimate." A major point of divergence between him and Michael was that Michael saw potential for improvement of the *Post-Dispatch* in "public" or "civic" journalism approaches being tested by some newspapers. Public journalism was a movement—called "a cult" by some critics—that sought to redefine the role of newspapers by having journalists "step out of their roles as experts on public affairs to listen more closely to what members of the community are saying." It considered outmoded the traditional definition of the press as society's watchdog against abuses of

28. ERP to MEP, December 5, 1995. Memorandum given author by Mrs. Pulitzer. In May 1996, with Michael Pulitzer as the source, it was reported that when Woo was replaced, he would take "a senior editorial position, allowing him to continue writing his Sunday column, and to make national speaking appearances" with a title such as "contributing editor/distinguished journalist." His immediate superior would be the new editor, with authority to dismiss him. *SLBJ*, April 29, 1996; *SJR*, July–August 1996, 1.

power. Instead, it urged newspapers to make fundamental changes by having reporters initiate conversations about public issues with citizens in focus groups or other settings, and report the conclusions reached. The end result would be "new possibilities and outcomes for the community."[29]

Woo was highly skeptical. It seemed to him that these changes could undercut traditional journalistic ideals such as "objectivity, detachment, independence [and] the courage to print stories that are unpopular and for which there is no consensus."[30] Even so, he said in a lecture in 1995: "Public journalism has potential to help us see through to a better day.... But it poses hard questions for traditions and values that we have held and respected for a long time. I fear that we are abandoning these too easily,... without sufficient examination." At newspapers where public journalism practices had been adopted, he said, "editors sit on public boards or action committees. Newspapers are becoming the conveners of their community, the master of ceremonies of the new democracy. Journalists no longer serve or inform the electorate; they become it."[31] He questioned the approach:

> We now privatize prisons and public schools. Why not privatize democracy itself? Soon we may be able to say: Tuesday's election is brought to you by the friendly folks at the *Post-Dispatch*; the American Dream Realty—where every home is a castle—and the Foreclosure National Bank—see us for your next auto loan.
>
> What are the implications when profit-seeking newspaper companies, either privately held or publicly owned, declare that they have become the electorate? What if IBM or the Yellow Pages or Bill Gates were to assert themselves as the convener of the community?

"Public journalism has yet to demonstrate itself as the penicillin of daily journalism," he said shortly before his resignation. "When public journalism is criticized for hiring community activists or doing things that are seen by common assent as egregious, the public journalism proponents always say that it was a bad experiment that didn't work. It never reflects on the original premise." It had long been his premise, he said, "that the

29. *St. Louis Post-Dispatch*, April 6, 2000, and *SJR*, July 2001. Unless attributed specifically, other material about public journalism comes from these sources and *SJR*, April 1997 and September 1998, and MEP interview, October 31, 2003.

30. Quoted in "Angels in the Newsroom," *Congressional Quarterly Governing Magazine*, August 1996, 20.

31. "As Old Gods Falter: Public Journalism and the Tradition of Detachment," number 30 in the Press-Enterprise Lecture Series, delivered February 13, 1995, at the University of California, Riverside; published by the *Press-Enterprise*, Riverside, California, and *SJR*, July 1995, 10 and ff.

paper should be activist and have a moral compass. I am much surer about what is meant in the *Post-Dispatch* platform, written in 1907 by the first Joseph Pulitzer, where it says 'never tolerate injustice or corruption.' . . . It does not embarrass me to say that the platform of the *Post-Dispatch* essentially makes it a paper with a social mission. These are things we don't really say out loud today: that you have a mission."[32]

In the 1990s it was common practice, although perhaps not in the 1907 sense, for both public and private institutions to develop "mission statements," often in conjunction with projects such as Odyssey; Pulitzer Publishing was no exception. Its statement blended the newspapers into the company as a whole, using broader terminology than Woo's, with a common commitment to such principles as "fairness and accuracy," "public service," "innovation and growth," and "the restless pursuit of excellence."[33] Michael did not see public journalism as negating the platform. "I think public journalism is a much maligned concept," he said. "If it means knowing about your community and being a leader in your community, well, that's the platform. You can make the case that the *Post-Dispatch* platform is a platform for public journalism. I especially think of the phrase 'never be satisfied with merely printing news.' It seems to me that that encompasses a lot of what public journalism is all about. A newspaper that's not plugged into the community just is not doing its job."

He said that in 2003, after the *Post-Dispatch* had spent more than three years trying—and failing—to retool its news and editorial functions to conform with public journalism principles. In 1996 a search committee of Michael, Emily Pulitzer, and James Snowden unanimously selected Cole C. Campbell, forty-three, editor of the *Virginian-Pilot* in Norfolk, Virginia, and a promoter of public journalism, to replace Woo. Campbell had been at the *Pilot* since 1990, serving consecutively as senior editor, managing editor, and finally editor for three years. The *Pilot*'s story on his departure said he "brought sweeping change to the [paper's] design, reporting style and the personality of its newsroom" during a "sometimes-controversial" tenure.[34] Emily said that from the beginning of the search process she felt "a very great responsibility to maintain the journalistic and other family traditions." Snowden thought that she might have been concerned that he

32. Quoted in Alicia C. Shepard, "After the Fall," *American Journalism Review*, July–August 1996, 40–41.

33. In full, it reads: "The people of Pulitzer work together to be the premier provider of news and information to the communities we serve. We are dedicated to the public interest, to fairness and accuracy, to innovation and growth, and to the restless pursuit of excellence." "Pulitzer Publishing Company, 1996 Annual Report," 3.

34. *Virginian Pilot*, August 24, 1996.

and Michael might out-vote her by favoring "a business type [over] some-one interested in the journalistic tradition." As it turned out, however, all three picked Campbell as "clearly the superior candidate" of all those considered, internal and external. But in hindsight, Snowden conceded after Campbell was gone: "We didn't do a very good job," adding that the committee discovered "no clues in the interview process—and shame on us—that Cole was going to be so disruptive, and that his management style was going to be so different." Snowden said Campbell's "homework" on the Pulitzer family "and the tremendous respect and regard that he said he had for the Pulitzer tradition" had impressed the search commit-tee. But "as it turned out, his idea of journalistic excellence was pretty dif-ferent from what we thought it was going to be."

A newsroom staff eager for guidance welcomed Campbell to the *Post-Dispatch* in October 1996.[35] "Cole couldn't have had more support when he got here," investigative reporter Carolyn Tuft recalled. "All any of us wanted was an improvement. Some leadership. When Cole gave his first speech, he got raucous applause." Initial concern about his keen interest in public journalism moderated as staff members found him to be highly perceptive as well as an impressive speaker and leader of meetings. "If you came to one of our quarterly meetings, you'd think he was really terrific," said columnist Bill McClellan. But at other times, he said, "there was all this [Master of Business Administration] talk. We could have been a widget factory. There was very little discussion about news. Any ques-tions or criticisms or suggestions were met with this arrogant 'You are being resistant to change.'"

Campbell pursued change at every turn. He "abolished the concept of general assignment reporter to cover breaking news; did away with the city editor's position; made everyone 'reapply' for their jobs; hired more of what he called 'visual journalists,' otherwise known as graphic design-ers; and put reporters on 'teams' headed by 'team leaders' instead of edi-tors." Five of the managing editor's senior staff were designated assistant managing editors with changes in title and responsibilities. The metro edi-tor, for example, became assistant managing editor of all local coverage—the metro desk, business, and sports. Campbell held many meetings at which he spoke in "New Age management jargon many found difficult to grasp." He also employed outside specialists to motivate the editors and staff. One was nonjournalist Richard Harwood, head of a Bethesda,

---

35. Alicia C. Shepard, "The End of the Line," *American Journalism Review,* July–August 2000, 44–51. Unless otherwise cited, observations and quotations about Campbell are from this source.

Maryland, consulting firm, who had worked with communications scholars "to develop a new and specialized vocabulary for journalistic practi-
tioners" and had written a workbook on public journalism. Neil R. Peirce,
a nationally syndicated columnist and urban journalist, was another. Both
were public journalism advocates who contended that journalists could
motivate citizens to reorganize and revitalize their cities—things political
and business leaders had failed to do—"by thinking differently about
how to gather and present the news."[36]

Many staff members found the jargon of Harwood and Peirce unclear.
"I don't even know if we are talking about the same things," said Margaret Freivogel, an assistant managing editor. "Do you think there's some
common values, some common ground we share?" Editorial page editor
Christine Bertelson said it frustrated her that "we put a lot of things up
here [on a flip chart] and never get to a point." Some of the terms were
"connections," "personal context," "room for ambivalence," and "sense
of possibility." The term "ambivalence," defined as "a gray area in debate
in which to discuss and test ideas," was one of the most troublesome.
Reporters were told that because "most of the American populace is
ambivalent," they should "write stories that include comments from the
ambivalent" and were told: "In the new newsroom culture of public journalism, [both] reporters and editors must learn to feel comfortable with
ambivalence."[37]

Bewildered by such directives, staff members became increasingly
uncomfortable with and distrustful of Campbell's reform efforts; they
also found him immune to criticism. "Histrionics will get you nowhere,"[38]
he advised the staff on the cover page of a 1999 document describing news-

36. *RFT,* June 7, 2000. See also *SJR,* July–August 1999, 1, 13. *St. Louis Post-Dispatch,*
February 2, 1997. Campbell also appointed two deputy editors reporting to him, one
responsible for technology initiatives, the other for readership research, strategic planning, and internal communications. *SJR,* June 1998, 16. Peirce, a Princeton graduate
who edited *Congressional Quarterly* for nine years, was the author of a series of books
about the people and politics of all the country's regions. He and Curtis Johnson, his
writing partner, had studied fourteen cities prior to coming to St. Louis, but did not
consider themselves consultants who prescribed solutions. "We're saying, 'This is
the situation. Now get together and make your own plan,'" Peirce said. Quoted in
"The Peirce Report: A Call to Action," *St. Louis Post-Dispatch,* March 9–16, 1997 (reprint
edition), 20; See also *SJR,* October 1997, 1 ff. and December 1997/January 1998, 10–11.

37. *SJR,* June 1998, 1, 16, citing Arthur Charity, author of *Doing Public Journalism*
(New York: Guilford Press, 1995). The best-known spokesman on behalf of public jour-
nalism has been Jay Rosen of New York University, author of *What Are Journalists For?*
(New Haven: Yale University Press, 1999). See also Edmund B. Lambeth, Philip E.
Meyer and others, *Assessing Public Journalism* (Columbia: University of Missouri Press,
1998).

38. Quoted in *SJR,* July–August, 1999, 1.

room reorganization. But that was what he got—indirectly—on March 24, 2000, when seven veteran reporters asked relatively new *Post-Dispatch* publisher Terrance C. Z. Egger to meet with them at the Missouri Grill, a bar across the street from the *Post-Dispatch*. Egger, to whom Campbell reported, had been hired as the paper's general manager in 1996, and was elevated to publisher after Nicholas Penniman retired in 1999.[39] The reporters were dismayed because nineteen reporters and other staff members had left the paper in the previous eighteen months. It was an emotional session, Harry Levins, a twenty-nine-year employee, said afterward. "It was the first time we pissed and moaned out loud about Campbell instead of sly innuendo and a joke here and a minor bitch about this or that in the newsroom. We just let it hang out." None at the meeting believed, however, that their complaints brought Campbell down. Egger agreed: "There was no *one* meeting," he said. "In general, you pick up comments in the hallways, in the elevators, and just try to be very open in conversation with all of our employees to get an idea of what's right and what isn't working."[40]

39. Egger had been vice president for advertising at TNI Partners in Tucson, a joint operating agreement agency that ran the business operations of the *Arizona Daily Star*, owned by Pulitzer, and the *Tucson Citizen*, owned by Gannett Newspapers. Penniman stepped down to became a consultant to Pulitzer in 1998, and retired the next year. *St. Louis Post-Dispatch*, January 21, 1996, and July 22, 1999.

40. Quoted in *RFT*, June 7, 2000, 10, 12. See also *SJR*, September 2000, 17. One item circulating around town, as well as in the paper's hallways, was talk that Campbell, then married, had had a personal relationship with editorial page editor Christine Bertelson (daughter of former managing Arthur Bertelson), whom he recommended for promotion from metro columnist to the editorial page position. "The editor and I have a social relationship.... We've gone out. So what?" she told a *St. Louis Journalism Review* interviewer. Shortly before the article appeared in February 1998, Campbell sent a "personal and confidential" letter to *SJR* editor Ed Bishop emphasizing that her appointment to the editorial page position was based on her professional credentials, not a personal relationship. "If you publish any statements alleging that her appointment was made for personal reasons, that will be libelous on its face—to her and to me....I know this as a seasoned journalist and have confirmed it...with counsel for the *Post-Dispatch*." He said the letter was "not for publication or any other dissemination." Bishop replied: "Thank you for your instructions on libel....You omitted at least one aspect of libel, however, and failed to fully develop another....First a plaintiff in a libel case must prove that 'actual harm' resulted from false published statements. Simply being embarrassed is not considered harm by the courts. Second, a plaintiff must prove that the false statements were published with 'reckless disregard' for the truth. If a reporter refused to accept a denial and continued a line of questioning, for example, that would not necessarily be construed as reckless disregard for the truth." He added that *SJR* "will always rely on the first, and absolute defense against charges of libel—publishing the truth." He assured Campbell that in the upcoming profile of Bertelson, "*SJR* will do its utmost to be fair, responsible and accurate in its reporting." In a note to readers, he said that over the years, "scores of letters marked 'not for publication'" had not been published. He explained that Campbell's letter had "wide

Less than two weeks later, on April 5, 2000, Campbell resigned after serving three and a half years as editor. "There was a certain logic to his thinking on paper," Margaret Freivogel said, "but when you tried to make it function in the real world of daily journalism, it was at cross purposes. The reorganization took so much energy to make simple decisions and left no time for the really difficult things in our business. . . . In the end, he didn't seem to be able to differentiate between the inevitable complaining that accompanies change and helpful criticism that should have led to necessary adjustments. He dismissed it all as resistance and, as a result, never adjusted to the reality that was in front of his eyes." A group consisting of the paper's four top editors was appointed to run the paper until Campbell's successor was hired.[41] As had Foster Davis, Campbell joined the Poynter Institute for Media Studies in St. Petersburg, Florida, where public journalism was a topic of major interest. In July 2004 he was appointed dean of the Reynolds School of Journalism at the University of Nevada. He was at that time a doctoral candidate in public discourse and democratic practice at the Union Institute and University, an Internet-based distance-learning college where students design their own degree programs.[42]

Many believed management realities had more than anything else to do with Campbell's departure. If his effort had any effect on readers, most, apparently, were negative. The paper's daily circulation fell by 12,000 during his tenure, to 307,000, and on Sunday by 31,000 to 509,000. His main Sunday initiative was to replace the "News Analysis" section with "Imag-

---

distribution," both at the *Post* and other media outlets. "It was not *SJR* that circulated Campbell's letter." The profile said its reporter, Ellen Harris, asked Bertelson about "what St. Louisans have been talking about for four months. She begs off the question four times." It was widely assumed, as news staff member Tom Borgman observed, that the relationship issue "hurt [Campbell's] image, and hurt a lot in terms of his standing in the newsroom that I don't know he ever got back." *SJR*, February 1998, 1, 4, 14–15; *American Journalism Review*, July–August 2000, 50.

41. They were executive editor Richard Weil, his deputy, Virgil Thompson, managing editor Arnie Robbins, and editorial page editor Christine Bertelson. *SJR*, April 2000, 1, 11.

42. "Nevada News" (news release), University of Nevada, Reno, April 27, 2004; *St. Louis Post-Dispatch*, April 28, 2004. Quoting Campbell: "In the next five to ten years, this school can leverage its commitment to media ethics and media technology to become a beacon for journalism as a practice and journalism education." He added: "I think journalists will always have to use certain conventions and rituals and routines to get through the day. The question is how are we going to revisit them to see if they work for us effectively?" The *Post* story said of his time as its editor: "He is best remembered for his abstract thoughts about journalism and attempts at institutional change. As one longtime staffer put it: 'He was more interested in the newspaper of tomorrow than tomorrow's newspaper.'"

ine St. Louis," which presented a single subject in detail each week with the intent of opening community dialogue. Combating illiteracy and the question of building a new baseball stadium were among the issues. The section ran for two years, but never caught on. When the paper arranged a public forum on the stadium issue, only two citizens came. The *St. Louis Journalism Review* called the section "an ill-fated experiment in public journalism that came to represent the gobbledygook mindset of its mastermind, Cole Campbell." *Review* editor Ed Bishop criticized it as "naive to the point of absurdity. It was based on a simplistic notion that democracy works by having a group of well-informed citizens get together and arrive at a solution to a problem. Democracy is a lot more complicated than that."[43]

Campbell also overspent his budget in 1999, not taking into account the expense of the reorganization's overtime and training costs. This clashed with the Odyssey mandate to operate within a centralized chain of authority and accountability as well as with the company's focus on the future. Since 1996 Michael and other executives had concentrated on strengthening the company financially, both in and outside of St. Louis. That year they made the largest acquisition in company history by buying thirteen Scripps League daily newspapers in California and ten other states for $216 million.[44] The papers' combined circulations were 185,000 daily and 145,000 Sunday, were located in noncompetitive markets, and had "considerably higher" profit margins than those in St. Louis. In 1999 the company bought the 50,000-circulation *Pantagraph* in Bloomington, Illinois, and nine smaller newspapers from the Chronicle Publishing Company of San Francisco for $180 million.[45]

Closely related to these acquisitions was the decision reached between the two newspaper deals to sell all the company's broadcast stations. A financial analyst described the five radio stations and nine network-affiliated television stations as "cash-cow, high-margin" properties. The

43. The section ran from April 1999 to July 2001, when it was discontinued by Campbell's successor. *SJR*, May 1999, 1, and July–August 2001, 3 and 16.

44. From Lihue, Hawaii, to Newport, Vermont. The most costly transaction before this was the purchase of television stations in Daytona Beach, Florida, and Des Moines, Iowa, for $165 million. *St. Louis Post-Dispatch*, May 29, 1993; JMS interview.

45. The Scripps family, whose newspaper business was founded by Edward Wyllis Scripps (1854–1926), whose journalistic philosophy matched that of the first Joseph Pulitzer, asked Pulitzer to bid on the properties because of the similarity of their journalistic traditions. The smaller newspapers in the *Pantagraph* group were weeklies and one monthly, with circulations between 740 and 31,000. *St. Louis Post-Dispatch*, May 7, 1996, and October 6, 1999; Annual Reports, Pulitzer Publishing Company and Subsidiaries, 1996, 3, and 1999, 3; JMS interview.

buyer, for $1.85 billion, was Hearst-Argyle Television Inc., a broadcasting company majority owned by descendants of William Randolph Hearst, Joseph Pulitzer's rival in the 1890s.[46] The process started in 1997, during a discussion between Michael and James Snowden while they were attending the opening of new facilities at Pulitzer's New Orleans television station. They were concerned about the prospect of needing in a relatively short time to replace the company's top three management executives— Ken Elkins, Nicholas Penniman, and Ronald Ridgway, all approaching retirement age—and the company's future in network television broadcasting. They were uneasy as well about the competitive implications of relaxed federal limits on the number of television stations a company could own.[47] This made clear, Snowden said, that network television "was going to become a business where scale mattered" and that to stay competitive, Pulitzer would have to spend as much as $1 billion to buy more stations: "We did not have, frankly, the stomach to want to take on that much debt."

Snowden, Michael, Emily, David, and company counsel William Bush concluded that the more attractive alternative was to sell the stations. They decided that the best option would be to become solely a newspaper company by adding assets such as the recently acquired Scripps group. This would eliminate the concerns about incurring substantial debt and replacing the management executives as they retired. It also would increase the amount of cash that could be invested in smaller newspapers in growth markets with circulations ranging from ten thousand to one hundred thousand, and in associated Internet/new media ventures. Hearst-Argyle agreed to pay Pulitzer $1.15 billion in stock and to assume all of Pulitzer's $700 million in debt. The sale had other advantages, the primary one being that it increased the company's stock value for shareholders by about $730 million, which they received in stock without having to pay any cap-

46. When not attributed specifically, material about the Hearst-Argyle transaction is from the *St. Louis Post-Dispatch*, February 28 and May 26, 1998, and January 19, 1999; *SJR*, April 1998, 1; Morton Research Inc. "Newspaper Newsletter," February 27, 1998; *Pulitzer Magazine* (company publication), Summer 1998, 2–4.

47. The Federal Communications Commission rule at the time restricted company ownership to stations reaching no more than 35 percent of the national audience. The Pulitzer group of stations ranked twenty-third in size nationally, reaching about 5.5 percent of American households; Hearst-Argyle ranked fifteenth, reaching 11 percent. The limit was raised to 45 percent in 2002, after some media giants exceeded the 35 percent cap. *St. Louis Post-Dispatch*, May 26, 1998; *Washington Post*, June 3, 2002; Center for Digital Democracy/News, www.democraticmedia.org/issues/mediaownership/chart.html.

ital gains tax.[48] Another was that it diversified the holdings of all share-holders, a matter of particular importance for Emily, Michael, and David—who held substantial amounts of Pulitzer stock they had chosen not to sell. Ownership of Hearst-Argyle shares enhanced their financial flexibility by giving them the choice of selling Hearst-Argyle shares, to which they did not have the same attachment as Pulitzer shares, and to diversify.

With no broadcasting interests, Pulitzer was the smallest among the publicly owned major newspaper-oriented companies, but was financially sleek with no debt and $450 million in cash, and ready to expand its newspaper holdings.[49] The decision to get out of broadcasting came at the height of the 1990s seller's market frenzy to acquire major network television properties, which peaked just before cable competition began to take a substantial number of viewers away from the ABC, CBS, and NBC networks with which Pulitzer stations had been affiliated. "Michael was right in seeing the competitive situation that has now evolved," Snowden said in 2003.

Part of the process of shedding the broadcast properties was changing Pulitzer's corporate name to Pulitzer Inc., a more modern descriptive not confined to publishing. Michael, nearing seventy, was ready to step down as chief executive. He had concluded that in all likelihood the company would be able to find a strong leader for a newspaper-only company more easily than one with expertise in managing both newspaper and broadcast properties. Accordingly, the company searched for a person with a record of success in running newspapers. In December 1998 the company hired Robert C. Woodworth, fifty-one, vice president for newspapers at Knight Ridder Inc., as company president and chief executive officer, the second non-Pulitzer to have both those titles.[50] Michael remained chairman of

48. The Hearst-Argyle stock was distributed to Pulitzer shareholders, the largest of whom were Emily Pulitzer, Michael Pulitzer, David E. Moore, and Pulitzer executives. Michael and Pulitzer Broadcasting president Ken J. Elkins became members of the Hearst-Argyle board of directors. After the transaction, Hearst-Argyle owned twenty-four television stations and ranked second in national household coverage, at 16.5 percent, among television groups not owned by networks. Sinclair Broadcast Group was first. *St. Louis Post-Dispatch* and *New York Times,* May 26, 1998.

49. Michael quickly dismissed speculation that the newspapers would soon be up for sale: "The answer to that is no. The reason it's no is the ownership structure," he said, explaining that he, David Moore, and Emily Rauh Pulitzer control 95 percent of the company's votes. *St. Louis Post-Dispatch,* May 26 and December 19, 1998.

50. Snowden explained how the broadcast properties transaction was structured so as to get tax-free exchange of stock treatment for Pulitzer Publishing shareholders: "We dropped our newspaper assets down into this new company, Pulitzer Inc., and then we did a tax-free merger of the Pulitzer Publishing Company with Hearst-Argyle.

the board. Woodworth had managed multiple newspapers for Knight Ridder and was publisher of the *Kansas City Star* when Knight Ridder bought the paper from Capital Cities/ABC Inc. and promoted him to vice president. There were other major personnel changes at Pulitzer Inc. between 1998 and 2001. Penniman, head of the company's newspaper division since 1984 and *Post-Dispatch* publisher since 1986, stepped down in 1998 to become a company consultant and retired in 1999. General manager Terrance Egger became publisher, and Matthew G. Kraner, who had worked under Woodworth in Kansas City, replaced Egger as general manager.

During Woodworth's first four years at Pulitzer, the company "committed to or invested more than half a billion dollars in the St. Louis marketplace," Snowden said, while continuing its search for properties nationwide.[51] Michael and Woodworth agreed in 1999 that the company should try again to do what had failed before: to reduce the Newhouse interest in the *Post-Dispatch*. In the agreement made when the *Globe-Democrat* was sold in 1984, Newhouse retained its right to 50 percent of the *Post*'s profits, a total of $177 million by 1999. "I see tremendous potential in St. Louis," Snowden quoted Woodworth as saying. "I don't feel like working all that hard only to give away 50 percent of the profits." The earlier discussions came to nothing either because Newhouse did not want to sell at the time, or considered the offer too low. This time, however, a legal team headed by Pulitzer attorney William Bush helped put together "a structure that enabled us to bridge the gap between what the Newhouse family said they wanted and what we felt was an affordable and appropriate price for us to pay," Snowden explained. The company paid $306 million for 45 percent of the Newhouse stake. On May 1, 2000, the company and Newhouse contributed their respective interests in the *Post-Dispatch* to a new joint venture, in which the company holds a 95 percent interest and

---

Pulitzer Publishing at that time had no newspaper assets [but] had all the [broadcasting] assets and all the debt." Hearst-Argyle shares were then issued to Pulitzer Publishing shareholders in exchange for their Pulitzer Publishing shares. At the same time, "the Pulitzer shareholders received as part of the spinoff [of the stations] shares of Pulitzer Inc., which contained the newspaper assets and the [approximately] $450 million in cash." JMS interview. See also *St. Louis Post-Dispatch*, May 31, 1998; Sara Brown, "Hearst-Argyle Picks Up Pulitzer," *Broadcasting & Cable Magazine*, June 1, 1998, 3.

Pulitzer Publishing veteran Glenn A. Christopher held the titles of company president and chief executive officer between 1984 and 1986. *St. Louis Post-Dispatch*, May 12, 1993. Unless attributed specifically, material about and quotations from Woodworth is from Pulitzer Inc. annual reports for 1998 and 1999; Mark Fitzgerald, "St. Louis News," *Editor & Publisher*, June 30, 2001, 15–19.

51. This included the $306 million to buy out Newhouse, $165 million to buy the Suburban Journals, $10 million for new production facilities, and several million for other capital expenditures. JMS interview, November 4, 2003.

Newhouse retains a 5 percent stake. As part of this arrangement, New-house received a cash payment of $306 million, which was borrowed by the new joint venture for a nine-year term and guaranteed by both parties. The 5 percent Newhouse retained would either be redeemed at its option in 2010 based on a formula price or repurchased by Pulitzer in 2015 based on a formula price.[52]

Woodworth then negotiated the purchase of the thirty-eight *Suburban Journals* of greater St. Louis, the company's major local competitor—serv-ing six hundred thousand households weekly in five counties—from the Journal Register Company for $165 million. The transaction boosted its percentage of local advertising dollars by 6.3 percent, from 24.8 percent to 31.1 percent. The *Post-Dispatch* and *Suburban Journals* news and advertis-ing operations continued to operate separately.[53]

In January 2001, Ellen Soeteber, fifty, a native of East St. Louis, Illinois, who grew up reading the *Post-Dispatch,* became the paper's sixth editor in its 122-year history. It was the third time she was hired into a position for-merly occupied only by men. She was the first woman to become metro editor of the *Chicago Tribune*—where she worked for twenty years—and managing editor of the *Sun-Sentinel* in Fort Lauderdale, Florida, where she had been since 1994.[54] Her approach to the task of *Post-Dispatch* editor differed from Campbell's. "She didn't come out and criticize Campbell," Harry Levins said, "but it's clear from what she's done what she thought of the way things were." Rather than running the newsroom with "a cer-tain ideological rigidity," he said, she "reinvented the newspaper in the traditional form, dismantling the team approach and reinstalling a tradi-tional city desk. . . . It was Ellen's first big operational change. I think she did a phenomenal job."

It was nothing out of the ordinary for Soeteber. "I've always worked in news environments that were oriented to being very aggressive in terms of investigative, breaking, and other enterprise news," she said. "I'm an aggressive journalist, a very competitive journalist." She had been part of a prize-winning investigative team at the *Tribune.* "The best investiga-tive projects don't exactly fall into your laps," she said. "You make them

52. William Bush and Richard A. Palmer to author, June 8, 2004.
53. The Journal Register Company, based in New Jersey with most of its holdings in the Northeast, was the seller. It acquired the Suburban Journals in 1990, when Ralph Ingersoll, Jr., relinquished ownership to the Warburg Pincus investment company, which in turn created the Journal Register Company. *St. Louis Post-Dispatch,* June 27, 2000. Pulitzer used some of its Hearst-Argyle cash to make the purchase, as it had for the Chronicle Newspapers acquisition and some capital improvements.
54. When not attributed specifically, material about Soeteber is from Dawn Grodsky, "Tough Broad," *SJR,* March 2001, 16–18.

happen." As assertive as she might be, in Harry Levins's opinion, she had a soothing influence on the operation. He described the newsroom atmosphere on September 11, 2001: "When I came in that day, the atmosphere was calm and purely professional. If it had been fifteen years ago, people would have been running around with their hair on fire. It starts at the top. I credit Ellen." She also replaced "Imagine St. Louis" on Sundays with "NewsWatch," a news analysis section, and discontinued the reader's advocate position. To spread accountability throughout the newsroom, she gave the responsibility for dealing with reader questions and complaints to all editors.[55]

It is likely that Joe would have been relieved that public journalism did not succeed at the *Post-Dispatch* and gratified that the editor selected at the end of that experiment decided to take the job after going through a thought process that was similar to his own as a young man. "It started to get to me after a while," Soeteber said, "thinking about that it was the *Post-Dispatch* and everything it had meant to me and everything it could mean.... This was the paper I grew up with, and the paper that inspired me to be a journalist." With Soeteber's hiring, every top day-to-day administrator of 1993, the year of Joe's death, had retired or been replaced. Looking back in 2003, Michael credited the Odyssey project for making it possible for everyone in the company "to step aside and...look at who we were and what we were doing." The effort, he said, was "one of my major contributions to the company."

How Joe might respond to the divestiture of broadcasting and the advent of Pulitzer Inc. is unknowable. Yet company legal advisers Richard Palmer and William Bush thought he likely would approve. "You know, the captain of the ship deserves significant credit for decisions taken during his watch," Palmer said. "In a strange sort of way, it's those decisions that Joe made on a kind of lonely basis [that] put the company in a position to be pretty valuable in 1985 and 1986, and made the minority shareholders probably a lot more money than they would have ever dreamed ten years earlier they would [get] out of their investment.... It was during Joe's watch that [the company] really went into the television business in

---

55. Levins is quoted in D. J. Wilson, "Short Cuts," *Riverfront Times*, March 14, 2001, and Kevin Kipp, "Ink by the Barrel," *St. Louis Commerce Magazine*, November 2001, at *www.stlcommercemagazine.com*. See also Readers' Advocate column, *St. Louis Post-Dispatch*, December 10, 2000.

Soeteber said she concluded on the basis of some of her past experiences that having the reader's advocate position "could lead [staff members] to say, 'I don't have to deal with readers.'" She added that she would keep open the option of reinstating the position in some form "if my plan doesn't work." Quoted in *New York Times*, July 9, 2001.

the late sixties...and it was the growth in the television business that really contributed to the financial position that let Joe and his leadership meet head on the enormous challenges on the newspaper side that the *Post-Dispatch* confronted all those years....I don't think anyone appreciated how difficult those decisions were; to make investment decisions when it was a tough thing to do; to survive the challenges of the sixties and seventies and into the eighties."

Bush described him as "very reflective. If you think of someone who's shown his kind of [expertise] in collecting art—anyone that I've ever seen who's very good at that—their personalities are very thoughtful, studying. And Joe approached business the same way. He analyzed; he would go back and review, and I think those talents were applied across the board; the way he thought about art; the way he thought about business issues and the like. That's the way the man was made."

Selected Bibliography

Bingham, Sallie. *Passion and Prejudice.* New York: Knopf, 1989.

Bradlee, Benjamin C. *A Good Life.* New York: Simon and Schuster, 1995.

Brenner, Marie. *House of Dreams.* New York: Random House, 1988.

Chandler, David Leon. *The Binghams of Louisville.* New York: Crown Publishers, 1987.

Csillag, Andras. "Joseph Pulitzer's Roots in Europe: A Genealogical History." *American Jewish Archives* 39 (April 1987): 54–64.

Dudman, Richard. *Forty Days with the Enemy.* New York: Liveright, 1971.

Emery, Edwin, and Michael Emery. *The Press and America.* 5th and 8th eds. Englewood Cliffs, N.J.: Prentice-Hall, 1984 and 1996.

Gillmor, Donald M., and Jerome A. Barron. *Mass Communications Law, Cases and Comment.* 4th ed. St. Paul, Minn.: West Publishing Company, 1984.

Graham, Katharine. *Personal History.* New York: Vintage Books, 1997.

Halberstam, David. *The Powers That Be.* Updated reissue. Urbana: University of Illinois Press, 2000.

Harris, Roy J., Jr. "The Gold-Medal Crusade Years." Booklet: The James C. Millstone Memorial Lecture, Saint Louis University School of Law, 2002.

Hohenberg, John. *The Pulitzer Diaries.* Syracuse, N.Y.: Syracuse University Press, 1997.

Hohenberg, John. *The Pulitzer Prizes.* New York: Columbia University Press, 1974.

Hoopes, Roy. *Ralph Ingersoll.* New York: Atheneum, 1985.

Isaacs, Norman E. *Untended Gates: The Mismanaged Press.* New York: Columbia University Press, 1986.

Juergens, George. *Joseph Pulitzer and the New York World.* Princeton, N.J.: Princeton University Press, 1966.

Kirschten, Ernest. *Catfish and Crystal.* New York: Doubleday, 1960.

Lent, John A. *Newhouse, Newspapers, Nuisances.* New York: Exposition Press, 1966.

Lundberg, Ferdinand. *America's Sixty Families.* New York: The Citadel Press, 1937.

Maier, Thomas. *Newhouse.* New York: St. Martin's Press, 1994.

Markham, James W. *Bovard of the Post-Dispatch.* Baton Rouge: Louisiana State University Press, 1954.

Meeker, Richard H. *Newspaperman.* New York: Ticknor and Fields, 1983.

Modern Painting, Drawing and Sculpture: Collected by Louise and Joseph Pulitzer Jr. Vols. 1–3. Cambridge, Mass.: Fogg Art Museum, 1957, 1958, and 1971.

Nasaw, David. *The Chief.* Boston: Houghton-Mifflin Company, 2000.

Overbeck, Wayne. *Major Principles of Media Law.* Fort Worth, Texas: Harcourt Brace, 1998.

Pfaff, Daniel W. "Joseph Pulitzer II and Advertising Censorship, 1929–1939." *Journalism Monographs* 77 (July 1982).

Pfaff, Daniel W. *Joseph Pulitzer II and the Post-Dispatch: A Newspaperman's Life.* University Park: Pennsylvania State University Press, 1991.

Polk, William J., Jr., and John W. Curley. *Uncle Polky.* St. Louis: Virginia Publishing Company, 2002.

Primm, James Neal. *Lion of the Valley.* 2nd ed. Boulder, Colo.: Pruett, 1990.

Rammelkamp, Julian S. *Pulitzer's Post-Dispatch 1878–1883.* Princeton, N.J.: Princeton University Press, 1967.

Rudenstine, Angelica Zander. *Modern Painting, Drawing and Sculpture: Collected by Emily and Joseph Pulitzer Jr.* Vol. 4. Cambridge, Mass.: Harvard Art Museums, 1988.

Seitz, Don C. *Joseph Pulitzer: His Life and Letters.* New York: Simon and Schuster, 1924.

Swanberg, W. A. *Citizen Hearst.* New York: Scribner's, 1961.

Swanberg, W. A. *Pulitzer.* New York: Scribner's, 1967.

Tifft, Susan E., and Alex S. Jones. *The Patriarch: The Rise and Fall of the Bingham Dynasty.* New York: Summit Books, 1991.

Tifft, Susan E., and Alex S. Jones. *The Trust.* Boston: Little, Brown, 1999.

Unger, Sanford J. *The Papers and the Papers.* New York: E. P. Dutton, 1972.

Wells, Katherine Gladney, and Gayle R. McIntosh. *Symphony and Song: The St. Louis Symphony Orchestra.* Tucson, Ariz.: Patrice Press, 1993.

Wilensky, Harry. *The Story of the St. Louis Post-Dispatch.* St. Louis: St. Louis Post-Dispatch, 1981.

Index